# The Silver State

*Wilbur S. Shepperson Series in
History and Humanities*

# The Silver State

## Nevada's Heritage Reinterpreted

*Third Edition*

James W. Hulse

University of Nevada Press
Reno and Las Vegas

Wilbur S. Shepperson Series in History and Humanities

Series Editor: Jerome E. Edwards

Initial publication of this book was funded in part by the
Nevada 125th Anniversary Commission.

The paper used in this book meets the requirements of American National
Standard for Information Sciences — Permanence of Paper for Printed Library
Materials, ANSI Z39.48-1984. The binding is sewn for strength and durability.

The Library of Congress has cataloged the second edition as follows:

Hulse, James W.
The silver state : Nevada's heritage reinterpreted / James W. Hulse — 2nd ed.
p.   cm. — (Wilbur S. Shepperson series in history and humanities)
Includes bibliographical references and index.
ISBN 0-87417-318-3 (pbk. : alk. paper)
1. Nevada—History.   I. Title.   II. Series.
F841.H83   1998
979.3—dc21        98-21770
CIP

University of Nevada Press, Reno, Nevada   89557   USA
Copyright © 1991, 1998, 2004 University of Nevada Press
Designed by Kaelin Chappell
Printed in the United States of America

ISBN 0-87417-592-5 (3rd ed. pbk.)

13   12   11   10   09   08   07   06   05

5   4   3   2

# Contents

*Preface / vii*

**1.** The Space and the Natural Setting / *1*

**2.** Native Americans / *18*

**3.** The First Explorers / *33*

**4.** Settlers on the Move, 1841–1850 / *43*

**5.** Three Cultures in Collision, 1850–1860 / *57*

**6.** The Early Comstock and Statehood / *74*

**7.** Colorado Steamboats, Eldorado Canyon,
and the Second Wave of Mormons / *91*

**8.** The Era of the Boomtowns, 1865–1878 / *101*

**9.** The Railroads and Their Towns / *114*

**10.** The Livestock Oligarchy and
the Agricultural Frontier / *133*

**11.** Crusaders for Silver, Indians' and Women's Rights / *149*

**12.** The Second Mining Boom / *162*

**13.** The Second Era of Railroad Building / *180*

**14.** New Urban Experiments:
Reno and Las Vegas Since 1940 / *203*

**15.** Land and Water: Changing Policies and Uses / *223*

**16.** Nevada Governments: Federal, State, and Local / *242*

**17.** Gambling and Tourism / *261*

**18.** Community Building in the Silver State / *277*

**19.** The Struggle for Equal Rights / *297*

**20.** The Twelve Northern Counties / *313*

**21.** The Five Southern Counties / *333*

*Selected Bibliography / 351*

*Index / 363*

# Preface

**M**ORE THAN twenty-five years ago, when the University of Nevada Press was in its infancy, its founders asked me to prepare a general history of the state for use in the public schools because the only textbook available at that time was a quarter century old and was thought to be inadequate for the needs of that generation. I wrote *The Nevada Adventure: A History* and tried to make it adaptable for various levels of classroom use. About three years ago, the staff of the press convinced me that the time had come to attempt yet another generalized history of the state: one which explores the more remote corners, which tries to do justice to the southern regions that might have been previously neglected, and which puts the events of the last fifty years into a tidy conceptual framework.

The approach of the 125th anniversary of Nevada's statehood (1989) prompted this effort, in much the same manner that the approach of the centennial (1964) encouraged the writing of *The Nevada Adventure*. The work of a score of scholars has surfaced since that centennial year. Among the most impressive is the scholarship of Russell R. Elliott, teacher and colleague to three generations of Nevada students and scholars. He has explored the spectrum of Great Basin history with a thoroughness that no person, with the possible exception of Leonard Arrington of Utah, has ever done; Elliott has pre-empted the western half of the basin, and Arrington the Utah part, for the scholarly audience. They have, between them, surveyed the vast social landscape in the tradition of the classical historians and have given us a body of excellent historical analysis of Nevada and Utah for this generation. The ambitions of the present work are more narrowly focused.

There has been an avalanche of important new scholarly material on Nevada and its environment within the last few years, which is worth mentioning in a book for the general reader and students in the schools. The excellent series on the natural history of the Great Basin, published by the University of Nevada Press with the generous assistance of the Fleischmann Foundation, should be tapped for use in the historical community. The outstanding volume in the *Handbook of American Indians* series, edited by Warren d'Azevedo and published by the Smithsonian Institution, has brought the cultures of the Native Americans into better focus than ever before. There are also several new social interpretations of the peculiar social organism called Nevada.

It is assumed that there is room for a general updating that will condense the earlier periods into smaller scope and encourage more thorough study of recent developments, since so much has happened in and to Nevada during the past twenty-five years. Our population has nearly tripled, gambling activity has more than quadrupled, and the memory of the early period has faded even further into oblivion in the places that have grown most rapidly. We have drunk more deeply from the waters of Lethe here in Nevada than elsewhere. Our old mining towns, ranches, public buildings, and roads once faded gradually from the scene under the forces of time and weather. Now we bulldoze them. The work of trying to preserve our natural and historical heritage needs more energy and talent than have heretofore been available. Fortunately, there are more hands working these veins than ever before. Interest in the state history has increased within the past quarter century, much of it stimulated and cultivated by the Nevada Humanities Committee, the Nevada Arts Council, the Nevada State Historical Society and museum, the local museums and libraries, and many others.

In the present work, I have assumed that a reinterpretation is in order, one that is careful not to overemphasize the early mining frontier, squander too much time and prose on the politicians, and neglect the burgeoning southern communities. It is also assumed that the time has come for a fresh emphasis on women who have contributed to the social fabric, the changing institutional climate, and the social problems and challenges that emerged in the 1980s.

A state poor in resources but pretentious in ambitions, Nevada has fashioned for itself an unusual role in the American Union. Things are looser here, and they change more rapidly than in most parts of the country; society is more fluid, moral standards are more easily altered or abandoned, apologies for ethical aberration are more easily accepted. Perhaps this is one reason why the study of history is popular.

The history of this state has largely involved a minority of more-or-less "permanent" residents, who have tried to maintain a political and economic commonwealth in a largely inhospitable land, with a majority of short-term "itinerants" constantly passing through. Thousands of Nevadans of the modern era have something in common with those pioneers who erected trading stations in the early days along the Carson River or in the Las Vegas Valley in hopes of doing business with the emigrants. The commercial resources of the land are meager, yet they have attracted those frontiersmen and speculators who wanted to make their profits as quickly and efficiently as possible—and often have left the social and natural damage behind. Perhaps the new evidence that has accumulated in recent years is worthy of the attention of that growing minority who have chosen to be long-term Nevadans.

My intellectual debt to colleagues and friends grows ever larger as the years pass. The community of scholars and amateurs has undergone a quantum expansion in recent years. It is of course impossible to name all the librarians, members of the Westerners' Corral, journalists, writers of bureaucratic reports, curious and thoughtful "buffs," and others who have contributed to the expanding reservoir of data and ideas. But in the evolution of this effort, the greatest responsibility goes to my long-term colleagues Russell R. Elliott, Wilbur Shepperson, Elmer Rusco, Jerome Edwards, and William Rowley, who are always ready with suggestions, arguments, and data when they are needed. Elmer and Mary Rusco have been most generous with information and suggestions about Native Americans. The recent book by Eugene Moehring from Las Vegas, *Resort City in the Sunbelt*, is the most important new addition to Nevada history in many years and has been indispensable.

Special thanks are due also the Alan Bible Center for Applied Research, and especially to Lorena Stookey, who did much to improve the prose of this text. With commendable diligence, Chris Ryan carried out the cartographic research and Nancy Peppin prepared the maps in their final form. Richard Adkins helped locate and select the photographs with his characteristic energy. Several other readers, some unknown to me, provided excellent criticism as referees for the University of Nevada Press. Cindy Wood of the press has applied her high professional standards as copy editor, to the great benefit of the manuscript. Tom Radko and Nicholas Cady, the press's director and editor in chief respectively, have shepherded the manuscript to completion with fine professional care. My former colleagues, Bob and Paule-Colette Fricke, provided the hospitality and facilitated the quiet hours for final editing in the Île de France, for which I will always be grateful.

Finally, my wife Betty has endured not only the long silences but also the frequent readings and re-readings with almost-saintly patience. And in this instance I have also had the kind help of our daughter, Jane Hulse Dixon, who has been an excellent proofreader and troubleshooter. No author is entitled to so much kindness.

Reno, July 28, 1990                                                    J. W. H.

## Preface to the Second Edition

Since I began the process of mining, milling, and smelting the ore of Nevada history nearly a half century ago, the state has been radically transformed. Much of that change has occurred since 1990, when the first edition of this book went to press. After seven years, it was badly in need of revision.

As always, I am indebted to people throughout the state who have generously responded to my probing and requests for information. Special thanks must go on this occasion to Bobby Shaw, my energetic graduate assistant; to Jean Ford, the foremost historical resource person on Nevada women; and Michael Green of the Community College of Southern Nevada.

My partnership with the competent people at the University of Nevada Press has been a high privilege for me for a third of a century.

Reno, January 15, 1998                                        James W. Hulse

## Preface to the Third Edition

In this revision, I have had the competent assistance of Cameron Sutherland, for which I am grateful.

Reno, November 11, 2003                                       James W. Hulse

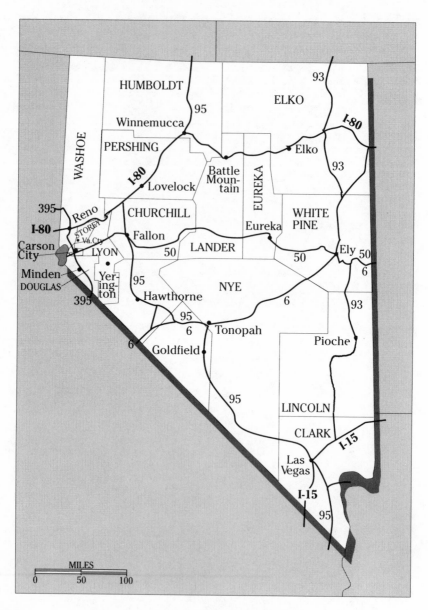

*Nevada Counties and Principal Highways*

# 1

# The Space and
# the Natural Setting

**H**ISTORY IS primarily a record of the tug-of-war between people and their environment. Half of their environment—the social milieu—humans construct for themselves. The other half they come to accept after settling in a particular locale. This chapter concerns Nevadans and the uses they have made of the state they have created.

The elemental components of the Nevada heritage are land, water, and the habitat that nature has provided. Since the days when Jedediah Smith and Peter Skene Ogden first probed the edges of this region in 1826, our predecessors cursed the desert and mountain terrain; they feared the blistering heat of summer and the blizzards of winter. But also, by steps as slow as those of the earliest pioneers, Nevadans have come to realize that the geology, the ecology, and the atmosphere of Nevada and the surrounding area are, in combination, greater treasures than all the precious metal of the Comstock Lode or the wealth of the gambling casinos.

Nevada is part of a new world that is still being explored. Columbus did not finish the work of discovery in those famous voyages he made five hundred years ago. He and his half-forgotten seamen simply advanced a quest as old as history—the search with new techniques for new opportunities somewhere beyond familiar terrain. Christopher Columbus was the first prospector and the first gambler of the New

World. His work continues in a land that would have been too strange for his imagination to contemplate, but in a place that now bears many names taken from the Spanish landscape from which he set sail—names such as Sierra Nevada (snow-capped mountains), Colorado (red), and Las Vegas (the meadows).

Nevada, with its 110,000 square miles, would cover more than half of Spain if it were moved across the Atlantic and laid down on the Iberian peninsula. Nevada is not the largest state in the Union, but it is big enough to inspire awe in its visitors. If one could pick it up and transport it eastward across the United States, its southern tip could touch South Carolina, and its northern boundary would reach the Great Lakes and include all or parts of seven or eight states. Or, we could fit all of Great Britain within it and still have room for most of Ireland.

Yet Nevada is not like Iberia, or the American East, or the British Isles from which it has drawn so much of its culture—the language, the system of justice, and several place names. It is part of one of the world's most extensive and diverse desert regions, into which have come explorers and adventurers from many lands. Like desert dwellers of other ages, Nevadans and their predecessors have shaped a special type of society, one which has adapted to a harsh environment. This book describes the efforts that people have made on behalf of a province named Nevada—a land of little water, much alkaline soil, and barren mountains that rise like giant sentinels in the landscape.

The story begins in the ancient past, long before there were written records among the people who lived here; it continues through the age of atomic testing and space exploration, in which the writings and the mathematics are so sophisticated that few can understand them. Nevada's desert terrain resisted the explorers and emigrants longer than most other parts of the United States because it seemed so harsh and barren in the early years of the American Republic. For the same reason, it has become a unique science and sociology laboratory for contemporary America.

Nevada has a short history. The Native Americans did not write chronicles to communicate their values to later generations. The majority of its present inhabitants arrived from some other part of America. Most are descendants of people who came during the span of this century, or only two or three generations ago. In their haste to make a living, they thought little about the local ecology or history until only recently. People often tend to think of the world in terms of the use that they make of it *now*. The Nevada topography does not yield many crops or provide many opportunities for manufacturing. Nevadans of the modern era, like the aboriginal inhabitants who preceded them, had to develop special skills for their livelihoods.

About 86 percent of the land in Nevada was still under the control of the federal government as the year 2000 opened. It was mainly managed by Washington because it had been largely unpopulated and unclaimed since the days of the pioneers. The land has been utilized by Indians, miners, livestock owners, sportsmen, and tourists with special interests, but otherwise Nevada has offered little of commercial value to the nation's marketplaces. There are more than 230 mountain ranges within its boundaries, all flanked by valleys that run in a north-south direction, and many of them are virtually unknown even to longtime residents of the state. Most Nevadans seldom stray from their valley cities, and when they do, they usually follow the roads in an east-west direction, crossing the mountain ranges or following the river valleys without exploring them.

Because of its vast, semi-arid expanses, Nevada has often been described as a "desert waste." Yet the state's economic history provides numerous examples which illustrate that the land unwanted by one generation will prove valuable to another. The history in these pages will reveal that people have been able to extract valuable minerals, raise animals and crops, devise commercial enterprises, and find opportunities for advanced technology within the same "desert waste" that previous generations regarded as useless. The land offers many advantages as a recreation center in a country where open space is becoming increasingly difficult to find. In addition, it is a laboratory for space exploration and high technology military experimentation. It is both a backwoods and a scientific frontier.

## Mountains, Deserts, and Precious Water

Geologists use two terms to describe the region of North America of which Nevada is a part: (1) the Great Basin, and (2) the Basin and Range province. The Great Basin is the "land of interior drainage," embracing most of northern Nevada, half of Utah, and fragments of California, Oregon, Idaho, and Wyoming, where the streams run inland toward sinks or lakes rather than flowing toward the sea. The Basin and Range province includes the Great Basin, but it also extends across southern Nevada, Arizona, New Mexico, western Texas, and into Mexico — where some of the waters move southward to the ocean and where the terrain and flora resemble that which surround the Las Vegas region. As the geologist Bill Fiero wrote:

> The hydrologic Great Basin, then, is that portion of the geo-logic Basin and Range with no drainage to the sea. The two great rivers of the West, the Colorado and Columbia, are gnawing away at the flanks. But the rainfall is too sparse, the rivers have too little energy, and the uplift of the inverted bowl is too recent for the big rivers to breach the defenses of the Great Basin—yet. (Fiero, *Geology of the Great Basin*, p. 7.)

The rugged highlands are the result of eons of geologic change. Every-where there is evidence of nature's turbulence in past ages. Jagged mountain peaks are the legacy of gigantic earthquakes that occurred millions of years ago. Black volcanic rocks testify to smoking mountains of lava that once scorched the earth. Broad, fan-like masses of dirt and rubble, stretching out onto valley floors from canyons, give evidence of relentless erosion over hundreds of centuries.

Nature played violent games with the American West in the millennia before humans appeared on the scene: mountain ranges rose and disap-peared several times; massive seas or lakes formed and evaporated; and the giant ichthyosaur swam, prospered, and perished above the lands that are now central-Nevada deserts. On a few occasions over the years, there have been startling reminders that this is a land that is still shift-ing. Small "seismic events" happen every day; the big earthquakes have seldom occurred in recorded history. Yet the evidence of such events is abundant in about two hundred north-south mountain ranges within the state. As Alvin R. McLane wrote:

> When viewed from afar, the surface of the Great Basin appears like a sea gone mad, the tumultuous waves roll east—from the Sierra Nevada to the Wasatch Range. (McLane, *Silent Cordilleras: The Mountain Ranges of Nevada*, p. 11.)

Within the past few decades, geologists have developed new theories about how the land of the great interior basin and the Colorado pla-teau was formed. It is now commonly believed that a process known as "plate tectonics" is operating, which accounts for gradual movements in the earth's surface. The plates form an eggshell-like crust around the core of the globe, and they virtually float around and across the inner core, colliding at times to form mountain ranges. The process is still highly active in the Far West, and it was graphically described by James McPhee in his popular book *Basin and Range* (see the list of Suggested Supplementary Readings at the end of this chapter).

Nature holds several reminders of past eons in her bag of tricks. Until recently, there were many people still living who remembered the San Francisco earthquake and fire of 1906. In Nevada, several times during the summer and autumn of 1954, huge forces within the earth's crust twisted and moved, shaking the towns of the central Great Basin, doing damage that could hardly be measured in dollars. Had these occurred directly beneath a city or town, many lives might have been lost.

These seismic events have stimulated intensive research, in which the University of Nevada has been an active partner. It is now known that a massive fault zone exists between Susanville, California, and the Spring Mountain Range west of Las Vegas, and another zone lies beneath the Reno–Carson City area. The possibility that heavy earthquakes could occur, similar to the ones that have damaged California cities, is taken for granted by scientists who work in this field. This concern is now reflected in Nevada's standard building codes.

Beneath the earth's surface in the Great Basin are huge reservoirs of hot water, which are accessible when they either boil to the surface or are tapped by deep drilling. Several hot springs in northern Nevada have long been known as desirable places for health and recreational uses. Between 1975 and 1985 an important geothermal industry began to emerge when companies started testing the possible uses of this energy to generate power. Seventy wells were drilled, and the prospects for beneficial use in the future were realized.

One need not look far into the paleontological or archeological records to realize that many species of plants and animals were temporary tenants in this region before *Homo sapiens* established wickiups, subdivisions, public domain, and real estate. At one time huge mammoths walked in the valleys, probably in a semi-tropical setting. Large pieces of petrified wood indicate the presence of giant trees that once flourished in the northern ranges.

The Nevada that stretches beyond the cities and towns is mainly the product of very recent natural change. Mt. Charleston, Wheeler Peak, the Rubies, and the Sierra Nevada are young, as geologists reckon things — only about a million years old. They are even now eroding, surrendering inch by inch to the lands below.

The traces of dry lakes and shorelines that are so prominent in many places are infants by comparison; their waters covered the land only tens of thousands of years ago. The Pleistocene epoch was the era when the great ice sheets covered much of the northeastern United States, when the Pacific Coast was a zone of volcanic activity, and when much of the Grand Canyon was cut away by the waters of the Colorado River. The shorelines in northwestern Nevada are the remnants of Lake Lahontan; in northeastern Nevada they are reminders of Lake Bonneville. This body of water covered 20,000 square miles—most of western Utah—and Lake Lahontan covered some 8,600 square miles of northwestern Nevada. During the wettest period of the Pleistocene era, at least a dozen lakes in central and northern Nevada grew larger than present-day Pyramid Lake or Lake Mead.

## The Northern Basin

With the climatic changes of the last several thousand years, the Great Basin assumed the appearance that now greets the hiker, motorist, or airline passenger. Not far from any city or town in the northern region is the familiar sagebrush and grassland terrain, or the "gray ocean," as James A. Young and B. Abbott Sparks called it in their book *Cattle in the Cold Desert*. The "ocean" is broken by those hundreds of mountain ranges, scores of which are sprinkled with the Utah juniper, piñon pine, firs, aspens, and dozens of lesser-known varieties of trees.

The motorist who speeds along the interstate highways isn't always aware of the splendid flora and fauna hidden in the mountains. The freeways do not bring us near the five million acres of national forests that exist in Nevada. Ronald M. Lanner, a Utah author and forester, described the region's hinterland in *Trees of the Great Basin*:

> No apology is necessary for our Great Basin forests and woodlands. On the whole, their trees are smaller and less varied than those to the west of our region, and less numerous than those to our east. But, forming a welcome cover of green and gold on our high ground, they serve us well. They give us relief from the relative treelessness of our low-lying lands. They provide us with a modicum of wood, forage, and game, and with most of our water. And they inspire us. We have, after all, the oldest trees known to man; and trees that persevere under a variety of stresses. Trees that cling to precipices above the timberline, trees that withstand devastating droughts, trees that tolerate the sterile soils just above the salt flats: the Great Basin has examples of them all. (Lanner, *Trees of the Great Basin*, p. xiv.)

A companion volume in the Nevada series on the life-forms of the Great Basin was prepared by Professor Hugh N. Mozingo, who has described more than sixty species of small plants that appear on the local deserts. In his studies of the life-forms that now exist in Nevada, Mozingo reached conclusions that complement those of scientists in other fields. He wrote:

> The Great Basin has a large number of very successful herbaceous forms, annual as well as perennial, but the really conspicuous and characteristic plants on our enormous vistas of both desert and steppe are the shrubs—so much so that we talk about the shadscale desert, greasewood association, or big sagebrush community. Shrubs are our constant companions here; basically, this is because the major factor limiting plant growth is the relative lack of water. Trees take in more water and evaporate more, and except for our mountain ranges, towns, and waterways there is simply not enough water to allow them to survive, let alone grow. From an airplane, in fact, many of our cities appear to be the only forests at low elevations. (Mozingo, *Shrubs of the Great Basin*, pp. 5–6.)

Another important contribution to the scientific and ecological understanding of the Basin and Range has come from University of Nevada, Reno, biologist Fred A. Ryser, one of Nevada's foremost ornithologists. Ryser writes:

> Whether seen or not, numerous kinds of birds frequent these desert shrublands and woodlands. This is magnificent country for raptors, and during the winter eagles, hawks, and falcons often concentrate in such numbers as to apparently defy the limitations imposed by a pyramid of biomass. . . . The shrublands are also the natal home of an array of distinctive birds, including the Black-throated Sparrow, Sage Sparrow, Lark Sparrow, House Finch, and Burrowing Owl. In sagebrush-dominated shrublands, the courtship displays of Sage Grouse are performed on ancestral strutting grounds. Some of the finest bird actors in the world—a troupe of corvids featuring the Black-billed Magpie, Common Raven, and Pinyon Jay—are on stage in the shrublands and woodlands. (Ryser, *Birds of the Great Basin*, p. 1.)

Despite its status as the most arid state in the American Union, Nevada has a rich variety of fish species, ranging from the rare and endangered cui-ui of Pyramid Lake and the Devils Hole pupfish to the more familiar varieties of trout, suckers, carp, minnows, catfish, killi-fishes, and other varieties introduced in recent decades. Several kinds of fishes have almost vanished in Nevada, partly because of diversion or pollution of their native waters and partly because of the introduction of competitors from other regions. Yet Nevadans have learned to regard the fisheries as a valuable resource and have taken an interest in preserving them.

The drama of the desert is there for those who are willing to watch it. The remarks of Lanner, Mozingo, and Ryser usually describe the high, cold, northern desert, but in many cases they can also be applied to that portion of southern Nevada where the interior basin merges with the low-lying land near the Colorado River.

## The Southern Triangle

In the southern portion of the Great Basin and across the lower Colorado basin lies the wide Mojave Desert, a beautiful, superficially barren expanse distinguished by its huge, ragged, mostly naked mountains and broad valleys. The most familiar botanical symbols of this southwestern landscape are the creosote bush, the yucca plant, and the Joshua tree, which repeatedly command the attention of the desert motorist who searches, from the comfort of an automobile, for some reassurance of the presence of life on the apparent moonscape beyond the windshield.

The most exciting way to reflect on the Mojave of southern Nevada is to see it from an airplane descending into the Las Vegas Valley, a view that millions of tourists enjoy each year. For the airline passenger arriving on a clear day, an appreciation of the arid vastness of the land is almost inevitable. And the Las Vegas Valley—though it holds well over a million people—still appears as a small oasis in a desolate land. The occasional patches of greenery and even the massive casino complexes shrink to lilliputian dimensions when viewed from 20,000 feet.

Mt. Charleston and Sunrise Mountain have not been diminished by the metropolis between them. Mt. Charleston, which rises to an elevation of 11,918 feet, is the most prominent peak in the Spring Mountains west of Las Vegas. Seven of its neighbors stand over 10,000 feet tall, a cluster of highlands that presents a sharp contrast to the surrounding Mojave terrain. Here, hikers can readily imagine themselves to be in the high country of the northern Sierra Nevada. Only a half hour's drive from Las Vegas, in Kyle Canyon, there are forests of piñon, Jeffrey pine, and white fir; deer and bighorn sheep roam the land, and dozens of species of

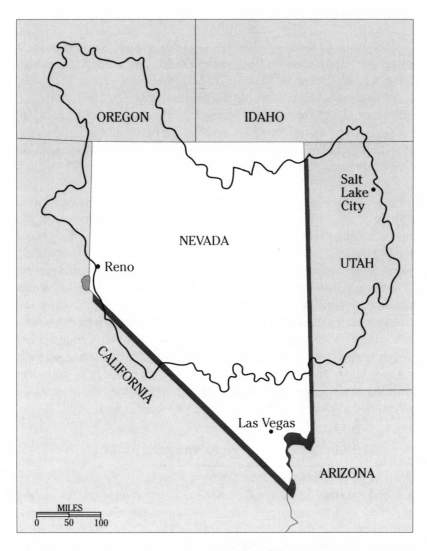

*The Great Basin, incorporating the Great Basin Desert,
a cold desert lying in the northern part of the Basin and Range
Province of North America*

birds, which do not frequent this latitude elsewhere in the Mojave, thrive in this region. At the higher elevation are stands of bristlecone pine. Lee Canyon has enough deep snow to be a popular winter recreation center for skiers.

Even more so than the rest of Nevada, the Mojave is a land of harsh extremes. Lake Mojave on the Colorado River, only about 90 miles from Mt. Charleston, is more than 11,000 feet lower in elevation. The summers in most areas are too hot for human comfort without the aid of air-conditioning. The rains are infrequent, but often torrential when they come. Native American peoples and pioneers avoided the region when they had a choice; the first emigrants who stumbled through its most barren section—the Manly party of 1849—gave its frightening topography the name "Death Valley."

Yet even the Mojave, where the United States found room for its main atomic testing site and where it has contemplated the creation of a nuclear waste depository, has abundant records of animal and human habitation. This land, like the Lahontan and Bonneville basins to the north, once had lakes and oases teeming with animal and human life. Tule Springs near Las Vegas may have been a feeding place for camels, mammoths, and giant ground sloths in the uncounted millennia that preceded human presence on this continent. It also may have been the site of human activity several thousand years ago. The Mojave River, which rises in the San Bernardino Mountains of California and provides forage and cover for many birds, rabbits, and squirrels, must have been a richer biological setting in past ages. Perhaps the Amargosa River, which Nevada and California share, was once much more lush.

## The Colorado River Basin

For the first hundred years of Nevada's history, the Colorado River seemed to be nothing more than a wild and sometimes destructive torrent that had no significance for people who were building a society further north. In the past half century, it has proved to be the crucial natural asset for the sagebrush state.

This mighty waterway flows for 1,450 miles and draws its waters from 244,000 square miles of the most arid part of the United States, including parts of Wyoming, Colorado, New Mexico, Utah, Arizona, Nevada, and California, as well as Mexico. Those who first visited its southern banks thought that it could never be tamed for human use. Yet because of government intervention, it became in less than fifty years the most tightly regulated waterway in America; the management of its flow became a crucial matter for the entire Southwest. Natural and human geography have been restructured along the Colorado River because of the building of Hoover Dam, Davis Dam, and a half dozen other large reclamation projects. Nevada's historical orientation has been decisively changed because of that fact.

The destiny of southern Nevada is closely linked with that of the other Colorado basin states, and especially with southern California and central Arizona. Nevada shares a small fraction of the river's length and uses about 2 percent of its water; most of it belongs to other states. The Colorado flows between Nevada and Arizona for only 125 miles, yet this stretch and the Nevada share of the river's water play an important role in the state's history.

Water experts have said for a quarter century that the river is over-allotted, i.e., that more water has been promised by law to the users than will be available during drought years, and it is only a matter of time until there will be severe shortages. Because the entire Southwest through which the Colorado flows has experienced rapid economic development in recent decades, competition for its life-giving current has accelerated just as rapidly. Planners in the Las Vegas Valley have started looking farther afield for the water that will be needed in the twenty-first century. The Colorado River cannot be expected to provide any more, and even the present allotment cannot be taken for granted. (For further discussion of the Las Vegas Water Project, see chapter fifteen.)

The lower Colorado River derives a tiny portion of its flow from the southeastern corner of Nevada. One of its lesser-known tributaries is the Meadow Valley Wash, whose waters originate near Pioche, more than 180 miles north of the main channel of the Colorado. It also gathers the Muddy and Virgin rivers, which drain basins north of Las Vegas. The natural flow from the eastern slopes of the Spring Mountain Range into Las Vegas Valley also descends through the Las Vegas Wash into the Colorado. Although the runoff from these streams is usually insignificant, all are prone to heavy flooding in some seasons. Old-timers may recall that floods can be more destructive than the heat.

## The Smaller Rivers of the North

The small rivers of northern Nevada had a primary role in directing the history of the state for almost a century before the waters of the Colorado became available. Four of them won special notice in the early annals of the West: the Truckee, the Carson, the Walker, and the Humboldt rivers.

The Truckee became well known because of its association with the

Donner tragedy of 1846–1847 and because it has been connected with the rise and reputation of Reno. Since the Truckee's main source is Lake Tahoe and its destination is Pyramid Lake, its history is completely intertwined with these two bodies of water and the controversies surrounding them. It flows for about 105 miles, dropping more than 1,700 feet through the rugged and heavily forested Sierra of California before it enters Nevada. Then it drops more gently through the Truckee Meadows (Reno) and the desert for the last 60 miles of its path to Pyramid Lake. Samuel G. Houghton, a thoughtful, nonprofessional historian, wrote the following condensed description of the river system:

> The upper portion of the Truckee River Basin resembles a funnel with a remarkably broad flare, 50 miles north-south from Henness Pass to the vicinity of Carson Pass, and all draining eastward into Nevada. The 790 square miles lying in California gather most of the water in the system from melting snow and rainfall on the surrounding slopes and ridges, and the 1,340 square miles lying in Nevada—including Pyramid Lake—use most of it up. This unbalanced condition has been the basis of sporadic dispute ever since the political boundaries were determined. (Houghton, *A Trace of Desert Waters*, p. 61.)

Years later, this river was the focal point of some of the most extended water conflicts in the history of the West.

The basin of the Carson River forms the next extensive drainage system south of the Tahoe-Truckee region on the eastern slopes of the central Sierra Nevada. Its east fork originates high on the slopes of Sonora Peak, more than 11,000 feet above sea level; its west fork begins near Kit Carson Pass. The two branches then flow northward to merge in the Carson Valley just inside the boundary of Nevada, providing the western Great Basin with one of its richest agricultural sections. Here, beneath the majestic peaks that encircle Lake Tahoe, the first emigrants entered the Sierra in 1841, the first temporary settlement was established in 1850, the first experiments with government began in 1851, and the capital of the territory and later the state was eventually established. Before the introduction of reclamation dams, the Carson River flowed another 60 miles into the desert, ending in the Carson Sink northeast of the present city of Fallon.

The Walker River, like the Carson, originates in two places on the high slopes of the central Sierra and flows northward to form a single watercourse within Nevada, meeting about 5 miles south of Yerington. Mason

Valley is the main beneficiary of this flow, which then continues in a large loop—first northward, then eastward, then southward—ending in Walker Lake, the sister of Pyramid Lake. The Walker River system never gained the notoriety of the Truckee or the Carson, partly because it was not on the main emigrant trail to California, and also because the population along its banks was much smaller than that along the other rivers. Yet it gave economic life to a vast region of western Nevada that otherwise might not have prospered.

The Humboldt River defies the larger pattern of Nevada and western geography. It flows mainly from northeast to southwest for about 280 miles, entirely within the boundaries of the state. It drains most of the northern third of Nevada, from north of Wells to the Humboldt Sink, with tributaries stretching more than 600 miles on the ground. Although a very small river by national standards, it has had an importance far beyond its size because it dictated the route of the westward-bound immigrants of the 1840s, the railroad builders of the 1860s, and the highway builders of the 1900s. Historian Dale Morgan described it as a paradox: "It was almost the most necessary river of America, and the most hated" (*The Humboldt: Highroad of the West*, p. 5).

There are several smaller "rivers" in Nevada, most of which are hardly equal to the designations they have been given. We have mentioned the Amargosa, which flows within and near Death Valley, mostly underground, but because it creates a few oases, it deserves a momentary recognition in the history of Nevada. The Owyhee and Jarbidge rivers in the far north would hardly be noticed in a more luxuriant region. They are assets to Nevada simply because of the small amount of moisture they provide before they flow northward into the Columbia River Basin. Water—whatever its form and quantity and regardless of the direction of its flow—is a most crucial resource in a desperately dry state.

## The Open Spaces: Asset or Burden?

Because Nevada has so much arid, open space (i.e., about 86 percent of its total area) still under the jurisdiction of the federal government, several large parcels of land have been marked for military use and atomic testing. No other state among the contiguous forty-eight has a greater part of its territory under the direct control of the federal government. The state has been selected or proposed at various times as the site for ammunition depots, air bases, livestock management, bombing ranges and the training ground of fighter-plane pilots, atomic testing, rocket development, the home base of hundreds of intercontinental ballistic missiles (the so-called M-X), and the deposit of high-level nuclear waste. For many years, because their land was so poor and their economy so unstable, Nevadans welcomed federal projects of this kind. But by the 1980s, many Nevadans had become much more skeptical about the long-range value of such activities. Some people believed that politicians from other states regarded Nevada as a dumping ground and junkyard for enterprises that are not welcome elsewhere. The debates on these issues became a central factor in Nevada politics in the late 1980s.

To emphasize the contrasts, let us consider the recent events that revolved around two of Nevada's most publicized upland regions—Yucca Mountain and Wheeler Peak.

## Yucca Mountain and Nuclear Waste

In the late 1980s, one part of Nevada that received intense public and scientific interest was Yucca Mountain, located about 85 miles northwest of Las Vegas. This arid, remote part of Nye County—basically unknown even to most Nevadans—was selected in the early 1980s by the U.S. Department of Energy (DOE) as a possible site for the underground storage of high-level radioactive waste, which will remain hazardous for 10,000 years. The Congress authorized an intensive study of the geology of the area in 1982. The DOE decided in a preliminary report in 1988 that this region was relatively free of earthquakes and volcanic activity, and that it had little water or other useful resources. It therefore concluded that this location warranted further analysis as a possible storage site for as much as 70,000 tons of dangerous refuse from the nation's nuclear plants. For several years, the department also considered possible sites in Texas and Washington State, but it dropped these from its list in 1987. This conclusion, based at least as much on political considerations as on scientific data, provoked a storm of protest in Nevada. In 1989, the U.S. government announced that it would begin new studies because it did not have confidence in those that had previously been conducted by the DOE.

Nevada politicians, who were custodians of little federal power and much federal land, sensed that other states were trying to dispose of their radioactive refuse without adequate assurance that the proposed transportation and deposit of the nuclear refuse was safe. The lesson of the Colorado River development—that one generation's wasteland may be another generation's oasis — was not lost on Nevada's leaders.

In 2002, President George W. Bush and his Secretary of Energy Spencer Abraham authorized the opening of the nuclear repository. Nevada's U.S. senators and representatives were unable to block this action in Congress, but the state's political leaders continued to oppose the decision in the federal courts.

## The Magnificence of Wheeler Peak

One of the natural cornucopias of the Nevada landscape was finally added to the national park system in 1987 with the creation of the Great Basin National Park. Located in White Pine County near the Utah border, this park includes Wheeler Peak, the 13,063-foot high jewel of the Snake Range. It has several nearby neighbors which reach above the 11,000-foot level — Mt. Baker, Mt. Washington, Mt. Lincoln, and Mt. Moriah — each of which is a majestic example of the natural mountain West. The whole region is remote from the cities and commerce for which Nevada is famous. Not all of these sites are within the new park, which was limited by Congress to 76,800 acres, but all are witness to the abundant natural variety of Nevada's eastern borderland. Its streams are wild; they offer the hiker a passage through natural life zones that dazzle both the senses and the intellect. The wildlife is close at hand, elusive, and abundant.

Within the park is Nevada's most remarkable cavern. Lehman Caves is the largest limestone opening still undergoing formation in the Far West. Some chambers invite the senses upward like the apse of a Gothic cathedral; the walk through the caves has induced a sense of reverence in generations of visitors who never had the privilege of visiting Europe. In the same region is Nevada's only permanent ice field. The world's oldest known bristlecone pine tree survived on Wheeler Peak until a few years ago, when an overzealous curiosity seeker cut it down.

For decades before the 1980s, the wonders of the Wheeler Peak area were known to a fortunate few, and it was proposed as a national park several times. However, the actions of a lone Nevada congressman in the 1960s managed to prevent the addition of this landscape to the national park system for many years to come.

Early in 1988, the National Parks and Conservation Association, an important private conservation group, recommended a significant expansion of the national park system. It proposed eighty-six new national historical and natural parks across the country, including four in Nevada. Those regions identified as potential park sites were located at Lake Tahoe, the Black Rock Desert in northern Washoe County, and the Owyhee Canyonlands and Ruby Mountains, both in Elko County. In the past, it has required many years for such proposals to be approved.

## The Question of Wilderness

While Nevada has been a favorite site for expansive military and technical experiments, it has received very little attention for its wilderness heritage.

Nevadans have been slower than most of their western neighbors in the formal recognition of the natural wonders of their state and in the effort to preserve some of them. Not until the middle 1980s was there a strong, successful drive to establish the Great Basin National Park and to set aside a significant number of unspoiled "wilderness areas" for permanent preservation. Even then, a prolonged debate developed between the proponents of wilderness designation and the miners, cattlemen, and sportsmen who had long regarded the open lands as their privileged domain.

A wilderness area is different from a national park in that it is a region that is basically in its natural state, essentially unaffected and undamaged by human activities, which has been set aside by Congress as a permanent natural preserve. The purpose of a wilderness designation is to select some regions as permanent natural enclaves for the wildlife and for future generations, and to reduce the damage by vehicles and commercial exploitation. As of 1985, Nevada had only one small, remote region in this category, a 64,000-acre preserve near Jarbidge in northern Elko County.

On the other hand, the state had, at that time, more than 5.1 million acres of national forest, and about 3.6 million acres were roadless. At least 1.5 million acres, located in twenty-one different areas of the state, were worthy of consideration as wilderness. The majority of Nevada's congressional delegation responded to local mining and ranching interests and tried, in the mid-1980s, to limit the wilderness protection to 136,000 acres, leaving Nevada with the smallest proportion of wilderness land among all the western states. However, Senators Harry Reid and Richard Bryan and Congressman James Bilbray fashioned a bill in the summer of 1989 that selected fourteen areas of unspoiled scenic highlands — a total of 733,400 acres — for wilderness designation. Both houses of Congress passed this bill late in 1989, and President George Bush signed it into law.

The debate about the future of Nevada's most precious natural regions grew stronger in the late 1990s. A Utah senator proposed that the Great Basin National Park be abandoned because it was less popular than other scenic sites in the same category. The areas designated as wilderness continued to be controversial because commercial interests wanted to exploit them. Most serious of all, pressures intensified for designating Yucca Mountain as the site of a "temporary" repository for high-level nuclear waste, even though scientific studies about the geology of the area were not complete.

## Suggested Supplementary Reading

Fradkin, Philip L. *A River No More: The Colorado River and the West*. Tucson: University of Arizona Press, 1984.

Houghton, Samuel G. *A Trace of Desert Waters: The Great Basin Story*. Foreword by Samuel I. Zeveloff. 1976. Reprint, Reno: University of Nevada Press, 1994.

Lambert, Darwin. *Great Basin Drama*. Niwot, Colo.: Robert Rinehart Publishers, 1991.

McPhee, John. *Basin and Range*. New York: Farrar, Straus, Giroux, 1981.

Reynolds, Deon, and Jon Christensen. *Nevada*. Portland, Ore.: Graphic Arts Center Publishing, 2001.

Ronald, Ann, and Stephen Trimble. *Earthtones: A Nevada Album*. Reno: University of Nevada Press, 1995.

Smith, Scott T. *Nevada: Magnificent Wilderness*. Foreword by Hal Rothman. Englewood, Colo.: Westcliffe Publishers, 1996.

Solnit, Rebecca. *Savage Dreams: A Journey into the Hidden Wars of the American West*. San Francisco: Sierra Club Books, 1994.

Titus, A. Costandina, ed. *Battle Born: The Federal-State Conflict in Nevada During the Twentieth Century*. Dubuque: Kendall Hunt, 1989.

Worster, Donald. *Rivers of Empire: Water, Aridity, and the Growth of the American West*. New York: Pantheon Books, 1985.

# 2

## Native Americans

B Y THE standards of world civilization, Nevada's recorded history is very short, but the prehistory of its inhabitants reaches back to the Old Stone Age. It is now commonly believed that the first immigrants from Asia reached the valleys of the Basin and Range province at least 12,000 years ago.

The time scale of Nevada's prehistory is stunning; this region has some of the earliest sites of human habitation in America. Leading archeological institutions, such as the American Museum of Natural History and the University of California, began extensive research in the 1930s. The Nevada State Museum in Carson City has long been a leading institution in the search for information about the prehistoric era in the Great Basin. In more recent years, the Nevada university campuses, both in Reno and Las Vegas, have sent skilled researchers into the field to seek data on ancient peoples, and the results are exciting.

The most intriguing evidence of Paleolithic (i.e., Old Stone Age) humans has been found at Tule Springs in the Sheep Range about 15 miles from Las Vegas. Scientists identified eleven bone tools that they believed humans used between 12,000 and 13,000 years ago. Another site at Gypsum Cave near Frenchman Mountain has also been identified as a possible site for early settlement, but the investigations conducted there in the 1930s are controversial and thought to be erroneous.

In various regions throughout the state, rock hunters have occasionally found "Clovis points," believed to have been made 10,000 years ago. These are stone dart points, apparently used as hunting instruments long before the invention of the bow and arrow. They were discovered near the Carson Sink, near Tonopah and Beatty, and in Washoe Valley. At Winnemucca Lake and near the Humboldt Sink in northwestern Nevada, scientists have identified dart points that may be 7,000 years old and hand-woven baskets that rested in caves for 5,700 years before they were uncovered.

Much of the evidence about Nevada's earliest inhabitants comes from places where they camped or hunted. Early humans searched out caves and rock shelters for safety, gathered together food stores and their most precious objects, and often died there. Many sites of this kind exist in Nevada because the region was once quite wet, with vast lakes and big inland rivers, and then gradually became dry under conditions that preserved human artifacts. Scientists have uncovered the remains of ancient civilizations in several places: near Winnemucca Lake, at the Humboldt Sink, at Frenchman Mountain, at Etna Cave near Caliente, at Lehman Caves in White Pine County, at Jarbidge Cave in Elko County, and at Hidden Cave in Churchill County. The list is long, and the challenge to the archeologists and anthropologists is great.

Much information has been retrieved about these societies. For example, the people who lived in the Lovelock Cave near Lake Lahontan 3,000 years ago knew nothing about the bow and arrow; they relied upon the dart as their main weapon for killing game. They were, however, talented basket makers, and they created nets for catching rabbits and woven bowls for storing their foods. Because the Lovelock Cave was quite dry for centuries, scientists had the good fortune to find many well-preserved tools, rabbit skins and feathers fashioned into clothing, and decorative items. The archeologists found decoy ducks made of tule reeds, which were painted with appropriate colors for attracting other birds.

The Lovelock Cave people knew nothing of agriculture; their lives must have been especially difficult as the waters of Lake Lahontan receded. Did they perish, to be replaced by other bands, or did they adapt slowly to conditions, accept migrating groups from elsewhere, and become ancestors of the modern Northern Paiutes? The answer is not clear.

## The Anasazi Record

The most remarkable legacy of the prehistoric inhabitants of Nevada was left by a people sometimes called the Pueblo dwellers, or the Anasazi. Their settlements were centered at Mesa Verde near the Four Corners area and once stretched across northern New Mexico, Arizona, southern Colorado, southern Utah, into part of southern Nevada near Overton. Artifacts from their homes have been found along the banks of the Muddy and Virgin rivers. The Anasazi civilization lasted for about 1,500 years and is often divided by scholars into four periods.

In the first period, from about 300 B.C. until A.D. 500—or approximately the same period as the Roman Empire—people were living in pit houses near the Muddy and Virgin rivers. They used only darts for hunting and made crude knives and scrapers from stone. They apparently did not learn how to make pottery or bows and arrows at this early stage. They did, however, know how to fashion fine baskets—an art which they practiced for centuries.

In the second period, probably A.D. 500 to A.D. 700, the Anasazi began to use pottery. The design suggests that they probably obtained their first vessels by trading with distant neighbors in other parts of the American Southwest. There is evidence that they mined salt, which they may have exchanged for products that were not available locally. Their craftsmen also built pit houses with masonry walls made of adobe and rocks. They had bins for storing foods, and eventually some learned to use the bow and arrow, a device much superior to the dart for hunting animals. As family members died, they formally buried their dead, leaving pottery in their graves. These innovations may seem to be only rudimentary elements of civilization, but they represented fundamental steps toward a more complex society. Some peoples of Asia and Europe were far ahead of the Anasazi in culture and technology fifteen centuries ago, but nonetheless, remarkable advances were occurring along the Virgin and Muddy rivers.

These riverbank communities were theaters for the transition from the Paleolithic to the Neolithic (i.e., New Stone Age) cultures. The greatest achievement of the Anasazi in southern Nevada—and perhaps the most important before the arrival of the Europeans in North America—occurred during their third period, in the years between about A.D. 700 and 1100, when inhabitants of the Muddy and Virgin river valleys began to cultivate the soil. They raised corn, beans, and squash. The Anasazi also developed an irrigation system, an achievement that marked a major transformation in many prehistoric civilizations around the world.

Some Anasazi builders constructed homes above the ground, using adobe for building material. The ruins of about a hundred of these "pueblos" have been found in Nevada, some of them having only one or two rooms, but a few having more than a hundred chambers. The city flourished because it had a more reliable food supply provided by agriculture. The remains of these buildings were discovered in 1924.

The Anasazi did not cease their hunting when they learned to plant and harvest vegetables. They killed deer, mountain sheep, and rabbits for meat. They gathered wild nuts (including piñon pine nuts), but these only supplemented their diet. They wove elaborate baskets and made more attractive pottery than the earlier pit dwellers had been able to fashion.

Scientists who dug into the ruins of this community—usually called the "Pueblo Grande of Nevada" or the "Lost City"—also found evidence that the Anasazi engaged in mining and trade. They extracted salt from underground deposits near their pueblo community and they mined turquoise nearby. They probably carried or sent these items to the east and west, getting pottery or seashells in exchange. It is believed that the Anasazi of the Lost City traded with other tribes in Death Valley, who probably obtained shells from the California coastal peoples. The Anasazi most likely obtained pottery from their distant neighbors living in Utah, northern Arizona, and New Mexico. It is possible that, in times of peace, a kind of common market existed.

In the salt mines of Anasazi country, scientists found rocks that had been fashioned into pick-like instruments, as well as crude ropes, and gourds for carrying water underground. All these implements testify to the skill of the adobe-house pueblo dwellers.

In the 1930s, the National Park Service established a museum near Overton to draw attention to this long-lost culture. In the 1980s, the Nevada State Museum assumed responsibility for this center, where visitors may obtain an impression of how the Anasazi lived a thousand years ago. Here, one can see the reconstructed displays of their dwellings and artifacts. The site of the original Lost City has been covered by the waters of Lake Mead since the 1930s, when Hoover Dam was built.

For reasons that we do not now understand, the Anasazi culture perished rather rapidly in southern Nevada. In the fourth period, sometime around 1150, they abandoned their homes and fields, making way for the Southern Paiutes. The Paiute bands had probably been moving into

*Indian house reconstructed on museum grounds in Overton, 1936.*
*(Pueblo Grande Collection, University of Nevada, Las Vegas, Library)*

southern Nevada gradually for several generations, and there may have been wars or conflicts between them and the Anasazi. About 1100, the Anasazi built a large house of eighty-four rooms in an elevated site above the valley floor, possibly a defense mechanism against an anticipated attack. It was constructed around a central square with limited entrance facilities—somewhat like an ancient Greek citadel or a medieval European fortress.

Did the Anasazi feel the need for castle-like bastions because they feared the Paiutes? This is speculation, and archeologists have not yet found tangible evidence of a battle. Perhaps disease, internal social dislocations, or a changing climate ruined the Anasazi civilization of the Lost City.

Before they disappeared, the Anasazi learned to domesticate dogs, cultivate cotton, and make decorative baskets, sandals, and netting. They had achieved the level of the Neolithic, or New Stone Age, culture in all major respects.

The Southern Paiutes who followed the Anasazi did not have many of the higher arts and skills of the pueblo dwellers. They were primarily a wandering people, spreading over a vast area, instead of confining themselves to the banks of the rivers. They did learn to grow crops— one of the few Nevada tribes to do so—but this was a less important source of food than hunting and gathering seeds. Probably their descendants gradually moved northwesterly, along the eastern edge of the Sierra Nevada, until they reached northwestern Nevada. These Northern Paiutes did not carry with them the tradition of agriculture. The Paiutes made relatively little technological progress from the time they reached Nevada, nearly a thousand years ago, until the arrival of the people of European descent.

## Mysterious Rock Art

Ancient Nevadans left one important and baffling reminder of their existence which may someday reveal more about their cultural patterns. In many locations, strange designs have been hammered, scraped, or painted on large rocks or the sides of cliffs. In some places there are only odd circles, spirals, or crisscrosses; in others, there are crude but clear representations of men, deer, and mountain sheep. Archeologists call these *petroglyphs* if they are cut into the surface of the rock, or *pictographs* if they are painted.

No one now fully understands the meanings of the symbols. Contemporary Native Americans have been unable to explain why or when they were created, and scientists have tried frequently to discover patterns that will give a clue to the mystery. It seems clear that the petroglyphs/pictographs were not intended to be the written form of a spoken language.

Rock pictures, scattered throughout the state, have been found in more than a hundred places. Some of the most remarkable are in the Valley of Fire near Overton; perhaps they were created by the people who lived in the Lost City. Some pictures resemble the kinds of large animals that the pueblo dwellers hunted. Other dramatic designs exist in Condor Canyon near Panaca, the Meadow Valley Wash south of Caliente, near the Truckee River east of Sparks, near Fort Churchill on the Carson River, on steep cliffs near Walker Lake, and several places in Churchill and Pershing counties. It is now believed that much of this design came into existence only a few centuries ago.

In 1962, Robert F. Heizer and Martin A. Baumhoff of the University of California made a careful study of places where rock pictures are found and developed some ideas about their meanings. Those pictures that can be identified often represent large animals like deer, antelope, or mountain sheep, and they often occur in places where such animals existed. There are few symbols of rabbits or fish. None of the rock art seems to suggest seed gathering, although for thousands of years people hunted rabbits and gathered seeds for food. Putting these facts together, Heizer and Baumhoff decided that the representations of the game must have had some special meaning related to hunting. In certain locations, the pictures seemed to be near hiding places where people could lie in ambush, waiting to surprise the large animals so they could hurl rocks or darts at them. Such practices were perhaps necessary before the bow and arrow came into common use. Patterns of rock art differ in northern and southern Nevada, which may reflect the different climates and hunting conditions in the two regions. The California scientists concluded that ancient hunters believed that a magical power was created when they carved the image of a deer on a rock cliff near the site of their hunt. Those who created the rock pictures were careful in their work; it is more logical to speculate that the ancient people attached some importance to their designs than to believe that they were merely "doodling."

In addition, there are some artifacts, identified and described by Donald R. Tuohy of the Nevada State Museum, that represent a rich spiritual life blending into daily needs of the unknown artists. In Lovelock

Cave, Professor Mark Harrington found a "composite monster" with the fins of a fish and the tail of a rattlesnake. Freestanding stone objects—statuettes—have been found throughout western Nevada. They could represent any real or imagined creature ranging from a fertility goddess to a grasshopper. Until the scholars help us with the puzzle, this must remain among Nevada's many mysteries.

## Nevada's Indian Peoples of the Modern Era

The Native Americans who lived in Nevada at the beginning of the historic period developed some basic skills to enable them to cope with a difficult environment. For all the peoples of this desert region, the problem of finding enough food was a perpetual challenge; they roamed a wide area in search of game and plants. Autumn was a time of intense activity because the nuts of the piñon pines ripened in the northern mountain ranges, and the northern bands gathered these nourishing delicacies in great quantities since the nuts could be stored for many months. In spring and summer families harvested cattails and tules at the edges of marshes, gathered chokecherries, and hunted rabbits, small rodents, squirrels, birds, antelope, or deer. Even insects, including grasshoppers, were a welcome food source at times. Near the rivers and lakes, fish were a crucial and abundant source of nourishment, especially at spawning time in the spring.

No clearly identified tribal organizations existed among the Nevada Indian peoples; they tended to live and move in bands of approximately fifty to a hundred people made up of several families, gathering in larger numbers when and where food was most plentiful. The bands worked together to drive the rabbits into large nets at the mouths of canyons, spear fish, and gather nuts. Their rituals and ceremonies, directed by a shaman, were meant to invoke the spirits that would aid in the hunt. Since the peoples moved so frequently, they had no permanent homes, but they often fashioned shelter from mud, sagebrush, or other handy materials. As winter approached, the wickiup was prepared with more care, with a pit in the center and a hole in the top to allow smoke from the essential fire to escape. A rabbit-skin robe was a great luxury.

Native Americans from Nevada were generally peaceful; no tradition of great warriors existed among them. At times various bands demanded tribute from strangers passing through their regions, but normally they were not aggressive. No formal social organization was apparent until

Anglo-Americans found a need to negotiate with "headmen." When they banded together to fight, it was normally an act of defensive desperation. They developed a reputation for thievery among the white population because they occasionally took their food and clothing, or drove off their livestock, but their societies lacked the sense of private ownership that the explorers and settlers from the East brought with them. And often, after the white-skinned population came in significant numbers, the Indian peoples were desperate for the necessities of life.

Because of the nomadic, precarious existence of the Native Americans in the early nineteenth century, the Anglo-American observers who first described them were quick to pass judgment, without realizing that the very earliest contacts with whites were devastating for the Indian peoples. The first waves of explorers and immigrants killed more wildlife, trampled more grass, and polluted more watering holes than had Native American tribes for centuries past, and European diseases caused much loss of life among the Native Americans everywhere in the West. The explorers and immigrants quickly disturbed an ecosystem on which the Indian peoples had relied for centuries.

At the time of the earliest European and American penetration of the Great Basin in the 1820s and 1830s, five main groups of Native Americans lived in the region that later became Nevada. The Southern Paiutes, who followed the Anasazi into the Colorado River Basin, were Numic people, related linguistically to the Shoshones—who roamed over much of central and northeastern Nevada, northern Utah, southern Idaho, and western Wyoming—and to the Northern Paiutes—whose domain stretched across the northwestern portion of Nevada and the Great Basin. Each of these three tribal groups belongs to the Uto-Aztec family of peoples and languages, which is widespread in western North America. The fourth group was composed of the Washo bands, whose domain included the Lake Tahoe region, parts of the upper Carson and Truckee river basins, and the central Sierra valleys of California. The Washos belonged to a different language group, the Hokan-Siouan, more commonly found on the central plains. The fifth group, long overlooked by Nevada historians, was the Mohave of the Death Valley and Colorado River region.

In all probability, there was a much higher, more serene Native American civilization living in the Great Basin province and northeastern Mojave Desert regions in 1810 than there was in the 1840s when "the Pathfinder," John Frémont, first described these bands systematically. Already by Frémont's time, several waves of travelers had crossed the more important rivers and meadows, killing game, trampling plants, and polluting water holes. A civilization of the kind he described in the 1840s was already being disrupted by the newcomers, even though they were only passing through.

It is impossible to know how many people lived in southern and northern Nevada 200 years ago, but some of the scientists have made thought-provoking guesses. Joy Leland, a Desert Research Institute scientist, theorized that perhaps as many as 40,000 people were scattered across the Great Basin 200 years ago. If that is so, the effects of the westward movement of explorers and pioneers were devastating in a very short period of time. Historians know this to have been the case in California.

By the time scientific anthropologists like Professor Julian Steward came on the scene in the 1920s to try to record prehistoric society, they were hearing the testimonials of a conquered, demoralized people. There had been, according to the best estimates, about 21,500 Native Americans in the Great Basin in the early 1870s; by the 1930s, when Steward was at work, there were 12,000, mostly disheartened and oppressed, who had only a folklorist memory of a better past.

## The Southern Paiutes

Before the arrival of European descendants, a dozen bands of Southern Paiutes lived north and west of the middle Colorado basin. Four of these—now designated as the Las Vegas, Moapa, Panaca, and Pahranagat tribes—lived in southern Nevada; others lived in southern Utah, northern Arizona, or adjacent parts of California. These groups were fluid and they roamed great distances across the arid landscape in search of food. Professor Steward assumed that they shared little communal activity in groups any larger than the family, and that they had no sense of community land ownership, although they did resent trespass by other bands. There may have been small, temporary villages at times, and even some small-scale irrigation along the Muddy and Moapa rivers.

The Virgin and Moapa river Paiutes cultivated crops such as beans, squash, and corn when the first Anglo-Americans came upon them in the 1820s. They occasionally propagated mesquite and grass seeds, and apparently they sometimes set fire to grass and brushlands to clear dead matter and encourage new growth. They engaged in modest trading with other bands, but all these activities supplemented their normal hunting for small game and seed gathering.

## The Shoshones

The Shoshone bands roamed across the widest expanse of territory within the Great Basin at the time that the first explorers arrived. It is customary to give the label "Western Shoshone" to those whose territory encompassed most of central and northeastern Nevada. They moved often and sought their food and clothing from the scarce birds, small animals, roots, and plants of the higher elevations. It was a great triumph to kill a large animal, such as a deer, since its meat could be dried and stored for months and its hide could provide a coveted blanket. More often, the Shoshones had to harvest the abundant rabbits, birds, gophers, and insects for their basic diet. Scores of edible plants—berries, wild carrots, wild onions, sego lilies, and some sage plants—will yield nourishment to those who know how to find and use them. The Shoshones, of necessity, were talented in this search.

In 1863, after more than a quarter century of exploration and emigration, when relations between "Anglos" and "Indians" were tense, two men made a treaty. The headman of the Ruby Valley Shoshones, named Te-moak, and the Nevada territorial governor and Indian agent, James W. Nye, signed a paper that seemed to respect the traditional rights of the Shoshones and also promised safe passage for emigrants and government officers. The Shoshones have since argued in federal court that they never yielded sovereignty to the land or to the aboriginal uses of it.

In the meantime, Native Americans were offered the chance to take up homes on "Indian farms" or "reservations," where—presumably— the government would give them the tools and the instruction to make them farmers and herdsmen. This policy became standard for the Shoshones and Paiutes for more than 25 years, from around 1859 until about 1887. Some Indian peoples settled into it, others continued their natural wandering ways.

## The Northern Paiutes

The Northern Paiutes, who are ethnically and linguistically related to the Southern Paiutes and Shoshones, ranged over an area of more than 75,000 square miles in western Nevada and adjacent areas of California, Oregon, and Idaho. There were twenty distinct bands when the first explorers arrived more than 150 years ago, each band consisting of 100 to 200 people and each identified with a region where their main food supplies could be found. They labeled themselves and their neighbors as "pine-nut eaters," "trout eaters," "cui-ui eaters," etc.

Recent studies of the Northern Paiutes indicate that these bands had very loose traditions of leadership and a peaceful, cooperative relationship with other groups. Shamans, or spiritual teachers, had considerable prestige because people believed they possessed spiritual powers. Warriors assumed authority on an ad hoc basis as necessary. The Northern Paiutes did not conduct wars of conquest; all the evidence indicates that they were a placid, hospitable people, willing to share their meager resources with others.

## The Washos

The smallest and perhaps least understood unit of the northern Nevada Native American groups was the Washo, who hunted, fished, and gathered foods in the vicinity of Lake Tahoe and the territory immediately north, east, and south of there. They were much more acclimated to the mountain environment than to the high, inland desert where the Paiutes predominated. They ranged into the Carson and Eagle valleys and the Truckee Meadows, sharing their resources at times (or occasionally competing) with the Northern Paiutes. Before the coming of the Anglo-Americans, they appear to have been more fortunate than the Paiutes because their Sierra hunting and fishing lands were richer. At the time of the arrival of the white man, the Northern Paiutes had apparently intimidated and dominated the Washo bands.

In spite of their seemingly inferior social status, the Washo won respect for their artistry in weaving splendid baskets from native fibers. From their ranks came Dat-so-la-lee, an outstanding basket maker among the artists of the Far West. She spent much of her life serving the family of a Carson City medical practitioner, Dr. S. L. Lee. If her name, and that of the doctor, are rattled off the tongue rapidly enough, we may come to understand that the name which history has given to this incomparable Washo artist may have originated as a matter of convenience: Dr. S. L. Lee became Dat-so-la-lee. Her work was made known to the outside world largely through the efforts of Abe Cohn of Carson City, who subsidized her artistic efforts. While we shall probably never know the Washo name of this talented woman, museums across the land recognized her creations, which became testimonials to the artistic instincts of the most downtrodden of Native Americans.

## The Mohave People of the Lower Colorado

There was one other community of Native Americans that had some claim to land within the present state of Nevada at the beginning of the historical era; some Mohaves had more or less permanent homes along the lower Colorado River near the present site of Davis Dam. Most of the country through which they roamed lay in California and Arizona, but their territory extended northward beyond Laughlin, into the southern tip of Nevada. They had villages on the eastern side of the Colorado River, which were visited by the earliest explorers of the region.

This group of Native Americans was remarkable for its agricultural practices, which had apparently been under way for several generations when the white man arrived. On a narrow band of territory adjacent to the river, they waited for the spring floods to fertilize the land and recede, and then they planted their gardens with corn, melons, pumpkins, and beans. The crops ripened quickly in this hot climate, and the produce provided the Mohave with a more varied diet than that available to their distant northern neighbors. They gained a reputation among the Spaniards of the California missions for being capable warriors when the need arose. In the 1980s, a few hundred members of this band continued to live on the Fort Mojave Reservation in the extreme southern tip of Nevada and on the Colorado River Reservation in Arizona.

From the 1940s until the 1980s, the American system of justice was highly sensitive to the rights of minorities, and in this social climate there were increased efforts to acknowledge Native American rights and traditions. This development followed several false starts in formulating a coherent policy in Indian affairs, and it served to re-awaken the self-determination among many Native Americans. The United States government took considerable pains to find some equitable means of compensating the Indian peoples for the injustices done to them a century or more earlier. Under the Constitution of the United States, the Native Americans of the West owned the lands which they occupied, and only the Congress, by treaty, could extinguish that ownership. The practices of the frontiersmen did not often honor the treaties when they were signed; the early cowboys and miners did not often wait for treaties to be negotiated before they made their claims. Yet the effort to do justice has been persistent in the last half of the twentieth century.

If land, game, or water was illegally taken from the Indian peoples,

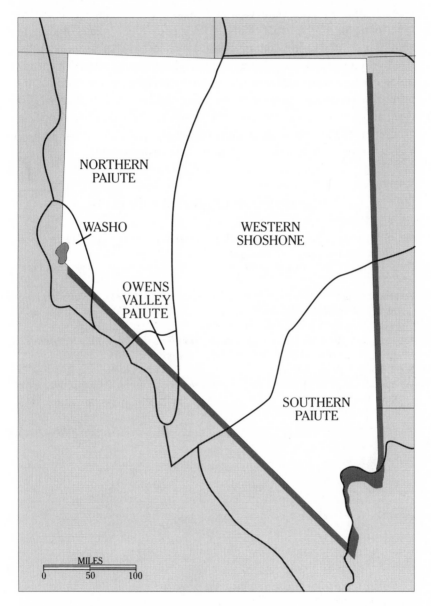

NORTHERN
PAIUTE

WASHO

OWENS
VALLEY
PAIUTE

WESTERN
SHOSHONE

SOUTHERN
PAIUTE

MILES
0    50    100

*Indians of Nevada*

what was the remedy? In 1946, Congress passed the Indian Claims Commission Act, which sought to find a legal way to compensate Native Americans for all the tribal claims of their peoples by means of a single, equitable formula. The commission established by this law was authorized to consider those claims that could be documented by anthropological and historical means and to set a value on the land for the purpose of compensating the tribes. It was a long and complicated process, and the results seemed unsatisfactory to several Native American groups more than forty years later. Yet the studies which resulted from this act have provided an important body of historical data.

## Suggested Supplementary Reading

Crum, Stephen J. *The Road on Which We Came: A History of the Western Shoshone.* Salt Lake City: University of Utah Press, 1994.

Forbes, Jack D., ed. *Nevada Indians Speak.* Reno: University of Nevada Press, 1967.

Knack, Martha C., and Omer C. Stewart. *As Long as the River Shall Run: An Ethnohistory of Pyramid Lake Indian Reservation.* Berkeley: University of California Press, 1984.

Kroeber, A. L. *Mohave Indians: Report on Aboriginal Territory and Occupancy of the Mohave Tribe.* New York: Garland Publishing Inc., 1974.

Scott, Lalla. *Karnee: A Paiute Narrative.* Reno: University of Nevada Press, 1966.

Wheat, Margaret M. *Survival Arts of the Primitive Paiutes.* Reno: University of Nevada Press, 1967.

# 3

## The First Explorers

THOSE WHO opened the Great Basin and the central Colorado River region to exploration and early settlement—the makers of the first maps—came from three directions and represented three cultures: Spain, the United States, and Britain or Canada. The entire Far West became an arena where the interests of these three competed, and the Nevada deserts were part of the stakes.

### The Spanish Expeditions

The Spaniards who conquered and partly colonized Mexico were the first representatives of European civilization to penetrate the spacious region between the Rocky Mountains and the Pacific Ocean. They entered New Mexico in the 1500s and established Santa Fe in 1609, at about the same time that the first English settlers landed 2,000 miles away on the Atlantic Coast. For more than 150 years, the Spaniards did not explore "upper" California or the Great Basin because their imperialistic attentions were diverted elsewhere in the Southwest and across the seas. In the 1760s, news of Russian explorations headed toward California from the Northwest reached Madrid and New Spain (i.e., Mexico). At the same time, a new spirit of evangelical zeal caused Spanish Franciscan fathers to look for new peoples to convert to Christianity. The combination of these events prompted authorities to send a joint military-missionary expedition northward along the coast from Mexico.

In 1769 the Franciscans, under Father Junípero Serra, established their first mission at San Diego, while Father Serra's military colleagues moved northward toward Monterey to create a presidio. Within a few years, missions and outposts stretched north along the coastline as far as San Francisco Bay; the village of Los Angeles was founded by a handful of outcasts in 1781. Father Serra, at first a California hero, became controversial in modern California history and in the deliberations of the Roman Catholic church, for when he was proposed for sainthood, there were lingering reports that he or his fellow missionaries abused and mistreated the Indian people.

By 1823, twenty-one missions had been established. They were small and, as outposts of the expansive Spanish empire, quite tenuous, but they did help spread seeds of Hispanic names and culture far inland, to places where Spanish feet had probably never walked. At times in the past, scholars have speculated that a few early Spaniards might have penetrated southern Nevada, but there is no strong evidence that they ever did so.

In 1776, the year of the Declaration of Independence, other Spanish padres tried to find routes between their colonies in New Mexico and the newly founded missions in California. One was renowned Father Francisco Garcés, who traveled from the mouth of the Colorado River northward, and then westward through the California desert to the coast. Nevadans have long speculated on the question of whether he saw the southern extremity of the state that would one day bear the Spanish name for "snow-capped"—i.e., "Nevada."

In that same year, two other churchmen from Santa Fe set out to search for a more northerly route toward California. Father Francisco Silvestre Velez de Escalante and Father Francisco Atanasio Dominguez, together with a few soldiers, traveled from Santa Fe into central Utah, saw a few small streams running westward, and observed the life of the Indians. Discouraged by bad weather, they decided not to go on to California. When later mapmakers compiled their information about the rivers that the priests had described, they guessed that there must be a majestic waterway flowing from central Utah to the Pacific Ocean because they had seen the Sevier River of Utah, and the missionaries of California had described the Sacramento River pouring into San Francisco Bay from the east. Nothing in their experience had taught them to contemplate a vast "land of interior drainage." Because of this incorrect guess, the cartographers of the early 1800s drew maps showing a large river, which they called the San Buenaventura, flowing from central Utah to northern California. It required several expeditions to correct this well-intentioned but overly optimistic blunder.

As the Spanish missionaries penetrated Alta California—as the present state of California was called in the eighteenth century—they stayed within a few miles of the coastline. There is no evidence that they or their military counterparts who represented the Bourbon crown in Madrid had much taste for exploring the inland valleys and mountains, and they certainly had no appreciation for the potential natural riches of the region they had opened. The missions were often short of food, and they were largely unsuccessful in converting the Native Americans to Catholicism.

In 1819, a band of Mohaves raided one of the missions in the Los Angeles area, and some people were killed. This episode led to a little-known expedition of revenge from the San Gabriel Mission, through the Cajon Pass, and into the Mojave Desert. A small army of fifty-five mounted soldiers directed by Gabriel Morara, one of the most adventuresome of the Spanish soldiers, marched to the northeast to punish the troublemakers. This troupe marched for at least ten days toward, and probably beyond, the Colorado River, but their exact route is unknown. The grass and water were too scarce for a unit of this size and their animals, so they returned to San Gabriel without satisfying their crusading vengeance. Did they touch or see the environs of Searchlight or Las Vegas? Perhaps we shall never know, but they belong in the annals of history, along with Garcés, Escalante, and Dominguez, who explored the adjacent regions.

One of Nevada's best-known creative writers, Walter Van Tilburg Clark, wrote an article late in his life in which he speculated on what the Spaniards might have thought if they had stopped at the Las Vegas springs:

They were nearly fearless explorers of desert, but this place made them afraid.

No, if any of the early Spaniards stopped at the springs, they probably squinted northward into that endless perspective of barren, wavering, dull-colored mountains, and turned away and stayed where they were. They rested and drank themselves back from what the desert had done to them, and then, if it was in the hot months, late some afternoon, when the sun was far down and weakened, started on west, unimaginably small, slow and insignificant upon that pale expanse, meaning to use the night and starlight to travel by. They would have looked north again, and seen the Unknown Land, just a little time before so forbidding, so nearly colorless and featureless, now assuming dramatic color and shape, stained by the late sunlight and carved by the shadows. They would have felt then an attraction of mystery; but they knew the desert too well to be misled. They kept on westward in the pleasant, dry air of evening, to California. (Clark, "Nevada's Fateful Desert," *Holiday*, 22, November 1957, p. 76.)

The Spaniards never penetrated Nevada at all, if contemporary interpretations of history are to be trusted. But they may have brushed its edges, and later generations gave Spanish names to places they never saw. In addition, their presence among the Indian people initiated the beginning of the dislocating of the Native American cultures. After Mexico declared its independence from Spain, California's forts and missions passed under Mexican jurisdiction in 1822, but its new rulers almost completely ignored them. California and the hinterlands were ripe for exploration by others coming overland from the north and east.

## The Anglo-American Quests

English settlers and their descendants lived on the North American continent for more than 200 years before any of them saw the mountains and valleys of Nevada. The Declaration of Independence was 50 years old and five presidents had completed their terms of office before any Anglo-American entered this terrain. It was the last large portion of the forty-eight contiguous continental states to be thoroughly explored and mapped. Yet it was the region in the Far West that evolved most rapidly from terra incognita to statehood within the American Union.

President Thomas Jefferson promoted the first early governmental exploration of the Far West when he sent Meriwether Lewis and William Clark across the northern plains, through the Rocky Mountains, and into the Columbia River Basin in the years 1803–1806. Although they did not come within 200 miles of what would become the state of Nevada, they brought back reports of rich lands and large rivers with plenty of fur-bearing animals. Within a few years after they wrote their reports, hundreds of energetic young men were following their tracks into the Rocky Mountains. Fur trapping and trading was a risky business, but it attracted people as adventuresome as the astronauts of the twentieth century.

Between 1826, when the first Anglo-American explorers entered Nevada, and 1845, most of the region's topographical and geographical features were discovered by hardy groups of mountain men, fur trappers, and government agents. The first English-speaking explorers were no better prepared than the Indians to survive the rigors of the desert. In fact, the earliest explorers occasionally experienced much hardship because they were ignorant of the water holes that sustained the Native Americans.

The fur-trapping and trading business was one of the first enterprises that offered large profits on the frontier, from the opening of the Virginia frontier in the early 1600s until about the 1840s. Women and men of New York, London, and Paris regarded fur hats and coats from the "wild west" as fashionable items, and those who brought them to the trading posts occasionally became famous figures in the popular journals of the nineteenth century.

In 1826, small bands of these fur traders touched the extremes of the southern and northern Great Basin, which in their day was almost as remote as the moon. Both the British and American governments had claims on the Columbia River Basin of the Northwest under a joint occupation agreement signed in 1818, and two representatives of rival fur companies carried the hopes of their politicians into the Great Basin. British-Canadian trappers, on behalf of the famous Hudson's Bay Company, tried to establish a monopoly on the beaver resources of the Columbia River Basin. In 1825, a new American organization known as the Rocky Mountain Fur Company was penetrating the Far West to challenge this assertion. The British interests decided to extend their operations southward from the Columbia to kill as many animals as possible and thus to discourage the Americans. Hence Nevada's written history begins with a struggle to exploit the resources of land as rapidly as possible. That struggle has recurred several times throughout Nevada's history.

The first American expedition, composed of fifteen men under the leadership of Jedediah Strong Smith of the Rocky Mountain Fur Company, located the eastern and southern extremes of the Great Basin in the summer of 1826, without, of course, identifying it. Trekking southwestward from the Great Salt Lake, they entered Nevada on the Virgin River, followed it approximately to the site of the present town of Bunkerville, and then passed along the eastern edge of the Colorado River southward to a point near Needles, California. There they met Indians who guided them westward across the Colorado River and through the torrid desert of southern California to the San Gabriel Mission, which the Spaniards had established near the present site of Los Angeles. The land was as barren as any he had ever seen, and Smith found no new regions for fur trapping. He had, however, wandered into lands controlled by the Mexicans, who had won their independence from Spain only a few years earlier. Technically, he was trespassing on the territory of a foreign power, but he was casual about that infringement.

The Mexicans treated Smith's party well enough, but they insisted that the Americans leave by the same route they had used to enter California. Disregarding this order, Smith took his party northward into the San Joaquin Valley early in 1827. Finding that it would be difficult to cross the snow-covered Sierra in the spring, Smith decided to leave most of his party in California, proceed directly toward the Great Salt Lake with only two men, and return later for the remainder of his party. He apparently hoped that once across the Sierra, he would find the San Buenaventura River, which had been mentioned by the Spanish explorers.

The route that Smith and his two companions took across Nevada in 1827 was a mystery for many years, but in the 1960s a manuscript copy of his journal came to light in St. Louis. It now seems certain that Smith and his men crossed the Sierra approximately on the route of present-day Highway 89, followed the West Walker River, and saw Walker Lake. The three then proceeded eastward across the arid, life-threatening center of the Great Basin. When they could not find game, they killed and ate their mules. In some places they struggled across high mountain passes, in others they encountered deep sand. Often they had to ration their water carefully, and one day they dug themselves into the ground to get relief from the blistering heat. One of the explorers nearly died when they failed to find water for several days. Through a combination of bravery and desperation, they finally reached the Great Salt Lake and reestablished contact with their company. They had crossed the Sierra, the middle of Nevada, and half of Utah in about six weeks, one of the most remarkable feats in the history of western exploration.

Smith returned to California in that same year to rejoin the companions whom he had left behind. He followed his original route down the Virgin and Colorado rivers and westward across the Mojave Desert again, after a battle with Indians near the Colorado River in which ten of his men were killed. He made contact with his former party in California as planned, but did not risk the perils of the central Great Basin for another eastward trek. This time he detoured far northward into Oregon, where once again his party had a bloody encounter with the Native Americans, and most of Smith's men perished in battle. Smith barely escaped with his life.

The leading trapper of the Hudson's Bay Company in this region at the time of Smith's first trek down the Virgin River was Peter Skene Ogden, a Canadian-born adventurer who made six expeditions into the so-called Snake River Country between 1825 and 1831. Three of these trips penetrated Nevada—the first in the spring of 1826, when Ogden's men explored those tributaries of the Snake River now known as the Bruneau and Owyhee rivers, which rise in northern Elko County.

Once again, because of newly uncovered documents, scholars have learned much about the probable paths that Ogden took into the Unknown Territory, as the interior basin was frequently called in the 1820s. The Hudson's Bay Company records in Britain show that Ogden not only explored almost the entire Humboldt River basin in 1828 and trapped beavers in the vicinity of Winnemucca, but also that he probably returned in 1829–1830. Although there is still some uncertainty about his route in this final "Snake Country Expedition," he and his followers probably explored the lower Humboldt River, the Humboldt Sink, the lower Carson River, the Walker Lake area, and the vast desert region between Walker Lake and the Colorado River. His journal suggests that he proceeded along the eastern edge of the southern Sierra, eastward to the Colorado, then southward to the Gulf of California, and finally westward across the Mojave Desert on a route similar to that followed by Smith.

If indeed Ogden's men did this, they made a trek that matches the most remarkable exploits of the great British explorers in the depths of Africa and the sands of Arabia. This expedition has not had the advantages of coverage by a romantic press, but it challenges the research and imagination of future scholars of far western history to probe the possibilities of this journey.

Several other explorers touched the southern edges of Nevada in this same era. Ewing Young, one of the leading fur merchants of the Southwest, passed through the southern regions in 1829. One member of his party was Christopher "Kit" Carson, later to become one of the most famous mountain men. In the same year, according to another recently discovered diary, Antonio Armijo, a Mexican trader leading about sixty men, penetrated the Las Vegas Valley while exploring the region between New Mexico and Los Angeles. After passing through southern Utah, he found the Virgin River and proceeded southward to the Colorado.

Las Vegas historian Elizabeth Warren has produced an excellent analysis of the Armijo expedition which has significantly changed the historical analysis of this trek. One young man in the party—Rafael Rivera—became separated from the main group for several days while exploring the Colorado River, and he is believed to have found Las Vegas Valley and to have led the main party into it. The group probably followed the Las Vegas Wash upland from the Colorado River, through the southern part of Las Vegas Valley, then westward to the Mojave River, and ultimately to the San Gabriel Mission.

Soon thereafter, George Wolfskill and George Yount made a trek similar to that of Jedediah Smith. By the early 1830s, there was a more-or-less established route between central Utah and southern California known as the Old Spanish Trail, although the Spanish explorers had never used it in its entirety. The eastern segment of this trail extended to Santa Fe and intersected other trails northward into Kansas and southward into Mexico. The southwestern portion became known as the Mormon Trail; it followed approximately the same route as Interstate Freeway 15 across the Las Vegas Valley.

Within three years after Ogden made his last expedition, another squad of fur trappers explored the northern river—sometimes called Ogden's or Mary's, but eventually Humboldt's River. In 1833, Joseph R. Walker, serving under the leadership of U.S. Army Captain Benjamin L. E. Bonneville in the Rocky Mountains, led an expedition of about forty men westward from the upper Green River into the Great Basin. This activity was unauthorized, but it may have been an espionage mission into foreign territory for the army. They traveled along "Ogden's" River from near the headwaters to the Humboldt Sink, and slaughtered some thirty or forty Indians there who seemed to be threatening their camps. They then passed over the Sierra and across the Central Valley to Monterey— then the capital of California. After a comfortable and friendly rest lasting several months among the "Californios," Walker and his men traveled eastward once more. Eventually he became a semi-heroic figure in the narrative that the popular novelist Washington Irving wrote about the adventures of Captain Bonneville.

So, during the decade between 1825 and 1835 several teams of fur trappers/explorers passed around or through the heart of the inland deserts of the West. They did not quite comprehend what they had found, and there was no systematic way of conveying their information to a larger public, which was poised at mid-continent for one of civilization's periodic migrations westward. But the awesome interior basin had been visited, and most of the visitors had survived. The hordes of Anglo-Americans were not far behind.

The first generation of explorers won only modest fame for their exploits, in part perhaps because they did not keep very thorough records or because their accounts were unknown to popular writers and politicians for generations. By the 1840s and 1850s, however, matters were quite different. Among those who came westward in those years were men who had government backing, political ambition, and a large measure of good luck. Historians have been abundantly generous in recognizing them.

## John Frémont, Kit Carson, and Joseph Walker

John Frémont holds a prominent place in national and western history not only because of several successful expeditions, but also because he led a rebellion in Mexican-controlled California, helped achieve the conquest of the Southwest for the United States, and was elected United States senator from California. In 1856, he became the first Republican candidate for president. He built his early reputation on the reports that he wrote after exploring the West, but he had much expert help in doing so from tough mountain men like Kit Carson and Joseph Walker. Frémont wisely hired Carson for $100 per month—three times the normal wage for an experienced trapper—to provide expert advice about the unknown territory.

Frémont mounted two significant expeditions that traversed Nevada. He renamed its rivers and lakes, described the fundamental physiographic features, and proved that there was no San Buenaventura River. His first foray into the Great Basin occurred in 1843–1844, when he moved southward from the Columbia River Basin, discovered Pyramid Lake together with its connection to the Truckee River, and then crossed the Sierra into central California. During their return trip eastward, they passed through the Las Vegas Valley by following the Old Spanish Trail. Although it was still early in May, they suffered from the severe heat and some of their animals died of thirst or were killed by Indians. One member of the party died in a scuffle with Native Americans on the Virgin River.

Frémont's second probing of the Nevada desert came in 1845, and this time he was accompanied by Walker and Carson, both experienced scouts. Crossing the center of the basin from east to west in two groups, they redefined the limits of the Humboldt, Carson, Walker, and Truckee river basins. By this time, they were certain of all the most important physiographic features of the Great Basin—which is the name that Frémont gave to this vast land of interior drainage. Frémont made a less important crossing of Nevada in 1853, traversing the region slightly north of the area crossed by the Manly party in 1849. Frémont made a much more thorough record of his travels and discoveries than any of his predecessors had done, and his reports and maps became important to later emigrant parties. For this reason, the names that he gave to the most prominent natural landmarks became official. It was he who gave Ogden's River the name of Baron Alexander von Humboldt, a German scientist of international renown (who never saw the region). He also designated the Carson and Walker rivers for his capable guides. Few natural features in Nevada bear his name, but in later years he would be memorialized by Fremont Street in Las Vegas.

Peter Ogden, Jedediah Smith, Antonio Armijo, Joseph Walker, and John Frémont—these were the "space explorers" of their day. The space into which they traveled was on the surface of the earth, but that does not make their ventures any less significant in the human quest for knowledge than the work of the astronauts in the late twentieth century. They took great risks, and many of their companions gave their lives in the search. But since the beginning of the human experience, this has been the drive of humanity: to explore the unknown and to add some additional fragments of knowledge to our understanding of the earth.

## Suggested Supplementary Reading

Cline, Gloria Griffin. *Exploring the Great Basin*. Norman: University of Oklahoma Press, 1963.

Frémont, John Charles. *The Expeditions of John Charles Frémont*. Ed. Donald Jackson and Mary Lee Spence. Vol. 1, *Travels from 1838 to 1844*. Urbana: University of Illinois Press, 1970.

Rolle, Andrew F. *John Charles Frémont: Character as Destiny*. Norman: University of Oklahoma Press, 1992.

Smith, Jedediah S. *The Southwest Expedition of Jedediah Strong Smith: His Personal Account of the Journey to California — 1826–1827*. Edited with an introduction by George R. Brooks. Glendale: Arthur H. Clark Co., 1977.

Stone, Irving. *Men to Match My Mountains: The Opening of the Far West, 1840–1990*. Garden City, N.Y.: Doubleday, 1956.

# 4

# Settlers on the Move,
# 1841–1850

**M**UCH OF the history of America is the description of the massive westward migration of people of European descent. The earliest colonists from England came westward across the Atlantic Ocean to Virginia in 1607. After the Europeans had established their first towns and farms in Virginia, almost 200 years elapsed before their descendants crossed the Appalachian Mountains to settle, and the westward movement gained momentum. Between 1800 and 1840, citizens of the new nation pushed westward through the forests, from the Appalachian Mountains to the middle of the continent, and then west of the Mississippi River. For a few years they stopped at that point, like water behind a dam, because the arid prairies and the "Indian Barrier" presented many hazards. But they were eager for new land since the East was becoming more densely populated. Between 1840 and 1850 the dam broke and the American nation spilled westward to the Pacific Coast. At first it was a trickle and later a relentless flood, not stopping until it reached the shores of the Pacific.

Powerful social forces were at work in the young American society, which encouraged the westward thrust. Land hunger was a chronic condition for the growing population, and Congress adopted a generous land policy on its public domain. The famous Preemption Act of 1841 even recognized the rights of squatters to claim land simply by using it. During the 1840s, Manifest Destiny became a political slogan and a social expectation, asserting that the Yankees had a natural right to claim territory from coast to coast.

The story of Nevada as a political and cultural entity is a relatively late chapter in the history of the westward movement because the Great Basin and the Colorado River were so remote from the eastern seaboard and so forbidding in appearance to the early explorers. Yet two important emigrant groups crossed the region in 1841—one in the north and the other in the south.

## The Bartleson-Bidwell Party, 1841

It was reports of abundant land in California that drew the original pilgrims to the Far West. By the autumn of 1840, hundreds of excited persons had joined the Western Emigration Society, which had publicized its intentions to make an organized trek westward in the spring of 1841 to the Central Valley near Sacramento.

When spring arrived and it was time to depart, only sixty-nine persons appeared at the designated meeting place near Independence, Missouri. The main organizer of the party was John Bidwell, a young man with almost no knowledge of the western frontier. "We knew that California lay west," he said later, "and that was the extent of our knowledge." Another leader was John Bartleson, an ill-tempered and irresponsible character who demanded and got the title of captain of the company. He knew no more about how to get to California than did Bidwell.

As they started up the Missouri River along the trail established by the fur traders, they met a group of Jesuit missionaries who were headed for Oregon. Their guide was Thomas "Broken Hand" Fitzpatrick, previously a fur trapper in the Rocky Mountains, who knew that region well. This was a piece of good luck, because he guided them more than 1,000 miles to the Bear River, north of the Great Salt Lake. At that point, however, the missionaries and Fitzpatrick turned toward Oregon, and the emigrants had to decide whether to follow them or set out on their own to the southwest over the unknown trail to California. About half the party abandoned their original goal, following Fitzpatrick to the northwest. Thirty-four others took their chances with the unknown deserts of the Great Basin. Among these were Nancy Kelsey and her small daughter—the first Anglo-American woman and child to make the trip across the Great Basin.

As they crossed the desert west of the Great Salt Lake, their troubles began. Wagon wheels often became stuck in the sand and tangled in the underbrush, the animals frequently became exhausted, and water was scarce. After a few days of slow progress, they were delighted to find a towering mountain, which yielded fresh water and good grass for their oxen and horses. This later came to be known as Pilot Peak (located in eastern Elko County, close to the Nevada-Utah boundary); it became a landmark for thousands of later emigrants who followed in the footsteps of Bartleson and Bidwell.

Westward beyond Pilot Peak, the heavy wagons exhausted their oxen, so the emigrants eventually abandoned most of the hardware they had been hauling. They pushed on across the Ruby Mountains into the Humboldt basin, most of them on foot because few had horses. During their tedious procession down the winding little river in the chilly autumn days, some men became impatient at the pace. Several who had horses decided to proceed ahead of the hikers and oxen. One day, near the present site of Winnemucca, they divided the food. Eight men, including Bartleson, went on ahead.

Bidwell and the cool-headed Benjamin Kelsey—the husband of Nancy —led the remaining party past the Humboldt Sink, across the frightening Forty Mile Desert to the Carson River, then southward until they found the Walker River, and on toward the awesome Sierra Nevada. Unexpectedly, they encountered Bartleson and his seven companions, who had taken a wrong turn and wandered into the desert. Some Indians befriended them and gave them pine nuts and fish, which saved them from starvation. Now they were willing to take their chances with the main party.

It required about two weeks for the party to struggle across the snowy mountains, probably by way of Sonora Pass. The narrative of their crossing is like the account of Smith's experience; they ran out of food, killed their oxen, and finally slaughtered their horses for meat. Indians took some of their livestock, and they suffered some painful falls on the steep mountainsides. But their plight ended happily on the last day of October when they arrived in the San Joaquin Valley, where they found antelope and wild fowl in abundance and the ranch of the promoter who had encouraged them to come. Without a map or a guide, they had safely crossed the western half of the continent.

In spite of their ignorance and poor organization, the Bartleson-Bidwell party proved that emigrants could make the long trek to California. No lives were lost, and there were few conflicts with Indians. It required six months to make the journey, but after it was finished the

California climate and opportunities seemed to make their ordeal worthwhile. Within months, back in the heartland of America, many others were preparing to follow.

## Rowland-Workman and Others, 1841–1845

Later in the same season in which the Bartleson-Bidwell party completed their journey, another contingent made a trip almost as remarkable from Santa Fe to Los Angeles, passing through the Las Vegas Valley en route. Two men who had missed the Bartleson-Bidwell departure from Missouri went southward and arrived in Santa Fe. There they joined a score of others under the leadership of William Workman and John Rowland to attempt a westward expedition on the Old Spanish Trail. They followed northwesterly from Santa Fe through Utah, then southwesterly along the route that Jedediah Smith had blazed fifteen years earlier. This route had been known by traders (including men herding Indian slaves) for several years, and was thought to be relatively safe. Workman and Rowland successfully drove a band of sheep with them, obtained land grants from the Mexican authorities, and became prominent ranchero builders in southern California near San Gabriel. Their trip from Santa Fe to San Gabriel required only two months in late summer and early autumn, but they were startled by the bleak landscape that they crossed.

John Rowland made another trip along the Old Spanish Trail during the following year, 1842, but this time there was much hardship and many animals died. This trail never attained the popularity of the Humboldt Trail, which offered a slightly better terrain for wagons and a milder climate.

No immediate stampede to the West followed on the heels of the successful Bartleson-Bidwell and Rowland-Workman parties. News traveled slowly and over the next few years, the numbers of emigrants to make the trip were small. However, one member of the Bartleson group, Joseph B. Chiles, went back to Missouri in 1842, and the following year he was ready to lead another contingent westward, this time with the veteran explorer Joseph Walker as an additional guide.

This caravan started with many wagons loaded with furniture, farm equipment, and other machinery; Chiles assured his followers that they could transport all those goods to California. The party divided at Ft. Hall, and most of those who went to California managed to get their wagons there after abandoning much of their portable property. The credit for their success belonged to Walker, who guided them down the Humboldt, then southward to the Walker River, and eventually across Walker Pass.

Several parties followed the Humboldt Trail in the early 1840s, among the most significant being the one led by Elisha Stevens, Martin Murphy, and John Townsend in 1844—the year that Frémont discovered Pyramid Lake and the Truckee River. This group employed the services of a venerable mountain man, Caleb Greenwood, who was commonly known as "Old Greenwood" because he was over eighty years of age, with more than four decades of experience in the western wilderness. This group did not follow the usual route from the Humboldt Sink southward to the Carson or Walker rivers; rather it took a virtually unknown trail across the Forty Mile Desert to another river, which Frémont called the "Salmon Trout" and which they designated as the Truckee River. The canyon was steep and narrow in places, sometimes so confining that they had to walk in the middle of the water. Their feet bled and their animals suffered. After refreshing themselves in the fertile Truckee Meadows where the cities of Reno and Sparks would later be built, they started the treacherous climb over present-day Donner Summit. Under the direction of Old Greenwood, they disassembled their wagons, made pulleys and windlasses, and hoisted their possessions piece by piece over the steep higher embankments. In the end, they reached the Central Valley of California with most of their wagons, equipment, and animals.

Other parties crossed Nevada by the Humboldt route in 1845, and the Frémont-Walker group made its second, most important survey of the Great Basin in that same year. The curious Native Americans who watched and sometimes harassed the struggling men and beasts of burden could not have known that these were the advance scouts of a race that would eventually overwhelm their aboriginal homes.

Anthropologists have assembled evidence that the earliest explorers and immigrants did extensive damage to the resources on which the Native Americans had traditionally relied. Even when they did not fight the Indian peoples, they consumed the grass, game, and other resources on which the Indians depended for their survival. As the wave of immigrants increased—when it reached flood tide in 1849 and thereafter—the food and fiber of the Native Americans were devastated.

## The Donner Disaster, 1846–1847

By the winter of 1845, the publicity about the wonders of California had spread far and wide. Middle America knew that several groups had successfully made the long trip across the plains, mountains, and deserts. Even at that time, there were land promoters like John Marsh and the Swiss immigrant John Sutter (who had built a fort at Sacramento), publicizing the rich lands of central California. They published promotional propaganda in the frontier newspapers of Missouri and other reports appeared in East Coast cities. There were also promoters ready to sell their services to those on the Missouri frontier who had heard the call of the California promoters. One such individual was Lansford Hastings, who was responsible for encouraging the Donner party.

Hastings had found an easy way to get to California—or so his hastily printed guidebook said. That little document described much of the route well, but it misled the emigrants about a cutoff through the Ruby Mountains. The followers of Hastings did not know that he had traversed only part of the trail that he was promoting; they did not expect him to begin as their guide and to abandon them when the trek became difficult.

Yet it is clear that the Donners themselves held much of the responsibility for the tragedy. Eighty-seven people left Missouri in May, and they experienced more than the usual trouble reaching their destination because they passed through a little-known rugged section of the Rocky Mountains, in spite of warnings that they should stay on the main trail. They struggled across the Bonneville Salt Flats and Ruby Mountains without a guide, and then down the Humboldt River during a scorching period when the waters were laden with bitter alkaline. Oxen choked and rebelled, Indians circled and drove off livestock, a murder occurred, and the travelers fought among themselves. Death seemed to hover over the hapless band as they crossed the Forty Mile Desert between the lower Humboldt River and the Big Bend of the Truckee River. Upon reaching the Truckee Meadows, they rested beside the cool waters of the river for several days.

The worst was yet to come. They entered the upper Truckee Canyon in October just as early, heavy snows began to fall. Most foundered at Donner Lake, just before the steepest part of the ascent to the summit. Fifteen tried to surmount the high mountain pass through the deep snowdrifts; seven got through and later returned to help their comrades. By that time, the desperate remnant had eaten shoe leather, dogs, and

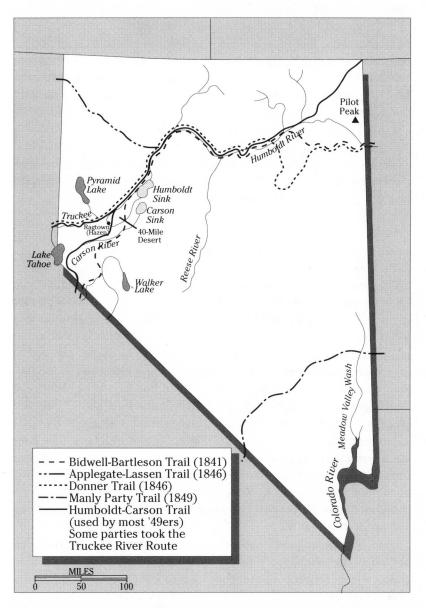

Emigrant Trails Through Nevada

decaying human flesh. Of the eighty-seven who had taken the Hastings Cutoff, forty-seven survived, including most of the women and children.

The experiences of the Donner party were even more widely publicized than the achievements of the mountain men and John Frémont. For two years, all the success stories of the earlier emigrants and explorers faded into the shadows cast by reports of the Donner tragedy. Like space explorations of 140 years later that were interrupted by a fatal malfunction in the Apollo program, western explorations temporarily lost their romantic appeal for the American public. The western trails became much more silent—and the Truckee Trail almost completely so—until 1849, when the great gold rush to California began. But before that time, there were other daring settlers who made the decision to establish a new dominion within the Great Basin.

## Utah and the Latter-day Saints

The history of the Latter-day Saints (Mormon or L.D.S.) church is an exciting and controversial episode in the evolution of the Far West. The history of Nevada is closely intertwined with the story of the Mormons' westward trek and their settlement in Utah, and Nevada's social and political life has been much influenced by Mormonism in recent years.

The Mormon movement began in upper New York State in the mid-1820s, at approximately the same time that Peter Ogden and Jedediah Smith were exploring the Great Basin, which the Mormons would eventually occupy. A young man named Joseph Smith claimed to have discovered "golden plates" containing holy scriptures, and he laid the foundations of Mormonism. After a series of conflicts with other religious groups, Smith and his followers moved his flock to Ohio, then to Missouri, and then to Illinois. During their exodus, the Latter-day Saints developed a social and religious ethic that was well suited to the desert valleys of the Great Basin.

A turning point in Mormon history came during the years when they settled in Nauvoo, Illinois, in the early 1840s. Smith began to build a theocratic and political power base there. The violence that followed and the murder of Smith in an Illinois jail produced echoes that were heard in the distant western deserts years later.

Brigham Young assumed leadership of the L.D.S. church soon after the death of Smith in 1844, and it was he who planned and led the great trek of 1846–1847. His biographer, Leonard Arrington, called him an "American Moses" who led his people out of oppression into a new land, a Zion in the Far West. He laid out his new "City of the Saints" in the valley of the Great Salt Lake in 1847. He also claimed a vast tract, including the western Great Basin and southern California, for the "State of Deseret," which he hoped would eventually be admitted to the Union.

Within a few years, Young was sending church missionaries and other settlers into the most remote corners of the inland desert—to the Carson Valley at the eastern edge of the Sierra Nevada near Lake Tahoe, and into the Las Vegas Valley. He wanted to keep as much territory as possible from the flood of new rivals on the horizon—the gold seekers who were on their way to California. Soon, this wave of pioneers swept across the West, establishing new claims for the United States and new challenges to the Mormon Zion.

In the meantime, the United States fought the Mexican War, which decisively changed the map of western America. At the times when Jedediah Smith, Peter Ogden, John Frémont, and all the emigrants mentioned earlier made their trips, they were intruding upon Mexican territory. Yet the government in Mexico City was disorganized and could exercise little control over its northern frontier. The penetration of increasing numbers of Anglo-Americans into New Mexico and California made it impossible to administer this sprawling frontier according to Mexican law. President James K. Polk, an imperialist who popularized the Manifest Destiny theme, led the country into the Mexican War in 1846 and took credit for the victories of 1847 and the Treaty of Guadalupe Hidalgo in 1848.

None of the events of the Mexican War occurred within the boundaries of the region now called Nevada, but Col. Frémont—who only recently had made his second expedition through the Great Basin as a military officer—was an active instigator in leading the Californians in a rebellion against Mexican authorities. Also, local envoys of the U.S. government encouraged Americans to assist the revolt to assure annexation. Under the 1848 Treaty of Guadalupe Hidalgo, Mexico surrendered to the United States the southwestern region that included the present states of California, Nevada, Arizona, Utah, and parts of Wyoming, Colorado, and New Mexico. This act became known as the Mexican Cession.

Also in the interlude between 1846 and 1849, the United States extended its dominion to the Pacific Coast with the addition of the Oregon Country to its northwestern border. President Polk's government reached a compromise with the United Kingdom over the long-disputed region, which both countries had claimed and jointly occupied for a quarter century.

## The Gold Rush of 1849

Soon after Guadalupe Hidalgo, the United States learned that its new western settlers had found a bonanza of gold in the new provinces. In the month before the peace treaty of 1848 was signed, a group of men from John Sutter's fort were building a sawmill on the American River east of Sacramento when they noticed some interesting specks of yellow sand. When they identified it as gold, they kept it secret, but the news spread with remarkable speed. The few Americans living in California became excited in the spring and summer of 1848, and reports began to circulate in the eastern states later that year. In December, President Polk mentioned the goldfields in a message to Congress.

With that official statement, the rush began. By the beginning of 1849, more than fifty ships had set sail from the East Coast to round the Horn of South America, bound for California. Even in London and European cities, people became excited about the rumors of the new El Dorado. There were frequent reports of men earning $50 a day by panning gold dust—a fantastic sum. The more prosperous class set out by sea to California; the poorer people, who could not afford the expensive ship fare, gathered along the Missouri River, as the Bidwell and Donner parties had done before them, and prepared for the voyage by team and wagon, by horse, or on foot. Thousands set out for California from mid-continent, hoping that if they reached the goldfields in time, they would quickly become wealthy.

About 25,000 people, scattered along the trail for a six-month period, are believed to have made the trip to California by land in 1849. Most of the emigrants followed the trail that took them up the North Platte River across Nebraska and into the Rocky Mountains of Wyoming. Then they crossed southern Idaho, reaching the northeastern corner of the present state of Nevada. From there, the most popular route went along the trails already established—by way of the Humboldt River. Then they proceeded either to the Truckee or Carson River, into the Sierra Nevada, and through the passes to the gold camps in the western Sierra Nevada foothills. The crossing of the Nevada desert and the Sierra often proved to be the worst part of the long trek. By the time they arrived at the upper reaches of the Humboldt River, people and animals were already exhausted from the months of slow plodding; cholera and other diseases took a heavy toll. Grass was hard to find by the time the later emigrants arrived; the Humboldt water was brackish and bitter late in the season. Even after the emigrants had survived the brackish river and the Forty Mile Desert, there was the challenge of following one of the small rivers—most chose the Carson in 1849—into the Sierra and across the rugged passes into the California Central Valley. (Some chose the Lassen-Applegate trail north of Pyramid Lake, but many considered that too far north of the direct route to California.) Later generations regarded these emigrants as heroic, sent by destiny to found a new American commonwealth. Thousands of others reached California mostly by sea, via the Isthmus of Panama.

## The Death Valley Party of 1849

One band of pioneers gained fame for a trek across the southern desert in 1849. This was a party of 107 wagons led by Lewis Manly and Jefferson Hunt which set out from Salt Lake City in the fall of the year. Because of the lateness of the season, they went southwesterly along the Old Spanish Trail into southern Utah, and then the party divided because of reports that a shortcut was available. Leading 7 wagons, Hunt insisted on continuing along the well-known trail through the Las Vegas Valley. They reached their destination by Christmas.

The other party of 100 wagons set out in an unmapped westerly direction and encountered the rugged Beaver Dam Canyon in Lincoln County, near the present Nevada-Utah state line. Later they endured the obstacles of the Meadow Valley Wash, the expanses of the northern Mojave Desert, and Death Valley—which they named. Among those who plodded through Death Valley were several families with small children, spending most of the winter in the driest and most barren part of the continent. Two heroes of the expedition were Manly and a companion named John Rogers, who scouted for water holes and once made a 200-mile trek to a California ranchero for food in order to save the party from starvation. Yet another hero was Mrs. Julia Brier, the mother of three small children, whose endurance became legendary. This fragmented band—with all the odds against them—reached their destination with the loss of only one life.

## The California Dream and Statehood

From the era of the gold rush onward, California became part of an expansive American dream. It was often perceived as a kind of El Dorado and Eden combined, where one might become rich quickly and live in a balmy climate with all of nature's bounty at one's doorstep. The hardships of the voyage by sea from the East, usually by way of the isthmus, or by land across the hostile Great Basin, were later romanticized; the dream survived a thousand instances of misery and violence. In due time the harsh desert land east of the Sierra Nevada, which had caused so much of the suffering, began to stimulate some dreams of its own. But before 1850, it was only a vast barrier to be endured—a purgatory on the way to paradise.

On the other side of the continent, the worst internal conflict in the nation's history was gathering force. The slavery question divided the nation along geographical lines, and politicians recognized that a showdown was approaching over the question of whether black slaves could be owned or imported into the newly acquired lands of the Mexican Cession. Congress bitterly debated the Wilmot Proviso, which would have prohibited the extension of slavery to the Cession. Although the measure did not become law, it sparked a debate that echoed all the way to California.

By 1850, more than 90,000 people lived in California, and newly transplanted immigrants from the eastern states were eager to play the political game that Americans had learned so well since 1776. They wanted to form a new state and gain admission to the federal Union as soon as possible. Therefore, a group of delegates met in Monterey, drafted a constitution that prohibited slavery, and petitioned for admission to the Union. The Congress, which normally passed an "enabling act" when it was considering the admission of a new state, did not have time to do so in this case because the energetic Californians had taken matters into their own hands. Faced with the problem of how to organize the region that had been won from Mexico, the Congress simply accepted the work of the Monterey convention and granted statehood to California as part of the famous Compromise of 1850.

This compromise did much to shape the destiny of the American Republic and of the newly annexed Southwest. Leaders of the slave-owning states of the Old South wanted to extend their institutions and privileges to the territory acquired from Mexico, to allow their culture to spread westward. Statesmen from the Northeast and Midwest opposed this idea, as they were already bracing for a crusade that would abolish slavery. The expansive spaces of the inland desert seemed to be of little value at the time, but they became important as a jurisdiction, even before they were populated.

During the Monterey convention, California's founding fathers debated about where the eastern boundary of their new state should be. Some delegates proposed the crest of the Rocky Mountains; others argued for the crest of the Sierra Nevada. After much discussion, the convention compromised and designated the line that forms the present eastern boundary. Had they selected a line one degree further east, the Comstock Lode and the valleys where Nevada was eventually born would have been within their jurisdiction, and California would have had yet another bonanza within its domain.

The Congress, in admitting California to the Union on its own terms, also decided to organize the remainder of the Mexican Cession of 1848 into two territories—Utah and New Mexico. The national lawmakers thus ignored Brigham Young's plan for a State of Deseret, but they did include within Utah Territory all of the Basin and Range province between the 42d and 37th parallels, west to the California border. By this act, the Congress put the northern 90 percent of present-day Nevada into Utah Territory. The southern 10 percent, including such sites as Las Vegas, the Muddy and Virgin rivers, and Beatty, were part of New Mexico Territory. At least theoretically, the jurisdiction of American territorial governments extended into the Great Basin and lower Colorado River region, but that jurisdiction had little meaning in 1850, when only Native Americans lived there.

Those who made the trek as explorers or emigrants from the Midwest to California in the 1840s were part of a migration older than history; the wanderlust of the human species is one of the elementary facts of social life. Those who walked with Jedediah Smith, or Frémont, or Bartleson and Bidwell, used the same techniques as the Israelites during the Exodus out of Egypt. Their technology was not much different from that of the barbarian hordes who descended upon the decaying Roman Empire 1,500 years ago. They walked or rode their animals, and they hauled their few possessions in wagons that would not have appeared radically strange to William the Conqueror. Their communications with the world they left behind were almost as rudimentary as those of medieval Europe.

But within the lifetime of some of those who began the westward movement of the 1840s, the modern industrial revolution would penetrate those regions that had been unknown, except to the Native Americans, for untold centuries. Within ten years after the rush of 1849, John Bidwell presided over a convention of 100 people in San Francisco to discuss the building of a railroad all the way from the Missouri River to the West Coast; in another ten years, that railroad was a reality. And the technology of industrial mining and extraction of precious metals was revolutionized in the mountains of California and Nevada.

## Suggested Supplementary Reading

Arrington, Leonard J. *Brigham Young: American Moses.* New York: Alfred A. Knopf, 1985.
Elliott, Russell R., with the assistance of William D. Rowley. *History of Nevada,* 2nd ed. Lincoln: University of Nebraska Press, 1987. Chap. 3.
Hardesty, Donald L. *The Archaeology of the Donner Party.* Reno: University of Nevada Press, 1997.
Johnson, Leroy and Jean. *Escape from Death Valley.* Reno: University of Nevada Press, 1987.
Stewart, George R. *Ordeal by Hunger: The Story of the Donner Party,* new ed. Boston: Houghton Mifflin, 1960.
———. *The California Trail: An Epic with Many Heroes.* New York: McGraw Hill, 1962.
Unruh, John D., Jr. *The Plains Across: The Overland Emigrants and the Trans-Mississippi West, 1840–1860.* Urbana: University of Illinois Press, 1979.

# 5

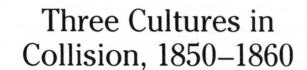

## Three Cultures in Collision, 1850–1860

I N THE middle of the nineteenth century, two groups of people established themselves and their industries within the territory that would eventually become Nevada. They were, first, members of the Latter-day Saints church who had been sent by Brigham Young to expand the new Zion, and, second, a ragtag collection of mining men—accompanied by their camp followers—who had not done well in the California gold rush and were testing their luck in the mountain ranges of the Great Basin. These two contingents collided with each other and with the Indian peoples. After a brief skirmish, the Mormons withdrew to their Utah bases. It was a temporary, tactical retreat, not a complete surrender. In the case of the Native Americans, they were overwhelmed and their society was shattered, but they survived with an ethnic and social identity that is still being reaffirmed more than 150 years after the initial confrontation.

The California mining fraternity was the most aggressive arm of American social imperialism in the 1850s, and at the end of that decade a few lucky prospectors discovered the Comstock Lode, which proved to be one of the richest natural treasures of silver and gold ever found in North America. It was this contingent that gave Nevada its original social and political structure; even now the mining legacy casts a long shadow over Nevada's history. Before the onslaught of the "miners' frontier," the

Native American peoples retreated, as they had been forced to do so often in other parts of America.

## Mormons in Carson Valley, 1850–1857

The first Mormons to establish themselves on the western edge of the Great Basin arrived in 1850 and built a crude, temporary station to engage in trading with the growing number of emigrants. Joseph Demont, the captain of this organization, and his clerk Hampton S. Beatie, proved that they could profitably transport flour, bacon, and other supplies across the mountains from California to Mormon Station in Carson Valley. There they could trade or sell their merchandise for profit to the California-bound emigrants for a tired horse, cow, or other object of value. The Demont-Beatie group withdrew as winter approached late in 1850, but the enterprise produced such encouraging results that another Mormon party established a permanent station the following year.

Since the eastern boundary line of California fell just west of Mormon Station, this trading post was in Utah Territory, even though it was nearly 500 miles from Salt Lake City. The second contingent of businessmen from Utah, who reached Mormon Station in Carson Valley in 1851, came with the intention of plowing fields, erecting fences, and building a fort to secure the region for Utah Territory and Mormonism. This group, led by a merchant named John Reese, brought ten wagons loaded with supplies. Within a few months, he had a thriving business, selling the emigrants locally produced foodstuffs as well as items imported from California.

From the beginning, the Mormons had competition; they may not have been the first to found an outpost in the vicinity. Twenty miles down the river near the mouth of Gold Canyon, trekkers on their way to California had found signs of the precious metal, and a trading post was established near the site of Dayton. Its residents now claim the title "first in Nevada," using the diaries of emigrants to assert that a community existed there even before Mormon Station was built. A lively controversy has arisen over the question of which town is older. Another station was founded later in Eagle Valley, where Carson City arose soon afterward in the 1850s.

It may have been Mormons who made the first discovery of precious metal in Gold Canyon. The carefree young Abner Blackburn later claimed to have identified the "yellow metal" there in 1849; other accounts suggest that William Prouse and John Orr, members of a wagon train traveling from Salt Lake City to California, washed some gold-bearing sand in 1850. The question of the identity of the original discoverer may never be resolved, but the later facts are clear. The Mormons did not benefit from the gold discovery; most of them disregarded it because the church discouraged them from joining the search for precious metals, which might divert them from their religious duties.

But the quest for El Dorado could not be denied in this part of Utah Territory. Hundreds of men came to Gold Canyon in the next few years to try their luck, bringing their pans for washing gold, their crude tools and pack animals, and their wandering habits. They were not settlers, but searchers for a quick and easy fortune. Almost none of them kept records, and very few became rich. But they created a subculture in Gold Canyon that posed a potential threat to Mormon Station and other small settlements that the Latter-day Saints established in Eagle Valley, the Truckee Meadows, and other valleys along the eastern edge of the Sierra Nevada.

Because they were so remote from their political leaders in Fillmore City and their religious authorities in Salt Lake City, the Mormon settlers in Carson Valley decided to form a local "squatters' government." Like the Pilgrims who created the Mayflower Compact in 1620, and like American frontiersmen of all eras, the early traders and farmers assembled in democratic meetings to make essential rules for dealing with the immediate challenges of society. In November 1851, they held three meetings at Mormon Station and established a plan for surveying and selling property, keeping formal records, and settling disputes in a local court.

The prospectors and non-Mormon settlers from California had other ideas. Most had no desire to be governed from Salt Lake City or even from Carson Valley. A few newcomers decided as early as 1851 that they could get better laws and government from the California legislature in Sacramento. In 1853, forty-three settlers signed a petition asking California to annex their valleys and to establish law and order in Carson Valley.

This brought a predictable response from Governor Young, who wanted to preserve this region for Utah Territory and the Mormon church. Under his leadership, the Utah territorial legislature created Carson County in 1854, and Young appointed Orson Hyde, an apostle of the church, as probate judge to administer the county. Hyde reached Carson Valley in June of 1855 together with a new band of Mormon settlers. He arranged for an election and a boundary survey to assure that Mormon Station was within Utah Territory. By the end of 1855, the Mormons seemed to have established their authority; the earlier squatters' government disappeared without ever having functioned, but some of its records were recognized by Carson County.

For approximately two years, Hyde and his followers tried to build a society in western Utah Territory according to Mormon principles. They gave Mormon Station a new name, Genoa, in honor of the birthplace of Columbus and made it the county seat. They created a settlement in Washoe Valley called Franktown, and Hyde built a sawmill there. More than sixty additional Latter-day Saints families came from the older towns of Utah Territory to take up land in 1855 and 1856, raising the Mormon population to more than 500 in the valleys near the eastern slopes of the Sierra by early 1857.

The Mormon rule was to be short-lived. The miners panning for gold a few miles away resented the self-styled "Saints" and occasionally defied their authority. Judge/Apostle Hyde became frustrated with his duties, and late in 1856 the church called him back to Salt Lake City. In his absence, Mormon and Utah authority began to falter. In 1857, the Utah territorial legislature moved the seat of government from Genoa to Salt Lake City, and some settlers decided to return east. Finally, in September of 1857 during the so-called Utah War, when it appeared that a federal army was marching on Salt Lake City from the east to enforce national law, Brigham Young summoned the Mormons from all the outlying territories to return and help protect the new Zion in case of a military battle.

The "Utah War" came about because of misunderstandings and misinformation. President James Buchanan, beseiged by reports that the Mormons were harassing emigrants and defying the orders of federal judges, dispensed an army of 2,500 with orders to enforce federal jurisdiction. Most of the reports were unsubstantiated, but the army was real, and it created panic among the Latter-day Saints.

The battle that Young feared never came, but the crisis caused most Mormons to abandon their homes and farms in Carson Valley. In many cases, non-Mormons moved onto the improved lands and into the abandoned homes without payment, which was easy since Carson County had no effective government.

## Emigrant and Indian Conflicts

As the number of emigrants along the Humboldt Trail increased during the 1850s, there were repeated acts of violence between whites and Indians. Many Anglo-Americans who went to the frontier were prone to violence; like Joseph Walker and John Frémont, they were disposed to use their firearms against the Native Americans with only slight provocation. The Indians did not have the same concept of personal property as the whites, and they often "stole" cattle or other supplies when the opportunity arose. By the late 1850s, there were frequent reports of "depredations" by Indians against whites in the official reports of the U.S. government. The Native Americans operated according to mores that the Anglo-Americans did not understand, and at times they stole as a result of desperation. They were also, however, victims of racist attitudes of a conquering nation whose army leaders and emigrants had little regard for the Constitution that was intended to protect their rights.

In the meantime, the U.S. government initiated a policy of establishing Indian reservations in an effort to gather the wandering bands in safe locations and to teach them agriculture, thus removing them from proximity to the emigrant trails. Much of the early information about the Washos and Paiutes of northwestern Nevada came from an Indian agent named Frederick Dodge, who represented the Utah Superintendency of the Office of Indian Affairs in the region in 1858–1860. Dodge arrived from Salt Lake City with instructions to make a survey and establish one or more "Indian farms," upon which the Indians could be taught to cultivate crops and raise livestock. This, it was hoped, would reduce the conflicts with the emigrants and teach Native Americans the skills of Anglo-American civilization.

Dodge tried to determine the number of Indians and select the most suitable land for them to farm. His first choice in 1859 was the Truckee Meadows, that rich valley through which the Donner party had passed in 1846 and in which the city of Reno began to grow a decade later. Unfortunately for his plan, he sent his recommendation to Washington at the beginning of the same year that marked the discovery of the Comstock Lode, and settlers began to arrive in the adjacent valleys in growing numbers before the government acted. In 1860, therefore, he selected the lower parts of the Truckee and Walker rivers and the two lakes into which they flow as the sites for permanent settlements. Many years later, in 1874, President U. S. Grant confirmed these suggestions, thus formally recognizing the two oldest and largest Indian reservations in Nevada—those at Pyramid Lake and the Walker River.

While the westward migration of the 1850s produced many conflicts and much violence between the Indian peoples and those whom they regarded as intruders, there were also many instances in which friendship developed between the Caucasians and the Native Americans, and there were those who worked diligently to soften the impact of the Anglo-American conquest. One such man was Warren Wasson, who settled in Long Valley northwest of the Truckee Meadows and who "bought" his land twice—once from the Paiutes and once from the Washos. He later moved to Genoa and became U.S. marshall and a troubleshooter who tried to keep the peace throughout the region. He had a keen sympathy for the Indians and in a few cases managed to help them.

## The Las Vegas Mission, 1855–1858

A scenario roughly similar to the one that occurred in the Carson Valley was played out in the Las Vegas Valley in the same period; it was of shorter duration, and some of the details were different. But both events featured a struggle between dedicated Mormons, a mining enterprise, and an unpredictable Indian population.

The Mormons who settled in the Las Vegas Valley had an assignment unlike the one undertaken by the first settlers of Carson Valley; they had been summoned by the church leadership to visit the "Lamanites," as they called the Native Americans, and convert them to the church's teachings. The missionaries were under the immediate direction of Young in his capacity as head of the church, not as governor of the territory. They were also expected to extend the jurisdiction and the influence of the Mormons as far south as possible along the Old Spanish Trail. Church leaders also intended the Las Vegas colony to be a supply station and resting point on the road between central Utah and a large ranchero that the church had established at San Bernardino.

In the spring of 1855, the church called thirty men to a mission and directed them to set out for Las Vegas Valley. This meant they had to leave their families and the homes they had started only a few years earlier in the Utah valleys. Young selected William Bringhurst to serve as president of the mission, with complete authority over all its affairs. Thus the Las Vegas Mission was founded as an autocracy from the beginning, unlike the Carson Valley outpost.

Travel from Salt Lake City to Las Vegas required thirty-five days—approximately the same length of time as a trip from Salt Lake City to Genoa. (With modern highways and automobiles, the same trip can be made in nine or ten hours.) The most difficult part of the trek to the prospective mission site was the crossing of the last fifty miles northeast of Las Vegas, which was even more challenging than the dreaded Forty Mile Desert of the western Great Basin. The waters of the Las Vegas springs were most welcome when the missionaries reached them in mid-June.

On the first day, they built a small bower for religious services; on the second, they divided the land for farming and picked the site for a fort. Each man received a small plot for a garden, but each also had regular duties in the building of the adobe bastion that would serve them as a place of defense in case of an attack from Indians or hostile emigrants. Like Teutonic knights of the Middle Ages in northern Europe, they had come to stake out a "mark," or frontier defensive post, in potentially hostile territory, and they meant to stay.

Almost immediately, Bringhurst and his men became friendly with the Indians, and the history of the mission was essentially peaceful, even though there were some fundamental misunderstandings. The records of the mission show that the Native Americans often "stole" food and cattle; they had no sense of individual property rights of the Anglo-American type. On the other hand, the missionaries had taken a prime spot at their traditional watering place.

These settlers had to overcome a host of difficulties in building a settlement in the blistering, isolated valley in July and August of 1855. For the first few weeks, they had little to eat except the bread they brought with them. The heat made it impossible to work more than a few hours a day, and there was very little shade. Bringhurst sent a group into the Spring Mountains to the west in search of timber, which they found about 20 miles from the Las Vegas springs. Since no roads existed, it was a tedious chore to haul the timber to the mission site. Most of the original fences for the gardens consisted of mesquite brush, and the missionaries used mud as the main building material for their adobe fort.

After they had been in the valley for about a month, one of the missionaries wrote:

> The country around here looks as if the Lord had forgotten it; the mountains are very high—some as high as 1,000 feet of sandstone standing up edgeways; some cliffs seem to lay in regular strata, but for the most part they seem as disjointed fragments, some standing out in bold defiance of the parent rock.

Here we found some of the scattered remnants of Israel; they
would stand upon the highest mountains and hollow; they sent
us a present of pine nuts by a young Indian that we had along
for a guide. (Jensen, "History of Las Vegas Mission," *Nevada State
Historical Society Papers, 1925–1926*, 1926, pp. 152–153.)

The "scattered remnants of Israel" were, of course, the local Indians, who spoke a Shoshone-Ute dialect and were distantly related to
the Paviotso or Northern Paiutes near Walker and Pyramid lakes. The
Mormons intended to convert them, but they were frustrated when the
Native Americans generally proved unreceptive to their evangelical message.

These first missionaries found Las Vegas to be a depressing place to
live, primarily because it was so isolated. They longed for their families,
and Bringhurst constantly urged them to keep busy with their gardens
and their communal chores. He administered the mission with a firm
hand and got most of the men to work well together. A few members of
the colony left at the end of the growing season, but most stayed on for
the winter, in the hope of having their families join them in permanent
homes during the second year.

The first year's harvest brought several disappointments. On one
occasion, as a party of emigrants passed through the valley on the way
to California, their cattle broke into the fields, eating corn and trampling
crops. At other times, Indians took vegetables without permission. In
spite of this, the missionaries harvested enough to sustain themselves
during the winter months, and by spring they had partially completed
their fort. Feeling that providence had blessed their efforts, the church
president in Salt Lake City praised their work.

In the second year, the missionaries completed their fort and built a
few homes, and it was possible to bring some families to the valley. They
raised two crops of grain and vegetables, which would have provided
an abundance if there had not been a new, heavy burden placed on the
little community.

This new challenge resulted from an effort to establish a mining community as a satellite to the mission. The Mormon leadership began a
search for industrial metals in 1856, and Indians had guided missionaries
to a site in the western mountains where they identified lead ore. (They
did not know that it also contained silver, and they were not interested
in that metal in any case.) When church authorities in Salt Lake City
heard of this resource, it seemed to be a godsend, as they wanted to be
able to manufacture their own metal tools—including bullets. Brigham

Young sent five men, led by Nathaniel V. Jones, who had studied met-allurgy in the Midwest, to mine the ore with the help of men from the mission.

This directive caused a conflict because Bringhurst would not accept Jones's word that he had authority to reassign missionaries to the mining enterprise, and the two had a bitter quarrel. Weeks passed before the matter could be resolved by a message from Young, who eventually supported Jones. In the controversy that followed, Young dismissed Bringhurst and assigned another missionary, Samuel Thompson, to his place. To add to the troubles, Jones learned that the lead ore was not easy to mine and refine. He expected to build a furnace near the excavation by using rocks, but found that he lacked the essential equipment.

The entire venture was a dismal failure. Jones was an unpopular taskmaster, and he apparently knew little about the galena ore with which he was dealing. During the same season, Indians and insects took a heavy toll of the gardens, some of which suffered from neglect because men had been called to the mines.

This venture killed the hopes of the Las Vegas Mission. During the winter of 1857–1858, most of the men asked to return to their Utah homes, and Young granted them permission to leave before the beginning of the 1858 growing season. Most did depart, but a small contingent remained through the following summer under the leadership of Benjamin R. Hulse. There was continuing trouble with Indians and emigrants, and at the end of the summer, the last group of missionaries decided to abandon their outpost.

A few years later, the site where Jones had labored and failed became known as the Potosi Mine, presumably because the galena rock proved to have silver ore and one of the great silver mines of early colonial Mexico had been called the Potosi. This property did yield some ore to the war effort of 1917–1918, and thus Young's dream of a metal industry eventually had a small vindication—sixty years too late for his purposes.

In one sense, the Las Vegas Mission experiment was a microcosm of the venture which the Spanish Franciscan fathers undertook in California about eighty years earlier. Under the leadership of Junípero Serra, representatives of the Catholic church set out in 1776 to establish a string of outposts from San Diego to the San Francisco Bay, both to claim the region for the Spanish Empire and to carry Christianity to the Native Americans. The enterprise was a failure; those who undertook it endured much discomfort and frustration. But they left a legacy and tradition that later Californians have honored.

## Placer Mining in Gold Canyon:
## Prelude to the Comstock Discovery

From 1851 to 1858, a small band of placer miners panned for gold in the canyons of the Virginia Range northeast of the Carson Valley with modest success. Most of them built small cabins from sagebrush, rocks, and juniper branches for shelter and spent their days crushing and washing the gravel in the gullies to extract four or five dollars worth of ore per day. It was common practice for these wandering prospectors to spend several weeks or months in the mountains during warm weather, until they had enough gold to return to California for a while or prospect elsewhere. They bought their wheat and potatoes from the farmers in Carson Valley and salted pork, when it was available, from trading stations along the Carson River. They planned no permanent improvements, because most of them did not intend to stay.

The records of those pre-Comstock years are very scarce. The mining regulations which the men adopted were almost as crude as the cabins in which they lived. The population in Gold Canyon and Six Mile Canyon on the slopes of Sun Mountain (later Mt. Davidson) ranged from a few dozen men to two or three hundred in those years. Only a few of them left any testimonials to their activities, and those are dubious.

Two men whose stories have long fascinated chroniclers of Comstock history were Ethan Allen Grosh and Hosea Ballou Grosh, two young brothers from Pennsylvania who arrived in the Virginia Mountains at least as early as 1853 and spent the next two or three summers there. They not only panned for gold, but may have secretly explored for silver as well; they were probably the first miners to do so systematically. Perhaps they identified one remote ledge of the Comstock Lode in the lower part of Gold Canyon, but both of them died before they could make use of their discovery. Hosea struck his foot with a pick in the summer of 1857 and died of blood poisoning within two weeks. Ethan tried to cross the Sierra in a snowstorm a few months later, was trapped in a blizzard, and died when he refused to allow his frozen legs to be amputated. Later the letters of their father and the testimony of their friends indicated that they had talked and written of a "monster ledge" of silver.

More fortunate members of the Gold Canyon prospectors were Eilley Orrum, a daughter of the Scottish highlands, and her husband Lemuel (Sandy) Bowers. Eilley came west with the Mormon settlers and stayed behind when they departed in 1857; Sandy drifted in with the flotsam from California. They each claimed a few "feet" along the rich vein of ore in the canyon, became partners in mining and matrimony, and emerged as the first millionaires in the region. Eager to enjoy their new wealth, they arranged for the construction of a handsome sandstone mansion at one of the most beautiful spots in Washoe Valley, and they went to Europe to enjoy the fruits of their good luck.

But these first millionaires experienced the fate that has often followed Nevada speculators. Sandy died in 1868, their property lost its value because of poor business practices, and Eilley spent her last, impoverished years telling fortunes for a few pennies. Their mansion, however, survived as a restored historical monument and a reminder of the earliest luxury, extravagance, and bad management in Nevada history.

## The Discovery of the Comstock Lode

In the meantime, the "monster ledge" that the Grosh brothers may have identified attracted new prospectors at two points in 1859—at the Ophir claim on the northeastern slopes of Mt. Davidson and at the "Old Red Ledge" about two miles to the south in Gold Canyon. The men who made these discoveries in 1859 had no notion of the wealth that lay beneath their feet. Their names became western legends: "Old Virginny" Fennimore, Henry Paige Comstock, Patrick McLaughlin, and Peter O'Riley. Their fame was not the result of any particular skills or contributions, but because they happened to find the first small bonanzas in a region that would one day be famous for its mines and gambling casinos. By historical accident, the ledge of silver-and-gold-bearing ore was named for Henry Comstock, a prospector who had nothing to do with the discovery, but who demanded and got some recognition as "owner" of the land on which it was found.

Almost immediately, several new towns arose on the mountainsides, the most important being Virginia City near the Ophir Mine. Perhaps named by Old Virginny Fennimore when he accidentally broke a bottle of whiskey, Virginia (as local residents usually called "her") was situated in a steep natural amphitheater, which faced eastward and extended down into Six Mile Canyon. The main traffic lanes evolved roughly like bleacher seats in a stadium, with A Street at the top and, as the city gradually expanded downward into the canyon, P Street near the bottom. At first the business places and residences consisted only of tents or hovels of mud, sagebrush, stone, or whiskey barrels. Gradually, timber from the Sierra, finery from California, and technical mining outfits arrived by the wagonload. Within months, Virginia was a ramshackle assortment of humanity, animals, carts, houses large and small, saloons, hotels, and ever-more-complex machinery and expanding mine dumps. More than 800 buildings arose on the slopes of Sun Mountain in the first year.

Virginia held the place of honor on her lofty perch. From almost any street one could look eastward into the Great Basin, with its rows of purple-gray mountains and deserts so different from the Sierra at her back. She soon had several neighbors—Gold Hill just outside the amphitheater to the south, Silver City farther down Gold Canyon, and the milling towns of Washoe City and Ophir on the opposite side of Mt. Davidson.

The first discoverers soon passed from the scene, to be replaced by groups of capitalist entrepreneurs, technicians, and politicians—mostly from the depressed California goldfields. Scores of those who arrived in 1860 and 1861 began to think of themselves as the builders of a new dominion. Knowing they were beyond the boundary of California and not willing to acknowledge the authority of Utah Territory with its capital 500 miles away, they soon petitioned the government in Washington for a government of their own. In the next chapter we shall become more familiar with William Morris Stewart, Adolph Sutro, John Mackay, and William Sharon, among others, who transformed the so-called Comstock excitement into a state of the Union and promoted a speculative adventure of international interest.

As the mines of the Comstock Lode drew wealth seekers across the Sierra, they stimulated the development of one small intermediary community, which called itself Carson City. Until 1858 its locale was known only as the Eagle Ranch, but then a promoter named Abe Curry came along, laid out a midwestern-style town with a substantial central plaza, and announced that he intended to erect a state capitol there. Situated in a charming valley halfway between Genoa and Virginia City, it attracted much of the through traffic from the former and the wealth of the latter. It soon became a business and market center for the entire region that had been abandoned by the Mormons.

But before these developments had proceeded very far, a disastrous confrontation erupted between the newly arrived Anglo-American population and the Native Americans.

## The Battles of Pyramid Lake, 1860

The spring of 1860 brought the first and decisive instance of violence to the Washoe country—a clash between the reckless frontier mining society that was just discovering the extent of the Comstock Lode and the disoriented Indian population of the northwestern Great Basin. It was one of the tragedies of the early West, which resulted in much loss of life in two battles near Pyramid Lake.

On the Carson River about 30 miles east of Virginia City, James Williams had established a typical trading station. While he was absent one day, some of his companions kidnapped two young Indian women and took them to the station, provoking an attack from the Indians in which three white men were killed. This deed was probably the work of Bannock Indians who were temporarily in the area, not by the generally peaceful Paiutes. When Williams returned to find his friends dead and his station burned, he concluded that Indians were on the warpath, without making any distinction about which bands were involved.

When news reached the Comstock towns, no one bothered to check the details; exaggerated reports spread like a raging forest fire. Rumors circulated that hundreds of Indians were on the warpath, and men formed military companies in Genoa, Carson City, and Virginia City. Settlers feared for their lives and their meager homes. Most were badly prepared for a military expedition, and they had no single leader whom they all recognized and respected. Major William Ormsby of Carson City was an informal commander, but no discipline existed in the ranks. In many cases the "soldiers" were simply overzealous young men, ready to steal horses and kidnap women.

On May 12, when this informal army of about a hundred men proceeded down the lower Truckee Canyon toward Pyramid Lake, they did not anticipate that the Indians would be ready for them. The Paiutes, who were innocent of the assault on Williams's Station, were nonetheless determined to protect their home territory. They descended on Ormsby's disorganized "army" in a frenzy, killing seventy-six men, including Major Ormsby. Twenty-nine others, wounded and humiliated, fled toward Carson City to tell of the horror.

This episode was especially tragic in view of the fact that for many years whites and Indians had been living and working peacefully together in western Utah Territory. Sarah Winnemucca Hopkins, the daughter of the Paiute leader known as "Old Winnemucca," had lived in the Ormsby home and received an education from his family. Sarah's brother tried unsuccessfully to save the life of Major Ormsby in the battle. "Brave deeds don't always get rewarded in this world," Sarah wrote later in her famous book about the tragedy of the Paiute people.

The initial battle was followed by a period of panic, and then another slaughter—this time of Indians—as an act of revenge. Immediately after the first battle, fright and hysteria multiplied in Virginia City, Carson City, and elsewhere on the newly settled slopes of the eastern Sierra Nevada. Calls for help went over the mountains to California. Hordes of settlers in the Comstock mountains and ravines fled westward. The more hearty and the desperate settlers awaited reinforcements from the U.S. Army and the governor of California. Later in May, more than two hundred regular soldiers and five hundred volunteers marched toward Pyramid Lake again, and this time the Indians dispersed. There is disagreement among historians about the casualties in this encounter; the Indians claimed that only four of their people died, while some recent accounts have concluded that more than 160 Native Americans were killed.

The fear caused by the Battles of Pyramid Lake did not pass quickly. For many months, the Indians were still regarded as a menace. Troops of the U.S. Army built a small base near the Carson River—Fort Churchill— and maintained garrisons there for a few years. The Indians never threatened seriously again, however, and Fort Churchill eventually became a colorful state park and historic interpretation area.

Only gradually did the facts of the Pyramid Lake battles and the misunderstanding that led to them come to light. Most early Nevada journalists and historians who wrote of the episode saw only one side—that of the white settlers—and did not consider either the needs of the Native Americans or the irrational panic of the prospectors and settlers. There was no doubt, however, that the events of Pyramid Lake had decisively established the domination of the white man in the western Great Basin. They were now ready to expand their commercial ventures.

In the same season that the Battles of Pyramid Lake occurred, the first "high speed" communication between California and the midwestern heartland began—by means of the famous Pony Express. A private mail-carrying company connecting St. Joseph, Missouri, and Sacramento, California, established relay stations every fifteen miles to allow for the exchange of horses and riders on a regular basis. About twenty of these stations operated at intervals across central Nevada; the ruins of several of them can still be seen along U.S. Highway 50.

The owners of the Pony Express promised their clients that they would carry a letter from Missouri to California in ten days at a cost of five dollars in gold. The swift horses and their riders often covered 200 miles a day in 1860 and 1861, but the venture never prospered. Within eighteen months it had been rendered obsolete by the building of a transcontinental telegraph line. Even the remote western fringes of the Great Basin were being penetrated by modern technology by the time the Civil War began in the East.

## The Quest for Law and Order

By the middle of 1860, there were about 7,000 people of European descent in the mountains and valleys of Carson County, most of them exploring for gold and silver or trying to extract it from the stubborn rock in which it occurred. A few had taken up land for farms and ranches; some operated the crude trading stations for the transients. This was not yet a settled society. It did not yet have a name except for the vague designation of "Washoe" after the Indian community that roamed the region in prehistoric times. It had no effective government because Utah authorities had virtually abandoned it. All previous efforts to hold court or to establish a functioning local government had been short-lived.

The miners of Gold Canyon assembled as early as the spring of 1859 to create a mining district, with regulations about the staking of claims, the settling of disputes, and the punishment of criminals. This was common practice in the frontier mining districts, but seldom did such ad hoc groups provide governmental stability.

There were brief attempts by local citizens to form territorial governing offices in 1857 and 1859, but both efforts failed quickly. Utah territorial authorities who tried to hold court were equally unsuccessful. But during the rush of 1860, there arrived in Washoe several men who eventually gave the region a semblance of law and order, and it became possible to form a separate territory during the early months of 1861.

The first presiding territorial judge who was able to exercise effective judicial authority in the western Utah district was John Cradlebaugh, a "tall, lean middle-aged lawyer from Ohio," who reached the Salt Lake Valley with federal judicial credentials in November 1858. Cradlebaugh moved to Carson Valley soon after the Comstock Lode was discovered and soon after the Battles of Pyramid Lake. By this time, quarrels and litigation between miners and speculators had increased to flood proportions. Although no one at that time had any understanding of how vast or rich the lode was, there were already a myriad of disputes over titles to the outcroppings. Cradlebaugh stepped in to a judicial responsibility that was as dangerous as a battlefield, as most of the disputants carried sidearms. Not only were many mining titles in dispute, but also the population was divided between Northern and Southern sympathizers in the chaotic pre–Civil War election which pitted Abraham Lincoln against Stephen A. Douglas and two other opponents.

> Judge Cradlebaugh . . . opened court at Genoa, Carson Valley, on September 3, 1860, in the only available room, a badly lighted chamber, over a livery stable. The town was filled to overflowing with lawyers, litigants, witnesses, and jurors. A bundle of straw in a barn was eagerly sought as a bed, and the judge slept contentedly between rival attorneys, while the humbler attendants spread their blankets on the sage-brush. (Lord, *Comstock Mining and Miners*, p. 101.)

The two most prominent attorneys among the high-spirited population were William M. Stewart and David Terry, both large and physically vigorous men. Stewart was a former attorney general of California and a Union supporter, Terry a one-time justice of the California Supreme Court and a southern sympathizer. They represented clients who had conflicting claims at both ends of the Comstock Lode, and they agreed to try their cases before Judge Cradlebaugh soon after his arrival. As the tangled litigation was proceeding, President James Buchanan abruptly ordered the removal of Cradlebaugh from the bench and appointed Robert P. Flenniken, a southern sympathizer, as his replacement. Cradlebaugh refused to accept this arrangement on the grounds that the president had no right to remove a sitting judge, and (according to Stewart's memoirs written forty years later) Stewart and Terry agreed to proceed with their cases before Cradlebaugh, with the understanding that one of his rulings would be appealed to the Utah Supreme Court to assure the validity of his jurisdiction. However, when Judge Cradlebaugh ruled in Stewart's favor on an important issue, Terry had second thoughts and sought out Judge Flenniken. In the meantime, seventy-five armed men who supported Terry and the southern cause had seized the property in dispute.

Stewart's remembrance of this incident in later years paints him as a bold knight in defense of virtue, receiving the appropriate ruling from the territorial capital in Salt Lake City, averting bloodshed, and nobly forcing

Judge Flenniken at gunpoint to go to the telegraph office and transmit his letter of resignation as a judge. The rebellious rebels who had seized the property then obeyed the lawful order of Cradlebaugh's court.

Historians have had reason to question the authenticity of Stewart's account of these events, but there can be no doubt that the foundations of lawful society were laid in 1860 in this region where anarchy had prevailed for several months.

## Suggested Supplementary Reading

Egan, Ferol. *Sand in a Whirlwind: The Paiute Indian War of 1860.* Foreword by A. B. Guthrie, Jr. Garden City, N.Y.: Doubleday, 1972.

Elliott, Russell R. *Servant of Power: A Political Biography of Senator William M. Stewart.* Reno: University of Nevada Press, 1983.

Hohmann, John W., comp. *The Old Las Vegas Mormon Fort: The Founding of a Desert Community in Clark County, Nevada.* Carson City: Department of Conservation and Natural Resources, 1996.

Jenson, Andrew, comp. "History of Las Vegas Mission." *Nevada State Historical Society Papers.* Reno: Nevada State Historical Society, 1926. Pp. 117–284.

Richnak, Barbara. *Silver Hillside: The Life and Times of Virginia City.* Incline Village, Nev.: Comstock Nevada Publishing Co., 1984.

# 6

# The Early Comstock and Statehood

T HE CRUCIAL years in the shaping of the Silver State were 1860–
1865, the period in which the Union endured the tragedy of the
Civil War. During the time between the election of Abraham Lincoln and his death four years later, a society that called itself "Nevada"
materialized on the western fringe of the Great Basin. Its path to statehood was greatly accelerated by President Lincoln's struggle to save the
Union. The constitutional provisions and symbols of Nevada were inspired by those years. The official slogan of Nevada, emblazoned on its
flag, is the phrase "Battle Born."

In a sense, this motto is misleading because no Civil War battles were
fought in this region, and the events that threatened the survival of the
Union had little direct impact on the Great Basin, except politically. At
one time, popular history books asserted that the silver and gold of
Nevada's mines financed the Civil War; this is an exaggeration and a misunderstanding of government financial practices of the time. Yet without
the crisis of the war, Nevada would not have evolved through territorial
status to statehood as rapidly as it did. Only the wartime emergency
and the absence of the southern senators and representatives in Congress made it possible for a thinly populated region like Nevada to be
organized as a territory and a state.

Following the discovery of the Comstock Lode in 1859 and the "rush
to Washoe" in 1860, there were occasional demands for territorial status.

The unsuccessful effort to form a separate government in 1859 was led by Isaac Roop of Susanville, California (which was then believed to be part of Nevada), but the region had no effective judiciary or law enforcement agencies during the following two years. Only in March of 1861, in the last days of the administration of President James Buchanan when the Civil War seemed imminent, did Congress pass a law to establish Nevada Territory. In the meantime, those who had rushed to the newly discovered ledges of the Comstock Lode had more immediate interests.

## The Technical Challenge of the Comstock

The Comstock Lode proved to be the most puzzling and challenging, as well as one of the richest, ore bodies in the history of America. When its discoverers finally realized in 1859–1860 that they had found a great slice of ore-bearing rock extending down the side of Mt. Davidson, they knew very little about how to extract it, how to separate it from the "waste" material in which it was blended, and how to refine it into pure silver and gold. Some of the techniques used in California helped in the beginning, but an essentially new technology was necessary for the Nevada ores. America's mining and metallurgical industry developed a new technology for producing and refining precious metals on the Comstock Lode by trial and error.

An important new fact was that most of the riches of the Comstock— and this was true of the later Nevada mining towns as well—lay deep underground. The two-mile-long ledge that was discovered at the Ophir diggings and in Gold Hill resembled a great pancake, standing on its side and wedged into the ground. From the surface outcroppings, it folded under Sun Mountain, first plunging toward the west and then, a hundred feet or so below the surface, curving in an easterly direction as it descended. In places the lode was barren; in other locations, there were fabulously rich bubbles of silver-and-gold-bearing rock the likes of which no living man had ever seen. The pockets of ore discovered in the 1860s, although they seemed marvelously rich, were minute compared to the Big Bonanza that John Mackay and his associates found below the 1,300-foot level in the 1870s.

At first the miners lifted the ore from the shallow shafts with windlasses, but this became more difficult as the diggings got deeper. A critical problem was how to prevent the sides and tops of the shafts and tunnels from collapsing as the miners dug; an elaborate system of timbers became necessary, culminating in the famous "square-set method" devised by a German-born engineer named Philip Deidesheimer. As the excavations probed ever deeper into Mt. Davidson, ventilation became a chronic problem and increasingly oppressive heat made working conditions arduous.

Once the ore had been extracted from the earth, the mine owners had to separate it from the "county rock" or "waste" in which it was confined. At first the engineers used a practice that the Mexicans had devised much earlier for pulverizing the rock with horses' hooves and allowing its precious metal to be baked out by the hot desert sun. This process was slow, and many charlatans tried to sell magic formulas for getting the "values" out of the rock quickly. It required more than a year to find a satisfactory solution, but with typical frontier ingenuity and impatience, a California mining man named Almarin B. Paul invented the "Washoe pan process" in 1860, which involved crushing rock with iron stamps and washing the pulverized earth through a series of settlers and traps.

All this required wood, water, and machinery that were in short supply on the thinly wooded slopes of Mt. Davidson. On the other hand, there was too much water underground, where it was a nuisance, and in the earliest years the mining men tried to lift it from the lower levels in buckets. As the mines went deeper and this method failed, it became necessary to install pumps designed for the mines of Cornwall in western England. Expensive hoisting machinery for lifting the ore and waste rock and transporting the miners became essential. This meant the purchase and hauling of cumbersome steam engines to the Comstock, which needed large quantities of wood, chopped and transported from the nearby Sierra. In the meantime, scores of mills appeared along the Carson River, and ore wagons hauled their precious cargo down the canyons for processing.

Because of all the technical requirements of the Comstock, the small miners who made the original discoveries could not meet the costs or provide the diverse, necessary skills. In a short time the large financial speculators, based mainly in California, appeared on the scene and won controlling interests in the mines all along the lode. A stock exchange opened in San Francisco in 1862, stimulated primarily by the wealth of the Comstock and the companies that were formed to exploit it. A short time later, stock boards came into existence in Virginia City and Gold Hill, and speculative fever ran high on the streets of those towns. Soon, financial companies and individuals from the East invested heavily in the Comstock mines, and Nevada became an economic colony of outside financial interests, a pattern which existed across most of the mining frontier in the Far West.

## Foundations of Nevada Society

In 1861, a California printer compiled a directory of Nevada that described a society only two years old. The population was about 6,800 in the summer of 1860; men outnumbered women by a ratio of sixteen to one. A year later there were 16,300 residents, and a more stable society had emerged. By this time, the ratio of men to women was ten to one, and more than half the population was under thirty years of age. The directory said of Virginia City:

Located against the side of an arid and barren mountain, its position, saving proximity to the silver mines, was the most unpropitious possible. Yet, on this site so unfavorable, within a little more than two years from the time it was founded, has sprung up a city abounding with large and substantial fire-proof buildings, a multitude of comfortable houses, and a great number of costly mills and reduction works, while through its streets water flows in abundance, and luxurious gardens are cultivated in its suburbs. That a spot so desolate and forbidding, and withal so remote from the great central depot of the Pacific, should have been transformed in so short a time into a thrifty and populous city, speaks well for those who have had the work of building it up in hand. (Kelly, *First Directory of Nevada Territory*, p. 107.)

Virginia City had (in August 1861) a population of 2,704 people; it was already assuming the aspects of an inland political and commercial center. Within four years its population had increased, tripled, and quadrupled, and its citizens had organized scores of community groups: fire brigades, churches, fraternal orders, theaters, lively newspapers, innumerable saloons, a miners' union, and schools for the children of the families that eventually appeared on the scene. Similar patterns occurred in the neighboring communities of Gold Hill, Silver City, Dayton, and Washoe City. In the valleys that could be irrigated, settlers took up land for agriculture. In addition, as some prospectors found Virginia

City too crowded or lacking in the immediate rewards they wanted, the Comstock became the jumping-off point for scores of new inland mining districts.

## New Bonanza Towns, 1860–1863:
## Aurora, Unionville, and Austin

Hundreds of additional communities materialized on the rugged mountainsides of the Great Basin during the next half century; their residents were inspired by reports of the fabulous wealth of the Comstock. Stories are legion about the drama of the western mining camps—the vibrant, often-lawless places that sprouted like weeds in the springtime. All across the West the quest for El Dorado sent miners, promoters, and human parasites of all types scrambling into the unexplored mountains, and Nevada attracted some of the most colorful. It was common practice for the discoverers to stake their claims, organize a mining district, establish some local regulations for law and order, and then try either to produce gold or sell their claims.

Most camps died quickly, but a few flourished long enough to become county seats and thus to serve as market towns, where people gathered to socialize, buy the essential supplies, and engage in that chronic American pastime—politics. About a dozen of these hamlets survived and gained important institutional status within Nevada society; they provided a high proportion of its political officers, artists, writers, and businesspeople. Most gradually crumbled or burned, leaving intriguing imprints on the landscape.

One camp in the latter category was Aurora, which was founded in 1860 on the eastern slopes of the Sierra about 80 miles southeast of the Comstock, by three prospectors from San Jose, California. These men had a preference for romantic titles, choosing the name of the Greek goddess of dawn for their new town (Aurora), and the Spanish name for "emerald" (Esmeralda) for their mining district. Located in a rugged terrain where the boundary between Nevada Territory and California had not yet been surveyed, Aurora endured a short-lived boundary war between the partisans of each jurisdiction. It had a brief and spectacularly rich history, producing nearly $30 million worth of ore in the first ten years and then lapsing into oblivion. Its boosters claimed a population of 6,000 in 1863, but then its fortunes waned as the ore "pinched out." A series of financial failures and fires followed, and Aurora—like scores of sister towns—died a slow death.

The prospectors who laid out Unionville in the Humboldt Range about 100 miles northeast of Virginia City had a more pleasant setting for their enterprise. The Buena Vista Valley long had a reputation for its high desert beauty, sustained by one of those small streams that make the Nevada backcountry delightful. This was the era of the Civil War, and the Confederate sympathizers who arrived there first in spring of 1861 called the place Dixie. The Union sympathizers who followed formed a rival faction that insisted on applying a name that would affirm their loyalty to the Northern Union cause. Unionville did not produce nearly as much wealth as Aurora, and it faded even more quickly.

Yet another offspring of the Comstock excitement was Austin, which proved to be more durable than Aurora and Unionville. Located in the Toiyabe Range approximately in the center of the state, Austin was originally only a point near the Pony Express trail of 1860–1861. Men who operated a supply and relay station for horses and riders in the Reese River Valley discovered the silver ores of Austin in the spring of 1862, and the typical rush soon began. Within a few weeks the Reese River Mining District had been formed and hundreds of prospectors had trekked from Virginia City and the California camps. Most were disappointed; Austin produced less ore even than Aurora—only about $20 million in its first 75 years.

But Austin had an advantage that proved much more significant than its silver ledges—its strategic location in the center of the Great Basin. For more than a hundred years, it was also the seat of Lander County, which in the middle 1860s covered all of northeastern Nevada. In addition, its early settlers built well. Austin's main churches, business structures, and courthouse still stood 125 years after they were built. At least three churches were of considerable architectural interest in the late twentieth century. In the long run, Austin made a greater contribution to the Nevada heritage with its physical reminders of the 1860s than with its precious metal from that era.

## Territorial Status and Statehood

This first phase of Nevada's history as a political organization began in 1861, less than two years after the discovery of the Comstock Lode and only a few months after the rush to Washoe. Early in that year, the Congress examined the status of the western frontier regions and created three new territories—Dakota, Colorado, and Nevada. In the latter case, it had become obvious that Utah's Carson County with its rapidly growing mining communities was too far from Salt Lake City to be governed effectively. There was bitter resentment among most of the prospectors and settlers of Carson County over the efforts of the Utah authorities to enforce their laws, and residents of Carson County had made two attempts to secede from the jurisdiction of Salt Lake City in the late 1850s.

The earlier efforts to form a separate territory had been stymied partly because the southern states resisted the establishment of new territories in the West without an agreement stating that slavery would be tolerated there. With the secession of the South in the winter of 1860–1861, the main obstacle to the creation of Nevada Territory disappeared.

President Buchanan, the hapless chief executive who witnessed the gathering of the clouds of Civil War in the winter of 1860–1861, signed the bill that established Nevada Territory just before he left office in March of 1861. This law designated a north-south line approximately halfway between Salt Lake City and Genoa to separate Nevada Territory from its parent. Less than three weeks later, President Lincoln appointed one of his political supporters, James W. Nye of New York, as governor of the new territory.

Nearly eight months passed from the time Congress created Nevada Territory until a formal government was fully established. Governor Nye reached Carson City in July and chose it as the place from which to organize a territorial government. There, Governor Nye met another of Lincoln's appointees, Territorial Secretary Orion Clemens of Missouri, and his younger brother Samuel. Nye and Orion Clemens had primary responsibility for governing the territory until an election could be held and a legislature convened, a process that took until late November 1861. Nye invited the men in all the settlements to choose representatives to a legislative session to be held in Carson City to adopt basic laws. The elected representatives met from October 1 until November 29, passed various legal codes, made some arrangements for paying a few public bills, and began the process of organizing a public school system.

The leading figure in the 1861 legislature was William M. Stewart, who claimed credit for the compromise that designated Carson City as the permanent territorial capital and which provided for the creation of eight county seats and nine counties. They were Aurora (Esmeralda County); Genoa (Douglas County); Carson City (Ormsby County); Washoe City (Washoe County); Virginia City (Storey County); Buckland's (Churchill County); Unionville (Humboldt County); and Dayton (Lyon County). The ninth was to have been Lake County in the northwest corner of the state because it was assumed that Susanville and the Honey Lake region of California would become part of Nevada. No seat of government was designated there, and it was attached to Washoe County, first for administrative purposes and later on a permanent basis.

This first legislature created the new counties in the manner of the eastern states, and in the expectation of prosperity for all of them. Around the Comstock, county seats were close together because it was believed that the seat of local government should be within a few hours ride by horse or team and wagon from any mine or ranch. Stewart and Nye wanted to make each important town a county seat as part of the bargain to assure that its representatives would agree to retain Carson City as the capital. The vast eastern districts—embraced within Esmeralda, Churchill, and Humboldt counties—were expected to fill with people at some later time. The legislature formed Lander County in 1862 following the rush to Austin.

## Constitution Making: The False Start of 1863

When the territorial legislature met for the second time, late in 1862, a majority of its members were eager to prepare for the transition to statehood. Although the population was still small in comparison to existing states, the growing wealth of the Comstock and the discovery of mines at Unionville and Aurora seemed to promise a bright future. The legislators arranged a special election for September 1863, to decide whether the residents of the territory wanted statehood and to allow them to elect delegates to a constitutional convention. The vote for statehood was overwhelmingly favorable, with more than 6,600 in favor and only 1,500 in opposition.

It was normal, in the forming of western states, for Congress to pass an enabling act to authorize the people of a territory to hold a constitutional convention. However, Californians had ignored this practice in 1849 when they framed their constitution in Monterey, and Congress had accepted the results in 1850. Nevada politicians of 1862–1863 had a similar goal, and although Governor Nye visited Washington early in 1863 to lobby for an enabling act, he was obviously interested in the cause for personal as well as political reasons because he had ambitions to become a United States senator. Even though Congress failed to act in this instance, territorial voters chose thirty-nine delegates who met for thirty-two days in November and December and drafted a document similar to the one then in effect in California. The two leading figures in the convention were the attorney William Stewart and the former surveyor general—now a territorial judge—John North.

Most of the work of the delegates was routine and noncontroversial, but some of their decisions aroused the resentment of the voters and brought a rejection of the proposed constitution in its original form. The most controversial matter involved a decision to tax mining property in the same manner as all other property. Stewart, a friend of the San Francisco mining interest, strongly opposed this provision, but Judge North, the president of the convention, argued that mining property should be taxed in exactly the same manner as ranches and homes. His position prevailed and was adopted by a substantial majority.

Judge North was one of the most honorable and influential early leaders in the territory. He had become territorial judge because of the respect the local attorneys had for him, but he had to face an explosive issue involving a geological problem at the very time the convention was under way. The large mining companies believed that the Comstock Lode consisted of a "single ledge" or lode, all of which they owned according to local mining regulations. Other "wildcat" prospectors had staked claims to the east and west of the main lode, claiming that they had identified separate ledges and therefore were entitled to stake separate claims. In one of his preliminary rulings from the bench in December 1863, Judge North held that the single-ledge theory had not yet been proven, and he refused to grant an injunction to the famous Ophir Company to remove its rivals from adjacent property.

This ruling pleased the small wildcat miners, and it was reasonable in view of the level of geological knowledge at that time. It was an opinion that encouraged the efforts of the latecomers to the Comstock who had located claims on the hills adjacent to the lode on either side. But this view was obviously a challenge to the older mining companies, many of them by then under the control of San Francisco financiers and represented by Stewart. This became the hottest political controversy in the territory as Nevadans began the process of designing a state government. And Stewart set out to ruin North's reputation, drive him from the bench, and secure approval of statehood in order to assure a new judiciary that would be more sympathetic to his clients.

Stewart and his followers supported the final draft of the constitution, but the mining companies and most of their workers opposed it, and when it was submitted to the voters on January 19, 1864, they rejected it by a vote of 8,851 to 2,157.

Another reason for popular opposition to the constitution of 1863 was the fact that the convention provided for the nomination of candidates for the newly created offices to be included on the ballot. The Union party of Storey County, led by Stewart, was the strongest political organization in the territory, and it offered a slate of potential officeholders who were closely allied with Stewart. North sought and failed to get the party's nomination for governor. There was much resentment over the manner in which Stewart's slate was selected, and the unsuccessful faction led the campaign to defeat the constitution.

In the meantime, Stewart accused North of a variety of judicial irregularities, including the taking of bribes. A committee of local lawyers later found North innocent of any wrongdoing, but in the course of the bitter fight, North's health failed, and once he had cleared his name, he left the territory. Stewart went on to an influential career in state and local politics.

## Constitution Making Resumed: The Successful Efforts of 1864

The decisive vote against the 1863 Constitution might well have spelled the end of the statehood movement if there had not been pressure from Washington to push ahead. President Lincoln and the Republicans were in political trouble; as the 1864 election approached, they worried that they would not be able to carry enough states to win the presidency and bring the Civil War to a successful conclusion. In the spring of that year, the Congress passed and President Lincoln signed legislation authorizing the citizens of three territories—Nebraska, Colorado, and Nevada—to hold constitutional conventions and to form state governments. He obviously wanted additional votes in Congress for his programs, and he believed that the new western states would support the Republican ticket in the 1864 presidential election. In all three territories such conventions met; only Nevada completed the process, becoming the thirty-sixth state.

The speed with which these pioneer Nevada political architects proceeded with their work was remarkable. Governor Nye called for an election of delegates to be held on June 6. Thirty-nine men were chosen, ten of whom had participated in the 1863 convention. Thirty-five participated in the drafting of the document, although they had no budget and received no salary for their labors. They met on July 4 and finished their task on July 21, compiling 829 pages of debate in the process. J. Neely Johnson, a former governor of California, presided; the old rivals, Stewart and North, were absent.

The level of the discussion and the quality of their political thought was often excellent; the 1864 delegates did not have as many distractions as their predecessors. In the end, they made one decisive change in the 1863 Constitution by providing that mines would *not* be assessed in the same manner as other property, but that only the proceeds of a producing mine could be subjected to taxation. They finished their document with considerable doubt about how the electorate would react, but when it was submitted to the voters on September 7, they approved it by a margin of 10,375 to 1,284. They telegraphed the document to Washington, and President Lincoln proclaimed Nevada a state on October 31, 1864—just in time to participate in the presidential election and to allow its senators and congressman to vote for the Thirteenth Amendment to the Constitution.

In the first election, held only a week after Nevada became a state, the voters selected Henry G. Blasdel—a Virginia City mine and mill superintendent—as governor, and they chose a legislature that met in December and named Stewart and Nye as United States senators. They immediately went to Washington to participate in the affairs of the embattled Union.

Even as the politicians worked at building the territorial and state governments, the eastward and southward migrations of the miners and their camp followers continued. Several hundred pressed inland in search of another Comstock Lode.

## Mark Twain's Nevada

The most famous participant in the mining rushes of the territorial period was Samuel L. Clemens, who later became internationally known as Mark Twain. Although he spent less than two years (1861–1863) there, Twain experienced the vitality of the early Comstock and its satellites. He wrote a delightful series of sketches in *Roughing It*, in his correspondence, and in his later reminiscences.

Twain came from his Missouri home to Washoe in 1861, the first year of the Civil War, after having tried his hand as a printer and as a riverboat pilot on the Mississippi. Because his brother Orion had been appointed secretary of the newly created territory, Mark accompanied him and thus avoided the hazards of military duty in the war. At first he hated the desert country, and even his later writings contain caustic remarks about it, but eventually he regarded it with good humor and even affection.

When he reached Carson City in the late summer of 1861, he found it to be a quaint village "in the shadow of a grim range of mountains overlooking it, whose summits seemed lifted clear out of companionship and consciousness of earthly things." And he continued:

> We arrived, disembarked, and the stage went on. It was a "wooden" town; its population two thousand souls. The main street consisted of four or five blocks of little white frame stores which were too high to sit down on, but not too high for various other purposes; in fact hardly high enough. They were packed close together, side by side, as if room were scarce in that mighty plain. In the middle of the town, opposite the stores, was the "plaza" which is native to all the towns beyond the Rocky Mountains—a large, unfenced, level vacancy, with a liberty pole in it, and very useful as a place for public auctions, horse trades, and mass meetings, and likewise for teamsters to camp in. Two other sides of the plaza were faced by stores, offices, and stables. The rest of Carson City was pretty scattering. (Twain, *Roughing It*, vol. II of *The Works of Mark Twain*, p. 155.)

It was a strange, violent place when Sam Clemens arrived. (His accounts are not always to be *completely* trusted because he was prone to exaggeration. But most of his anecdotes and descriptions were at least approximately based on episodes that he witnessed or heard about.) It was a land of casual shootings, tarantulas, crude living conditions, and loose talk. But it was also a land of marvelous beauty and high hopes.

Soon he and a companion climbed over the mountains to Lake Tahoe, where they camped for several days and considered building a house:

> Three months of camp life on Lake Tahoe would restore an Egyptian mummy to his pristine vigor, and give him an appetite like an alligator. I do not mean the oldest and driest mummies, of course, but the fresher ones. The air up there in the clouds is very pure and fine, bracing and delicious. And why shouldn't it be?—it is the same the angels breathe. (Twain, *Roughing It*, vol. II of *The Works of Mark Twain*, p. 164.)

Next Clemens "was smitten with the silver fever" and followed the rush to the Humboldt district. In his innocence and excitement, he stumbled upon some "fool's gold"—worthless mica that glittered in the sun. He and his partners staked claims and dug holes with crazed enthusiasm, only to be frustrated and disappointed at every turn:

> We had not less than thirty thousand "feet" apiece in the "richest mines on earth" as the frenzied cant phrased it—and were in debt to the butcher. We were stark mad with excitement—drunk with happiness—smothered under mountains of prospective wealth— arrogantly compassionate toward the plodding millions who knew not our marvelous canyon—but our credit was not good at the grocer's. (Twain, *Roughing It*, vol. II of *The Works of Mark Twain*, p. 201.)

Clemens soon became disappointed in Unionville and rushed southward to Aurora with the same result. But then came the opportunity—at first it seemed a poor substitute for hunting a gold mine—that changed his life. He took a job as a writer on Virginia City's *Territorial Enterprise*, where he was able to share the stimulating life of the Comstock, write stories true and half-true, report on and poke fun at the work of the territorial legislature, and practice the artistry that would one day make him one of America's best-loved novelists and the creator of Tom Sawyer and Huckleberry Finn. He served briefly as a secretary to the territorial legislature and as a clerk in the 1863 constitutional convention. He was on the Comstock less than two years, but Bernard DeVoto wrote of this period:

> One may say, at least, that Washoe perfectly satisfied and agreed with the compositor-pilot-prospector who here came into his heritage. It was Washoe that matured Sam Clemens, that gave him, after three false apprenticeships, the trade he would follow all his life, and that brought into harmony the elements of his mind which before had fumbled for expression. In the desert air a writer grew to maturity. Sun Mountain brought him to recognition of himself. In Washoe he took the name that is known more widely than any other in our literature and will be known as long as any. It was in Washoe on February 2, 1863, that Mark Twain was born. Not, one thinks, by chance. (DeVoto, *Mark Twain's America*, p. 133.)

During Twain's time in the territory, a boundary dispute flared between Nevada and California. Californians themselves had set the eastern boundary of their new state in 1850, but when Congress established Nevada Territory in 1861, it defined the "dividing ridge" that separates

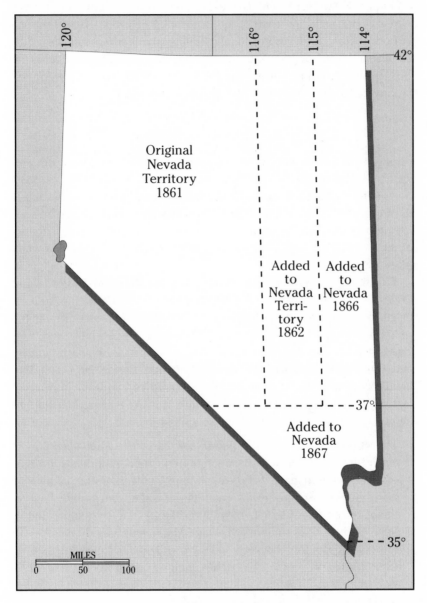

120°    116°  115°  114°

42°

Original
Nevada
Territory
1861

Added
to
Nevada
Terri-
tory
1862

Added
to
Nevada
1866

37°

Added to
Nevada
1867

35°

MILES
0    50    100

*Changing Boundaries of Nevada*

the waters of the Carson Valley from those that flow westward to the Pacific as the western boundary of Nevada, on the condition that California would yield the eastern Sierra slopes to Nevada. Trouble arose in both Aurora and Susanville, California (which some considered to be part of Lake County), and violence seemed imminent, but a formal survey and settlement was reached in 1864–1865. This survey found Susanville to be in California and Aurora in Nevada.

## Prospectors Push Eastward

Hundreds of others who were less articulate than Mark Twain pressed further inland on the mining frontier and helped establish the claim of Nevada to the vast center of the Great Basin and into the watershed of the Colorado River. Some pioneers kept diaries, wrote letters or mining reports, or composed imaginative stories that preserved fragments of their experience; such works are the basic fabric of modern Nevada tapestry.

To Austin, for example, came an Ohio couple named Martha and James Galley, who arrived in 1864 on their way to California and decided to stay. For ten years they struggled to make their stake in mining, ranching, freighting, speculation, and politics—all of which were tangled together. They raised children, huddled against the cold in shanties, and—in their leisure hours—wrote letters and diaries. Dr. Galley had been a dentist in the Midwest but did not practice that trade in Nevada; instead he tried his hand at journalism and creative writing. Martha sent her impressions eastward in 1865:

> The country is new & the population heterogeneous—you see every grade of every nationality represented—Americans from everywhere that have been everywhere—elderly portly capitalists that are here to invest—keen elegant speculators that have been successful—hairy, hungry "hard" looking miners, some that have "struck it" & some that haven't. Mill-owners & mill hands— merchants, doctors, lawyers, sailors, saddlers, "butcher & baker" every thing and everybody—riches & rags. (Lewis, *Martha and the Doctor*, pp. 32–33.)

The Galleys were lucky; they persevered for ten years as Austin declined, then "hit it lucky" in a pay streak at Tybo and sold out in time. They moved on to California before the collapse of the entire silver-mining economy on which Nevada depended at that time.

Austin's newspaper, *The Reese River Reveille*, served as the main source of information on central Nevada for the mining and business fraternity in the middle 1860s. Based on the reports and rumors printed here, scores of hopeful gold and silver seekers set out for points further south and east.

## The Pahranagat Episode and Boundary Changes

One of the false booms was in the Pahranagat mountains, about 200 miles southeast of Austin and 100 miles north of Las Vegas in 1865. At that time, the boundary line between Nevada and Utah Territory had not been surveyed, and it was unclear which had the right to govern the new district. Also at that time, land south of the 37th parallel in the southern triangle adjacent to the Colorado River belonged to Arizona Territory.

When Nevada Territory was created in 1861, Congress fixed the eastern boundary about halfway between Carson City and Salt Lake City. In the following year, it moved the line one degree to the east to incorporate the prospective mining districts in that jurisdiction. The revised boundary was expected to be somewhere near Pahranagat, but its exact location was unknown.

Reports of ore discoveries began to come from Irish Mountain, telling of a fabulous bonanza. Although information was fragmentary, the Nevada legislature was sufficiently impressed in 1866 to create a new county named Lincoln, and Governor Blasdel led a party into the region to try to form a local government. (He was interested in doing a little prospecting or investing in the mines himself.) Utah's territorial governor also visited Pahranagat in 1866, and for a time there was strong competition between Nevada and Utah officials for jurisdiction.

Because Nevada was a state, it had two senators and a representative in Congress; Utah Territory had only a powerless delegate in the House, and the polygamy sanctioned by the Mormon church was highly unpopular among the nation's leaders. Nevada's congressman was Delos R. Ashley of Austin. He, together with Senators Stewart and Nye, were able in 1866 to have the state's boundary moved eastward by one additional degree of longitude to ensure that control of the Pahranagat district came from Carson City rather than Salt Lake City. The mines themselves were almost worthless, but they did open this region to some of the men who eventually found important silver deposits at Pioche, about 50 miles to the north.

The Congressional Act of 1866 contained a bonus for the Silver State.

In the same law, Nevada's congressional delegation managed to attach to Nevada that part of Arizona Territory northwest of the Colorado River, which also was thought to include some good mining prospects and which would give land-locked Nevada access to a navigable river flowing into sea—or at least into the Gulf of California. This was a decision of incomparable significance to the new state.

## Suggested Supplementary Reading

Abbe, Donald R. *Austin and the Reese River Mining District: Nevada's Forgotten Frontier.* Reno: University of Nevada Press, 1985.

Bowers, Michael W. *The Nevada State Constitution: A Reference Guide.* Foreword by Frankie Sue Del Papa. Westport, Conn.: Greenwood Press, 1993.

———. *The Sagebrush State: Nevada's History, Government, and Politics.* Reno: University of Nevada Press, 1996.

Jackson, W. Turrentine. *Treasure Hill: Portrait of a Silver Mining Camp.* Tucson: University of Arizona Press, 1963.

Johnson, David A. *Founding the Far West: California, Oregon, and Nevada, 1840–1890.* Berkeley: University of California Press, 1992.

Lord, Eliot. *Comstock Mining and Miners.* Introduction by David F. Myrick. 1883. Reprint, Berkeley: Howell-North, 1959.

Ostrander, Gilman. *Nevada: The Great Rotten Borough 1859–1964.* New York: Alfred A. Knopf, 1966.

Paul, Rodman W. *Mining Frontiers of the Far West: 1848–1880.* New York: Holt, Rinehart and Winston, 1963.

# 7

## Colorado Steamboats, Eldorado Canyon, and the Second Wave of Mormons

**N**EARLY 500 miles southeast of Carson City, another piece of the Nevada tapestry was fashioned even as the state was being born, although this region did not yet belong to the new territory and state. Within the watershed of the Colorado River—where the Mormon Trail left the Colorado Basin and where the Mormon missionaries had abandoned their Las Vegas outpost in 1858—other prospectors were probing the Mojave.

### Eldorado Canyon

Even before the Mormons arrived, at least one explorer had considered the possibility of gold along the Colorado River. He was Francis Xavier Aubrey, a merchant from Santa Fe who tried to finish the work of the Spanish padres; he wanted to find a more direct trail between northern New Mexico and central California. He drove a large herd of sheep into southern California by way of the Gila River, but he thought that a railroad across northern Arizona might be more practical. He made two trips in 1853 and 1854, searching for a route roughly along the 35th parallel.

Aubrey is believed to have crossed the Colorado River at Eldorado Canyon, about 20 miles south of Boulder City, because he reported finding gold in the canyons that rise above the river on the west side. He did not live to witness the development of a mining district, but he has been recognized as a pioneer in the discovery of the precious metal in the Mojave Desert. He represented a new generation and new commercial interests in the Far West.

During the 1850s, settlers appeared along the lower Colorado River in California and on the opposite bank in territory that would later become Arizona.

By gradual stages, a steamship service had matured under the direction of George A. Johnson and, by 1856, he was trying to persuade the government to finance an expedition to navigate the river as far northward as possible. Congress accepted his idea, appropriated money for an expedition, but then chose someone else—a West Point graduate named Joseph C. Ives—to conduct the expedition. These two men competed for the honor of proving that the Colorado could be navigated, and they soon proved that steamships could operate some 500 miles up the river from the Gulf of California. This meant that normally they could take a small steamboat as far north as the Las Vegas Wash, and at high water as far as the Virgin River. By the early 1860s, Johnson and his rivals were jockeying for the privilege of trading with the Mormons of Utah.

In the meantime during the spring of 1861, a former trapper named Johnny Moss found gold in Eldorado Canyon about 65 miles north of Fort Mojave—probably the same outcropping that Aubrey had seen a few years earlier. He spread the news to the California towns as quickly as possible in an effort to promote his claims, and, within a few months, hundreds of men came scouting for gold-bearing ledges up and down the river. In Eldorado Canyon alone, seven hundred mining claims were staked in a short time.

Like Pahranagat, Eldorado Canyon yielded only a modest amount of gold during the next few years, but by 1864 promoters built a stamp mill and later a furnace. There was still enough interest in 1866 for Nevada's congressional delegation to push for the addition of the southern triangle south of the 37th parallel as they arranged for the addition of another slice of Utah Territory to Nevada. And when the Pahranagat district opened, some of the unused milling equipment from Eldorado was hauled there—a distance of more than 100 miles. Thus the two Nevada mining frontiers, from north and south, met on the slopes of Irish Mountain, some 125 miles north of Las Vegas.

# The Mormon Communities of the Southeast

In the southeastern corner of Nevada, not far from the Utah and Arizona borders, the terrain is unfit for agriculture except in the narrow valleys immediately adjacent to the Meadow Valley Wash, the Muddy River, and the Virgin River, but the experiments of the peoples who made their homes there have added an unusual segment to the mosaic of the state's history.

As we have seen, the Virgin River was an important link along the Mormon Trail from central Utah to southern California; it has several sources in the mountains of southern Utah, and most of them funnel together near St. George. It then proceeds southwesterly through the northwest corner of Arizona and into Nevada near Mesquite. After passing through a few miles of sandy, increasingly parched terrain, it bends southward to empty into the main channel of the Colorado River (or, since the building of Hoover Dam, into the northern tip of Lake Mead). Some 25 miles south of Mesquite, it received (before the building of the dam), the flow of the Muddy River.

The Muddy River was misnamed, or at least it was given its label at flood time. (At times it had been called the Moapa, a more appropriate label.) It is not a river, and it is seldom muddy. But if heavy precipitation falls upstream, it can be both at once. Usually its waters are clear, but occasionally its northern reaches, the Meadow Valley Wash, have produced flash floods that have made it dangerous and destructive. Like most desert streams, both the Virgin and the Muddy–Meadow Valley have sometimes behaved well for years and then dumped tempestuous volumes of water into towns and fields along their banks within a few hours.

## Upper Meadow Valley, Panaca

At the same time that Mormons were withdrawing from Carson Valley and Las Vegas in 1857, leaving their homes and fields to the Indians or miners, others of their denomination were seeking a place of refuge in a green oasis called Meadow Valley, about 150 miles north of Las Vegas. The church presidency ordered a search for a place where the leaders might hide if the U.S. Army did occupy the Salt Lake Valley and try to persecute them. For this purpose, the Mormon scouts selected the site of Panaca and laid out ditches and fields there in 1857. As we have seen, it did not become necessary for the church leaders to retreat from Salt Lake Valley. After the compromises between them and Johnston's army, the advanced parties of Mormons abandoned the place of refuge, and the Meadow Valley fields lay idle for several years.

In 1864, just as statehood for Nevada was being fashioned in Washington and Carson City, new contingents of Mormons arrived in these southwestern fringes of Utah Territory. Young sent settlers into Meadow Valley under the leadership of Francis Lee to establish a community known as Panaca, under the direction of Erastus Snow, president of Dixie Mission, which had its headquarters in St. George.

Panaca was not only the first but also the most successful Mormon community founded in the 1860s in the region that later became eastern Nevada. These settlers believed they were in Utah Territory, and until Congress changed the Nevada-Utah boundary in 1866, they were.

Even as they arrived and began to establish a townsite, Lee and his party met a squad of soldiers who had come from Camp Floyd in Utah to search for a suitable route for a wagon road from central Utah to the Colorado River. They were also prospecting for precious metals, as gold fever had already reached into the heart of Mormon country. Missionary Snow admonished the settlers "not to suffer themselves to be overcome by a spirit of covetousness and a desire for riches to the exclusion of the Spirit of the Lord" (Lee and Wadsworth, *A Century in Meadow Valley*, p. 3).

The Panaca farmers generally resisted the lure of the mines, but later they found good employment for their young men and a ready market for their crops in Pioche, a mining town that opened 11 miles to the north in 1870. They introduced a communal irrigation system strikingly different from that which evolved in western Nevada, formed a co-operative store for the sale and purchase of products, and thus maintained their community identity during the onslaught of the mining frontier on their neighborhood. Panaca remains one of eastern Nevada's most idyllic examples of a pioneering Mormon town, with many descendants of the original settlers still in residence more than 140 years after their ancestors arrived.

## Callville and the Muddy Mission

The Latter-day Saints church founded missions in the upper reaches of the Virgin River in southwestern Utah for the purposes of converting the Indians to Christianity in the 1850s, even before they built their fort at Las Vegas. In 1861, Brigham Young visited the region, known as "Utah's Dixie," and decided to send permanent settlers there—including Orson Hyde, the former probate judge of Carson County. The objective was to establish a cotton mission to produce the raw materials for a textile industry. By 1864, the Mormons were branching outward down the river, both to open additional productive agricultural land and to establish a line of communication.and settlement to the Colorado River.

In October 1864, the same month that Nevada was admitted to the Union, Young designated Anson Call to lead a party to explore the Colorado River and choose a site for a warehouse and shipping center, because he wanted to take advantage of trade opportunities offered by the steamboats that were plying the river below the Las Vegas Wash. It was his hope that navigation on the Colorado River would make it possible to ship supplies upstream from the gulf, thus avoiding the costly overland freight hauling from the Midwest or California. Call established a community, which he named Callville, on the big bend of the Colorado River about 25 miles east of Las Vegas. (The location is now covered by the waters of Lake Mead.) For a short time, small steamers operated up and down the river, but the venture was never a success because the river was too dangerous. A few years later, in 1869, when the transcontinental railroad connected northern Utah with both California and the East, the need for Callville and the riverboats disappeared.

The decision by the Latter-day Saints' leadership to establish the Muddy Mission was prompted in part by Call's favorable report on the possibility of navigating the lower Colorado. Also in October of 1864, the church decided upon the establishment of missions in the Muddy River Valley, about 50 miles northeast of Las Vegas. During the following year, Thomas S. Smith and more than forty families founded St. Thomas, and Joseph Warren Foote established St. Joseph about 8 miles upstream. This mission was much more successful in the short run than the Las Vegas Mission had been a decade earlier. Hot-weather crops could be grown almost year-round. The settlers produced enough wheat, corn, and cotton to justify the construction of a mill to grind the grain and to operate a cotton gin.

Missionary Foote—he preferred to be called Warren—was a tenacious representative of his denomination. Although his immediate mission ran into political trouble after a few years, his example became a testimonial to future generations who were willing to challenge this environment. Warren and his wife Ann located a new settlement a few miles north of St. Thomas, which Brigham Young suggested they name St. Joseph in his honor.

Forty-five additional families joined them within two years. Church authorities expanded the mission by assigning more families to it in 1867. Thousands of pounds of agricultural products went northward into Utah. The settlers planted orchards and developed fine herds of cattle.

Life was not easy for those who operated the Dixie Mission in the 1860s. The severe summer heat helped some crops, but it drove many of the settlers away after a year or two. Malaria was a common and frequently fatal disease. There was no local timber for home building, so the missionaries fashioned houses of adobe with roofs made of cattails that had been harvested from the river. The distance to market was great and the missionaries often felt that they were not receiving enough equipment and supplies from the church in exchange for their products. Yet the settlers built more than a hundred homes and cultivated five hundred acres of cotton. There were occasional complaints about the threats and the thievery of the Indians, but their relations with the Native Americans were usually friendly, and a few of the Indians accepted the religious message of the Mormons.

When John Wesley Powell, the famous explorer and ethnographer, made his first trip along the upper part of the Colorado River in 1869, he accomplished one of the remarkable feats in the history of American exploration. Riding rafts with his companions down the treacherous waters of the Grand Canyon, he completed his wild three-month escapade at the mouth of the Virgin River, where he unexpectedly found three Mormon men fishing. Soon he and his four surviving companions had been fed heartily on a banquet of fish, beef, melons, butter, and cheese—a testimonial to the abundance that the settlers on the Muddy River had been able to provide for themselves.

By the time the federal census of 1870 was taken, more than 750 settlers lived in the region that had been denominated "Rio Virgin" in southern Lincoln County. Nearly all of them had homes along the Muddy. The census for that year counted only 8 residents at Las Vegas.

But there on the Muddy River, the mining frontier and the Mormon Zion collided once again. The fatal blow to the mission came from the tax assessor of Lincoln County in 1870. These settlers, like those in Meadow Valley to the north, believed they were within Utah Territory, and the Utah legislature even created a separate county, named Rio Virgin, to serve their governmental needs. But a boundary survey made in 1870 showed that they were within Nevada, and the county officers from Lincoln County insisted on collecting back taxes that were much higher than those imposed by Utah. The Nevada authorities also wanted the payment in gold, which the Mormons did not have. More than a hundred persons signed a petition to the Nevada legislature seeking the abatement of taxes, and they appealed for the creation of a new county to be called "Las Vegas County."

When officers from Pahranagat threatened to seize the Mormon property if the taxes were not paid, the church released the missionaries from the assignment, and most returned to the Utah farms whence they came. Brigham Young himself visited the Muddy settlements in 1870. This old veteran of so many religious and political encounters wanted to learn the facts. Should there be another retreat, as there had been from Nauvoo in 1846, and from Carson Valley and Las Vegas in 1857? Or should the "children of Zion" make a stand on the banks of the Muddy, as they were doing successfully in Meadow Valley? In the end, these stream banks were too sandy, the climate too hot, and the faithful too few in number. So in December 1870, he encouraged them to withdraw.

As their predecessors had done in the previous decade in Las Vegas and Genoa, the Mormons of the Muddy Mission abandoned their homes and cultivated fields. Only two people, Daniel and Ann Bonelli, remained after 1870 and operated a ferry across the river. Warren Foote, who had built a "permanent" home and spent six years cultivating his vineyard and fields, was stoical at the time of departure. He wrote in later years:

> In leaving the Muddy, my faith did not fail me . . . I felt that the Lord had not forsaken me, but that He would open up the way before me in such a manner that we would not suffer. (Quoted in Arrington, *The Mormons in Nevada*, p. 45.)

Foote and many members of his family lived into the next century and knew of the eventual return of other members of their denomination to these valleys.

The Mormons were a persistent people, and ten years after their departure from the Muddy, in 1880, some of their numbers returned to the lower Muddy River, rebuilt homes, and replowed the fields. St. Thomas and St. Joseph (renamed Logandale) rose again, and the town of Overton emerged between them, soon to become the most important community of the region. The industrious settlers soon had virtually all the land that could be easily irrigated under cultivation. In the next century, the transportation revolution diminished the isolation of these towns and they became a successful center for the production of tomato plants and early spring vegetables.

## Octavius Decatur Gass and Las Vegas

In the meantime, an outpost of society had returned to the abandoned fort at Las Vegas. When the Civil War broke out, the U.S. Army considered placing units of cavalry and infantry there and calling the place Fort Baker. A company from the California Volunteers began preparations to occupy such an outpost, but never went there, and as the war ended, the old Mormon property fell into the hands of a miner named Octavius Decatur Gass.

Gass, like so many of the early Comstock miners, was a forty-niner who had met disappointment in the California goldfields. He was among those who shared the excitement and the disappointment of the rush to Eldorado Canyon. He once also worked in Eldorado County, California, staked claims many times, and "saw the elephant." (Prospectors like Mark Twain who had tried several rushes and had turned to other jobs to make a living used this expression to indicate that they had tried and failed at mining.) So Gass took up the Las Vegas ranch. He tore down some of the old Mormon buildings, planted an orchard, and plunged into the elementary chores of raising a garden and a herd. He acquired 640 acres at Las Vegas and also the 160-acre Spring Ranch southwest of Las Vegas.

The energetic Gass also plunged into politics and served four terms in the territorial legislature of Arizona from 1865 to 1868. He drafted a bill to create Pah-Ute County with the seat of government at Callville. The fact that this region was officially attached to Nevada by the boundary change of 1866–1867 did not immediately convince Gass that he should change his political allegiance, and Pah-Ute County sent representatives to the Arizona legislature for another three years. He resisted the payment of Nevada taxes for a time, but finally capitulated.

When Gass sought a wife, he found a promising possibility in Moapa, 50 miles away. Mary Virginia Simpson, a young woman from Missouri, had been traveling southward with her sister's family from central Utah

*Old Ranch, Las Vegas. (Ferron-Bracken Collection, University of Nevada, Las Vegas, Library)*

to Arizona in 1871, when they became aware of the abandoned Mormon property on the Muddy River. They bought it for a low price and settled there, and Octavius began to court Mary Virginia across the sandy stretches that separate Las Vegas from Moapa. When the time for their marriage arrived, they traveled 175 miles to Pioche for the license and the exchange of vows. They lived at the Las Vegas ranch for another nine years and had six children there. Then they fell into debt and lost their ranch.

The western frontier was a harsh place, and no part of it was more challenging than southern Nevada. The barren mountains and valleys, the heat, and the lack of timber and other useful resources defeated most of those who tried to build outposts of American civilization there in the nineteenth century. But the twentieth century brought new technologies, and in the meantime, Nevada continued its evolutionary development in the north.

## Suggested Supplementary Reading

Arrington, Leonard J. *The Mormons in Nevada*. Las Vegas: Las Vegas Sun, 1979.

Edwards, Elbert B. *200 Years in Nevada: A Story of People Who Opened, Explored, and Developed the Land*. A Bicentennial History. Salt Lake City: Publishers Press, 1978.

Lingenfelter, Richard E. *Steamboats on the Colorado River*. Tucson: University of Arizona Press, 1978.

Townley, John M. *Conquered Provinces: Nevada Moves Southeast, 1864–1871*. Charles Redd Monographs in Western History. Provo: Brigham Young University Press, 1973.

# 8

## The Era of the Boomtowns, 1865–1878

I N THE fourteen years between October 1864, when Nevada attained statehood, and the end of 1878, the early Nevada mining frontier enjoyed its greatest era of production and prosperity. For several of these years, it was hailed as the most important center for the production of precious metals in America. Several exciting new mining districts opened in the eastern counties, and the residents of the Comstock Lode witnessed the discovery of one of the biggest ore bodies in world history—the fabled Big Bonanza. It produced tens of millions of dollars and many scandals, and then—with greater speed than it had arisen—the boom collapsed, leaving the state in *borrasca*—the Spanish term for "a bad wind," which the miner translated as "out-of-ore and out-of-luck."

This period profoundly influenced the political and social structure of the state for the next hundred years. The mining boom pushed the borders of the state eastward and southward. It led to the creation of new counties and the building of courthouses which became symbols of law and order—and sometimes of extravagance—in a new zone of the frontier. The speed with which the mining companies found and lost their "luck" contributed to social instability. Large financial fortunes rose and fell, and the mania for speculation in mining and other forms of gambling became ingrained in the social mentality. The land and people of the new state were often considered to be easy targets for exploitation by ambitious financial manipulators.

*Virginia City at its peak. (Nevada Historical Society)*

The Comstock investors who controlled the richest mines in the 1860s had an important ally in Washington in the person of Senator Stewart. He carried with him to the nation's capital a keen understanding of the needs of the larger mining companies and his forceful way of getting things done. Early in his first term, he authored the country's basic mining law.

The National Mining Law of 1866 institutionalized what the mining fraternity was doing in the desert West. It gave legal validity to mining district regulations that were enacted on the spot and approved the principle that miners could preempt parts of the public domain and its waters simply by laying claim and making use of them. The basic principles of this law remained in effect as the twenty-first century opened, to the despair of governmental planners and conservationists.

## The Tyranny of William Sharon, 1864–1875

Even in the early period, the wealth of the Comstock Lode drove many of its boldest men into a condition of speculative madness. One of the most famous cases is that of William Sharon, the notorious agent of the Bank of California in San Francisco. He arrived in Virginia City during an economic slowdown in 1864 and worked systematically to gain a monopoly of the mills, the richest mines, and the transportation that served the Comstock. He almost succeeded by the early 1870s because when he could not gain ownership of the mines, he tried to control the milling and smelting of their ores, the supply of timber, and the water system of the Comstock.

Standing behind Sharon in his quest for wealth and power was William Ralston of San Francisco, the energetic founder of the Bank of California and other leading oligarchies of the Bay Area. The "bank crowd" came to be feared and hated by common people and smaller businessmen of Nevada because they insisted on control of all aspects of the Comstock economy. They wanted a "vertical monopoly" that would give them total control of the region's resources, from extraction of the ore to the controlling of its benefits. The bank crowd wanted no competition and no middlemen.

Sharon, as the local agent of the Bank of California, promoted the building of the Virginia and Truckee Railroad down the steep slopes of Mt. Davidson to the mills on the Carson River, and eventually through the Washoe Valley and Truckee Meadows to connect with the Central

Pacific at Reno. He wanted to be able to control and set the prices for the movement of ore. He used his influence to persuade the voters of Ormsby (now Carson City) and Washoe counties to issue bonds to pay for the extension line to Reno, without any assurance of repayment. He eventually gained control of the *Territorial Enterprise*, the most famous Nevada newspaper.

Sharon's objective at every stage was to gain a more complete stranglehold on the wealth of the region. In 1875 he crowned his political achievements by manipulating—or rather purchasing—his election to the U.S. Senate in the Nevada legislature. After winning the office, he almost never tended to his duties in Washington because he was more concerned about the bank's and his own private financial affairs in California and Nevada.

In the same year as his election to the Senate, Sharon and Ralston saw their financial empire rocked to its foundations. Their wild speculation put too much of their depositors' money into unsafe ventures, and in the summer of 1875 his clients started a run on the bank that could not be stopped. California's largest financial institution closed its doors and Ralston resigned his administrative office. He then went swimming in San Francisco Bay and did not return—an apparent suicide. Sharon patched up the tangled financial affairs and did manage to have the bank open again after a few weeks, but business enterprises in all parts of the West, and especially in Nevada, suffered losses. Because of Sharon and other smaller manipulators, the Comstock got a bad name for financial dealings.

Ralston and Sharon belonged to that class of financial oligarchies that would engage in almost any kind of business arrangement for their own profit, without any regard for the consequences for the public at large. They were brilliant businessmen without a conscience. They won public acclaim while they were perceived to be creating jobs, but in the end the public tried to restrict and regulate men of their type.

## Adolph Sutro and His Tunnel

One of the pioneer speculators and experimenters in the milling of ore was a German immigrant named Adolph Sutro. After spending several years in small-time trading in California, in the early 1860s, he brought to the Washoe country a plan for building a mill on the Carson River only a few miles from the mines to reduce the high cost of shipping the ore over the mountains. Several other investors followed his lead, and most of them failed to process the ore successfully, but the experiments added much to the metallurgical science of the Far West.

Sutro became the mastermind of one of the most ambitious schemes of his day when he proposed to dig a four-mile-long tunnel from a point near the Carson River into the heart of Mt. Davidson to penetrate the ore bodies, drain the excessive water from the mines, and provide better ventilation. (The mine shafts became uncomfortably hot as they extended deeper beneath Mt. Davidson.) Sutro spent most of the 1860s seeking legal authority from the state legislature and Congress to build the tunnel, and searching for the necessary financial backing. It became one of the most controversial enterprises of the era because in the early stages he got contracts with the mine owners which promised that he would be paid a special fee for each ton of ore extracted after the tunnel was finished. Some of the large mining companies supported him at first, but later tried to block his project when they realized the great value of the ore. His most bitter enemy and chief obstruction was William Sharon, who feared the challenge to his control of the wealth of the Comstock. Sharon obstructed Sutro's efforts in Congress whenever possible, and the bank crowd successfully blocked Sutro's efforts to raise capital anywhere in the western or eastern financial centers for several years, so Sutro sought financial backing in Europe.

A Gold Hill mine tragedy in 1869 provided the impetus, the rationale, and the initial financing that enabled Sutro to begin his tunnel not far from Dayton on the Carson River. A disastrous fire broke out in the Yellow Jacket Mine and killed forty-five men deep below the surface when the timber in the shaft ignited. If Sutro's tunnel had been in existence, the doomed men might have had an escape route. The miners' union then made the first large pledge of money for Sutro's scheme. Soon afterward, other investors offered their support.

The tunnel project was widely publicized as one of the outstanding engineering projects of the age. Ironically, when Sutro's workers finally reached their goal at the 1,600-foot level beneath Virginia City in 1878, all the rich ore of the lode was gone and the mining companies were digging vainly, almost desperately, in the hot depths of the earth further down. Later, he sold his interest in the tunnel, prospered by investing in San Francisco real estate, and became mayor of that city.

## The Triumph of the Bonanza Firm, 1873–1877

The story of the four Irishmen who found and developed the famous Big Bonanza is somewhat happier. One of these "Bonanza kings," John Mackay, became legendary for his honesty in business and generosity to less fortunate miners. But another of them, James G. Fair, had a reputation almost as bad as that of William Sharon. The other two members of the Bonanza Firm—William O'Brien and James C. Flood (the latter was born in New York of Irish parents)—made little mark on history, but they stand as two of the very rare early mine promoters who realized great wealth from their efforts. Mining was, in a sense, much like the contemporary gambling business. Risks were great and only a few managed to gain large fortunes and keep them.

Mackay, like two of his partners, was an immigrant from Ireland. He started his Comstock career as a hard-rock miner in Gold Hill, and by gradual steps he and Fair acquired an interest in one of the mines that Sharon did not control—the Hale & Norcross in the center of the lode. When that property produced a small bonanza, they bought control of other claims further north, which became the renowned Consolidated Virginia and the California. It was there—some 1,300 feet below the surface—that their crews discovered the Big Bonanza.

This massive block of rich gold-silver ore extended downward for 300 feet and consisted of the richest large body of "high grade" ever found in America. Mackay directed the mining carefully; this was unusual practice on the Comstock or anywhere in the West. In the next nine years it yielded more than $100 million and paid dividends to its stockholders of more than $74 million. The total group of Comstock mine owners reported production of nearly $40 million in a single year—1877, and it was widely known that most companies under-reported their actual production in order to avoid paying part of the state government's tax on the proceeds of mines. In that same year, the budget of the entire state government was less than $600,000.

## The Cities of the Comstock

The cities that evolved on the side of Mt. Davidson and in Gold Canyon became an American phenomenon—publicized across the nation as places of millionaires and wild frontier extravagance. Virginia City claimed some of the finest mansions, opera houses, banks, churches, and schools in the entire West. It also had the most ornate saloons. Its wealthy magnates lived high on the mountainside, near or above C Street, which was the main business thoroughfare. Below, in alphabetical order, were streets where one could find the brothels, the bustling railroad station, the large hoisting works, the Chinese and the Indian communities. Most residents lived close enough together on the rocky slopes to be constantly within earshot of the business bustle on C Street, the riotous life of the saloons, the roar of the mine hoists and stamp mills, and the constant to-and-fro surging of humanity.

Virginia City was never a large community by modern standards; there have been many exaggerated generalizations about its population. A basic problem for demographers is that both in 1870 and 1880, when the decennial federal census was taken, the Comstock was experiencing economic stagnation; the greatest prosperity occurred between those years. Reports that the area had 40,000 people in its most prosperous days cannot be trusted; probably its total population never exceeded 20,000. Yet it attracted famous visitors by the dozens: three former presidents and assorted politicians on their way to California, military heroes and preachers, traveling actors and performers, and scores of writers who spread the word about its wonders. Gold Hill and Silver City, further south along the Comstock Lode on the other side of "the divide," were less famous and less elaborate, but they were nonetheless well-known and prosperous communities.

Men greatly outnumbered women in the Comstock towns at the peak of the bonanza period, but the wives of the wealthy class tried to set a social standard that would be worthy of larger, more cosmopolitan cities. They furnished their homes and adorned themselves with the finest luxuries that San Francisco and Europe could provide. Nevadans were eager participants in the "gilded age" when they could afford to be, and even beyond that point.

Although the number of women was relatively small, they provided an important stabilizing influence in the bonanza camp. The wives and daughters of the executives and businessmen often played important roles in establishing churches, schools, and cultural events. Another category of people who came to the Comstock to seek their fortunes just as the miners did were those who served in the theaters, dance halls, hurdy-houses, and brothels. Prostitution was a recognized and tacitly accepted institution in the Comstock, as in many other parts of America. The sexual and economic exploitation of these women was assumed to be a standard part of the frontier experience.

One morning, on October 26, 1875, that most dreaded nemesis of the densely packed mining towns struck Virginia City—fire. It roared from street to street in the center of the town, swept by the famous "Washoe zephyr" blowing over Mt. Davidson, and fed by the timber of thousands of trees that had been cut in the Sierra to build the city. It blazed for several hours before it could be contained, consuming most of the business center and civic buildings. Mackay fortunately saved the mine shaft that gave access to the Big Bonanza, and the Comstock money rebuilt Virginia City with even more elegant trappings. The main buildings that have become famous since the rise of the twentieth-century tourist economy were constructed after the great fire of 1875.

Several factors worked together to destroy the Comstock's prosperity at the end of the 1870s. Not only were the treasures of the Big Bonanza exhausted and the confidence of the financial community shaken by the manipulations of Sharon, but also the price of silver began to fall and the U.S. Congress stopped minting silver dollars in 1873. Suddenly, Nevada's greatest mineral resource was being overproduced and no longer had the prestige of former years. In many parts of the West, other mining camps had opened and were pouring their "white metal" onto the financial markets in such quantity that its price fell dramatically.

## Mining Rushes to Eastern Nevada

During the late 1860s while Sharon, Sutro, and the Bonanza crowd fought for supremacy on the Comstock, there were several mining rushes into the mountains of central and eastern Nevada, but only a few of them had any lasting importance. In nearly every case, the discoverers and early developers hoped for another lode like the one on Mt. Davidson, but none ever approached it in scope and wealth.

In chapter 6 we observed that Austin had been the jumping-off point for the exploration of much of central and eastern Nevada. Although it was not one of the great camps in terms of its gold or silver, Austin produced more than its share of historical, governmental, and architectural legacy. Its most promising early offspring, Pahranagat, failed, but the prospectors, with their undying optimism, continued to fan out in the "great east," and within a few years their hopes were rewarded in the discoveries at Belmont, Eureka, Hamilton, and Pioche.

## Belmont and Eureka

Most of the town names that arose in the 1860s have long since vanished from the public view, like the ephemeral desert flowers that appear after a spring rain and perish in the summer's heat. Belmont, in the Toquima Range of central Nevada, yielded $2 or $3 million worth of ore in the late 1860s before the "pay streaks" disappeared. During its brief hour, it was designated by the legislature as the seat of a new county named for the popular Governor Nye. A fine courthouse rose there, and its noble ruins are now a national historical landmark.

The outcroppings at Eureka, about 60 miles east of Austin, first came to the attention of the mining fraternity in 1864, but these ores could not be refined easily because they included large quantities of lead. The discoverers lacked both the knowledge and investment capital to develop their claims, which led to several false starts before a practical technique was developed in 1869. A successful smelter went into operation in that year, and Eureka enjoyed a fifteen-year period of prosperity—a long time in the history of the mining towns.

Throughout the 1870s, Eureka had the most consistent record of production of any Nevada mining town. According to official records, its mines produced between $2 million and $5 million in gold and silver, and was the leading producer every year from 1871 through 1882. While this was modest compared to the Comstock Lode during the years of the Big Bonanza, it rivaled Virginia City during the early 1880s. As other mining camps fell silent, Eureka's unique reduction works and furnaces transformed millions of tons of raw ore into silver and lead bars, consuming thousands of cords of wood from the mountains and employing hundreds of men. But by the middle 1880s Eureka, like the other camps, felt the pinch of disappearing ore bodies and declining silver prices.

In 1873 the legislature created Eureka County, and a few years later the local government authorized the building of one of the finest courthouses in the state—a handsome red brick edifice that became the center of one of the most admired architectural clusters in the West, which included the Jackson House, the *Eureka Sentinel* newspaper building, and an opera house. All were intact, but in need of urgent attention, more than a hundred years after the fading of the boom of the 1880s.

At its peak, Eureka had a population of about 6,000 people. It suffered less trouble with gunfighters than other camps, probably because the vigilante committee 601 chased out the troublemakers at an early stage. But the town did not completely escape violence; its history was marred by an ugly example of ethnic-inspired hatred directed against the large number of Italian immigrants who had congregated in the district.

This 1879 episode became known as the "charcoal burners' war" or the "Fish Creek war." Because the ores had to be smelted in furnaces at high temperatures, charcoal was in great demand. Hundreds of men— many of them from Italy, where the craft of the "carbonari" had a long and admirable tradition—made their living by cutting juniper and pine trees in the distant mountains and carrying them to large beehive-like ovens that they had erected for transforming the wood into charcoal. When the smelter owners in Eureka tried to reduce the price of charcoal, they decided to pay the workers less. The woodchoppers organized a boycott and attempted to prevent the delivery of wood to Eureka.

The smelter owners, without good cause, worried that the Charcoal Burners' Association might march on Eureka and destroy property, so they telegraphed Governor John Kinkead in Carson City and asked for a militia to keep the peace. There was no serious trouble, but after a week of tension, an overeager sheriff's posse went to the Fish Creek charcoal burners' camp 30 miles south of Eureka, attacked a group of workers, and killed five. County officials inquired, but never fixed the blame for the murders. Despite the violence, a compromise was reached without further bloodshed. It left a bloody reminder, however, that when men take the law into their own hands, innocent people can die.

## Hamilton

Southeast of Eureka, at an elevation of 8,000 feet in the White Pine Mountains, prospectors found another silver vein in the fall of 1865. As in the case of Eureka, full development of the district did not begin until three years later. When systematic work began in 1868, there was wild speculation and wasteful exploitation far in excess of anything that happened in Eureka. The prosperity of Hamilton and its neighbor, Treasure City, lasted only two or three years—from 1869 to 1871. After that, the towns and the White Pine district declined rapidly, because the ore body did not extend very far downward.

Yet while it lasted, the White Pine boom provoked some of the greatest investment extravagance ever known in the Far West; the excitement became known as "White Pine fever." Prospectors filed thousands of claims with the county recorder within a few months, and about 170 companies were created—many of them listed on the San Francisco Stock Exchange—with capitalization of nearly a quarter billion dollars.

British speculators in London became excited about the prospect, providing much of the capital that went into the mines. Their money kept the camp barely alive for many years after the boom had passed. Few of them ever saw any return from their investments. An elaborate system for pumping and piping two million gallons of water into Hamilton each day was financed in San Francisco; the investors in this enterprise likewise "lost their shirts."

At the height of the boom in 1870, the official census showed that Hamilton had nearly 4,000 people and Treasure City nearly 2,000, but local booster newspapers characteristically claimed five times that number. The Nevada legislature responded to the rush in the usual manner in 1869 by creating a new county, named White Pine, and the taxpayers financed yet another fine brick courthouse. Hamilton retained its status as a county seat until 1887, when the courthouse burned down and the county offices were transferred to Ely.

## Pioche

The ores of Pioche, like those of Hamilton and Eureka, were first located in 1864, but no town appeared until 1869–1870. Then there followed a rush and a two-year period of extravagance and lawlessness that had few equals in the Far West. For a year or two, it seemed likely to surpass the Comstock Lode—which was then in a relatively quiet phase—as a producer of silver. The Raymond-Ely Mining Company and the Meadow Valley Mining Company became two of the most successful corporations, with shares traded on the San Francisco Stock Exchange. But no boomtown of the 1870s in Nevada was more distant from Carson City or from a railroad, and none had a weaker local government. There were about 5,000 or 6,000 people, including several hundred "rowdies," as the vandals of that day were called. Forty murders went unpunished in the first two years, and unnecessary expenditures for local government set records.

During the prosperous years, the county officers built a $16,000 courthouse—rather modest in size and fixtures—which they financed in such a manner that it eventually cost more than $600,000 to pay the bills. Pioche is still known primarily for its "Million Dollar Court House"— now a rustic quartzite and red brick museum devoted to the memory of a once-vigorous camp.

The bonanza at Pioche lasted for about five years. By 1876 it was virtually finished because excessive amounts of water had flooded the mines at the 1,200-foot level and the price of silver was falling. But the town survived because it had become the seat of the largest county in the West in 1871, because a series of investors repeatedly explored its mines over the years, and because it was the center of vast and productive livestock ranges. Decades later it was the scene of a second productive period, extending from 1937 until 1958, based upon the successful mining of lead-zinc and silver ores.

## The Role of the Immigrants

One aspect of the early Nevada mining frontier, mostly neglected by the state's first historians, was the importance of foreign-born men in the development of the industry. Nevada in general—and its mines in particular—attracted a high percentage of immigrants. Not only were many of the mine operators from overseas (all four Big Bonanza owners were Irishmen), but also 2,000 of the 2,770 Comstock mine employees working in 1880 had been born abroad. Most of the immigrants were from Ireland or Britain, but hundreds came also from Canada, Mexico, Italy, Germany, the Balkans, and elsewhere. They often organized social clubs based upon their ethnic or linguistic backgrounds and gave to the mining camps a diversity that many other frontier groups lacked. Each of the early camps had a significant Chinese population, which suffered much discrimination and exploitation at the hands of the white community but offered a colorful part of the mosaic of early Nevada.

Because the social structure of Nevada was so fluid, white foreigners who settled there often had good opportunities to succeed in business or politics. Two early U.S. senators (John P. Jones and James G. Fair) were foreign-born mining men, as were two early governors (Reinhold Sadler and John E. Jones). Nevada retained its multi-ethnic character well into the twentieth century, despite the decline in the mining economy.

The first Nevada mining boom lasted only about sixteen years, from 1861 until 1877. By the end of that latter year, the economy of the Comstock was in a tailspin from which it never recovered. Production from the mines of Virginia City and Gold Hill dropped from $37 million in 1877 to $20 million in 1878 to $7 million in 1879, and the plunge continued. Likewise, every other important camp except Eureka declined sharply, and that boomlet lasted only a few more years. Every town that had become a county seat on the basis of a mining boom—Belmont, Austin, Eureka, Hamilton, and Pioche—had economic trouble, and a twenty-year "Rip Van Winkle sleep" settled over the Silver State's mining industry. It came to be known as the "twenty-year depression."

## Women and Their Contributions

The early mining camps had relatively few women, but their numbers grew as the communities became more stable, and they played important roles in giving these towns the amenities of civilization. Historical evidence is sketchy, because women usually did not own property, participate in politics, or even have their activities reported often in the newspapers in the early years. Popular mythology and the media have distorted the record by focusing attention on prostitutes and dance-hall girls. Recent research, however, has revealed the many important service roles of women, especially during the years of the Comstock bonanza.

Women in the wealthy and middle-class families were often founders of schools, activists in the churches, and supporters of charities. Hundreds not only served their families but also worked as seamstresses, dressmakers, nurses, servants, and operators of boardinghouses and lodging houses. They were also leaders in the temperance movement. In a society that was unstable, highly mobile, and often violent, they provided a measure of culture that the predominantly male world sorely needed.

## Suggested Supplementary Reading

De Quille, Dan (William Wright). *The Big Bonanza.* 1876. Reprint, New York: Alfred A. Knopf, 1947.

Jackson, W. Turrentine. *Treasure Hill: Portrait of a Silver Mining Camp.* Tucson: University of Arizona Press, 1963.

James, Ronald M., and C. Elizabeth Raymond, eds. *Comstock Women: The Making of a Mining Community.* Reno: University of Nevada Press, 1998.

Long, Walter S. *Brushwork Diary: Watercolors of Early Nevada.* Text by Michael J. Brodhead and James C. McCormick. Reno: University of Nevada Press, 1991.

Molinelli, Lambert. *Eureka and Its Resources.* 1879. Reprint, Reno: University of Nevada Press, 1982.

Richnak, Barbara. *Silver Hillside: The Life and Times of Virginia City.* Incline Village, Nev.: Comstock Nevada Publishing Co., 1984.

Shepperson, Wilbur S. *Restless Strangers: Nevada's Immigrants and Their Interpreters.* Reno: University of Nevada Press, 1971.

# 9

## The Railroads and Their Towns

CONTEMPORARY NEVADA owes more to its railroads than it does to its mines. The most durable and prosperous communities in Nevada in the twentieth century have been those towns that were established by the railroad companies. Reno, Las Vegas, Sparks, Elko, Winnemucca, Lovelock, and Caliente all came into existence and ultimately survived because they had important stations along transcontinental "bands of steel." Virginia City, Gold Hill, Carson City, Minden, Pioche, Eureka, Austin, Tonopah, Goldfield, and Hawthorne all shared, at times, the advantages of a branch railroad. Nevada witnessed the building of more than a hundred mining towns between 1860 and 1910, but only a few of them continued to exist in the 1990s.

Nearly all of the communities founded by the railroad developers survive in the present era, and one of them, Las Vegas, parlayed its strategic location into a world-famous city. We shall deal with that transformation in a separate chapter.

A close reading of history will remind us that the first great western railroad, the Central Pacific, came into existence partly because of the capitalistic daring of some western financiers, and partly because of the toil of workingmen, many of them Chinese, who put their lives on the line in the Sierra and the deserts of Nevada.

# The Central Pacific

Early in the Bonanza era, well before the Comstock approached its peak, Nevada businessmen became excited about the news that the first transcontinental railroad would be built along the Humboldt-Truckee Trail. For many years before the 1860s the idea of such a railroad somewhere in the West was tentatively discussed, and there were surveys done to identify the most feasible route. There were outspoken supporters of a far northern route to the Pacific Northwest and still others, such as Secretary of War Jefferson Davis, who wanted a route from New Orleans to southern California. Either of these routes would have bypassed Nevada. During the Civil War, with the southern states in rebellion and the far northern territories still undeveloped, politics dictated a central route between Omaha and Sacramento. The route contemplated by Congress in the Pacific Railroad Act of 1862 passed only 30 miles north of Carson City and 25 miles north of Virginia City. It was almost the same as the trail that had been first used by the Stevens-Murphy-Townsend party less than twenty years earlier.

Such a railroad, spanning half a continent of wilderness, was a vast undertaking, particularly at a time when the country's resources and energies were being consumed in civil war. To encourage the developers, Congress granted them generous loans and a vast tract of land—alternate sections on either side of their road for a distance of 10 miles. The government hoped this would enable the companies to sell some of the property to settlers and thus to recover much of their costs. The railroad men were thus given some five million acres in Nevada, and their successors are still the largest landowners in the state more than 125 years later.

Railroad fever—a psychological condition as contagious as gold fever—affected thousands of people in both the East and the West, and the project began even as war was spilling the blood of the nation's young men on the battlefields of the South. Construction started in 1863. The leaders of the Central Pacific—building eastward from Sacramento—and the Union Pacific—progressing westward from Omaha—came together at Promontory, Utah, in the spring of 1869.

The individual most responsible for the promotion of the Central Pacific and for the final transcontinental plan was a California engineer and entrepreneur named Theodore Judah. It was he who arranged the crucial financial support in California and who did much of the effective

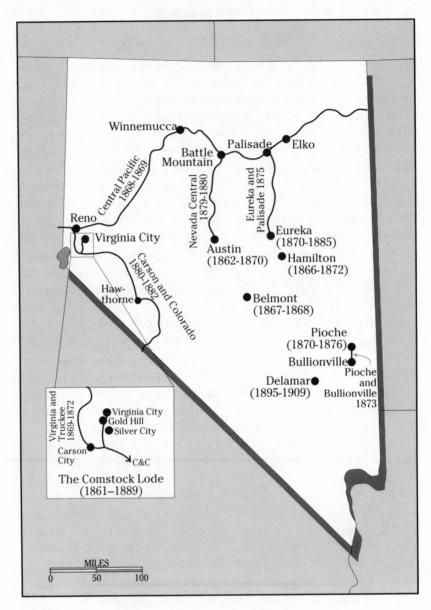

Winnemucca

Central Pacific 1868-1869

Reno

Virginia City

Battle Mountain

Palisade

Elko

Nevada Central 1879-1880

Eureka and Palisade 1875

Carson and Colorado 1880-1882

Haw-thorne

Austin
(1862-1870)

Eureka
(1870-1885)

Hamilton
(1866-1872)

Belmont
(1867-1868)

Pioche
(1870-1876)

Bullionville

Pioche and Bullionville 1873

Delamar
(1895-1909)

Virginia and Truckee 1869-1872

Virginia City
Gold Hill
Silver City

Carson City

C&C

The Comstock Lode
(1861–1889)

MILES
0    50    100

*Bonanzas and Railroads (Before 1900)*

lobbying for federal governmental help in Washington. Although Judah did not live to see even the beginning of construction—he died of yellow fever in Panama in 1863—he provided the spark of inspiration for the Sacramento businessmen who guided the Central Pacific, the "Big Four": Collis P. Huntington, Mark Hopkins, Charles Crocker, and Leland Stanford. These men became famous and powerful in California history, and the Silver State owes much to them, and to Judah's initiative as well.

Work on the Central Pacific began in Sacramento in October 1863, but the line did not reach the California-Nevada boundary until four years later, in December 1867. The struggle to prepare a roadbed and lay the tracks through the forested foothills east of Sacramento, over the granite bluffs of Donner Summit, and down the Truckee Canyon could not be rushed. The terrain was rugged and equipment was scarce. Most of the backbreaking work was done by Chinese laborers, who were usually paid $30 or $35 monthly for twelve-hour days, and they provided their own food. The Chinese workers were not exactly regarded as slave labor, but they did seem to the promoters to be a cheap, expendable resource. Only recent generations of Nevadans and Californians have been inclined to erect monuments to the Asians for their exhaustive work in building the main traffic link between the Missouri River and the Far West.

## Reno

By May of 1868, the tracks reached as far east as the Truckee Meadows, the greenest and most promising valley on the eastern edge of the Sierra. The construction superintendent, Charles Crocker, decided to establish a town there, at a spot previously known as Lake's Crossing. Businessman Myron Lake owned an inn on the south bank of the Truckee River and had a territorial franchise to operate a toll bridge (later the Virginia Street bridge). That bridge connected the main east-west emigrant road through the Truckee Meadows with the road to Virginia City, and Lake had a good income from the fees that he charged to freighters and travelers.

Lake sold about 80 acres of land north of the river to the Central Pacific, which laid out the town of Reno; he kept much real estate on the south bank. Town lots went on sale to bidders on May 9, 1868; more than a thousand people appeared for the auction, and some paid as much as $1,000 per lot. Within a month, a hundred business buildings and homes had been built or were under construction. Crocker chose the name of Reno to honor a Union general, Jesse L. Reno, who died in battle at South Mountain, Maryland, during the Civil War.

*Downtown Reno, circa 1906. (Nevada Historical Society)*

One obvious advantage of the Reno site was its location in a pleasant valley that was a natural eastern entryway to the Sierra Nevada, near the place where the Truckee River emerged from the mountains into a relatively flat, well-watered basin. A second crucial advantage was its proximity to the bustling industries of Virginia City and Gold Hill. Within weeks, Reno was a thriving distribution site, with teamsters hauling their cargo between the depot and the Comstock towns. Yet another bonus was the promise of agriculture, because cattle and small gardens had been raised successfully for nearly a decade by the first settlers. Several groups of settlers formed ditch companies to divert water onto newly plowed fields. And nearby to the west were the bountiful forests of the Sierra. Few places in the inland West offered such a promising combination of ample water, timber, grazing, and mining possibilities in close proximity.

It is little wonder that Reno boomed immediately and that it soon surpassed its neighbors to the south in commerce and population. Here, as in so many other western railroad towns, the saloons came first. They were ready to serve their clients even before Charles Crocker placed the parcels of land on sale. Reno's early reputation was at least as notorious as those of the mining towns. One early history of Nevada said of the beginnings of Reno:

Those were the palmy days of Reno; work for all who sought it; plenty of money; good prices paid for labor and goods. The number of men, animals and wagons necessary in transacting this immense freighting business, assured employment and prosperity for the merchant, farmer and mechanic, and, it may be remarked, to the saloon keeper also. Where there is a large number of men, well employed and receiving good wages, especially when the majority of them are unmarried and free from the restraining care of the home circle, there the saloon finds its most inviting field. There also will be found a class of human cormorants who live upon the labor and toil of others by robbing them at the gaming table, or by the many devices of which money is extorted from the unwary, or failing that, by open violence and crime. (Angel, ed., *History of Nevada 1881*, p. 635.)

As in many western towns, citizens found it necessary to form a vigilante group to impose order because the local and state governments were no match for those who came to live by theft or other forms of exploitation.

In 1873, when the town was less than four years old, Reno already had a certain notoriety. A national railroad tour book published in Boston said:

> Of this place every one has heard. It is situated sixteen hundred and twenty miles west of Omaha, and a hundred and fifty-four miles east of Sacramento. This lively town is said to contain two thousand inhabitants, has a little paper called "The Crescent," and boasts itself a great city. (John Erastus Lester, *The Atlantic to the Pacific: What to See, and How to See It*. Boston: Shepard and Gill, 1873, p. 53.)

Almost from the beginning, Reno presented a second, urbane face to the world to counterbalance its appearance as a wild frontier outpost. It had to pass through the frontier boom period and the unregulated bustle of commercial activity in the 1870s before it completely established its more cultivated identity. It assumed early its pretensions to high culture which followed from being the commercial center of a "sovereign" state within the federal Union with the best connections to San Francisco and the East. It very quickly won the first political prize that every ambitious frontier town aspired to: the county commissioners approved the removal of the county seat from Washoe City to Reno in 1870. Myron Lake offered an acre of land next to his inn and toll bridge at a price of $1,500 as a site for a courthouse. The county commissioners accepted. The inn which he had built (later the Riverside Hotel) prospered for several decades under various owners.

Religious organizations grew almost as rapidly as the less respectable institutions. The Methodists led the way in the establishment of a church, founding a congregation in 1869; the Catholics were not far behind with their first parish in 1870. Father Patrick Manogue of the Catholic diocese, who became famous as one of the civilizers and benefactors of the poor in Virginia City, took an early interest in Reno, and contemplated building a college there. In 1877, the Dominican sisters opened a preparatory academy for women. In the previous year, the widely traveled missionary bishop Ozi W. Whitaker of the Episcopal church had managed to open a seminary school for girls in Reno, one of the few of its kind in the West.

Reno's strategic location gave it more long-term advantages than any other town of that day in Nevada. William Sharon's Virginia & Truckee Railroad connected Reno with Virginia City and Carson City by 1872, and it likewise became an important distribution point for freight on its way to Susanville and the other northern Sierra regions of California. Although Reno felt the effects of the decline of Virginia City after 1877, it was not totally dependent on the freight from that direction because it had become a distribution center to northern California, northern Nevada, and southern Oregon, even as the Comstock ceased to be productive.

The so-called twenty-year depression that affected the mining industry of the Silver State between 1880 and 1900 did little harm to Reno. Its growth was slow but steady. Railroad brochures advertised it as a place with a healthful climate, where hot springs and sanitoria for asthma could be found. Because of its readily available water, it had steam-generated electrical power as early as 1882. The legislature recognized and multiplied its assets by locating an institution for the mentally ill near the city in the same year, and Reno became the home of the state university in 1886 after that institution had failed to prosper on its original site in eastern Nevada. By 1890, the census takers counted a population of about 3,500 people. It was virtually the only town in Nevada that was still growing rather than declining.

As the nineteenth century entered its final decade, one of the rising financial moguls of California chose Reno as his home. He was Francis G. Newlands, who had married the daughter of former Comstock manipulator Senator William Sharon. Newlands had also become Sharon's business associate and the executor of his estate. He built a handsome home in Reno on a bluff overlooking the Truckee River and made it his primary business to promote Reno and western Nevada. He put his stamp on the city and the state for generations to come—long after the railroad which had created the town had laid the earliest foundations.

## Other Central Pacific Towns: Wadsworth, Lovelock, Winnemucca

When the Central Pacific was laying its track eastward in the spring of 1868, its second townsite selection was at the Big Bend of the Truckee about 30 miles east of Reno, near the point where the river ceases its eastward trend and turns northward to Pyramid Lake. John Frémont had visited this place twenty-four years earlier during his first trip into the western Great Basin. Crocker decided to name the place Wadsworth and to establish a division point, a place where crews and locomotives could be changed and water could be taken on.

It had required more than five years for the construction crews to reach this point, 188 miles from Sacramento. They put the next 500 miles of track in place, making the famous connection with the Union Pacific north of the Great Salt Lake, in less than ten months. Wadsworth was the jumping-off point and the fitting-out place for the crews as they built at breakneck speed across the Forty Mile Desert and up the Humboldt River.

Although Wadsworth held an important place in the strategy of Crocker and his crews, it never became a major town. There were no important mining or agricultural districts within easy freighting distance, and early in the twentieth century the corporate managers moved its shops and even some of the company-owned homes to Sparks, on the eastern edge of Reno.

As the railroad crews proceeded northeasterly from Wadsworth in the summer of 1868, they faced next the challenge of the dreaded Forty Mile Desert, which had caused the suffering of so many emigrants on their way to California less than twenty years earlier. The Chinese and American tracklayers were better equipped for their ordeal because the locomotives that came behind them brought the necessary food and supplies, but they worked at top speed in the scorching heat. Sixty-two miles northeast of Wadsworth, beyond the Humboldt Sink, they reached the Big Meadows. By this time there was a well-established stage station there, owned by the Englishman George Lovelock. The river at this point could be diverted to cultivate grassland beyond the natural meadows, and cattlemen had already begun to take advantage of it. There was a nearby mining district called Trinity that briefly generated the usual high hopes of the prospectors. It seemed a logical place to establish a small stopping point for the trains.

The town of Lovelock emerged later and more slowly; it did not suffer the rowdiness and disorder that most of the other railroad centers experienced during the construction period. Perhaps that was because it was only a minor point along the route, and the prospectors spent most of their time in the scattered camps in the distant hills. Only sixty people made their homes there as late as 1880. The town of Lovelock did not have a newspaper until the 1890s, and it did not become a center of local government until 1919, when Pershing County was created. In the meantime, however, it had evolved into an important center for the raising of livestock and alfalfa as the waters of the lower Humboldt were diverted onto the land around the old Lovelock ranch.

Winnemucca was the third town—after Reno and Wadsworth—to be established by the builders of the Central Pacific in the summer of 1868.

The crews took only 80 days to lay the track from Wadsworth to Winnemucca, a distance of 130 miles.

Crocker obviously chose this site for another town because it offered the most promising place from which stage lines toward eastern Oregon could depart, and he selected it also for another division point. The Humboldt Valley is wide at this location, and the Little Humboldt flows into the main channel here from the Santa Rosa Range to the north. During the days of the emigrant migrations to California, it proved to be one of the best crossing points on the river for several miles in either direction. It became known to the earliest travelers as Frenchman's Ford and was the site of one of the popular trading stations along the California trail in the 1860s.

Several years before the appearance of the Central Pacific, prospectors had explored the nearby mountains with little success. There was indeed gold in the region, but it was in microscopic form and was not to be identified and developed until the 1980s. Yet the prospects seemed so good to the lode miners of the early 1860s that an Italian entrepreneur named Joseph Ginacca planned a 90-mile-long canal, 15 feet wide and 3 feet deep, extending from Golconda to Mill City. His idea was to develop a mill to process the anticipated ores from the Humboldt Range and to irrigate the land in the vicinity of Frenchman's Ford. This might be regarded as northern Nevada's first ambitious reclamation project, or—according to some victims—the Humboldt country's greatest fraud. It was a typical, imaginative frontier scheme—based upon eastern and European experiences and capital, but far too ambitious for the resources of the western Great Basin. In some years the water in the Humboldt River is too shallow to float even the smallest of barges. Only about 30 miles of the canal were finished, but it did reach Frenchman's Ford, and a successful hay ranch had been established there by the time the railroad arrived.

The town received the name "Winnemucca" because the founders wanted to honor the Paiute leader who had been prominent and respected when the first emigrants appeared. It enjoyed its most prosperous early period between 1869 and 1874, when regular railroad service made it profitable to put cattle on the rangelands in large numbers and then ship them to distant markets.

The Central Pacific located a roundhouse and an icehouse at Winnemucca and arranged that engines and train personnel would be changed at that point. This was also the place where the earliest trains picked up cordwood to fire their steam engines, so a vigorous wood-hauling business developed immediately. However, wood is scarce in these mountains, and soon coal replaced it as the source of fuel all along the route.

In 1872, Winnemucca became the governmental seat of Humboldt County, preempting the honor from the declining mining camp of Unionville. The economic welfare of the community for the next several decades was almost entirely dependent upon county services, livestock raising, and railroading.

## Battle Mountain and Carlin

Sixty miles east of Winnemucca, Crocker selected another site for a town and gave it the name "Argenta," the Latin word for silver. In this case, however, his choice for a community did not match that of local people who gathered to take advantage of the new commercial opportunities, and within a few years, the town of Battle Mountain had emerged 12 miles to the west as the market and transportation center of the region. Its location at the point where the Reese River flows into the Humboldt River seemed more attractive for the homes and shops of the early settlers, and it was more accessible to the mining districts— including Austin 90 miles to the south—than was Argenta.

The name of Battle Mountain has often puzzled travelers because the town is located not on a mountain but along a flat stretch of the river valley. The peak that got its name for a skirmish between emigrants and Indians in the early 1860s is located several miles to the south. Unlike Winnemucca, Battle Mountain did not become a county seat quickly, because it was located in Lander County, and Austin tenaciously retained the privileges of hosting the local government for more than a century, even though its boom years were past and its population was slowly declining.

Before the end of 1868 the Central Pacific tracks reached as far eastward as Carlin, where Crocker located yet another roundhouse and additional workshops. There was rich river bottomland here, mining districts to the north and south, and—more important—good grazing ranges for livestock. Carlin soon had a hotel that became famous for stocking good cigars and whiskey.

## Elko

The Elko region in 1869 had all the assets of its Humboldt Basin neighbors, but in greater abundance; it had access to more excellent rangeland, more dependable small streams in the northern mountains, and more timber. In addition, this was the natural place for the freight lines that would carry goods to southern Idaho and to the new mining camps in the White Pine region of eastern Nevada.

Elko's foremost historians have emphasized, among its assets, the remoteness of their small city. In the 1860s, as in the 1980s, it was the center of a vast, mostly unsettled jurisdiction embracing 17,127 square miles. It is 240 miles west of Salt Lake City, 290 miles east of Reno, 235 miles south of Boise, and 475 miles north of Las Vegas. Elko County, created in 1869 immediately after Crocker's men had established the town, is larger than Massachusetts, Rhode Island, Connecticut, and Delaware combined. The very fact of its geographical isolation in a region of abundant high-desert resources has given the city a regional importance far greater than its size would warrant in other parts of the nation.

The early history of Elko resembled that of Reno, at least in the beginning. Railroad agents laid out streets and lots at the end of 1868, and the first town parcels were sold on January 15, 1869. Lots 25 by 100 feet in size sold for between $300 and $500 each. The railroad promoters presented to the town, as a gift, a block for a future courthouse. Here, the solution to the county seat question was obvious. Lander County then covered all of northeastern Nevada, but Austin was more than 200 miles away, so county division seemed mandatory. Fortunately, the legislature was in session within days after the town of Elko had been established and the bill to create the new county became law quickly. Tents had to be found to accommodate the county offices.

Elko, although smaller, was as rough-and-tumble a community as Reno. It had forty-five saloons and several houses of prostitution before it was six months old. But a respectable investor soon erected the fine Depot Hotel with 80 rooms and a dining room that would seat more than a hundred persons. One of the early amenities was an opera house. Substantial stone and wooden residences and stores replaced tents during the first year. By some accounts there were 4,000 people in the town before that first anniversary was observed. Elko soon had a flour mill, several furnaces that awaited ores from distant mines, and two semiweekly newspapers.

In 1870, when Elko was less than two years old, one of its local cattlemen won election as governor of the state. L. R. "Broadhorns" Bradley used his influence to have the legislature locate the proposed University Preparatory School there in 1874. But this did not become the economic or educational success that its founders hoped. It began with only seven students, and in the eleven years of its existence never had more than thirty. In 1886, the legislature and the board of regents moved the institution to Reno.

Elko had its periodic experiences with mining excitement. There were oil-shale beds, thought to be coal, not far away. A flurry of prospecting and gold-silver production occurred about 50 miles northwest of Elko at Tuscarora in the mid-1870s, but these developments were much more modest than the excitement at White Pine, Pioche, and Eureka. Elko had a more stable resource in its livestock ranges with their proximity to the railroad, but it experienced hard times during the twenty-year depression. Severe winters devastated the herds, high railroad freight rates restricted the town's trade, and the population dropped to 1,000 by 1900 and to about 800 in 1904.

There is one additional old Nevada community that owes its existence to the Central Pacific. The town of Wells, located on a site 50 miles east of Elko where Joseph Walker had camped in the 1830s and where thousands of emigrants had stopped to refresh themselves at the numerous springs (which they called the Humboldt Wells), was not established during the original construction of the Central Pacific in 1869. Several months after the closing of the gap between the Union Pacific and the Central Pacific in the spring of 1869, a town grew up to serve the mining districts that could be more readily reached from that point, and some railroad service facilities followed.

By the time the town of Elko was five months old, the transcontinental rail link had been established at Promontory, Utah. It was an occasion for nationwide celebration when the ceremonial golden spike from California and the silver spike from Nevada were driven into the last tie on May 10, 1869, just a year and a day after the auction of lots had been held at Reno. There were celebrations across Nevada as well, but the people of the state soon learned that the great railroad, beneficial as it was to northern Nevada, was an ambiguous and often greedy partner.

## The Smaller Railroads

The completion of the Central Pacific across Nevada stimulated the building of several small feeder lines to connect the outlying mining towns with the great railroad that had become a virtual east-west spinal cord for the nation.

The first and most famous of these was the Virginia & Truckee Railroad, built initially down the steep mountainside from Virginia City to Carson City in 1869, and eventually northward through Washoe Valley into Reno, connecting with the Central Pacific in 1872. This project was conceived and promoted by William Sharon and Darius O. Mills, the president of the Bank of California, to serve the bank's mining and milling empire, benefiting them much more than the communities through which it passed. It represented an engineering achievement of much importance because it required seven tunnels, a high trestle in Gold Canyon, and a serpentine route down the slopes of the mountains. At the peak of its operations, more than forty trains each day ran along its route, hauling ore, merchandise, and hundreds of passengers. It prospered with the Big Bonanza and fell on hard times later. But it also became identified with the efforts of Sharon and the Bank of California to get a stranglehold in all aspects of the Comstock economy.

Eventually, the V&T reached southward into the Carson Valley to serve the farming towns of Minden and Gardnerville, and its engines continued to move up and down the slopes of the Comstock until 1938. Its trains continued to run on the link between Reno and Carson City until 1950, when it died for lack of business. In the 1980s, the Nevada State Railroad Museum restored some of its colorful rolling stock and other early Nevada transportation memorabilia in Carson City, and in the 1980s an investor named Robert Gray reopened a few miles of the line in Virginia City.

Two short lines penetrated central Nevada during the period of the nineteenth-century railroad enthusiasm; the first reached southward to Eureka. In 1874–1875, when Eureka's mining prospects were still bright, Mills and his associates created the Eureka & Palisade Railroad. Palisade, on the Central Pacific line 10 miles west of Carlin, provided the easiest jumping-off point for tracks. The line was completed by October of 1875. Although Eureka's silver ore bodies had been exhausted ten years later, the railroad continued to function until it fell victim to the Great Depression in 1938.

The other famous short line into the geographic middle of the state was the Nevada Central, which extended up the Reese River Valley 90 miles from Battle Mountain to Austin. The successful developer in this case was Anson Phelps Stokes, who adopted the idea of such a railroad in 1879 and saw the job completed less than six months later. This railroad did not rescue Austin's declining economy, but it too survived long after the silver had faded from Austin's crown. It ceased to roll in 1938.

For a brief time in the 1870s, the mining boom at Pioche justified the operation of a 10-mile rail line called the Pioche & Bullionville. The boosters of that town dreamed of a link that would connect them with Eureka and perhaps with the Colorado River. But that was one of the bonanza fantasies that evaporated into the desert air once the boom had passed.

## Hawthorne and the Carson & Colorado

Yet another legacy, and a more enduring one, of the era of railroad expansion is Hawthorne and the other towns in Mineral County (Schurz and Mina are younger communities that also owe their beginnings to the railroad). Hawthorne came into existence because of the activities of the Carson & Colorado Railroad at the beginning of the 1880s. The founders of this line originally intended to lay rails all the way from Mound House, on the Virginia and Truckee line east of Carson City, to Fort Mojave on the Colorado River. The sponsors of this enterprise were the same men who had built and profited from the Virginia & Truckee and who had backed the Eureka & Palisade—Sharon and Mills. They expected to open vast new silver and gold districts along the neglected eastern slopes of the southern Sierra Nevada and to gain a monopoly on hauling ore and supplies.

The first goal of the Carson & Colorado promoters was Candelaria, a new mining town 200 miles southeast of the Comstock. It had produced several million dollars worth of precious metal in the middle 1870s, and for a brief time it seemed to promise a replacement for the declining Virginia City. That dream faded quickly, like so many others on the frontier, but in spite of this failure Hawthorne became yet another small commercial hub because of its railroad, the basis for another Nevada county that otherwise would not have existed. The Carson & Colorado was extended southward across Montgomery Pass into California's Owens Valley in 1883.

Although several mining districts sprang up within a day's wagon ride of Hawthorne, none of them yielded much ore in the next hundred years. When President Mills of the Bank of California made an inspection trip in the early 1880s, he was bitterly disappointed in the prospects. "We built this line either 300 miles too long or 300 years too soon," he commented. But while Hawthorne never enjoyed a boom, it never suffered the total collapse and exodus that was common elsewhere in the mining West. It had 337 people in its first official census in 1890, and 436 in 1900. It became the "market town" and the local administrative center for a vast stretch of desert. It survived in later decades because it was a county seat (of Esmeralda County in 1883–1907 and of Mineral County after 1911) and because its railroad managed to continue operating, relying more on hope than revenue.

## The Operations of the Railroad Oligarchy

Throughout the West, towns that were created by the railroads developed a love-hate relationship with them. They were the umbilical cords which gave birth to the infant towns, but they were soon regarded as domineering, exploitative parents. They controlled much of the land in and around the townsites, tried to dictate terms of state and local politics, and charged freight rates that hindered the economic growth of the communities they served.

The record of the Central Pacific in Nevada is typical of a western pattern. The company had received land grants totaling more than 5 million acres under the congressional acts of the 1860s, located adjacent to the railroad line in alternate sections. Thus the company had a vast checkerboard of land parcels stretching across the state, which still stands out on any land-use map of Nevada. The Central Pacific was able to sell a small amount of this land for a high price, as in Reno, but most of it was so arid that it was regarded as useless. But when developers and investors wanted to obtain desirable parcels, they often found the railroad's terms difficult.

Far more annoying was the matter of freight rates. Once the railroad company had driven the rival horse-drawn stage lines out of business, it raised its freight rates to the point that would extract the largest amount of money from the inland communities. It charged cities like Reno and Winnemucca, for example, far more than it did San Francisco for freight from the East, because the bay city had the alternative of bringing its necessary freight by sea. The Central Pacific imposed the notorious "back-haul rate," charging the Nevada towns for the price of shipment all the way from New York to San Francisco and back to Nevada, even though it was unloaded in Nevada. Thus the cost of shipping a carload of machinery from New York to San Francisco was $600, but the cost of sending the same load from New York to Reno was $818, and to Winnemucca $996. Nevada Congressman Rollin Daggett forcefully objected to this practice in Washington in 1881, and he accused the Central Pacific of overcharging its Nevada clients by $30 million in the previous ten years. "Nevada is an orange which for ten years these railroad vampires have been sucking in silence," Daggett said. "We have been, and are still, bleeding at every pore."

The bitterness mounted, but Nevadans had no legal or economic remedy. There was no national legislation in those years to regulate the rates charged by railroads, and the state laws that existed were ineffective. Efforts by state and local government to regulate shipping costs brought quick retaliation or threats, and the local agents of the railroad companies dabbled in election politics and used their money in Carson City during legislative sessions to assure that no anti-railroad legislation became law. H. M. Yerington, general manager of the Virginia & Truckee Railroad, and later C. C. Wallace, the Eureka County assessor, became notorious as manipulators of local politics for the benefit of the large and small railroad owners. This problem troubled the economy and politics of Nevada and other western states until well after 1900, when Congress passed effective interstate commerce legislation. Nevada's weak government was impotent to act on its own.

In addition, the Central Pacific developed a cozy, managerial relationship with Nevada's two most durable senators of the late nineteenth century. Senator Stewart, who sat in the upper house of Congress from 1864 to 1875 and again from 1887 to 1905, did the bidding of the Central Pacific regularly during his second career. His long-term colleague, Senator John P. Jones, a onetime Gold Hill mine superintendent who was elected to five successive terms beginning in 1873, likewise made his services and his Senate votes available to the Central Pacific.

This oligarchic arrangement existed because the state legislature elected the United States senators, and in most years a relatively small amount of money could assure the election to the state senate and assembly of majorities favorable to Stewart and Jones. Yerington and Wallace managed this business, and Nevada's scattered people had little voice in what their representatives did in Carson City. As the nineteenth century drew to a close, much popular bitterness arose over this system, and a populist movement emerged in response to it.

The populists consisted of an alliance of western and southern farmers, livestock men, laborers, and eventually leaders of the western mining industry that advocated regulation or ownership of the railroads by the federal government, free and unlimited coinage of silver, and direct election of United States senators. As we shall see in chapter 11, this movement became powerful under the "Silver" label in the 1890s.

Another legacy of the railroad-building era was a comparatively large Chinese population—mostly male—that remained and spread out through the mining frontier after the railroad construction had been completed. Chinese laborers had immigrated by the thousands during the 1860s. An upsurge of anti-Chinese sentiment occurred during the bonanza years because so many people of oriental descent had gathered in the "Chinatowns" for the mining and railroad camps. They often operated restaurants, laundries, and small retail businesses, and they encountered the greatest animosity when it was perceived that they were taking the jobs of white men—as wood cutters, gardeners, and auxiliary workers. In 1880, the census counted more than 5,000 people of Chinese origin within the state—about 8 percent of the total population.

Virginia City and Carson City both had sizeable Chinese communities during the boom years. "Chinatowns" were as crowded and as colorful as any similar ghetto anywhere in the Far West except San Francisco. The men with their traditional pigtails and bamboo hats, and the women with their red and blue gingham scarfs, moved about at their typical trades: wood gathering, rag picking, laundering, and restaurant management. They were barred by law and custom from the mining business, and they had their own physicians, pharmacists, shoemakers, barbers, and prostitutes. They tended some of the best tiny gardens in the district and their vegetables were in great demand, but they were infamous for the opium trade that flourished among them.

State and local governments passed discriminatory legislation against them, including many laws that were unconstitutional. On several occasions Nevada's lawmakers sent petitions to Congress asking for stronger action to curb Chinese immigration. Only the gradual decline of the Chinese population in the 1890s and early 1900s eased the hostile feelings of the majority in the white community. Not until the middle of the twentieth century did Nevada officials give recognition to those from the Orient who had helped to build the economic basis of the state.

During the 1980s, several groups interested in railroad memorabilia restored some of the equipment and symbols of the state's railroad heritage. The Nevada State Museum opened a specialized exhibit south of Carson City to refurbish some of the rolling stock of the Virginia & Truckee Railroad and other antique equipment with historical ties to Nevada. By gradual stages the museum restored a locomotive and railroad cars, opened a station building that formerly served Wabuska in Lyon County on the Carson & Colorado, and installed a loop of track to allow tourists to take a short ride. The display soon became one of northern Nevada's most popular tourist sites. The restored portion of the Virginia & Truckee in Virginia City was likewise popular with visitors.

Also, in East Ely local railroad enthusiasts managed the reopening and restoration of the station and a locomotive of the Nevada Northern Railway. This accomplishment occurred in 1987, in conjunction with the centenary of the designation of Ely as the seat of White Pine County and seventy-one years after the original dedication of the line. The Northern Nevada Railroad Museum also inherited a large collection of records and other historical artifacts from the line.

Other smaller memorials were the Jim Lillard Railroad Park in the center of Sparks, with a locomotive and several cars, and in Caliente the Boxcar Museum and the old Union Pacific Depot. In the Las Vegas Valley and Boulder City, steps were under way to revive at least a replica of the trains that operated in that region during the 1930s, when Hoover Dam was under construction.

## Suggested Supplementary Reading

Kneiss, Gilbert. *Bonanza Railroads*. Stanford: Stanford University Press, 1941.
Land, Barbara and Myrick Land. *A Short History of Reno*. Reno: University of Nevada Press, 1995.
Myrick, David F. *Railroads of Nevada and Eastern California*. Vol. I, *The Northern Roads*; Vol. II, *The Southern Roads*. 1962-63. Reprint, Reno: University of Nevada Press, 1992.
Rowley, William D. *Reno: Hub of the Washoe Country*. Woodland Hills, Calif.: Windsor Publications, 1984.
Townley, Carrie Miller. "Helen J. Stewart: First Lady of Las Vegas," *Nevada Historical Society Quarterly* 16 (winter 1973), 214–44; 17 (spring 1974), 2–31.

# 10

## The Livestock Oligarchy and The Agricultural Frontier

THE FABRIC of Nevada society that emerged from the 1860s and 1870s consisted of more than mining camps and railroad towns. These latter outposts—together with the mining speculators and railroad barons—got much attention from the pioneer press and therefore from the early historians. But beyond the tumult of the more notorious towns were those communities devoted to husbandry or those isolated ranches where women and men tried to force the desert to yield to the plow and sustain their livestock.

The traditional pattern that the early Mormons brought to Genoa and Las Vegas—of small gardens and carefully tended livestock herds that would sustain a colony and provide a surplus for trade to travelers—did not have many successful imitators after they departed in the 1850s. Pioneer settlers established few productive farms like those in Utah or the Midwest. A few families did raise crops along the banks of the Carson, Walker, and Truckee rivers, but in most places the soil was too dry and akaline and the growing season too short for the cash crops that flourish in California and the East. In addition, the local markets were too small, except when a nearby mining camp provided an outlet during a few brief seasons. During the 1860s fruit orchards occasionally yielded bountiful crops in the valleys of western Nevada, but frequently the unseasonal frosts took a heavy toll. The fruit farmers could not be certain that they would have buyers for their products in this thinly populated region, even if the harvest were bountiful. The number of families engaged in this branch of agriculture dwindled as the century advanced.

Yet across the northern half of the state, a scattered subculture emerged, based largely on the raising of cattle and sheep on the open range and the growing of hay either for export or, later, to maintain the herds during cold winters. This business became at least as important and probably brought more long-term benefit than either the mining bonanzas or the railroads.

## The Western Valleys

The first successful experiments with livestock grazing occurred along the western edge of the Great Basin in those valleys that are bunched together inland from Lake Tahoe, where the Sierra sends its river and streams eastward into the desert. Here, the East and West Walker rivers, the East and West Carson rivers, and the Truckee invited not only the first settlers but also the first herders.

Three names became prominent locally even before Nevada had attained territorial status. Henry Fred Dangberg entered Carson Valley in the mid-1850s and laid the foundations of a vast livestock enterprise when the Mormons were still there. His descendants influenced the social life of that valley for more than a century. H. N. A. "Hock" Mason first saw Mason Valley in 1854 on his way to California and returned in 1859 to establish a vast grazing domain along the Walker River. In this same year—during the summer when the Comstock Lode was first being mined—R. B. Smith, T. B. Smith, and two partners drove their herds into Smith Valley because they believed that the winter range was better there than in California. In the meantime, tenacious sheepherders had driven bands numbering several thousand across the Humboldt-Carson Trail or the Old Spanish (Mormon) Trail to California. They, like Mason, had seen the Nevada rangelands, remembered its grasses, and had come back to take their chances.

### Genoa, Dayton, Smith and Mason Valleys, and Washoe City

Every settlement, trading station, and ranch in western Nevada felt the influence of the Comstock Lode. Genoa, Nevada's first town, quietly made the transition from a trading and governmental center to an agricultural community. During the early 1860s, when the Comstock boom was young and much of the freight from California came over the passes south of Lake Tahoe, it bustled with commerce. It had the region's first stage station, the first newspaper, and the first telegraph link with the outside world. But when Governor Nye selected Carson City for the territorial administrative offices, and especially after the Central Pacific shifted the Comstock-bound trade through Reno in 1868, Genoa settled into a bucolic pattern that was compatible with its green fields and majestic mountains, reminiscent of the early days of Mormon occupation. Genoa remained the county seat of Douglas County until 1916, when its neighbor, Minden—founded by the Dangberg family in 1904—became more popular with the valley's settlers.

Another station on the Carson River that evolved into a permanent community was Dayton, which was earlier known as "Chinatown" because Asian-Americans had tried to pan gold there in the 1860s. Located at the mouth of the gulch which descends from Gold Hill, Dayton became a supply station for the Comstock (less than 10 miles away), a focal point for the Carson River farms, and a residential community for those who worked in the Carson River mills that processed the Comstock ores. With such a diversified economy, it had a population of nearly a thousand people in 1870. When the Comstock bonanza ended, Dayton—like Genoa—survived as a tiny village due to its agricultural resources. Its several bonanza-era buildings have increasingly become tourist attractions.

Two other agricultural settlements appeared southeast of Carson City in the same period. In Smith Valley on the West Walker River, the cultivation of land and the raising of cattle got a boost from the mining excitement at Aurora and nearby Bodie, California. Settlers initially scattered their homes and farms widely across 60,000 acres, and a trading station named Wellington opened in 1865. In Mason Valley to the east, other settlers took up land along the West and East Walker and the place first known as Pizen Switch, then Greenfield, and then (when it appeared likely that the Carson & Colorado Railroad might pass through it) Yerington, named in honor of the general manager of the railroad. The compliment to the shrewd Carson City businessman did not achieve its goal, however, because he ordered the construction of the line through the northern edge of the valley, several miles north of the town which had just been renamed in his honor.

On the other side of the Comstock Lode, between the Virginia Mountains and the western edge of the Sierra Nevada, lies Washoe Valley.

Its rich lands attracted a few early Mormon settlers, and its waters and timbers were crucial assets for the Comstock industry. Here, the little communities of Franktown, Ophir, and—most important—Washoe City bustled during the bonanza era. In the earliest years, teamsters freighted their ores over the Jumbo Grade from Virginia City into Washoe Valley and hauled timber in the opposite direction. The few hundred settlers in the valley rejoiced at the coming of the Virginia & Truckee Railroad in 1872, but it proved to be the downfall of the little towns they had built. After the linkup with the Central Pacific and Reno, all three declined rapidly. Washoe City, the original seat of Washoe County, virtually dissolved into a cattle-ranching community.

These satellite entities on the edge of the mining frontier were not instant towns thrown together in ramshackle fashion like the mining communities, which usually were built in haste and often abandoned within a few months or years. On the whole, the agricultural communities avoided the violence and some of the more seamy aspects of the railroad towns. Traditional family life flourished here, and Nevada found its most stable population and often its most effective social leadership in such places.

## Carson City

At the hub of this early agrarian activity was Carson City, which also had the advantage of being located only 15 miles from the heart of the Comstock Lode, and at the approximate center of the other valleys mentioned above. Although Eagle Valley, in which Carson was located, did not have the broad sweep of flat land which characterized its neighbors to the south and east, it enjoyed ample water and close access to the forests of the Sierra.

By 1871, the state government had erected an imposing two-story granite capitol building in the center of the plaza that Abe Curry, the founder of Carson, had provided at the outset, and where Mark Twain had witnessed horse trading, shootings, and public auctions only a few years earlier. Its residents soon constructed the fine homes that befit a capital and lined their streets with shade trees that drew admiring comments from scores of visitors. In due course, other service institutions clustered there: fine inns, the state orphans' home, the state prison, the state printing office, the United States Mint, the bureaucracy of Ormsby County, the federal courthouse, and—not far distant in Eagle Valley— a regional school for Indian children. After the Virginia & Truckee Railroad connected Carson with both Virginia City and the main line of the Central Pacific in Reno, Carson's status as a commercial center accelerated. It soon had a stockyard, and it regularly sponsored state and district fairs.

By 1880, Ormsby County had 5,400 residents, second only to the Comstock as an active community. Yet it too shared the agony of the depression years. By 1900, the population had shrunk to fewer than 2,900, and the prospects in all the surrounding valleys, except the Truckee Meadows, seemed dubious.

## The Search for a Land Policy: Part One

Nevada did not have—perhaps it did not want or have a chance to develop—a coherent land policy during the Bonanza era, and when it got around to developing one in the 1880s, the result was little better than a costly giveaway program.

Upon entering the Union in 1864, Nevada was entitled under federal law to approximately 3.9 million acres for the support of public schools, and another 660,000 could be selected for internal improvements, for support of a college of agriculture and mechanic arts, and for other purposes. The school-grant law had been designed for the humid eastern states; most of this land that was theoretically available had to be selected from the 16th and 36th sections of each township. Therefore, it was necessary to wait for surveys to be completed, but much of Nevada's land was not worth surveying because it could not be irrigated. The large 3.9-million-acre grant, which seemed generous in 1864, seemed a hollow gift a few years later. The 660,000 acres from the other land grants were grabbed up quickly within a few years because they could be selected along the stream banks.

As we have seen in the previous chapter, the Central Pacific Railroad received 5 million acres within Nevada; hence it, not the state, was by far the largest single landowner, with some of the best agricultural acreage adjacent to the Humboldt and Truckee rivers. The irrigable land along the railroad right-of-way was already gone or went quickly after the trains began to run; some of the remainder had value as rangeland, and grazing rights were eventually sold to cattlemen. But millions of acres were virtually worthless for any other purpose because there was no way of transporting water to the region.

How was Nevada to develop if it could not get productive land into the hands of farmers and settlers? The 1879 legislature proposed a solution; it offered to surrender its 3.9-million-acre grant for a special 2-million-acre entitlement, if it could select those acres wherever its ranchers or settlers wanted them. Congress approved this idea in a special act in 1880, and for the next twenty years the surveyor general pursued the selection and sale of land by request in those spots where water was available. This seemed, at first, to be enlightened politics and economics.

But this policy proved to be a mistake, because the state government virtually squandered the land; most of it was sold, by law, at a price of $1.25 per acre to the first applicant, even if it were near the streams and springs, where a higher price might have been paid if there had been competitive bidding. The state legislature initially had tight limitations on the amount of land that could be claimed, but it relaxed this restriction, and the men who were on the spot to select these strategic sites were the cattle barons, mostly in northeastern Nevada. There was a rising demand for their beef in California; the railroad was handy to the rangelands of the Humboldt Valley. A few large livestock owners developed special relationships with the Carson City land-office agents, and their men were on the ground to identify the strategically located water holes. They could file on the prime land, pay only 25 cents per acre down, and then procrastinate in the making of additional payments without much trouble from state or federal authorities. And the educational funds that were supposed to be financed from the land sales received a pittance. By about 1900, most of the 2-million-acre grant had been selected, but much of it had reverted to the state for nonpayment, and the educational endowment funds had little to show for it. In addition, the cattle-ranching business proved to be as risky as the mining industry for most who tried it.

## The Ranching Empires

"Broadhorns" Bradley, the Nevadan who fought the large mining companies to require them to pay a fair share of the tax revenue, was a rare individual who managed to build a large cattle domain in the days before Nevada received the 2-million-acre grant in 1880. He had driven cattle along the Humboldt route to California as early as 1854 and had brought his herds into Mason Valley in the winter of 1861–1862. He expanded his rangelands further inland, first to the Reese River Valley and then to

Elko, where he became one of the leading citizens soon after that town was founded in 1868. By this time he was a prominent Democrat; he won election as governor in 1870 and again in 1874, so he presided over his distant cattle ranges in Elko County from afar for the next several years. Soon after he lost his bid for a third term in 1878, some 20,000 head of his cattle perished during the severe winter of 1878–1879. Frustrated and disappointed, he died during that same season.

In the early years of the depression, the situation was desperate even for those who had tried to diversify their activities. Franklin Buck, who had been so enthusiastic about Pioche in 1870, had a large herd in northern Lincoln County in the 1870s, but he recorded the gradual demise of the camp after borrasca set in. "This town has completely gone in," he wrote in 1878, "petered out. Everybody is leaving who can. As I am engaged in raising cattle and horses it doesn't make so much difference to me." But within a year, Buck himself packed up his family and went back to California, whence he came in the late 1860s. A small livestock operator and businessman could not make a living with no operating mines and no railroad close at hand. The few who prospered ran herds further north in the Humboldt Valley, where there was more water that was widely distributed and within reasonable distance of the Central Pacific.

Jewett Adams, Nevada's fourth governor, was one of those who gradually shifted their attention from the mining camps to cattle raising, and from western to central and then eastern Nevada in the 1870s. He ran Texas longhorn herds in northern Nye County, won election as lieutenant governor and then as governor, taking over the executive mansion in 1883. Adams served only a single term in that office, and this did not seriously interrupt the building of his rangeland domain. He later expanded his holdings into White Pine and Lincoln counties, and in 1896 merged his spread with that of another displaced Comstocker, William McGill. They had sheep as well as cattle on the range, and they gradually acquired nearly 100,000 acres of private land—a vast holding for the sagebrush state.

During the era when Bradley and Adams were serving in Carson City, another sprawling cattle dominion arose in northeastern Nevada. The originator in this case was Jasper Harrell, who grew up on a Georgia slave-owning plantation, rushed to California with the gold diggers, and turned to barley raising in the San Joaquin Valley. He began to acquire land adjacent to water holes in the Thousand Springs Valley of northern Elko County in 1870—the year after the driving of the golden spike at Promontory. By 1872, he had several thousand head of cattle on the ranges, most of them on land he did not own but could only be used by one who controlled the strategic springs and creeks. His ranch hands traversed the grasslands and sagebrush country on both sides of the Nevada-Idaho border, moving the cattle as necessary for grazing and warding off threatening intruders—especially sheepmen from Idaho—with their ever-handy rifles.

In 1883, when Harrell was well established, he sold his interests to a pair of Texas-based operators named John Sparks and John Tinnan. Both were southern-born veterans of the Confederate Army. Sparks had been especially successful at cattle raising even as a teenager and had expanded his operations northward to Wyoming after the Civil War. He did not find enough open rangeland there for his growing herds, so he entered Nevada and formed the partnership with Tinnan. Playing a business game that would later be called "take-over mania," the Sparks-Tinnan partnership soon absorbed most of Harrell's domain and called their spread the Rancho Grande. By the late 1880s they had between 80,000 and 90,000 animals on the range—twice as many cows as there were residents of Nevada.

Sparks not only co-managed the vast sagebrush realm in northern Nevada and southern Idaho, but he also operated a showplace ranch— the Alamo—in the Truckee Meadows south of Reno, where he proudly exhibited his animals and the trophies they had won. He, more than anyone else, was responsible for introducing the now-familiar white-faced Hereford cattle to the Great Basin, and he promoted their virtues with a well-planned publicity campaign. This breed proved to be much more durable than Texas longhorns in the harsh summer heat and winter snows of the high desert.

As the Sparks-Tinnan empire grew, so did its market. In the early 1870s most northern Nevada cattle were shipped live by railroad to California. Later, small cattle-butchering and dressing businesses emerged in Reno, Winnemucca, and Elko, but sending the animals "on the hoof" remained the standard procedure. As their enterprise matured, Sparks and Harrel marketed their animals as far east as Omaha.

Probably the best-known western ranching spread—based in California but operated in Nevada, Oregon, and Mexico as well—was the Miller & Lux outfit. Henry Miller and Charles Lux were immigrants from Germany. Miller started work as a butcher in California, entered the cattle business in 1857, and began buying large sections of San Joaquin Valley acreage when prices were low during the drought of 1862–1863. He and

Lux gradually penetrated Nevada—including preferred watering spots in Mason Valley and the Humboldt Basin—linking up with "Hock" Mason and buying strategic water rights. Eventually they controlled ranches in Nevada totaling at least 70,000 acres outright and hundreds of thousands of additional acres of grazing rights.

For several years, these and other cattle realms prospered almost as well as the bonanza mining companies had done in their heydays. They were less spectacular, but they provided evidence that the desert frontier offered more than one or two ways to join the ranks of the millionaires. Money brought fame, and fame occasionally brought political success. But like ex-Governor Bradley and dozens of Comstock mine owners, the livestock plutocrats learned that the god "mammon" can be fickle.

Three factors conspired to interrupt the palmy days of the ranching and livestock business in the late 1880s: drought, overgrazing, and severe winter weather. There was a shortage of snow and rain across the northern plains and deserts in 1886, at the very time when the herds owned by the cattle barons were reaching their peak numbers. In 1876, there had been only 180,000 head of cattle and 80,000 head of sheep on the ranches and rangelands; ten years later, there were 270,000 head of cattle and 337,000 sheep competing for the same grasses and brush. With no governmental regulation or control, the numbers rose steadily.

The winter of 1889–1890 produced a damaging blizzard worse than anything ever seen in the Far West. Snow stood in drifts four or five feet deep for several weeks, and cattle either froze or starved to death. Sparks said later that he had lost 60 percent of his herd on the range that winter. Hock Mason lost nearly all of his livestock and thereafter became a manager for Miller & Lux.

Sparks and Harrell were large enough to survive and rebuild their herds, and it was they who led the way in raising and baling hay on their patented land to enable their cowboys to winterfeed the animals in harsh weather. This meant securing even firmer control, whenever possible, of water rights. The big cattle spreads seemed to get stronger, despite adversity, as the nineteenth century came to an end.

Probably twice as many cattlemen as sheepmen roamed the richer rangelands of northern and eastern Nevada in this era, and often their struggle for control of the best brush-and-grass forage led to violence. The historical record does not tell how often these two castes shed blood on the desert or tried to destroy each other's herds. Not until Congress passed the Taylor Grazing Act in 1934 did it become possible to define range rights with precision and to reduce the overexploitation of the forage.

The beginning of the new century marked a transition point in the ranching business; some of the larger spreads were selling their interests to out-of-state investors. John Sparks transferred his half-interest in Sparks-Harrell for about a million dollars, part of which he exchanged for Texas cotton land. Then he turned his attention to politics and won two terms as governor of Nevada in the elections of 1902 and 1906. During his first term, he entertained President Theodore Roosevelt on his Alamo ranch near Reno in the same manner that a feudal baron of the German Rhineland might have entertained a visiting monarch in the Middle Ages. He died during his second term as chief executive in Carson City in 1908.

## The Mormons' Return: The Virgin Valley

Even as northern Nevada was entering its period of borrasca, some of the disciples of the Latter-day Saints church were pressing outward again, into the southeastern corner of the sagebrush state. About 30 miles northeast of St. Thomas, near where the state line crosses the Virgin River, there is a strip of rich bottomland that contrasts sharply with the surrounding sandy desert. Here, in 1877, a Mormon group known as the "United Order" undertook a co-operative settlement of twenty-three people under the leadership of Edward Bunker. Under their communal organization, members of this colony agreed to take their meals together, to assign all chores on a community basis, to put their crops into a common storehouse, and to tend and sell their animals collectively rather than individually. They called their town Bunkerville, and for two years it prospered on this basis. After that time, however, disagreements among members became acute on matters of work responsibility and the sharing of produce, and the order was dissolved, with individual members establishing separate homes and farms from the collective.

Five miles northwest of Bunkerville, on the narrow but fertile Mesquite Flat, another community began to form in 1880. The Mormon settlers here took up their land on an individual basis, struggled to build an irrigation system in the shifting and unstable sand, and within two years succumbed to the heat and the repeated flash floods. The lands of Mesquite did not become the site of a successful town until the 1890s, and

*Winifred Cutler and children. Sharp, circa 1911. (James W. Hulse)*

even a century later, these communities were occasionally victims of flash floods on the tiny, but often turbulent river called the Virgin.

One of the leading historians of southern Utah, Andrew Karl Larson, used the term "lonely villages" to describe these "outposts of Zion," and indeed they were as remote from Nevada's capital as any other part of the state. Yet in spite of the distances from the county seat (Pioche is nearly 150 miles away) and from Carson City (about 500 miles distant), the towns of the Virgin and Muddy rivers became gradually integrated into state and local society, and the old hostility between Mormons and non-Mormons abated. A church historian reported as early as 1892 that Nevada was spending more money on schools in this region than it was collecting in taxes, and that "both the state and county officers are very kind and considerate to our people." In 1897, voters of Lincoln County sent one of the settlers of Mesquite, George B. Whitney, to Carson City to represent them in the legislature.

## The Persistent Optimists

Nevada did not lack boosters and optimists, even in the most barren regions and in the darkest years of the depression. In 1889, the state's surveyor general, John E. Jones, estimated that of the 70 million acres in Nevada, about 6 million were capable of cultivation, but only 146,000 acres were being used. There was a broad consensus that if only irrigation water could be brought to the rich lands by large canals, hundreds of profitable small farms would arise. If, at the same time, the transportation problems could be solved for the remote regions, the economic woes of the commonwealth would dissolve—so the hangers-on believed and regularly repeated to one another. This was the theme of hundreds of political speeches and editorials.

Daniel Bonelli, the tenacious Swiss-born Mormon settler at Rioville on the Colorado River who was still at his post near the mouth of the Muddy River twenty years after his original co-settlers had left, can serve as an example. He could write with great enthusiasm in 1890 about the terrain around him and contrast its bleak appearance with its future promise:

> Along the southeastern border of the State of Nevada there is a belt or zone of country about fifty miles in width and 150 in length characterized by such peculiarity of climate and adaptability to the production of semi-tropical vegetation that it must be considered

separately from the rest of the State. This zone reaches northeast-
ward into Utah to the rim of the Great Basin, and southwestward
into California. This portion of the State ranges in altitude from
500 to 1,000 feet above the Pacific, and includes the fertile margins
of land along the Colorado and the valleys of the Rio Virgin and
the Muddy . . .

The temperature of this region for the average of the whole year
most closely resembles that of the south coast of Spain, although
the extremes assume a somewhat wider range. There is no reason
in climate or soil why the whole catalog of semi-tropical plants
should not prosper here . . .

The great want of the region, transportation to market, seems
in a fair way of being shortly supplied by the Union Pacific railroad extension now being planned to pass the north end of this
fruit belt, and the Denver, Grand Canyon and Pacific road recently
surveyed to follow the west bank of the Colorado to the gulf coast.

All the elements of success are here at hand, and it requires only
the application of energy and means to produce results that would
be fairly astonishing. (From the *Report of the Surveyor General and
State Land Register*, 1889–1890, Carson City, Nev.: 1891, p. 160.)

Bonelli's interest in the possibilities of a railroad that would open the
resources of the region were typical of those who clung to their frontier outposts in spite of the hardships. His vision was not foolish, as it
seemed to many at the time, but only premature. The railroad did not
pass through that region until fifteen years later. If it had been possible
for him to return to this region a hundred years later, he would have
seen most of his predictions validated. But his generation lacked the
means to transport the water, the resources, and the people that were
necessary to make this desert flourish. It was not a time or a place where
small husbandmen or the persistent Swiss-born ferryboat operator could
prosper.

## The Las Vegas Rancho and Helen Stewart

Bonelli's letter of 1890 did not mention the most promising valley of all,
perhaps because from his perspective it was a less obvious prospect for
large commercial enterprise than other sites.

As we have seen, the "rancho" became the property of Octavius D.

Gass in 1865, a disappointed forty-niner who settled there after having failed to strike it rich in the mining business. He could raise fine cattle and excellent fruit, but there was no market for it. More than once he tried to sell his property, but nobody would pay his price—although it was quite modest. He borrowed money, offering his ranch as collateral, and eventually lost it to another forty-niner.

Archibald and Helen Stewart were important transitional figures in the history of southern Nevada. They had followed the trail of the mining camps from California to Pioche and had taken up ranching near Pony Springs (30 miles north of Pioche). It was they—and especially Helen— who wrote a decisive chapter in the history of Las Vegas. Archibald was an enterprising jack-of-all-trades frontiersman, a businessman as well as a miner and rancher, and he could drive a hard bargain. After he gained control of the Las Vegas Rancho, he tried to manage it from Pony Springs—200 miles to the north—for a few months, but in the early 1880s, he decided to move his family there.

The Las Vegas Rancho had been described in officials reports as the most prosperous ranch in Lincoln County, with an abundance of water and fruit trees, and a longer growing season than any other large Nevada valley. Its main disadvantage was its remoteness—from the county seat, from schools, from any other town or active social life. Archibald and Helen had three children when they lived near Pioche; she was expecting the fourth when they moved to Las Vegas for a "temporary" stay, as Helen thought. Her fourth child was born soon after their arrival at the Las Vegas Rancho in the spring of 1882.

Only two years later, Archibald was shot and killed at the neighboring Kyle Ranch (today in North Las Vegas). It was a typical example of frontier justice or injustice; the facts have been told in several different versions. Helen went to the neighboring ranch, retrieved the body, supervised the building of the coffin, and read from the prayer book over her husband's grave. When she told the story in Pioche, a coroner's jury rendered a verdict of justifiable homicide. Her fifth child was born soon after these events occurred.

From the 1880s on, the Las Vegas Rancho became a minor business and communication center for the entire southern portion of Lincoln County. The Stewart home was the voting precinct for elections and the gathering place for Fourth of July celebrations and occasional dances. When the U.S. government opened a post office in 1893, Helen became postmaster.

She managed the property with the help of her sons and ranch hands

*Helen J. Stewart. (Doris Hancock Collection, University of Nevada, Las Vegas, Library)*

for nearly twenty years, preparing meals for travelers, sending her children to school in California, acting as postmaster, supplying foodstuffs to the miners of Eldorado Canyon, collecting Indian artifacts, and ministering to the needs of the Native Americans. She built a good collection of Native American baskets and gathered trinkets that she believed had been lost by Spaniards on the Colorado River a hundred years earlier. And, unlike most pioneers, she kept a journal.

In 1902, Helen sold her ranch (except a four-acre homesite) and most of her water rights to the Montana millionaire William A. Clark for $55,000. Clark was the mastermind promoter of a railroad from Salt Lake City to Los Angeles. The history of southern Nevada entered a new phase, as Daniel Bonelli had predicted it would.

## Suggested Supplementary Reading

Dangberg, Grace. *Conflict on the Carson: A Study of Water Litigation in Western Nevada*. Minden, Nev.: Carson Valley Historical Society, 1975.

Hohmann, John W., comp. *The Old Las Vegas Mormon Fort: The Founding of a Desert Community in Clark County, Nevada*. Carson City: Department of Conservation and Natural Resources, 1996.

Patterson, Edna B., Louise A. Ulph, and Victor Goodwin. *Nevada's Northeastern Frontier*. Sparks, Nev.: Western Printing and Publishing Co., 1969.

Townley, Carrie Miller. "Helen J. Stewart: First Lady of Las Vegas," *Nevada Historical Society Quarterly* 16 (winter 1973), 214–44; 17 (spring 1974), 2–31.

Townley, John M. *Alfalfa Country: Nevada Land, Water and Politics in the Nineteenth Century*. Reno: University of Nevada Agriculture Experiment Station, 1981.

Young, James A., and B. Abbott Sparks. *Cattle in the Cold Desert*. Logan: Utah State University Press, 1985.

# 11

## Crusaders for Silver, Indians' and Women's Rights

**N**EVADA WAS not alone in facing economic troubles between 1880 and 1900. All of the states of the inland Far West also endured hard times. This was the era when miners, farmers, and other producers of raw materials throughout the West and South found themselves trapped by a tight monetary policy imposed by the eastern bankers and industrialists. And in this period the abundant output of products from the earth drove prices downward. The more grain, cattle, and ore that laborers produced, the weaker the price structure for these items became. People in the younger states were regarded as colonists within the new American empire. As the nineteenth century approached its end, the discontent of these frustrated westerners jelled into the movement called populism. In Nevada, this movement took an unusual form because its spokesmen were leaders of the so-called Silver Crusade.

In addition, this was a time of nationwide reexamination of the U.S. government's policy toward Indians and of the beginnings of a movement for woman suffrage. Even though Nevada was the most thinly populated and, economically, the weakest of the western states, it produced influential leaders in the silver movement, in the Indian movement, and in the struggle for voting rights for women.

## Populism and Silver

A key point in the Populist program involved demand that a bi-metallic (gold and silver) monetary standard be adopted for the country, with the price of silver fixed at a ratio of one-sixteenth the price of gold. The eastern bankers, who were generally creditors, wanted a single standard (gold only) because this was not inflationary and it made their investments seem more secure. The western farmers, who were debtors, yearned instead for an increase in the quantity of money—i.e., an inflationary policy—because it would make it easier to pay their debts. One way to achieve this was to mint more silver coins.

In Nevada, the Populist movement was distorted because there were so few farmers and because of the predominance of the silver-and-railroad oligarchy in state politics. Even though the mining industry had withered, the old guard who had risen to power in Virginia City during the bonanza years continued to represent the state in the U.S. Senate—at least nominally—long after the silver boom had passed. The oligarchs served the large corporations and monied interests, and "bought" influence in the legislature, even as they preached for the cause of free silver.

At times two or three clans, like feudal duchies in medieval Europe, fought against one another for the senatorial toga. Such was the case when Adolph Sutro, John P. Jones, and William Sharon maneuvered for the same U.S. Senate seat in 1872, or when Sharon of the bank crowd virtually bought a place in the Senate in 1875, or when James G. Fair of the Bonanza crowd crowded out Sharon in 1881 for his place in Washington's "exclusive club," as the Senate was called. John P. Jones sat in one of Nevada's two seats for thirty years between 1873 and 1903, and during most of this time he did not even live in Nevada or trouble himself about his constituents. William Stewart held one of the seats—it would be inaccurate to say that he "served"—for twenty-eight years between 1864 and 1905. Both senators had as their main clients not the people, but the large mining interests and the Central Pacific Railroad. The popular will and the interest of the average citizens concerned them little.

Once in a while, a man from outside the ranks of the oligarchy could be elected governor or congressman. At times, a courageous governor would even challenge the power bosses. Such was the case when Governor L. R. "Broadhorns" Bradley, the Elko cattleman, tried to force the

Bonanza-crowd mine owners to pay their fair and legal share of taxes to the state. In 1877, he vetoed a bill that would have resulted in a tax giveaway to the big mining firms. He was bitterly denounced by the *Territorial Enterprise* and other newspapers that were controlled by the mining tsars. In the following election, when he was running for a third term, the governor lost his office. Ultimately, the matter went to the U.S. Supreme Court, and in 1883 the Bonanza firm lost its battle and was ordered to pay some of the back taxes and penalties.

Little did Governor Bradley and the Comstock millionaires know when they fought their bitter battle over the taxation of mines in the late 1870s, that the underground wealth of the Comstock was practically gone, and that the commonwealth called Nevada would soon be a pauper among the states, begging for federal help.

Governor Bradley also fought against the granting of taxpayers' money to railroad companies as bonuses to encourage them to construct lines. Occasionally county governing boards or legislatures were very generous in granting taxpayers' money to railroad promoters to induce them to lay tracks in their communities. Bradley recognized this as a dangerous practice, because a railroad, even if it were built, often cost more than it profited.

We have also seen that Rollin Daggett, the Nevada congressman in 1879–1881, passionately denounced the Central Pacific for its rate discrimination against Nevada towns, but his words had no effect in Washington. Such protests by high-ranking Nevada politicians were the exceptions to the general pattern.

As the silver prices fell during the 1870s—partly as a result of the large production in Nevada and other western states—political leaders became increasingly alarmed about what was happening to the state's main industry, and they found a scapegoat in Congress and in the federal monetary policy. In 1873, when Congress passed a coinage bill, it failed to authorize the minting of new silver dollars. Stewart was a member of the Senate at that time and did nothing to resist its passage. Later he charged that he was tricked by the author of the legislation. This act, which came to be known as the "crime of '73," emerged as a central issue for the silver crusaders, although in fact it had little to do with the basic economic problems. But the oligarchs used it effectively to wage their campaigns for political support.

By the early 1890s, the people of Nevada were desperate for economic help. Their population dwindled from 62,266 in 1880 to 47,355 in 1890. They had watched their mining towns crumble or burn, their cattle prices drop, and their railroad rates rise to the strangulation point. The size of the electorate fell even more rapidly than the population as a whole; nearly 20,000 votes had been cast in 1876, but fewer than 11,000 in 1892. Some voices were raised in Congress suggesting that Nevada did not have sufficient population or enough economic resources to continue functioning as a state. Senator Stewart countered with a proposal that parts of Utah and Idaho territories be annexed to Nevada to increase the population.

The year 1892 marked a turning point in Nevada politics. Most voters abandoned their allegiance to the Republican or Democratic parties and cast their votes for a national Populist ticket headed by James B. Weaver of Iowa, who had been nominated in Omaha at a national convention that pledged free and unlimited coinage of silver at the sixteen-to-one ratio, honesty and efficiency in government, reclaiming the excessive lands of the railroad, government ownership of railroads and telegraphs, and direct election of U.S. senators. It was the kind of panacea that voters in Nevada could not resist; more than two-thirds of them cast their ballots for the third party. Senators Stewart and Jones soon changed their party labels from Republican to "Silver" without changing their political theories.

The restlessness of the nineties touched Nevada in other ways as well. There was much concern in Reno and Carson City in 1894 when it was reported that "Coxey's Army," a disorganized horde of job seekers, would pass through Reno on their way from California to Washington in response to the call from a midwestern agitator. Nevada had no strong industrial unions at that time and no serious internal threats of violence, but the country was alarmed by a rising tide of frustration from the labor groups, and Governor Roswell Colcord received several requests to take action to assure domestic peace. In the end, the railroad company provided extra locomotives and railcars to hasten the "army" eastward as rapidly as possible.

One of the beneficiaries of the discontent of the 1890s was Francis G. Newlands, the attorney from San Francisco who had arrived in Nevada to manage the affairs of the late William Sharon. Newlands was the son-in-law of Sharon, so he had family as well as financial ties to the former boss of the Comstock. He was, therefore, also one of the San Francisco mining-investing oligarchy that had manipulated Nevada politics for thirty years. He possessed, however, a greater sense of social responsibility and a keener vision than Sharon, and he had broader economic interests. Newlands played an important role in making Reno an attractive and progressive city, and he won five terms in the House of Representatives (1893–1903) and three in the U.S. Senate (1903–1917). But to achieve his purpose, he had to build a political base gradually during the 1890s and mount an assault on the old oligarchy in the years of its senility. He and Senator Stewart fought a bitter battle for Stewart's Senate seat during the legislative session of 1899, and the old warrior prevailed for the last time. In 1903, Senator Jones retired, and Newlands replaced him in the upper house of Congress.

In the meantime, Nevada's voters attached their hopes even more firmly to the Populist-Silver cause nationally and locally. Nearly every person who won office during the 1890s—executive, legislative, judicial, and educational—ran under the Silver label. In the famous presidential election of 1896, Nevadans voted more than three to one for the Populist-Democrat William Jennings Bryan (who ran as a Silver-Democrat in Nevada) against Republican William McKinley, who advocated a gold standard. This election aroused more passion, more hope, and—when Bryan lost nationwide even though he won most of the West and South—more frustration than any other election in which the western states participated in the nineteenth century. Bryan's "Cross of Gold" speech became an American legend, and those Nevadans who heard it never forgot it.

Half a century later, during World War II, there were still old-timers who reminisced with fierce passion about that election and about how Nevada, which had been cheated by the crime of '73, had been denied its normal opportunities to develop as a sovereign commonwealth because of policies dictated by the "gold bugs" from the East. Much of Nevada's popular resentment of the East and of the federal government can be traced to the failure of the Silver Crusade.

This crusade consumed the energy of a generation of Nevada political leaders without producing any tangible results. It is doubtful that, even if the price of silver had been higher, the state's economy would have been much better. The silverite policy was, at best, a kind of price fixing; its purpose was to provide a guaranteed price for the mineral that Nevada once had in abundance. But what Nevada needed most was diversification of its economy and liberation from the old Comstock oligarchy. Early in the twentieth century, it began to experience both.

In the meantime, other reform and protest movements enlivened the social environment of the Silver State. The most tenacious problem, and one which the larger society was slow to address, concerned the Native Americans.

## Sarah Winnemucca Hopkins and the Paiutes

In chapter 5 we considered the writings of Sarah Winnemucca Hopkins in connection with 1860 Battles of Pyramid Lake. This "Paiute princess," as she was sometimes called, became the most articulate member of her tribe in describing the tragedy of her people.

No group on the Nevada frontier endured greater frustration than the Indian bands who saw their ancestral homes transformed before their eyes into a harsh environment which threatened their survival. The Paiutes, Washos, and Shoshones all lost their traditional hunting-and-gathering grounds in the late nineteenth century, a tragedy compounded by an inactive government and a generally indifferent white community.

Born about 1844, Sarah Winnemucca was the granddaughter of a Northern Paiute leader called Captain Truckee, who had befriended some of the first emigrants who passed along the lower Humboldt when she was a small child. Her father, the widely known Chief Winnemucca, leader of the Humboldt River band, consistently sought peaceful relations with the Anglo travelers and settlers. Sarah herself received rudimentary education in the home of Major and Mrs. William Ormsby in Carson Valley and attended a Catholic school in San Jose for a time in the early 1860s. She returned to her native Humboldt Valley to witness the displacement of her people by the settlers of the new state.

The Paiutes were promised reservations for "Indian farms" on the lower Truckee and Walker rivers, but the federal government did little to help the Native Americans establish them. The early maps were vague (surveyors located the exact boundaries only several years later), and in the meantime white squatters illegally moved onto the best land on the lower Truckee. White trespassers intruded on their lands and fishermen frequently poached in their waters. In spite of the protest of Sarah and others, no governmental action to defend the Indians' rights came from Washington. Similarly, in Oregon on the Malheur Reservation, Paiutes had been cheated and made hungry by a corrupt agent. When rebellion flared up in the so-called Bannock War of 1878, her people lost more of their lands at Malheur, and many were forced onto the Yakima Reservation in central Washington. Promises that were made to her people— even pledges made in Washington, D.C., when a delegation of Paiutes traveled there in 1880—proved to be empty. At each stage, the humiliation increased.

*Sarah Winnemucca. (Nevada Historical Society)*

Sarah's education empowered her to chronicle these wrongs and to make eloquent speeches about them. Her book *Life Among the Paiutes: Their Wrongs and Claims*, is a Native American classic. She worked peacefully within the American system, repeatedly trusting the whites and the government, repeatedly being frustrated by them. During the most active period of her career, she married a young officer of the American Army (Lambert Hopkins), traveled to the East, and became a celebrity with her book and lectures.

The Paiute princess visited Boston and won the respect of the prominent Peabody family, who agreed to assist her in the establishment of a special school near Lovelock—her native region—for Northern Paiute children. But the school never received enough support to function properly, and she endured repeated slanders from critics both within and beyond Nevada. She contracted tuberculosis, closed her school, moved to Montana where some of her scattered clan could care for her, and died in 1891, less than fifty years old.

## Wovoka and the Ghost Dance Religion

One of the strangest and most tragic movements in the history of the Native Americans, the "Ghost Dance Religion" of the 1890s, had its origins with a thirty-year-old Paiute man who spent almost all his life in Mason Valley. His Indian name was Wovoka, but like many Native Americans he had assumed the name of the family for whom he worked—he also used the pseudonym Jack Wilson. He was deeply troubled by the degradation that his people had suffered at the hands of the white men.

In January 1889, he spoke of having had a mystical vision. During a trance, he had been taken to a place of great beauty and had seen and talked with many dead relatives and friends. The experience also gave him instructions about how to roll back time and restore his people to a former state of happiness. According to his account, the living of a purer life and the performance of a sacred dance would enable the Indians to recover their lands from the white intruders who were despoiling it. His message seemed to blend Paiute beliefs with Christian Adventist ideas that were popular at the time.

Several other mystical teachers appeared among the Indians in that era; reliable witnesses said that even Wovoka's father reported visions and conducted dances in Mason Valley in 1870. But Wovoka's teaching had an almost instantaneous appeal that swept through the Native

American tribes all the way to the Midwest; some called him the Indian Messiah. His message was pacifistic, but it claimed to come from supernatural powers, and some of his followers assumed that by performing the ghost dance and wearing a magic shirt they could ward off the bullets of the white men. This led to one of the bloodiest tragedies in the history of the Indian wars—the massacre at Wounded Knee, South Dakota, in 1890, when two hundred men, women, and children of the Sioux nation were slaughtered by the U.S. Army.

Wovoka had no direct part in this event; he never traveled far beyond the Yerington area during his lifetime. But there was a connection between his teachings and the revivalist passion of the Sioux at Wounded Knee. Wovoka was a celebrity for the remainder of his life, the subject of several books and sociological studies. He died in 1932, still admired by a tiny band of disciples. Six decades later, his memory was still honored in celebrations in Mason Valley.

Sarah Winnemucca and Wovoka represent opposite extremes of the Indian movement. Both were pacifists because the Paiutes were basically a peaceful people and they had many friends among both races. But Sarah spent her life trying to win respect and fair treatment for her people through political action and publicity. Wovoka functioned in a different realm—the spirit world of the Numa—and was out of place in the political and social chaos that flowed from his visions. They both hold honored positions in the history of Native Americans and in the struggle for justice which has been waged by people of all races.

## Origins of the Woman Suffrage Movement

Nevada was one of the last western states in which an effective struggle for women's rights was waged. Because its economy depended so heavily on the mining, railroad, and livestock businesses in the nineteenth century, the number of adult men outnumbered the women more than two to one, and those males who held political office seldom took an interest in the stirrings that were occurring elsewhere in the suffragist movement.

One notable exception to this pattern came in 1869, when C. J. Hillyer, an attorney from Virginia City, won a seat in the state assembly in Carson City and used the legislature to make an emotional plea for the rights of women. His text appeared in the journal of the assembly and was a remarkable example of the speeches from that era.

In one of the most eloquent orations ever delivered in the Nevada legislature, Assemblyman Hillyer insisted that the burden of proof on the suffrage question should be on those who believed women should *not* have the franchise, since they were subject to the same laws, the same obligations of citizenship, and the same burdens as men. He argued:

And if there be those—and I know there are many—who think that intelligence is the natural guardian of the suffrage, and that it should be made a qualification of the right to vote, I shall demand of them to tell me how it is that they are willing to permit the tens of thousands who scarcely reach the qualification of barely writing legibly their names and reading laboriously the Constitution of the United States, and yet are willing to exclude the other tens of thousands of women who write our books and teach our schools.

Among the maxims which form the creed of American republicanism there is none more venerable by its age, more deeply cherished, more axiomatic by reason of universal consent, than this: that taxation and representation should go hand in hand. As an article of our political faith, it is fundamental. It is intimately interwoven with the birth and history of our Government. It was the keystone of the arch of the American Revolution . . .

Now, sir, in behalf of the women of America, I invoke the application of this doctrine; and I say that unless gentlemen see fit now, for the first time, to question its truth, the argument is complete with the simple ascertainment of whether or not the women of our land are taxed. Let the Constitution of the United States, the Constitution of our own State, the Acts of Congress, our own statutes, our judicial decisions, State and National, answer the question.

Hillyer went on to assert that the existing practice that kept women outside the political system was a form of tyranny:

Tyranny meaner and more contemptible than that of which our fathers complained—for theirs, at least, was a tyranny of men over men, and this is that cheaper and more cowardly experiment of a tyranny of the physically strong over the physically weak.

And Hillyer argued that the granting of voting rights to women would improve the sordid political scene throughout the country:

The politics of the country is corrupt. Corruption in the primary; corruption in the election; corruption in the deliberative body; corruption by money; corruption by bargain and sale of

position, corruption by all the avenues which lead to a supposed
self-interest. . . . Politics is a filthy pool. . . .

Sir, I shall not enter into any disquisition here to show that
woman is by nature more moral, more conscientious, than man. I
appeal to the observation of each one who hears me; I appeal to the
teachings of history in all time; I appeal to the received opinions
of every age and every people; to the declarations of universal literature. He who contradicts it must contradict all these witnesses.
(Appendix to the *Journal of the Assembly*, Fourth Session. Carson
City: State Printer, 1869.)

Hillyer's eloquent speech led to the passage of the woman suffrage measure by both houses of the legislature in 1869, but a proposed constitutional amendment in Nevada must pass two consecutive sessions of the
legislature before it can be placed on the ballot. In the 1871 session, the
measure failed in the legislature, so it did not go to the voters.

Another resolution to amend the constitution to allow women to vote
passed during the legislative session of 1895. During this campaign, national suffrage leaders—including Susan B. Anthony and Dr. Anna Howard Shaw—visited Nevada and helped organize a suffrage association
with Frances Williamson as president. The proposal to change the constitution failed to win passage in the 1897 legislature because of a tie vote
in the assembly.

Another cause promoted by energetic women was the temperance
movement, an effort to prohibit the manufacture and sale of alcoholic
beverages in Nevada. These efforts often complemented the attempts
to enact woman suffrage legislation. The Prohibition amendment to the
U.S. Constitution was ratified in 1919 and the national woman suffrage
amendment in 1920. Nevada women had won the right to vote in 1914
through a state constitutional amendment.

## Hannah K. Clapp

One of the most versatile women in the early history of Nevada and
an early leader of the equal franchise cause was Hannah K. Clapp. She
arrived in Carson City in 1860 at age thirty-six, observed that there
were no schools, and founded the Sierra Seminary, which she gradually built into a respected educational establishment. She and a friend,
Eliza C. Babcock, operated the school through the years of the Comstock
bonanza and eventually added a kindergarten. They prospered not only
because their private school attracted students from the wealthier fami-

lies, but also because they invested successfully in mining stocks. Clapp and Babcock won the respect of state officers and businessmen when they submitted the successful bid for supplying the material to fence the capitol grounds—a fence that remains in place more than 120 years later. When the Comstock boom collapsed, they—like their friends—lost most of their investments. They went to work at other jobs in order to hold onto their home and seminary. When the University of Nevada moved from Elko to Reno in 1886–1887, Clapp became one of the original faculty members on the Reno campus, a professor of history and English, librarian, preceptor, and advisor to young women who came to the college. She served the university for fourteen years.

Clapp was an aggressive political activist for her time. Because women had no rights in the political process, she never voted or held office, but she exercised a modest influence through frequent correspondence with Senator Stewart. She worked for equal franchise resolutions adopted by the Nevada legislature in 1883, 1885, 1887, and 1889—each time unsuccessfully. In 1895, she became a leader of the Nevada Equal Suffrage Association in Reno. By this time such national leaders as Susan B. Anthony and Mila Tupper Maynard (who was, for a time, a liberal minister in Reno) shared the work of organizing men and women for the cause. She did not live to see the movement succeed because she retired to California in 1901 and died in 1908. But she and Babcock helped to educate those who led the suffragists to their victory a few years later—including Anne Martin, Nevada's most famous feminist.

# The Progressive Era

During the first years of the new century, Nevada and most other states witnessed the enactment of several governmental reforms designed to reduce the power of the rich oligarchies and to give voters more control over those who made their laws and managed their public business.

In 1904, the voters approved an amendment to the Nevada Constitution, providing for the referendum. This amendment allows the registered voters to circulate a petition which can place on a general election ballot a question of approval or disapproval of any measure that the legislature may have enacted. The provisions for initiative petitions—which allow registered voters to propose and enact laws or constitutional amendments independent of the legislature—became law in 1912. A companion measure allowing for the recall of elected public officials before the end of their terms also won final approval from voters in 1912. The 1909 legislature provided for direct primary elections.

In this same period, the legislature created several boards and commissions to regulate public service, transportation, and financial institutions. The Board of Bank Commissioners, the Railroad Commission, and the Public Service Commission all reflected a popular reaction against the abuses of power that had been recorded by powerful companies or men in the previous decades. Lawmakers also passed significant legislation providing for the eight-hour day in many occupations, creating the office of mine inspector, providing for workers' compensation, and outlawing the "card system" restrictions on employment.

Perhaps the most important among these Progressive-Era changes was the Seventeenth Amendment to the U.S. Constitution, which was ratified in 1913, providing for the direct election of U.S. senators by the people instead of the legislatures. Nevada's legislature had provided for popular preference votes in three previous elections.

## Suggested Supplementary Reading

Canfield, Gae Whitney. *Sarah Winnemucca of the Northern Paiutes.* Norman: University of Oklahoma Press, 1983.

Forbes, Jack D., ed. *Nevada Indians Speak.* Reno: University of Nevada Press, 1967.

Ford, Jean, and James W. Hulse. "The First Battle for Woman Suffrage in Nevada: 1869–1871 — Correcting and Expanding the Record," *Nevada Historical Society Quarterly* 38 (fall 1995), 174–88.

Glass, Mary Ellen. *Silver and Politics in Nevada: 1892–1902.* Reno: University of Nevada Press, 1969.

Hopkins, Sarah Winnemucca. *Life Among the Piutes: Their Wrongs and Claims.* Edited by Mrs. Horace Mann. 1883. Reprint, Reno: University of Nevada Press, 1994.

Howard, Anne Bail. *The Long Campaign: A Biography of Anne Martin.* Reno: University of Nevada Press, 1985.

Johnson, Edward C. *Walker River Paiutes: A Tribal History.* Schurz, Nev.: Walker River Paiute Tribe, 1975.

Mooney, James. *The Ghost Dance Religion and Wounded Knee.* 1896. Reprint, New York: Dover Publications, 1973.

Zanjani, Sally. *Sarah Winnemucca.* Lincoln: University of Nebraska Press, 2001.

# 12
## The Second Mining Boom

I N THAT long interval between 1880 and 1900, when Nevada's economy was in desperate straits, hope for a revival in the state's basic industry never quite died. The newspapers continued to report the activities of promoters and prospectors, who from time to time spread the word of a remarkable discovery. Some truly believed they had made one; others were simply trying to find financial backers to keep them going. At the same time, Nevadans continued to look to the outside investors and the government for help with railroads and/or reclamation projects that would boost the development of the state's resources.

A handful of prominent politicians and businessmen brought their skills and money to the mining districts during those dreary years. Senator John P. Jones took time away from his duties in Washington to manage a search for ore in the old Comstock Mines—including the levels below the Big Bonanza—between 1883 and 1886. Other investors likewise plunged their dollars into the lower depths of the Comstock, buying costly pumps to fight the underground rivers of water. The miners whom they hired delved 2,000 feet beneath the level of the Big Bonanza in sweltering heat, but their hopes were repeatedly frustrated.

Other examples of this kind are sprinkled through the records. In Austin, in the center of the state, Anson Phelps Stokes, a well-known New York banker, financed the building of the Nevada Central Railroad in 1879 and sent his son, J. G. Phelps Stokes, to manage it. They never quite abandoned hope in that camp even though they constantly lost money. The Stokes family even financed a three-story stone "castle" with a parapet, from which to enjoy the magnificent view across the Reese River Valley. Isaac Requa, a famous Comstock mine superintendent, took an interest in Eureka's mines and railroads and put his son, Mark, in business there. Further east, William S. Godbe, the enterprising Salt Lake City businessman, kept hope alive in Pioche by reprocessing its tailings and organizing a company to promote its mines.

Such men dreamed of becoming the next "bonanza kings" of a second Comstock Lode, but it did not happen. There was one small success story in the Meadow Valley Range about 125 miles north of Las Vegas, where prospectors found gold outcroppings in 1892. Utah investors won the inside track there in a town called Delamar, where they extracted more than $12 million worth of gold within the next few years before the ore bodies were exhausted. The town became notorious because scores of young men died from silicosis after using new, power-driven drilling machines which had no provisions for controlling the dust in the mines. By 1910, Delamar had been virtually abandoned.

Finally, as the new century opened, a few dogged prospectors had their dreams fulfilled and brought the luster back to Nevada's reputation.

## Tonopah

Most Nevada historians have identified Jim Butler, a struggling central Nevada rancher, as the discoverer of the rich silver mines of Tonopah in 1900, but recent research suggests that he may not deserve exclusive credit for the strike. According to the most popular account, while Butler was prospecting in the San Antonio Mountains, his burro wandered away, and he found promising ore samples when he tried to retrieve the wayward animal. Butler did not have a reputation for great initiative, and he gave a higher priority to his ranching chores than to an apparently ordinary mining prospect. At first he could not find anyone to assay the rock without a payment that he could not afford, so he postponed the staking of the claim. Recent historical research identifies Butler's wife, Belle, who had spent much of her early life on the Nevada mining frontier and was knowledgeable about precious ore, as the crucial person in doing more thorough prospecting and taking the initiative in staking the claims that yielded the best silver since the Comstock days.

In the meantime, he showed his samples to a struggling young attorney named Tasker L. Oddie, who had come to Austin from New York to look after the interests of the Stokes family. Neither Butler nor Oddie had handy cash with which to pay for an assay of the samples, but Oddie arranged to have a friend in Austin do the work. The rocks he sampled indicated a vein of ore worth more than $300 a ton—bonanza-grade silver. Butler staked some claims and named the site "Tonopah," which in the Paiute language meant a place of little water.

The story of the opening of Tonopah in the winter of 1900–1901 became one of the legends of the new West. Butler allowed dozens of men to lease part of his ground on an informal basis and pay part of their proceeds to the owner. News of this opportunity spread rapidly through the fraternity of scattered prospectors. Hundreds poured in to take advantage of this chance to mine their own ore, and scores of others located claims nearby. For a year, a system of trust existed in Tonopah with nothing more than a handshake between Butler and the lessees to seal the bargain. In the mining business, it was often said, "a man's word is his bond," and there were few violations of that faith in the new mining town.

Soon Tonopah was the hottest camp in the West. Prospectors found themselves in richer diggings than they had seen for many seasons, and Butler became wealthy—one of the few hard-rock prospectors who realized a significant profit from his discovery. Early in the town's history he sold his interests and went to the gold country of California to retire. Eastern capitalists formed the corporations that extracted the tens of millions of dollars that made Tonopah famous.

Tonopah's residents had to solve many of the same problems of isolation, supply, sanitation, and social organization that the first Nevada camps had known forty years earlier, but technology had advanced by leaps in the meantime. Initially, an Austin surveyor and school superintendent laid out a town, and the miners pitched their tents. They bought water for 25 cents a bucket, suffered an epidemic of pneumonia during the first winter, and lived with highly unsanitary conditions.

Tonopah experienced problems of isolation in much the same way that Virginia City, Hamilton, and Pioche had in the previous era. Necessary supplies could be hauled by train as far as Sodaville, a station on the Carson & Colorado Railroad 60 miles to the west, and then carried by team and wagon. There was almost no timber and little other suitable building material in the region, and they had to be supplied by freight from great distances after the mineral wealth of the camp was proven. Even Reno, more than 200 miles away, saw business improve as Tonopah and the other "southern camps" flourished.

In the second year of its operation (1902), Tonopah reported the production of more than $1.5 million worth of ore—almost as much as all the other Nevada mining camps combined for that year. Ultimately, its output was valued at more than $9 million per year in 1914—the peak year of production. It never approached the Comstock Lode's richness, but it rekindled the mining spirit in Nevada and sent hundreds of prospectors back into the mountains in search of El Dorado. It generated a new era of energetic mineral exploration and stimulated new railroad building. Within six years of Butler's discovery, railroad crews were laying new lines toward Tonopah from three directions, and in short order it had direct rail connections with Reno and, later, with the newly founded town of Las Vegas (see chapter 13).

Tonopah was different from the older Great Basin mining camps in several respects; it belonged to the twentieth century and to the post-frontier age. It was one of the first mining communities in the West to overcome its isolation by means of the automobile. On July 4, 1903, Tasker Oddie drove one of the horseless-carriage machines from Soda-ville to Tonopah and proved that it could cross the desert terrain even without good roads. By 1905 motorcars were common equipment in the district. Much new technical machinery was available to the Tonopah miners, including improved drilling and hoisting machinery.

The eastern investors who bought Butler's claims organized the Tonopah Mining Company, which produced about $50 million worth of ore in the next forty years. Although the boom period passed quickly, Tonopah remained reasonably prosperous until the early 1920s. The inevitable decline became obvious after 1925, and the Great Depression of the 1930s reduced Tonopah almost to the status of the other communities that were relics of the first bonanza period.

From the beginning, Tonopah was a much more peaceful town than Virginia City or Pioche had been when they first came to life. Men no longer carried pistols on their hips by this time, and few instances of frontier violence marred its history. From the beginning, it had a more stable family population, with a Ladies Aid Society and a Women's Improvement League dedicated to working for better community services, sanitation, and opposition to prostitution. Mrs. Hugh Brown, the wife of a prominent attorney who later wrote a sparkling chronicle of her time in Tonopah, recalled with joy the acquisition of one of the first vacuum cleaners—designed after the model of a metallurgist's mill filter— which enabled her to fight the ever-present dust of the mining camp streets. And she enjoyed the luxury of sending her laundry by train to Reno. Twentieth-century amenities made Tonopah a much more pleas-

*Elks-Eagle Parade in Tonopah, 1907. (Nevada Historical Society)*

ant place to live than it would have been a generation earlier (*Lady in Boomtown*, pp. 52–54, 81–82).

Tonopah became the political center of Nye County in 1905, winning the county seat from Belmont. In the boom years before the bonanza faded, the stocks that represented ownership in the mines were traded briskly on the exchanges of San Francisco and Salt Lake City.

## Goldfield

One of the admirable traditions of the mining frontier was the "grub-stake." This term is now disappearing from the vocabulary of the American West. It is a traditional expression, which rose and fell with the early western mining business. When a prospector did not have the basic supplies and financial resources to prospect on his own, a more prosperous friend might provide his food, or "grub," and supplies for several months, on the understanding that if he found something valuable, he would share the profits with the benefactor. Usually it produced nothing for the sponsor, and only hard, frustrating work—plus a few weeks of hope—for the penniless prospector. But it was a noble tradition, and once in a while, it paid off for both.

In 1902, Jim Butler grubstaked two young men named William Marsh and Harry Stimler when they went southward from Tonopah looking for outcroppings of gold or silver. They were lucky enough to find a showing of gold about 25 miles from Tonopah, in a region that had been overlooked. The appearance of gold seemed unusual for this part of Nevada, and they staked a claim. Within a short time their location had been named Goldfield.

It took a few months for the mining fraternity to realize that Marsh and Stimler had found some of the most precious pieces of gold-bearing rock in the world. The Goldfield ore was some of the richest ever found in the American West, but it was confined to a very small area, and it occurred in a shallow geologic deposit. Millions of dollars worth were extracted from small sections of earth no larger than a baseball field.

Goldfield became the most publicity-minded mining camp of the early twentieth century, and for good reason. The average value of Comstock ore at the peak of the Big Bonanza was $65 per ton; the ore of Tonopah brought about $40 per ton in the early years. But in Goldfield, the value of the raw ore usually assayed at $100 per ton, and a few shipments brought as much as $12,000 per ton. Individual rocks were so precious that they came to be known as "jewelry ore," and unscrupulous miners tried to carry them from the shafts hidden in their clothing or lunch buckets. The mine owners lost tens of thousands of dollars through the underwear and "high pockets" of the miners. Thus another word came into the western mining vocabulary—"high-grading," or the stealing of high-grade ore from the underground workplace.

The two financiers who became the bosses of Goldfield, and eventually the new oligarchs of Nevada, were George Nixon and George Wingfield, both of whom had come from the Humboldt River cattle country to Goldfield to try their luck during the early boom period. Nixon had been a telegraph operator and later a banker in Winnemucca; Wingfield had been a cowboy from Oregon and a gambler in the northern towns. Together they built a mining empire and became the barons of the Goldfield Consolidated Mining Company, which produced more than $50 million worth of ore.

Because of this wealth, Goldfield attracted some of the more militant miners of the Far West—men who had joined the radical Western Federation of Miners or the Industrial Workers of the World (IWW). These labor unions developed reputations for militancy in other mining towns, and they decided to show their strength in Goldfield when Wingfield tried to crack down on the high-graders in 1907. He installed change rooms at his mine and ordered all workers to make a complete change from their work clothes to their street clothes in the presence of company inspectors at the end of each working day. This led to an outcry, a threatened strike, and finally a compromise in which the union members agreed to a change room, but with one of their own union comrades present as an inspector.

Later in that same year, Goldfield muddled through its most notorious period. When a slump hit the western mining camps and caused a shortage of gold and silver coins, which was then called "hard money," the Goldfield Consolidated tried to pay its workers with "scrip," or I.O.U.s. The result was another, more serious rebellion. This time, the workers called a strike, emotions became hot, and rumors about possible violence filtered through the camp. Wingfield and other mine owners became alarmed and warned Governor John Sparks that there was danger the union men would dynamite the mines and wreck the town. Governor Sparks telegraphed President Theodore Roosevelt, asking for federal troops to keep order. The president acted quickly to dispatch units of the U.S. Army to the richest camp in the West, and Goldfield was suddenly under military occupation. The population of the town at that time was probably only about 15,000, but its labor strife assumed national importance.

All this activity surprised local residents. Although the rhetoric was hot, there had been little violence, and the local sheriff did not call for help. Troops set up a bivouac for several weeks with nothing to do. In the meantime, Wingfield decided to destroy the union, reduce the miners' pay, and increase their daily working time. He invited strike breakers to come from neighboring states, offered them jobs if they would sign an anti-union pledge, and allowed the strikers to return to their former jobs only if they would sign an anti-union card. All these activities would be illegal if a company tried to use them today, but in Goldfield's heydey they succeeded for Wingfield and his partners because there was no federal legislation on the law books to protect the rights of labor organizations.

President Roosevelt became troubled by the fact that federal troops were being used as accessories in a union-busting enterprise and announced his intention to withdraw them before the end of 1907. Governor Sparks pleaded with the president to leave the troops in place, and after Roosevelt put pressure on him, Sparks agreed to call a special session of the state legislature to deal with the matter. The special session of 1908 created a token state police force, which replaced the federal troops. It also insisted that Wingfield abandon the card system, but by the time the troops left in March 1908, the radical union had been defeated by political and judicial means, and the company was in complete control.

In the Goldfield crisis, Nevada glimpsed the threat of labor violence and also the use of military and political power to crush a workers' movement. There was a shooting death on the streets of Goldfield early in 1907 and two union members—Morrie R. Preston and Joseph W. Smith—were charged, tried, and sent to prison on the basis of circumstantial evidence. More than seventy-five years later, diligent scholarship and formal reconsideration of their case concluded that they had been wrongfully convicted.

Neither the union nor the mine operators were free of blame for the Goldfield trouble of 1907–1908. Some miners had been stealing ore and the unions had defended them in the practice. On the other hand, the owners, headed by Wingfield, overreacted when they asked for federal intervention and imposed the card system, and Governor Sparks used his office to aid in the union-busting activity. This was the most highly publicized labor dispute in Nevada's history prior to the 1950s.

The mining companies of Goldfield reported production of about $30 million between 1904 and 1910, when the decline began. As was the case in most camps, the actual value of the ore mined was probably much higher because the gold and silver producers were notorious about understating the actual output of their mines.

Early Goldfield citizens obviously did not think of their rich town as yet another camp that would begin to crumble within a few years. Its residents not only built fine homes and a luxurious hotel, but they also demanded and won the privilege of having the seat of Esmeralda County relocated from Hawthorne in 1907, and they built a handsome stone courthouse. They counted among their number an unusually talented selection of bankers and profiteers. Tex Rickard, the famous prizefight promoter, boosted his career with the operation of a saloon and gambling den and by arranging a world champion boxing match between Joe Gans and "Battling" Nelson in 1906. Jack Dempsey, later heavyweight champion of the world, boxed in Goldfield on his way to the "big time." One of its young women, Clara Kimball Young, became a famous movie actress in Hollywood in 1916, early in the era of silent films. The Goldfield Women's Club was one of the most progressive social organizations in the community.

But Goldfield's "palmy days" were even fewer than those of Virginia City, and its prosperity faded even more rapidly than that of Tonopah. Production of the rich ores declined steadily after 1910, and nine years later the Goldfield Consolidated closed its mill because the known ore bodies were exhausted. In 1923, a fire destroyed fifty-two blocks of homes and business buildings as if to mark the end of an era that had begun with the discovery by Marsh and Stimler. Goldfield, like Tonopah, survived as a county seat and because U.S. Highway 95 brought a few motorists that way in later years.

## Training Ground for Politicians

From the streets of Tonopah and Goldfield came a fraternity of oligarchs who assumed political leadership and spoke for the state in the legislative halls of Washington during the next generation. Four men who served their political apprenticeships in the southern camps won terms in the United States Senate; two of them became political figures of great prominence. The "southern camps" had much greater influence in state and national politics than their populations ever justified.

George Nixon, one of the founders of the Goldfield Consolidated Company, won election to the U.S. Senate in 1905 (when the Nevada legislature still selected the senators and when it was customary to choose successful men from the mining frontier). Reelected by the legislature in 1911, Nixon died during the following year, without having time to build the seniority in the Senate that commands great influence. His partner George Wingfield was also mentioned for such an honor, but he preferred the role of backroom power broker to that of governor or senator. More than once he declined to seek high political office when friends encouraged him to do so. Instead, he moved to Reno and built a financial network based upon his Goldfield millions and a league of political associates that controlled much of the state's business for a generation. The "Wingfield machine," as his alliance was called, influenced state politics for nearly forty years, with prominent Democrats and Republicans both serving as his errand boys during much of that time.

Wingfield is best remembered in Nevada history for his activities during the Great Depression of the 1930s, when his chain of banks collapsed and many depositers lost their investments. In that era, no system existed for insuring bank accounts, and many investors were never reimbursed for their losses. Yet Wingfield continued to have influential business associates across the country.

The most famous politician to rise from Tonopah was Key Pittman, a Democratic attorney who sat in the U.S. Senate from 1913 until his death in 1940. A native of Mississippi, Pittman had followed the gold rushes to Alaska and Canada in the 1890s, before finding his fortune in the practice of law during the Tonopah rush. Like William M. Stewart forty years earlier, he converted his talent for politics into a career on Capitol Hill.

In the course of his twenty-eight years in Washington, Pittman managed to place his mark on several pieces of fiscal-monetary legislation, including the Pittman Act of 1918 and the Silver Purchase Act of 1934. These laws brought short-term benefits to Nevada and the West because they stimulated the mining industry. Due to his seniority, he became a prominent figure on the national scene during the Great Depression of the 1930s because, as chairman of the Senate Foreign Relations Committee, he could help shape international monetary policy for the advantage of the silver producers. He died within days after he had been elected to his sixth term in 1940—still thinking of Tonopah as his home.

Tonopah's first successful Republican politician was Tasker Oddie, the young attorney who had helped Jim Butler find an assayer for the ore that he discovered there in 1900. Oddie went first to the state senate (1905–1907), then to the governor's office (1911–1914), and finally to the U.S. Senate, where he served for two terms (1921–1933). He gained

most prominence for his support of legislation, as governor and as senator, that led to the building of a highway network to connect Nevada's
remote towns with one another and neighboring states.

The fourth man who spent a few years early in his political career
in Tonopah was Pat McCarran—although for most of his life his home
base was Reno, where he was born in 1876. He followed the mining
rush to Tonopah, became district attorney of Nye County, and eventually
ascended to a seat on the Nevada Supreme Court in 1913. After two unsuccessful attempts, he won election to the U.S. Senate in 1932, defeating
Senator Oddie. A conservative Democrat of independent instincts, he
quickly earned a reputation on the Senate Judiciary Committee by re-
sisting President Franklin Roosevelt's efforts to "pack" the U.S. Supreme
Court. His tenure in the Senate continued until his death in 1954.

## The Smaller Mining Towns, 1905–1910

As the dramatic success stories of Tonopah and Goldfield spread across
the West in the first decade of the new century, hundreds of prospectors moved into the mountains of southern and central Nevada with
new determination. Several discoveries brought excitement for a year
or two, but none ever approached these two in the volume or richness
of the precious metal. Prospectors still concentrated on gold and silver in these years; copper and the other industrial metals did not yet
have the luster that they were to attain through fifty years of successful
production in White Pine County.

In 1904, two prospectors found outcroppings of the precious metals
on the northern edge of Death Valley near the Amargosa River, 70 miles
southeast of Goldfield. The miners who arrived first named the district
"Bullfrog" and the town "Rhyolite." Within three years elaborate mills,
concrete and brick business buildings, and a handsome railroad station were erected. Investors plunged money into three different railroad
lines. Even Senator William M. Stewart, after he retired from Congress in
1905, joined the rush to Rhyolite and resumed his career as a prospector
near the end of his life. But the Bullfrog district yielded only about $2
million worth of ore over the next decade, and even by 1910—less than
six years after it had been discovered—most of its miners were gone
and its buildings crumbling.

An even more frustrating experience awaited those who rushed to or
invested in Rawhide, northeast of Walker Lake, in 1908. Seasoned mining

men knew that promoters often made more money from a camp than the miners ever did, but there were always suckers eager for the bait that they offered. Tex Rickard, the Goldfield boxing promoter, and George Graham Rice, a notorious huckster, publicized Rawhide far more than it deserved, and their bubble burst quickly. But in Rawhide's moment of glory, Rickard managed to arrange a visit to his Northern Saloon by Elinor Glyn, one of the most explicit novelists of the day, and promoted his business with suggestive publicity.

Another camp that had its brightest years in this period was Searchlight, about 50 miles south of Las Vegas. Although the discovery had been made before 1900, it reached its peak about 1906. It was never a large producer of the precious metals, but the town survived on the basis of small output and later because of its location on Highway 95.

Although most of the towns of the second mining boom were shortlived, in 1940 the Works Projects Administration's guide to Nevada published these words about Nevada's two main precious-metal towns of the early twentieth century:

> Tonopah is not merely a town and not merely the producer of $125,000,000. To almost every living Nevadan more than 40 years of age, Tonopah—with its lusty son Goldfield—stands for modern Nevada, for youth, excitement, hope, and the great adventure of a lifetime. It came into existence at a time when the mining West had long been going through hard times, when the population of the state was dwindling, when state finances were in a desperate condition, and hope was leaving all but those who remembered the days before 1880 and were sure they would return. When the great boom began here the whole state—and half the West besides, as well as part of the East—came flocking in, driving over hot dusty miles of desert. (*Nevada: A Guide to the Silver State*, p. 224.)

## The White Pine County Copper Industry

Gold and silver are the glamorous metals of the western mining business; over the decades, they have caught the imaginations of the big speculators and the most romantic prospectors. But through the first seventy-five years of the twentieth century, and especially after the decline of Tonopah and Goldfield, copper played a more important part in the economy of the Silver State. One county, White Pine, accounted for well over half the value of the Nevada copper production, and it produced more total wealth than any silver or gold district before that time.

Ely was not born as a boom camp; it had a more mundane beginning than most Nevada mining towns. Prospectors explored the mountains around Murray Creek as early as 1868, during the excitement at Hamilton and Treasure City (see chapter 8). They created the Robinson mining district, erected a stamp mill and a small furnace, only to learn that they could not process the ore by the usual methods. No important mining occurred before the end of the nineteenth century, but White Pine County did become a ranching and cattle-raising area during these years. Small mining enterprises emerged and faded at Cherry Creek, Ward, and Taylor. When Hamilton suffered a destructive fire in 1885, Ely inherited the county seat for lack of a competitor.

> "Ely at first was a sort of 'Western Sleepy Hollow,'" (according to White Pine historian Effie O. Read). "Its place as a town was rather precarious. A few shacks had been placed here and there, and there were some on the hillsides far away from the stream, and a familiar sight was an old Chinaman who drove two burros, each of which had a couple of sacks slung across its back in which water was carried to those shacks inconveniently situated. 'Water, water, fifty cents a bucket,' he would call out." (*White Pine Lang Syne*, p. 271.)

With the start of a new century, an expanding nationwide electrical industry needed much more copper, among other industrial minerals. Two areas west of Ely, known as Pilot Knob and Copper Flat, had large quantities of the "red metal" near the surface, and in 1900 two prospectors—David Bartley and Edwin Gray—theorized that the copper extended a considerable distance underground. Although they had only 75 cents when they reached Ely, they managed to take an option on some interesting claims, to find a grocer who would grubstake them, and to test their theory.

Their boldness paid off, while that of most other prospectors looking for silver and gold failed. Two years later, they attracted the interest of Mark Requa, the son of a famous Comstock superintendent and the owner of the Eureka & Palisade Railroad. He eventually took control of the property, absorbed adjacent claims, and formed the White Pine Copper Company. By 1904, Requa in turn established contacts with the famous Guggenheim family of Philadelphia, which was building one of the largest mining-smelting empires in the world, and he joined them in forming the Nevada Consolidated Copper Company.

The Guggenheims had financial resources much greater than Requa's; they acquired an excellent site for a mill and smelter to refine the ore. The location they chose, some 20 miles northeast of the main copper deposits and 12 miles north of Ely, was near the ranch that had been run by William McGill a few years earlier. On this location they built a massive reduction works to process the raw ore. This went into production in 1908, and within two years it had yielded a quantity of refined metal more valuable than all the silver of the famous old town of Hamilton, where the boom of 1869 had led to the establishment of White Pine County.

In partnership with the Guggenheims, Requa promoted the construction of a new railroad, the Nevada Northern, to connect the Robinson district with the Southern Pacific (the successor to the Central Pacific) main line 140 miles to the north at Cobre. The railroad ran through Ely, connecting the mines with the smelter. In a short time White Pine County had several new towns: Ruth, Kimberly, Riepetown, and Veteran near the mines to the west, and McGill northeast of Ely.

Early in their relationship, the Guggenheims crowded Requa out of the business and operated their White Pine property in a manner similar to that of their large copper deposits in Utah. There were other smaller companies, but they were of less importance than the Guggenheims' and the Nevada Consolidated Copper Company.

Because the copper-producing industry attracted a different kind of corporate organization than the gold-silver industry, the history of community development in White Pine County had little similarity to that of the ramshackle gold-silver camps. Once the Guggenheims had taken control, they and the other owners organized "company towns" in order to assure a stable, reliable labor force. Near the smelter at McGill's ranch, they laid out a town with fine homes for the executives, excellent concrete dwellings for skilled workers, and modest but decent housing for the mill and smelter workers and their families for a low rental cost. Thus the traditional "tent city" that had characterized so many mining and railroad towns was replaced by a planned community, with a company-owned store, saloon, hospital, water system, and other services. The company provided a fire department, a sanitation service, reading rooms, athletic equipment, and it assumed part of the responsibility for keeping the peace. The county government had little responsibility for providing the usual services, and there was no town government under this paternalistic system. McGill, Ruth, Kimberly, and Veteran (the last of which existed for only about five years) were all company towns. McGill and Ruth became larger than the others, with a broader range of services.

Although this system often brought criticism, it provided for neater and more orderly towns, with more dependable human services, than most Nevada mining camps enjoyed. The company towns did not tolerate prostitution within their boundaries (although it flourished on the fringes), and there was less violence and filth than in the typical gold-silver camp. Many former residents of the White Pine company towns testified to the benign rule of the companies.

One other new community, called Ely City, shared the White Pine revival of this period. A group of promoters affiliated with the Nevada Consolidated Copper Company and the Nevada Northern Railroad acquired a plot of land 2 miles east of the original town of Ely, platted a city of 250 acres, and offered lots for sale late in 1906. They acquired water rights in a manner that seemed to threaten old Ely and announced that the handsome new railroad station of the Nevada Northern would be placed there. The plan was to make homes and services available to the employees of the copper companies and to replace old Ely as the hub of the district. For two years, the new town threatened to overtake "sleepy hollow," but in 1908, the Post Office department—responding to the confusion about the similarity of names—redesignated "Ely City" as "East Ely." Thereafter Ely grew more rapidly, and the two towns blended without becoming a totally single social unit.

In 1900, all of White Pine County had a population of only 1,961. By 1910, the census takers counted 7,441 residents, with more than 2,000 in Ely, plus 738 in East Ely, and 1,900 in McGill. Even a few older mining districts and the livestock ranchers took new hope from the presence of the flourishing copper industry.

By 1912, the copper mines near Ely claimed first place in the revitalized Nevada mining industry, ahead of the more famous camps of Goldfield and Tonopah. Their managers brought new methods and techniques to Nevada's most famous industry. Open-pit excavations proved to be the most efficient way of extracting the huge bodies of ore near Ruth, but some work was done by means of conventional underground shafts. As the years passed, the Liberty Pit near Ruth became a massive hole, more than a mile wide and 1,000 feet deep, and the town itself had to be moved to allow for the expansion of the pit. In the words of

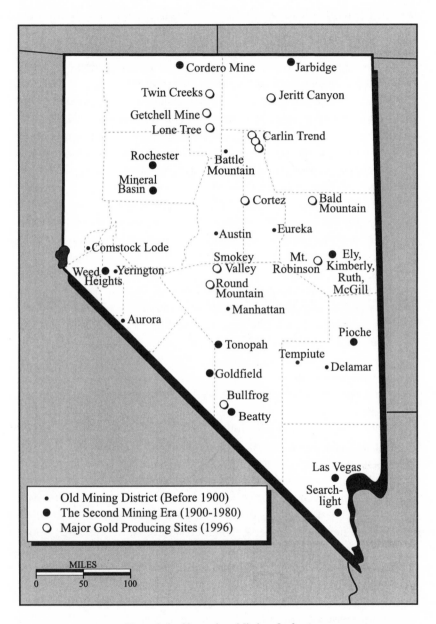

Cordero Mine •   • Jarbidge

Twin Creeks ○        ○ Jeritt Canyon

Getchell Mine ○

Lone Tree ○

                    ○○ Carlin Trend
                    ○
Rochester •    • Battle
              Mountain
Mineral
Basin •

              ○ Cortez      ○ Bald
                                Mountain

            • Austin    • Eureka

• Comstock Lode    Smokey      Mt.    ○  • Ely,
                   ○ Valley  Robinson    Kimberly,
Weed •  • Yerington                      Ruth,
Heights                                  McGill
                   ○ Round
                     Mountain

                   • Manhattan
• Aurora

                                        Pioche
              • Tonopah                   •
                        Tempiute
              • Goldfield    •  • Delamar

              Bullfrog
              ○○
                • Beatty

                              Las Vegas
                                 •
• Old Mining District (Before 1900)      Search-
● The Second Mining Era (1900-1980)      light
○ Major Gold Producing Sites (1996)        •

MILES
├────┼────┤
0    50   100

*Nevada's Changing Mining Industry*

Russell R. Elliott, a leading authority on Nevada history, copper was the "king" of the minerals.

During and after World War II, production climbed as giant mechanical shovels and entire trains operated in the bottom and along the sides of the pits, and the district gave employment to thousands of workers. In 1960, the Kennecott Copper Company, which had taken over most of the production from the older companies, was moving about 84,000 tons of rock every day and treating about one-fourth of that in its smelter in McGill. It was necessary to mine 500 tons of ore to produce 1 ton of refined copper. During the 1960s, the Ely district passed the $1 billion mark in terms of its total production.

Gradually, during the 1950s, 1960s, and 1970s, the prosperity of the district declined along with the rest of the domestic copper industry. Three factors—the long-term fall in the price of raw copper, rising production costs as the pits became deeper, and increasing wage demands from workers—made the continued operation unprofitable. Mines in Africa and South America could produce the red metal in greater volume at less cost. For several years, Kennecott gradually cut back production, and the company closed its mines near Ruth in 1978 and its smelter in McGill in 1983.

## Lyon County Copper

Across the state, near Mason Valley, Nevada had another large copper deposit. As early as the 1860s, a German immigrant named John Ludwig had discovered outcroppings in the Singatse Range west of Yerington and had made some shipments of the red metal to Virginia City for processing, but it was never a commercial success. With the post-1900 revival, several developers entered the region, built a railroad and a smelter, and opened new mines in 1912. The railroad, called the Nevada Copper Belt, ran from Wabuska on the old Carson & Colorado line, southward through Mason Valley and Yerington, and then northwesterly into the mining district.

This district produced copper from 1912 until 1918, reaching its peak during the period of American participation in World War I, 1917–1918. It never approached the levels of the White Pine region, and the mines either remained idle or produced only small amounts during most of the next thirty years. But Yerington had won a place on the maps of those who engaged in long-range mineral planning.

In the 1950s, when the Korean War threatened the nation with a shortage of strategic metals, the giant Anaconda Copper Company started open-pit mining and the district prospered for nearly twenty years. Weed Heights, another company town with many modern amenities, arose in the Singatse Range west of Mason Valley; it prospered only as long as the mining enterprise that it was created to serve. By 1980, Nevada's second copper district had followed the larger White Pine operation into the decline that had been the fate of so many other camps.

Recent research by Nevada historian Sally Zanjani has shown that the second mining boom was not the exclusive domain of men: a significant number of women prospected and mined in Nevada and throughout the West, especially during the period after 1900. While most of them failed to find the great bonanzas, they occasionally mustered the same skills and took the same risks as the men. They have only belatedly been recognized for their role in developing the wealth of the region.

## Suggested Supplementary Reading

Brown, Mrs. Hugh. *Lady in Boomtown: Miners and Manners on the Nevada Frontier*. 1968. Reprint, Reno: University of Nevada Press, 1991.

Elliott, Russell R. *Nevada's Twentieth-Century Mining Boom: Tonopah, Goldfield, Ely*. Reno: University of Nevada Press, 1966.

Glad, Betty. *Key Pittman: The Tragedy of a Senate Insider*. New York: Columbia University Press, 1986.

Reid, Harry. *Searchlight: The Camp That Didn't Fail*. Reno: University of Nevada Press, 1998.

Tingley, Joseph V., Robert C. Horton, and Francis C. Lincoln. *Outline of Nevada Mining History*. Special Publication 15. Reno: Nevada Bureau of Mines and Geology, 1993.

Zanjani, Sally Springmeyer. *Goldfield: The Last Gold Rush on the Western Frontier*. Athens: Ohio University Press, 1992.

———. *A Mine of Her Own: Women Prospectors in the American West, 1850–1950*. Lincoln: University of Nebraska Press, 1997.

Zanjani, Sally Springmeyer, and Guy Louis Rocha. *The Ignoble Conspiracy: Radicalism on Trial in Nevada*. Reno: University of Nevada Press, 1986.

# 13

## The Second Era of Railroad Building

THE TWENTIETH-CENTURY mining boom stimulated a new era of railroad building throughout Nevada. Between 1900 and 1910, at least a dozen companies laid more than 1,500 miles of track and sent trains through parts of the desert that had never previously been disturbed by the sound of a steam locomotive. At times there were more men working on railroad construction and operation within Nevada than in the mines or on the ranches. Although many of the small lines did not survive, the construction work of these companies had a more lasting influence on Nevada's history than did the mining booms.

In 1899, the Central Pacific—builder of the first railroad across California, Nevada, and most of Utah in 1863–1869—underwent a reorganization. It was absorbed into the Southern Pacific (with some of the same owners and managers). At about the same time, Collis P. Huntington, the last living member of the original "Big Four," purchased the almost-bankrupt Carson & Colorado Railroad to incorporate it into the Southern Pacific shortly before his death in 1900. He paid a low price for the old line because it had not shown a profit for nearly twenty years. But the crafty old man had made an excellent investment because soon thereafter came Jim Butler's discovery, and the rush to Tonopah was made partly by train. The Southern Pacific did much profitable business on this branch for several years.

## The Southern Pacific and Sparks

During the earliest years of the new century, the newly energized Southern Pacific (SP) virtually rebuilt its roads. It replaced the old narrow-gauged Carson & Colorado with standard gauge, and it rerouted that branch to take advantage of the Fallon reclamation construction. On the main line of the Central Pacific across Nevada, the SP relocated 221 of its 433 miles to reduce grades and make the curves easier.

The most important new community on the rerouted Southern Pacific line was Sparks, 4 miles east of Reno. When the new owners redesigned their line through the Truckee Meadows, they acquired several ranches as sites for large maintenance shops to replace the old ones at Wadsworth, and they moved virtually all the residents—nearly 700 of them— 30 miles westward to the new community in 1904. The railroad officers distributed homesites by lot and even made arrangements to move most of the buildings from Wadsworth to Sparks. Within a year, the state legislature granted it a municipal charter. Thus another city appeared on the map because of a railroad company's decision.

By 1910, Sparks was the fourth largest community in the state with 2,500 people, ranking behind Reno (10,867), Goldfield (4,838), and Tonopah (3,900). The stable railroad employment gave it a much more secure economic base than the old mining camps ever had. It soon had a well-organized labor union and a sense of community distinct from Reno.

## More New Railroads, North and South

The Tonopah-Goldfield-Rhyolite booms lured several railroad investors who were eager to take advantage of profitable freighting business generated by the new bonanzas. One new railroad from Sodaville (on the old Carson & Colorado line) to Tonopah began carrying freight in the summer of 1904. Within a few weeks another group put money into a track southward to Goldfield, and in the following year, these two groups merged as the Tonopah & Goldfield Railroad Company. Also in 1905, two different companies approached from the south—the Las Vegas & Tonopah and the Tonopah & Tidewater. In addition, a separate railroad was built between Goldfield and Bullfrog. All these lines were in operation in 1907—too many to allow prosperity for any of them when the mining activity diminished and the automobile became a common feature on the desert trails.

In that era, just before the car became a reliable instrument for moving goods and people, there were incentives to lay track almost anywhere that promised the possibility of producing raw materials for regional markets. The old Virginia & Truckee extended its line southward from Carson City to the new town of Minden in 1906. We have already mentioned the building of the Nevada Northern which connected Ruth-Ely-McGill and the Southern Pacific line at Cobre in 1906. That line continued its successful operation long after most of the other small companies had torn up their tracks and sold them for scrap.

Railroad speculators had so much cash and optimism as the new century opened that they were willing to build a second major line across northern Nevada between Sacramento and Salt Lake City. The Western Pacific, incorporated in 1903, had behind it the planning and money of George Gould, the son of millionaire Jay Gould, who owned a vast network of companies across the country. The route of the Western Pacific—from California's Feather River country, through northern Washoe County to Winnemucca, and to the Utah line at Wendover— ran parallel to the Southern Pacific for about half the distance across Nevada. Construction in Nevada began in 1907, and at times there were as many as 7,000 men on the labor crews. All of the towns along Nevada's northern tier, including Gerlach on the Black Rock Desert and Wendover on the Bonneville Salt Flats, took economic nourishment from this work. Eventually a branch line of the Western Pacific tapped the Reno commercial market from the north.

Nevada's open spaces on the continental chessboard fascinated the railroad millionaires. Financial giants like Edward H. Harriman, the New York stockbroker who took control of the Union Pacific in 1898, looked at the map of the Far West and studied the possibilities in southern Nevada, which was still untouched by the transportation revolution. There were several east-west transcontinental lines by that time, but no diagonals between Salt Lake City and Los Angeles. Overland rail freight between Chicago and Los Angeles, for example, would normally go through New Mexico and Arizona. The planning and building of the Panama Canal after 1901 stimulated much interest in the commercial prospects of southern California and encouraged its economic growth.

The Union Pacific had surveyed possible lines through part of southern Utah, Nevada, and California as early as 1890, and even laid a few miles of track in Utah, but the enterprise folded before reaching Nevada.

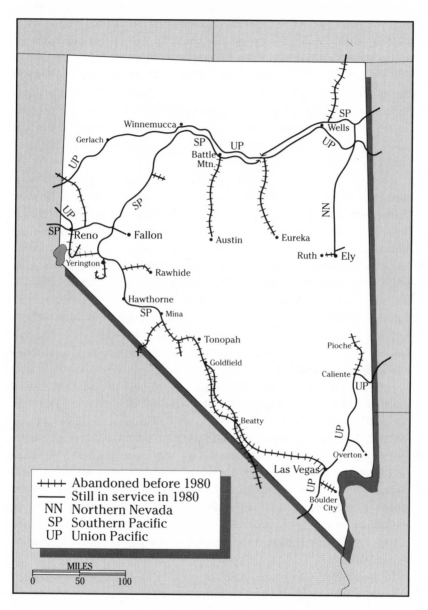

*Major Railroads of Nevada (1900–1990)*

Harriman projected a route through the dry, broken country west of the Grand Canyon and east of Death Valley. The most obvious—almost the only—choice was to send the line down the narrow Meadow Valley Wash to Moapa and across the broad Las Vegas Valley toward Los Angeles. About 200 miles of this projected route lay within Nevada.

It frequently was the case in the old West that when one millionaire had an enterprising idea, at least one or two more soon had the same notion, and a battle of the titans followed. They were like predators stalking the same game. In this case, Harriman's rival was Senator William A. Clark of Montana. Their struggle opened a new chapter in the history of Las Vegas.

Clark was the most ambitious oligarch to appear on the Nevada horizon after the passing of William Sharon and before the arrival of Howard Hughes. He was richer than any of the Comstock bonanza kings had ever been; his critics sometimes called him "the Midas of the West." It is not necessarily true that everything he touched turned to gold, but in the 1890s he transformed the Montana copper mines into millions for himself, and he bought a defunct Arizona mining district and made it one of the most prosperous in the country. It was widely rumored that he had a personal fortune of $50 million. From his own resources and without selling any stock, he incorporated a new company—known as the Salt Lake, Los Angeles & San Pedro Railroad, or more popularly as "Clark's line"—in 1900.

Harriman and Clark each acquired title to part of the right-of-way through Nevada, and their crews appeared in Clover Valley near the Nevada-Utah boundary in the spring of 1901. The rival factions had several fights with shovels and axes, and the sheriff came down from Pioche to try to prevent bloodshed. The "Clark-Harriman War" created more excitement in Lincoln County than anyone had witnessed there for a quarter century. Ultimately the battles were waged in the Nevada legislature, in the courts, and in the offices of the two financial giants. In 1903, they reached a compromise which involved joint ownership, and Clark's crews built the line through Clover Valley and down the Meadow Valley Wash.

In the interim, Clark's men laid out another town that was destined to become a division point and maintenance center. Caliente—originally called "Calientes" for the warm springs nearby—passed through the usual phase as a rowdy "tent city" construction camp, but soon it had a traditional row of attractive railroad workers' homes and a handsome station that gave an impression of permanency, and it quickly spread out into its cozy canyon. By 1910, Caliente was home to more than 1,700 people and a branch line had been built northward to revitalize the dormant mines of Pioche. In the meantime, construction crews extended "Clark's line" southward toward Los Angeles.

## Las Vegas: From Rancho to Whistlestop

Las Vegas was unusual among the railroad towns of Nevada because it had been settled as a Mormon missionary post fifty years before the first locomotive rolled into the valley in 1905, and it functioned as a working ranch in the interim. For another quarter century after 1905, it was practically unnoticed in the affairs of Nevada and the great Southwest because it was little more than a convenient place for taking on ice and water and a minor distribution point for the distant mining towns. But then something dramatic began to happen there, as America discovered a new part of itself, both physically and socially. With the help of Hollywood films and the publicity of the Union Pacific (which purchased Clark's interest in 1921), the nation slowly became aware of the wonders of the desert southwest. And, simultaneously, the speculative fever that had once been directed toward the mines and railroads began to find an outlet in other forms of gambling.

The history of Las Vegas and southern Nevada unfolded in four stages: missionary outpost, frontier "ranchero," railroad town, and casino resort center. As we have seen, the unsuccessful Mormon missionaries abandoned their fort and gardens in 1858 after three years in the blistering heat. After the last missionaries left the Las Vegas Fort in 1858, its adobe walls began to crumble into the desert due to the stout winds and monsoon torrents. Passersby referred to it as the Las Vegas "rancho," adopting the Hispanic description that was common in California. Octavius and Mary Gass struggled for fifteen years there before they lost their property to Archibald Stewart, but following his death the widowed Helen Stewart and her family made the place flourish as a farm and wayside stop for occasional emigrants for nearly two decades.

The official census of 1900 counted 30 people in Las Vegas. Two years later, Helen sold most of the rancho (1,800 acres) to Senator Clark for $55,000. She kept her home, including what was left of the old fort, and remained in Las Vegas until her death in 1926. She thus participated in the opening of the third phase, the railroad era, of Las Vegas history.

*Vegas Home Bakery, Las Vegas, circa 1911. (Squires Collection, University of Nevada, Las Vegas, Library)*

## The Clark Era

Some of the essential features of the town of Las Vegas were determined before the railroad arrived. Railroad surveyors decided to locate their town center a short distance west of the old fort. Helen Stewart hired a man named J. T. McWilliams to survey her ranch before the sale of the property to Clark. McWilliams discovered that about 80 acres of un-claimed land was available west of the Stewart ranch and adjacent to the projected railroad line, so he filed a claim for it in the courthouse at Pioche. He designated this as the "original" Las Vegas Townsite, and hundreds of men squatted there in a tent city in the spring of 1905, await-ing the sale of lots in Clark's Townsite. McWilliams sold lots earlier than Clark did, but without any water-distribution system, and after Clark's men conducted their sale, most of McWilliams's clients moved eastward across the tracks, leaving his townsite as a second choice. When Clark's crews built their roadbed, they deliberately constructed it higher than the surrounding terrain to make it more difficult to travel between the original townsite and Clark's Las Vegas. The McWilliams' Townsite later became known as the Westside.

There were about 1,500 people at McWilliams' Townsite when Clark's leading agent, C. O. Whittemore, auctioned the lots on May 15, 1905. The bidding was lively; the lots at Main and Fremont streets near the depot brought $1,750. In the first two days, Clark took in $265,000. "King Midas" had done it again.

A first priority for Clark's organization was to erect a depot at the hub of the new town. Other early investments included a water-distribution system and an ice-making plant that could produce fifty tons per day. This latter amenity was one of the crucial assets of Las Vegas in its earli-est months as a town because an abundance of ice not only served the railroad but also permitted regular delivery to residents, allowing them to cool their homes in the blistering summer heat.

Water is the ingredient in the remarkable success of Las Vegas. The presence of large springs in the center of an expansive valley had been the reason for the existence of "the meadows," for the building of the Mormon fort, for the success of the Stewart Ranch, and for Clark's selec-tion of the locale as a division point for his railroad. Las Vegas had a generous supply of the desert's most precious commodity. Just a short distance below the parched desert crust, there flowed a large under-ground river. Within the first ten years, hundreds of pumps raised large volumes to the surface for homes and flora. Even though the practice was

*Auction of Clark Townsite, Las Vegas, 1905. (Doris Hancock Collection, University of Nevada, Las Vegas, Library)*

wasteful, there was enough water to sustain the city's growth for forty years. And just beyond Sunrise Mountain to the east was the Colorado River, which southern Nevadans regarded with envy from the earliest days of Clark's Las Vegas.

Clark and Whittemore laid out the essential features of their new town in typical oligarchic fashion. The Las Vegas Land and Water Company managed the distribution of water—often in a wasteful manner—for the next fifty years. They arranged for the construction of typical railroad row-cottages in the southern part of their townsite. Whittemore believed liquor sales should be confined to one small area, so Block 16 was designated for saloons and the so-called restricted district. Hotels, restaurants, and wholesalers could sell liquor outside that area, but saloons were to be confined to that quarter by order of the railroad company. Violation of the rule was supposed to mean that title to the property reverted to Las Vegas Land and Water Company, but enterprising people in other parts of town soon opened "hotels" to evade the paternalistic restrictions.

Unlike Reno in 1868, Las Vegas did not have a mining district such as the Comstock Lode a mere 25 miles away. But on the other hand, several important mining booms of the early twentieth century occurred in the "southern camps," as Tonopah, Goldfield, Rhyolite, and their neighbors were commonly called, and part of their traffic went through Las Vegas in the boom years. Reno grew up as the gateway to the Comstock. In 1907 rail lines from Las Vegas extended into Goldfield, and picture postcards promoted Las Vegas as the "Gateway to Goldfield." Clark's associates established the first automobile rental service and tried to control the freighting business that served the southern mining camps. However, the bulk of the Tonopah-Goldfield traffic continued to pass through Reno.

Las Vegas fought its first notable community battle over the right to have its own county government. Lincoln County was one of the largest in the nation, embracing more than 18,000 square miles. Pioche—the county seat—was 175 miles north of Las Vegas, and the roads were crude even in the best of weather. For the recording of deeds and the conduct of court business, the old mining town was simply too far away. The promoters and political leaders of Las Vegas originally tried to wrest control of the county government from Pioche in the election of 1908, and when that failed, they persuaded the 1909 session of the Nevada legislature to create a new county. The county division bill became law just after Senator Clark's agents announced that he would construct large machine shops at Las Vegas, confirming its status as the main division point on the railroad between Salt Lake and Los Angeles. This prompted the decision to name the new county in honor of the former Montana senator. Two years later, in 1911, the legislature incorporated the city of Las Vegas.

Although some difficult years followed for the first residents, Las Vegas had greater economic momentum than most mining towns of the north had ever demonstrated. Like Reno thirty years earlier, it had a more or less dependable flow of through traffic between Utah and California. Even severe floods in the Meadow Valley Wash, which washed out the rail line in 1906, 1907, and 1910, did little more than interrupt the commercial progress for a few months because Senator Clark had the resources and the determination to rebuild promptly. For another ten years, until the Union Pacific bought the Clark interests in 1921, the Montana millionaire's associates promoted and encouraged Las Vegas. By the time Clark sold his interest in the railroad, Las Vegas had about 2,700 people.

Those who visited the small city in its first few years often considered it an improbable oasis surrounded by some of the most hostile landscape on the continent, as the Mormon missionaries said in the 1850s. To the east was the wild Colorado River and the virtually impassable Grand Canyon. To the north was the Muddy River and its tempestuous tributary, the Meadow Valley Wash, which provided a tenuous connection with the old towns of Pioche and Panaca more than 150 miles away. To the northwest, the vast desert called "Death Barren" by Nevada's first governor, separated Las Vegas from the state capital, which was 430 miles away. And yet another stretch of hostile, arid landscape to the southwest separated this valley from Los Angeles and the other important southern California towns.

But Las Vegas did possess a few distinct advantages that its neighbors to the north lacked—for example, a very long growing season. Despite the poor, sandy soil and blistering summer heat, scores of families took up land for farming, set out fruit trees, and in a few cases successfully raised alfalfa, grains, and vegetables. Agriculture never became a major part of the economy, but the greening of Las Vegas did become an important civic enterprise. The Mesquite Club—a women's community improvement society—organized the planting of more than 2,000 trees, which gradually made parts of this improbable outpost seem luxuriant.

As we have seen, the widely dispersed underground water supply was another advantage, as the proliferation of wells and pumps testified.

*Clark's private railroad car. (Ferron-Bracken Collection, University of Nevada, Las Vegas, Library)*

Yet there was another side to the story. The Las Vegas Land and Water Company, founded by Clark's men in 1905, soon had trouble keeping its customers in the center of town supplied because its wooden lines frequently broke and its owners—first the Clark interests and, after 1921, the Union Pacific—responded slowly to the obvious need for a more dependable system. Walter Bracken, a pioneer member of the Las Vegas business establishment, was water tsar for forty years after 1905. The public agencies waged a long struggle against the Las Vegas Land and Water Company to win control over this utility in later years.

In 1920, Las Vegas was the fifth largest community in the state, with a population of 2,688. Three of its larger, distant neighbors were about the same age as Las Vegas. Her more populous sisters on the Nevada map were Reno (13,263), Tonopah (4,144), Sparks (3,569), and Fallon (2,795). But judging from contemporary accounts, no city was more confident or more willing to write its own scenario for the future than Las Vegas. This was the era when the federal Constitution was amended to restrict the sale and transport of alcoholic beverages (the Eighteenth Amendment). Las Vegas, like Reno and a dozen other towns, blinked at this provision and went into the "bootlegging" business.

## A Period of Anticipation, 1920–1940

Several evolutionary trends tantalized the residents of Las Vegas into the notion that their town might indeed become a great city. In the 1920s, the Union Pacific advertised the entire Southwest in an attractive and systematic manner, and the state government took a keener interest in its neglected southern towns. The rapid growth of southern California caught the eyes of the country, and the U.S. government began methodically building an improved highway system in the Far West. The Nevada legislature opened the door to legalized gambling in 1931. But above all, the nearby Colorado River came to be recognized as a regional resource of prime importance.

Because the Colorado River in its natural state was such a wild and unpredictable watercourse, it had often been considered a detriment rather than an asset to the Southwest. In 1922, Herbert Hoover, the secretary of commerce, traveled through the region to negotiate an agreement among the states that would allow for damming the river and dividing of the waters. He visited Las Vegas and virtually promised that there would be a massive reclamation project in its backyard. In that year, the seven states that share the river signed a legal agreement that assigned them proportional shares of the flow. The Colorado River Compact and its later refinements allotted 300,000 acre-feet of water per year to Nevada —once the means could be found to transfer it uphill from the depths of the riverbed to the dry expanses of Las Vegas Valley.

Mr. Hoover, the first president to be born west of the Mississippi and the first to be elected from California, was also an engineer, and he had an active interest in the development of western resources. He not only promoted the building of the dam as a member of the cabinet of President Calvin Coolidge, but he continued his interest as president between 1929 and 1933. He emphasized that a large hydroelectric project could provide not only cheap power and more usable water for the entire region, but also flood control. Much of the crucial political support for the dam came from California interests who wanted both electrical energy and water.

Nevada had two governors and a congressman in the early 1920s who also took an active interest in the possibilities of reclamation on the Colorado River. The chief executives were Emmett D. Boyle (1915–1922) and James G. Scrugham (1923–1926), both engineers from the northern end of the state who helped direct the state's attention toward this project in the south. The congressman who most actively shared their work, Samuel S. Arentz (1921–1923 and 1925–1933), was also an engineer.

Through the 1920s, Las Vegas newspapers repeatedly carried reports about the prospects for a huge dam in a nearby canyon that would mean large payrolls and eventually more water and cheap electrical power for the entire region. Not until 1928 were all the pieces of the engineering and political puzzle fitted together, and Congress authorized the construction, which began in 1931.

In the meantime, local citizens learned more about the natural and cultural resources of their own area—such as the Pueblo Grande discoveries near Overton and the beauties of the Spring Mountains, which were made accessible by improved roads. And on the edge of Las Vegas, a French-born immigrant named David Lorenzi gouged two large holes from the desert, filled them with water, and started a resort and entertainment pavilion. Within a few years, some of the earliest Las Vegas experiments with stage shows, brewing (of illegal beer), and gambling were conducted there.

## Hoover Dam and the Mission Revival Era

Las Vegas went through its next important transition around 1930, when construction of Hoover (originally called Boulder) Dam was imminent and the city's leading citizens undertook the construction of several new private and public buildings worthy of a modern, prosperous regional center. The decennial census counted a population of 5,165 that year, and the city had become the focus of much publicity in the large metropolitan newspapers because of the size and scope of the project. Las Vegas received some dubious publicity because federal agents charged with enforcement of the prohibition laws made a sweep through the area in 1931 just as construction was beginning, closing twenty-five nightclubs and arresting ninety people for the illegal sale of alcoholic beverages.

The building of Hoover Dam began just as the grip of the Great Depression tightened and millions of men were out of work across the country. News that a thousand men would be hired on the project brought more than 12,000 applications. The federal government tried to discourage the unemployed hordes from rushing to the site, but they arrived anyway, giving southern Nevada more acute problems with migrants than the old mining towns had known in the days of the bonanza rushes. There were bread lines, soup kitchens, and "Hoovervilles"—all of which put social burdens on the local city and county governments.

In the long run, however, the project meant prosperity for Las Vegas businessmen and favorable publicity for the region. At the peak of construction in 1934, more than 5,000 men worked on the project and related facilities, and many spent their weekends and paychecks in Las Vegas. Construction of the 726-foot-high dam continued for four years and required the creation of a more massive block of concrete than had ever been poured before. Seventeen giant electrical turbines eventually went into the heart of the dam to create power for millions of homes and factories. The top of the dam was wide enough for a highway connecting Arizona and Nevada—and incidentally directing more traffic into Las Vegas.

Near the dam, just 25 miles from Las Vegas, the Bureau of Reclamation built a completely new community called Boulder City, to provide accommodations for executives and others who worked on the dam. A pleasant, well-landscaped town, it reflected advanced concepts of community planning and banned the saloons and other forms of entertainment that attracted the workers to Las Vegas.

This era has faded into partial historical obscurity over the period of growth that the southern Nevada valley has known since the 1940s, but the Las Vegas of the early 1930s—before it became famous as a gambling and entertainment capital—was a community bent on developing an urbane identity. Its government officials and residents invested in sub-

*Hoover Dam under construction. (Manis Collection, University of Nevada, Las Vegas, Library)*

stantial public and private buildings, usually designed in the attractive southwestern "mission revival" style, which had been vigorously promoted in San Diego a generation earlier by Bertram G. Goodhue of New York. The motif had spread rapidly in southern California, and it spilled into the Las Vegas Valley just as the little railroad town was seeking to show itself to the world as a place of comfort and culture.

Only a few buildings were still standing in the late 1980s as reminders of the Boulder Dam era. The Stephen R. Whitehead home on North Seventh Street, built in 1929, is one of the few surviving residential examples of this architectural pattern. The old Las Vegas Hospital on North Eighth Street, built in 1931 at a cost of $100,000, seemed doomed to removal in 1989. The Las Vegas Grammar School on South Fifth Street, constructed in 1936, was one of the best examples of the "mission revival" theme of that period. After its usefulness as a school ended, the buildings were adapted for service as a county government building; it has been recognized as historically important by its listing on the National Register of Historic Places. An innovative promoter opened a resort called The Meadows on the Boulder Highway in 1931—the year that Nevada's legislature re-legalized gambling. A handsome mission-style depot, erected by the Union Pacific in 1940 and built to replace the original Clark depot of 1905, marked the culmination of this architectural period.

## Reno: A Mixed Reputation

Throughout the first forty years of the century, Las Vegas lagged far behind Reno as a commercial and divorce center. The national publicity about the little community on the Truckee was more extensive, and its voice in national and state affairs was much louder than that of any other Nevada town. As late as 1940, the Reno area had three or four times as many residents as Las Vegas. As late as the 1950s, the political leadership of Nevada was still primarily centered there, and politicians from the north held nearly all of the most coveted offices.

Reno's slow but consistent growth from 4,500 people to 21,300 between 1900 and 1940 resulted from the fact that it was the financial and educational center for the western Great Basin. The advantages that it had gained from its proximity to the Comstock Lode did not disappear after the mines closed. It thrived on the trade generated by the Tonopah-Goldfield boom, on the construction of the Newlands Reclamation Project downstream on the Truckee River, and on the rebuilding of the railroads of northern Nevada and California. Yet through much of its history, Reno struggled with itself over the kind of city it wanted to be.

## The Newlands Era

The individual who did most to set the social tone of Reno at the turn of the century was Congressman (later Senator) Francis G. Newlands. Not only did he conceive of and get credit for the Truckee-Carson reclamation project (see chapter 15), but he made it his personal goal to give Reno an identity as the "city beautiful." Newlands also hoped to see Reno and Nevada become more like other, more traditional American communities. He encouraged city planning, supported the beautifying of the Truckee River, and arranged for the upstream storage of water to assure more dependable supply for Reno as well as for the Truckee-Carson Irrigation District. As William Rowley, one of the historians of the "Biggest Little City," wrote:

> Newlands had grand visions for Reno as the hub of an expanding agricultural and industrial development in western Nevada. Not only would the city nourish commerce, but also education, the arts, civic pride, and beauty. It would be the leader of a reform movement that would remake Nevada into Newlands' much-hoped-for "model commonwealth." (Rowley, *Reno: Hub of the Washoe Country*, p. 51.)

Such ideas were part of the Progressive Era of American politics. Congressman Newlands was typical of the civic-minded political leaders of his time in wanting to reduce the social evils of society by government action and planning.

In addition, Reno had become, after 1886, the home of the University of Nevada. Established as a preparatory school in Elko in 1874, the so-called university had not prospered in the northeastern corner of the state because there were not enough professors or students to make it an active place of learning. Even after the transfer to Reno, several years passed before the university could offer its students the range of courses in the liberal arts, mining, and agriculture that its constitutional founders had intended.

Between 1894 and 1914, the university had a president who clearly defined the role of an institution of higher learning and who set an ethical challenge for the city and state in a manner that few other individuals in Nevada have ever matched. He was Joseph Edward Stubbs, a scholar of the ancient classics and a man dedicated to the social and cultural improvement of the society around him. The tenure of President Stubbs at the university coincided closely with the leadership of Senator Newlands in the political field. Stubbs, in cooperation with women's groups, led a movement against gambling and prostitution in Reno, and in 1909 the legislature passed a law ordering that games of chance throughout the state be discontinued as of October 1, 1910. This began a twenty-year period in which most forms of gambling were technically illegal in Nevada, but the law was seldom vigorously enforced.

From 1918 until 1938, the university president was Walter E. Clark, an economics professor from New York. He and his wife likewise set a high cultural and ethical tone for the part of the community that sought to distinguish itself from the highly publicized activities that existed downtown.

From 1919 until 1923, Reno had a mayor, H. E. Stewart, whose civic ideas corresponded to those that Newlands, Stubbs, and Clark had proposed. He worked for better streets, more parks, and more schools, and participated in a movement to abolish the red-light district near the center of the city. He also tried to close the speakeasies that were infamous for selling alcoholic beverages contrary to the prohibition laws, but his message was overwhelmed by voices from the other side.

## The Wingfield Era

Historian William Rowley has effectively argued that the Newlands-Stewart aspirations for civic improvement ran afoul of the ambitions of George Wingfield, who transferred his wealth and profit-making ambitions from Goldfield to Reno after the ore bodies yielded their treasures. (Wingfield's partner, George Nixon, also moved to Reno and built a fine home near the Newlands mansion once he became senator.) Wingfield owned and managed a network of banks which, until they were rocked by scandal and depression, functioned as a financial control mechanism for much of the state's economy. Wingfield played the financial and political fields like an eastern "boss." He became a benefactor of the city by giving it land for a beautiful downtown park, but he had no interest in civic reform.

In Reno city government, Wingfield and his associates in 1923 threw their support behind E. E. Roberts, a former congressman from Nevada and a colorful orator, in order to unseat Mayor Stewart and sidetrack his reform movement. That municipal election, one of the most important in the history of the city, brought a resounding victory for Roberts and those who favored permissive social attitudes toward gambling, alcohol, and prostitution. Roberts got wide publicity by saying that he would be happy to see a barrel of whiskey on every street corner. He was reelected twice, served ten years, and died in office in 1933. He personified and encouraged the image of Reno as a city that would tolerate those practices that were banned elsewhere.

Even before Wingfield and Roberts established their grip on Reno's commerce and government, the city had gained notoriety for the ease with which its courts would grant divorces. In most states, it was difficult to dissolve a marriage, even when both parties wanted to do so. Either long separation before the divorce, or a long waiting period before a remarriage, or restrictive grounds for granting a divorce, or—most likely—a combination of these requirements complicated many lives. Reno had well-publicized divorce cases as early as 1906, and it became known that local judges were lenient on this matter. Nevada's laws required only six months of residency in the early 1920s and enabled the divorce to be granted easily if both parties agreed. The law also allowed vague grounds such as "mental cruelty" for ending a marriage and offered a means of avoiding ugly accusations and property disputes in one's hometown. By the mid-1920s, hundreds of women were coming from the East to be "Reno-vated," as the gossip columnists described it. They often spent their time on dude ranches at the edge of town, or in local hotels, or in homes of people who rented them accommodations and would testify in court that they were "permanent" residents of Nevada.

Getting a Nevada divorce became even easier after Mexico and other jurisdictions relaxed their laws, and Nevada divorce lawyers began to experience competition for their clients. The legislature reduced the Nevada residence requirement to three months in 1927 and to six weeks in 1931. Thousands of outsiders came every year for the "cure." Their ranks included movie stars, New York socialites, and foreign dignitaries. The legal fraternity prospered, and Reno claimed to have more lawyers per capita than any city in the nation. In addition, Nevada's easy marriage laws, with no waiting period and no requirements for medical examination, attracted thousands of additional couples from other states, where examinations and waiting periods were generally in force.

George Wingfield's Riverside Hotel (next door to the courthouse) prospered because much of the social and political life of the state swirled around it.

For a small city, Reno had a remarkably diversified economy in the 1920s and was not nearly as dependent on the divorce trade and tourism as it later became. It had two meat-packing plants, rock-products plants, an iron foundry, brickworks, furnace- and stove-producing facilities, lumber and planing mills, dairy and ice-cream plants, and scores of other light industries. The railroad companies employed more than 1,000 men, most of them living in Sparks.

In the middle 1920s, some dark clouds gathered over Reno's prosperous scene. A grand jury investigation showed that the state treasurer and a former state controller had conspired with an officer in one of Wingfield's banks to embezzle more than a half million dollars of the Nevada state government's money. After a special session of the legislature, the state received repayment of about one-third of the missing money from Wingfield. But the fraudulent activity cost Nevada taxpayers more than $400,000 in lost deposits and governmental expenses.

Later, during the Great Depression in the autumn of 1932, Acting Governor Morley Griswold declared a voluntary two-week "bank holiday" in Nevada because the Wingfield banks were in trouble, and shortly thereafter the Wingfield banks went into receivership. Hundreds of investors lost their assets, and another scandal erupted over the laxness of the state auditing and supervision of banks. By 1933, Wingfield's status as "boss of Nevada" was slipping. Early in the next year, President Franklin D. Roosevelt declared a national bank holiday because so many financial institutions were in distress.

At the peak of his power, Wingfield and his allies manipulated the affairs of both the Democratic and Republican parties from his bank office, and for many years thereafter it was alleged that Nevada's politics were largely managed by a handful of men from the banks and hotels on the edge of the Truckee River. The full story of this oligarchy has yet to be written.

When the Nevada legislature legalized gambling in 1931 and reduced the residency requirement for divorce seekers to six weeks, it gave the city's businessmen the tools with which to weather the economic storms of the 1930s. Reno continued to grow modestly during the depression years in spite of its scandals. Walter Van Tilburg Clark, one of Nevada's best-known novelists who lived there through part of this period, said cogently that Reno was both a "big city" (in relation to Nevada) and a "small town" (in relation to most other urban centers in the nation). "Reno stands in about the same relationship to the state of Nevada that New York City does to the state of New York," he wrote. The community's boosters erected a sign across Virginia Street, visible from the main highway and the passing trains, which read "Reno: The Biggest Little City in the World," and its residents took the slogan seriously. It continued to be a prosperous, attractive city, with a sophisticated social life nourished by its famous visitors, when World War II opened. It also continued to be ambivalent about whether it wanted to be a "sin city" or an average American market center and college town.

## The New Deal

As the Great Depression settled over the nation, Nevada seemed especially vulnerable in view of the collapse of the Wingfield banking chain in 1932. The election of President Roosevelt in that year and his inauguration the following March proved to be a turning point for Nevada as for much of the rest of the nation, because new forms of federal assistance became available for the struggling commonwealth. Although both Senators Pittman and McCarran had conflicts with President Roosevelt, both also had beneficial contacts with some of the New Deal administrators in Washington and helped funnel appropriations to the Silver State.

No state in the Far West had more help from the federal government during the years of the Great Depression than Nevada, if the expenditures are calculated on a per capita basis. In addition to the construction of Hoover Dam (which began during the Hoover administration) and the passage of Senator Pittman's 1934 Silver Purchase Act, Nevada communities received help from Washington in the form of loans, and money for such agencies as the Civil Works Administration and the Civilian Conservation Corps (CCC), which put unemployed young men to work planting trees, building dams, and improving parks and public facilities. Las Vegas received, for example, a new park at Stewart and Fourth streets and a new Las Vegas Memorial Building with a seating capacity of 1,600. Scores of other towns had similar but smaller projects, and hundreds of ranchers benefited from drought relief. In addition, the Nevada highway system underwent significant expansion and improvement during the depression years, again because of increased federal expenditure in this sector.

Nevada society had seldom paid much attention to its cultural assets and heritage before the Great Depression, but the Works Projects Administration (WPA) gave recognition to such activities in the late 1930s and sponsored the work of artists, musicians, and writers; some of the state's foremost painters, such as Robert Cole Caples and Richard Guy Walton, advanced their careers with the aid of this emergency governmental assistance.

In retrospect, the emergency work, public improvements, and cultural stimulation provided by the New Deal were pioneering efforts in conserving resources and encouraging humanistic enterprises. Nevada's heritage is richer in the twenty-first century as a result of the federal government's initiatives in the 1930s.

## Suggested Supplementary Reading

Moehring, Eugene P. *Resort City in the Sunbelt: Las Vegas 1930–2000*. Reno: University of Nevada Press, 2000.

Myrick, David F. *Railroads of Nevada and Eastern California*. Vol. I, *The Northern Roads*; Vol. II, *The Southern Roads*. 1962–63. Reprint, Reno: University of Nevada Press, 1992.

Nielson, Norm. *Reno: The Past Revisited*. Norfolk, Va.: The Donning Co., 1988.

Paher, Stanley W. *Las Vegas: As It Began—As It Grew*. Las Vegas: Nevada Publications, 1971.

Rowley, William D. *Reclaiming the Arid West: The Career of Francis G. Newlands*. Bloomington: Indiana University Press, 1996.

Stevens, Joseph E. *Hoover Dam: An American Adventure*. Norman: University of Oklahoma Press, 1988.

Townley, John M. *Tough Little Town on the Truckee: Reno 1868–1900*. Vol. I. Reno: Great Basin Studies Center, 1983.

# 14

## New Urban Experiments

### Reno and Las Vegas Since 1940

T HE SOCIAL and economic history of this desert state has changed so dramatically since World War II that an almost entirely new Nevada has emerged, with a distinctive economy and a set of expectations and priorities essentially different from those of the mining-railroading-ranching society that existed before 1940. The hybridized heritage retains much of the old landscape and the symbols of the earlier frontier, but these were gradually being adapted or erased by newer forms in 1990.

At the end of the 1930s, when Nevada was observing its seventy-fifth birthday as a state, it was still primarily a rural society; about two-thirds of its residents lived on ranches, in mining camps, or in railroad towns of fewer than 2,500 people. By the time Nevada celebrated its hundredth anniversary of statehood in 1964, Las Vegas and Reno had grown so rapidly that nearly two-thirds of the state's population resided in these cities or their suburbs.

By the late 1980s, the urban dwellers outnumbered the rural Nevadans by approximately nine to one. And the burgeoning tourist centers had problems and possibilities that the older Nevada never contemplated. The central fact of Nevada's social life was that the population had grown from 110,000 in 1940 to more than 1,700,000 in the late 1990s, and most of that expansion had occurred in or near the two larger cities. The rest of America had come to look upon Nevada as a place of sophiscated entertainment. Previously, for half a century it was also known as a place where prostitution flourished and where mobsters could hide behind loose gambling regulations to finance their criminal activities. In the 1990s, Nevada seemed to be shedding this image in favor of the many new family-oriented "theme resorts" that were being built, especially in Las Vegas. Its tourism managers were also trying to cultivate a wider appreciation of the state's natural attractions.

Also, it was a basic fact of intrastate life that Nevada was no longer understandable as a montage of twenty or thirty small, scattered mining and railroad towns and several hundred isolated ranches, remote from one another and everyone else, as it had been from the 1860s to the 1940s. Some outposts had changed little, but Reno had become a middle-sized urban area, and Las Vegas was a world-famous metropolis. From Europe to the Orient, on cruise ships and in desert wadis, gambling and resort centers borrowed names and images from Las Vegas. This dimension of Nevada history has had insufficient consideration because it is so strange in the historical context, both to Nevada and the nation as a whole.

## Reno: Ambivalence and Caution

Reno continued to be schizophrenic after 1940 as it had been from the beginning. The business core of Reno followed the course that its city fathers had charted for it in the 1920s and 1930s — a permissive, wide-open town catering to gamblers, divorcées, and temporarily single men and women — with some misgivings. But the other half of Reno, following in the footsteps of President Stubbs and Mayor Stewart, sought the high road of respectability. It was as though there were two cultures that interacted only superficially in the Biggest Little City and did not pay much attention to one another.

From pioneering days onward, Reno's remoteness and roughness were tempered by its beautiful setting. It was more fortunate in its topography than Las Vegas or virtually any other town in the state, nearer to its sheltering Sierra Nevada and therefore to the refreshing waters of the Truckee River. It was located on the most strategic transportation route between the East and the California goldfields, and its railroad — the Central Pacific — came through thirty-five years before Clark's Salt Lake line reached the Las Vegas Valley. As a town, it had a long season in which to mature before the 1940s.

Early in its history, Reno's residents were convinced that its high desert air and nearby hot springs had therapeutic value. Agriculture, especially livestock and hay raising, were rewarding to many families because water could readily be diverted from the Truckee or its tributary streams to turn nearly the entire bowl-shaped valley into pasture or garden land. The original townsite of 1868 was located in the northwestern corner of the valley, and it gradually spread outward—mostly into the eastern and southern flatlands, but also into the northern and western Sierra foothills. The railroad depot was the strategic center of town and the usual entryway into Nevada for temporary visitors, and this remained so for at least eighty years, until the 1950s.

When Max Miller described the Biggest Little City in his 1941 book entitled *Reno*, the railroad station was still the fulcrum of the place:

> When one stops at Reno, one knows one has stopped at Reno, and none other. He does not have to ask the conductor: "What town is this?"
>
> For Reno throws its worst face directly at the station, and appears to take pleasure at doing so, appears to take pleasure in indicating a turmoil of shack-stores, cheap saloons, a burleycue of gambling houses, even a tattoo shop, tough alleys—and a blur of constant excitement. This is the way it seems when one gets off the train. (Miller, *Reno*, p. 25.)

But Miller found that this dimension of the city was confined to only a few blocks. As one passed a short distance from the seedy center, he—or more usually she—found the handsome homes, the people fishing along the Truckee, the magnificent pastoral landscape of the high Sierra. He exalted:

> And this is the real Reno which gets into the heart of one, more the name of a region than of a town, so that the hurdy-gurdy of the gambling section becomes a minute speck indeed, an incident for meeting trains.
>
> Instead of Reno becoming smaller with intimacy as the days go along, Reno for a fact spreads and enlarges in focus. And this, I think, all this intangible mystery, all this gradual unfolding, is why people return to Reno for their second and third divorces, for their second and third honeymoons—and I am speaking of the region now, the whole region with its hundreds of miles, and with only this one strange little town in the center to serve as the pulse beat. (Miller, *Reno*, p. 32.)

Reno has long had a love affair with its mountains and the nearby desert, and by 1950 some of its more literate citizens had crystallized this affection in literature and scholarship. The novelist Walter Van Tilburg Clark—author of *The City of Trembling Leaves* (about Reno in the 1920s and 1930s), *The Ox-Bow Incident*, and *The Track of the Cat*—evoked descriptive natural moods and scenes that have respected places in the literature of the Far West. Dr. James Edward Church, the University of Nevada snow scientist and classicist, gained an international reputation as an interpreter and analyst of the Sierra watersheds. Robert Laxalt, the son of an immigrant Basque sheepherder, spread his neighbors' passion for the landscape and mountain people through the pages of numerous books and articles. The old, early families had two or three generations to settle in before the rapid growth of the late twentieth century hit Reno, and they were less quickly overwhelmed by the incoming hordes than was Las Vegas.

## Reno, World War II, and the Sequel

Forty years after the publication of Clark's *The City of Trembling Leaves*, one could still identify the essential regions of Reno as Clark had labeled them: the Court Street Quarter, the Mount Rose Quarter, the Peavine Quarter, the University Quarter, and so on. Many of the stately homes that he knew were still there, even if many newer buildings had crowded in among them. Reno and Sparks experienced only gradual change during the war years, unlike their sister city in the south. And while the rate of growth accelerated after the war, it left intact many symbols of the earlier, quieter Newlands Era.

Washoe County had no large wartime industry, as Clark County and many California regions did. It had as an immediate neighbor only one small military post a few miles north of Reno. The high, dry climate and proximity to California prompted the government in 1942 to establish the Reno Army Air Base (later renamed Stead Air Force Base). Its earliest mission was to train signal companies, and later radio and navigation schools developed there. Stead had a checkered career: deactivated in the late 1940s, reactivated again during the Korean War in the early 1950s as a survival training center, and then phased out again as a military base in 1965. The extensive military facilities—including a hangar, airport, and housing—passed under the control of local governments, the University of Nevada, and private business interests. William Lear, one of the most successful investors in the field of jet aircraft development, operated an experimental plant at Stead for several years.

There were other military bases at a distance: the Fallon Naval Air Station 65 miles away, the Herlong Ordnance Depot 65 miles north in California, and the Hawthorne Ammunition Depot, 130 miles to the southeast. Servicemen regularly made Reno their weekend recreation destination, but it was never a soldiers' or sailors' town to the extent that Las Vegas and many coastal California cities were because all these bases were small. However, because some servicemen frequented the Biggest Little City for recreation, the military authorities asked the city government to suppress the houses of prostitution, and it complied.

During the war years, and especially later, the Reno gambling business underwent a transition that influenced the entire state. Following the example of Raymond I. Smith, the founder of Harolds Club, casino owners began to advertise their establishments in other states. Smith took the initiative on hundreds of roadside billboards across the nation, with illustrations of covered wagons rushing to Reno. The advertisements did not mention gambling, but implied that fun and excitement awaited the traveler at this desert mecca. Smith also broke with tradition in hiring women dealers for his table games.

For thirty years after the war, Reno's city government made an effort to confine its gambling casinos to the downtown center of the city, with a "red-line" policy enclosing about a dozen blocks where table games could be licensed. This policy applied with few exceptions until the late 1970s, when a sudden surge in casino business and a desire to emulate Las Vegas brought a rash of new establishments along the main highways out of the city in all four directions.

There had been, from the early 1950s, a small gambling center in Sparks, and that railroad community shared the gradual growth of Reno in commerce and tourism. It became common, as they merged along their several miles of common boundary, to refer to the metropolitan region as Reno/Sparks.

Reno/Sparks capitalized on its location halfway between Lake Tahoe and Pyramid Lake early in the postwar period. Once automobile traffic became heavier after wartime gasoline rationing came to an end, the business community promoted the possibilities of winter sports, and several ski resorts became highly popular in the nearby Sierra. This effort culminated in the staging of the 1960 Winter Olympics at nearby Squaw Valley, and the entire Lake Tahoe–Reno/Sparks–Carson City area enjoyed a cornucopia of press coverage about its attractions. Television coverage of the games gave the region a bonanza of favorable publicity relating to the natural beauty of the area.

During the same period, California and the U.S. government were

*Scenic view of Lake Tahoe. (Nevada Historical Society)*

completing the interstate freeway across the Sierra Nevada, a result of the Interstate Highway Act of 1956, sponsored by President Dwight Eisenhower. The freeway replaced the narrow, steep slopes of old Highway 40, making it possible for tourists to rely upon open roads through most of the winter season. Businessmen felt triumphant when they approached their goal of making Reno/Sparks and Carson City a year-round destination for tourists. By the late 1960s, the reputation of Lake Tahoe as a resort center for outdoor sports in both winter and summer—as well as for showrooms and gambling—was well established.

When the Reno/Sparks area population approached 250,000 near the end of the 1980s, much community energy was being directed toward downtown redevelopment. As in many cities across America, time had dealt harshly with the city centers; many older commercial buildings fell vacant, having lost their occupants and their clients to the suburban shopping centers. Streets and sidewalks showed the effects of wear, and the unfortunate urban "street people" were in evidence. An official city report said that "economic stagnation and decline threaten future vitality of the downtown unless efforts are made to reduce and eliminate causes of blight." The city government pointed to such factors as age and obsolescence of facilities, existence of flood hazards, inadequate provision for open spaces, and lack of adequate planning in explaining this situation. The proliferation of suburban shopping malls also accounted for the problems downtown.

In 1983, the Reno municipal government designated a redevelopment zone of more than sixty blocks in the center of the downtown area. The purpose was to make the entire section more pleasant for investment, for the arts and other cultural functions, for tourism, and for pedestrian-oriented activities. By 1989, the city had made important strides in completing its goal. In the meantime, Sparks also redesigned part of its central business area with a Victorian theme.

At the end of the 1990s, a sturdy hiker could still walk across Reno/Sparks from north to south or from east to west in a couple of hours, with the mountains always in view and—except for the periods of rush-hour traffic—with a sense that the high country and the friendly deserts were still close at hand. And one could still see, from nearly every perspective, the trembling leaves that had evoked Walter Clark's lyrical praise sixty years earlier. This corner of western Nevada is urbanized, but the urban factor has not yet overwhelmed the basic features that Frémont saw in the mid-nineteenth century.

*Reno skyline, 1996. (Reno News Bureau)*

## Las Vegas: The Evolution of a Metropolis

Until World War II, the history of contemporary Las Vegas seemed to be a reflection of Reno's experience. In 1940, the Federal Works Projects Administration published a book in which the description of the social life of Las Vegas was a portent of things to come:

> The town is particularly lively at night. Neon lights call attention to the bars, gambling and night clubs, in which Hollywood celebrities, miners, prospectors, divorcees, corporation presidents, cowboys, and little old maids bent on seeing life at last, add to the stacks of silver dollars and watch the whirl of roulette wheels, or splash ink over the horse keno slips. Some restaurants are crowded till dawn. (*Nevada: A Guide to the Silver State*, p. 183.)

This was a quaint phenomenon in 1940, but strange only if one had not seen Reno. Las Vegas (with only about 8,500 people) did not then rival its northern sister as a divorce and gambling center. It was still clustered around the railroad depot at Main and Fremont streets where a new station had been constructed in 1940, and most of the gambling and other business activity had concentrated nearby. In local business circles, there was much concern that it would not be able to recover the momentum that it lost when the construction of Hoover Dam ended in 1935. Some thought, in 1938 and 1939, that the depression might tighten its noose on Las Vegas as it had on the mining towns.

At the beginning of the 1940s Las Vegas broke out of its isolated, small-town cocoon in three directions and with three new types of economic activity at once. First, new resorts and gambling houses appeared on the southwest outskirts beyond the city limits. Second, the federal government opened a vast new magnesium plant on the Boulder Highway. Third, a military gunnery range—the ancestor of Nellis Air Force Base—went into operation north of the city. All these additions to the Las Vegas economy started within a two-year period.

## The Origins of the Strip

During the war years, the "wild west" tradition that Las Vegas had adopted from Reno—the resort-saloon-gambling business—made a leapfrog expansion beyond the city, out along the highway toward Los

Angeles. The now-famous "Strip" was born almost accidentally in 1941 and 1942 when two roadside entertainment centers appeared just beyond the municipal boundary on U.S. Highway 91, offering landscaping, western flavor, gambling, and stage productions. Historian Eugene P. Moehring of the University of Nevada, Las Vegas, has pointed out that this was a crucial development in the city's evolution. A third, a fourth, and a fifth resort hotel-casino appeared by 1951, forming the basis of a new suburban grouping—linked to Las Vegas economically, but politically separate from it. Unlike Reno but like most larger American cities, Las Vegas had burst its original municipal boundaries and spawned distinct satellites; it had exploded outward, rather than expanding more or less symmetrically, as Reno had done.

Out on Highway 91, the new casinos were under the jurisdiction of the Clark County government rather than the city of Las Vegas. The fact that there was more available space, low county (as opposed to higher city) property taxes, and less restrictive licensing regulations beyond the borders of Las Vegas were the crucial factors. The Strip was closer to the airport that eventually became McCarran International, and it had the first chance to attract the automobile traffic from southern California that expanded during the postwar years. So there grew up a complement and a competitor to the "glitter gulch" of neon-garlanded casinos on Fremont Street. The construction of Interstate 15 along the Old Spanish Trail also made it possible to bring the heavy volume of automobile traffic to and from southern California in only a few hours. The larger property owners on the Strip successfully resisted annexation to the city by persuading the county commissioners to create a separate town government, thus fragmenting local political authority.

For forty years the Las Vegas tourist bonanza seemed to be a self-propelled economic machine; the more it prospered, the more investments and big-name entertainers flowed in. The more the community gambled on its future in the old Nevada way, the greater its financial rewards. In 1959, the local governments opened the largest single-story convention center in the world near the Strip, and they immediately grossed more than $20 million in convention revenue—several times the cost of the facility.

No place in America was more successful in attracting tourists and encouraging them to spend money. By the late 1990s, Las Vegas offered more than 100,000 hotel and motel rooms and a booming convention business. The population of the metropolitan area passed the one-million mark in 1995, and the central city was still growing at a rapid pace while most other large cities in the country were losing residents. The expansion was greatest in the southern and western parts of the valley, in regions adjacent to the Strip. As historian Eugene Moehring wrote, "the futuristic Strip 'Los Angelized' the metropolitan area [of Las Vegas]."

Many challenges confronted the sprawling metropolis: problems relating to race relations, crime, human services, and environmental quality. These will be discussed in later chapters. But here it must be emphasized again that it was not merely the tourist-gambling economy that accounted for the Las Vegas urban explosion of the 1940s and afterwards.

## Henderson and Nellis

In the meantime, two other leapfrog activities had started in 1941–1942 and stimulated new communities on the opposite side of Las Vegas from the Strip—out along the Boulder Highway to the southeast and near the Salt Lake highway to the northeast. Las Vegas suddenly began to have the community neighbors that it had lacked since the founding of the town. As Moehring wrote, "Fifteen years of frantic federal spending changed Las Vegas forever" (*Resort City in the Sunbelt*, p. 40).

In the first case, the cause was the development of the Basic Magnesium plant and the establishment of Henderson 13 miles from Las Vegas. Shortly before the Japanese attack on Pearl Harbor in 1941, the United States government recognized that this country had an acute shortage of magnesium, a metal of crucial importance in the manufacture of airplanes and incendiary bombs. Nevada had a large supply of magnesite and brucite, the necessary crude ore for magnesium, at Gabbs in the mountains of northern Nye County 300 miles away. The decision to build a huge processing plant in the Las Vegas Valley was influenced by the abundant supply of electrical power and water available at Hoover Dam. In addition, President Roosevelt favored decentralization of the defense industry, and the inland location seemed to be more secure than potential California sites.

Construction of the Basic Magnesium plant began in 1941 and production started less than a year later. The government built a thousand new houses, together with service establishments and schools, on the adjacent desert. The Henderson–Las Vegas area suddenly had a payroll for 10,000 men because of this industry early in the war—a larger employment base than any mining town of the state had ever known. Well before the war ended, the Basic Magnesium plant, the largest in the world of its kind, exceeded the production requirements of the government for this metal.

The construction of this facility pointed the way toward the solution of the most serious problem facing the Las Vegas Valley in 1941 — a growing shortage of water. As we have seen, the Colorado River Compact of 1922 promised Nevada 300,000 acre-feet per year of the flow of the Colorado River. However, until Lake Mead had formed behind Hoover Dam, there was no practical way for Nevada to get the water that had been allotted to it, and even then costly pumping equipment to carry the water up into the valley was too expensive for local or state governments. Las Vegas had depended since the beginning on the water that flowed from natural springs or could be pumped from rather shallow wells, but by 1940 these sources were already overtaxed for a community of 10,000 people. Part of the Basic-Henderson construction involved pumping millions of gallons of water per day from Lake Mead across the mountains. Much of the flow initially went for industry purposes, but in time more of it was available for domestic uses. After the war, the Basic plant became the property of the state of Nevada and eventually of private companies, and Henderson evolved into Nevada's largest and most diverse industrial city. By the late 1990s it had a population of more than 175,000 people.

The development of the military air base that was eventually named Nellis (for Lt. William H. Nellis of Searchlight, who died in World War II) was more gradual but even more decisive in the economic growth of Las Vegas Valley. Also, in 1941 before America's entry into the war, the U.S. Army chose a small air express runway 9 miles northeast of Las Vegas as the locale for a gunnery school for some of its pilots, largely due to the influence of Senator Pat McCarran. The empty desert space nearby and the normally good year-round flying conditions made this an ideal locale for trainees learning to fly fighter planes. Within two years several thousand airmen had received their instruction there.

Like Stead Air Force Base near Reno, Nellis underwent deactivation following the war, and reactivation a few years later when the Cold War led to American rearmament. During the Korean conflict in the early 1950s and under the jurisdiction of the U.S. Air Force, Nellis became the largest military fighter training base in the nation. In the middle 1980s, more than 12,000 employees worked there.

## The Atomic Test Site

The fourth major contributor to the contemporary Las Vegas phenomenon—after the gambling-tourism explosion, the Henderson industrial
growth, and the Nellis air base—was the opening of the Nevada Test Site
for experimental work on atomic weapons. This began in 1950 almost
ten years after the first three, and it brought to southern Nevada another
horde of skilled engineers, investigators, and planners on the forefront
of scientific experimentation. It also brought federal budgets amounting
to billions of dollars and huge payrolls. The atomic scientists concentrated their efforts on a 1,300-square-mile site located about 65 miles
northwest of Las Vegas.

Testing of atomic weapons on the Nevada desert began in January
1951, and during the next four years the Atomic Energy Commission
detonated more than forty bombs, mostly on the surface or above the
ground. People hundreds of miles away routinely saw the light and felt
the vibrations from the explosions, and once again Las Vegas basked in
the publicity of a unique new experiment.

After a two-year lull in testing at the Nevada site between 1955 and
1957, a new series of experiments began. As they proceeded and as
the British and Soviet governments started their own comparable programs, controversy arose about the level of radioactive pollution that
was being released into the atmosphere. Nevadans, who had occasionally been asked to wear badges to monitor the amount of fallout caused
by the tests, generally accepted governmental assurances that they were
safe—at least in the 1950s and 1960s. Nevertheless, because of public
and scientific concerns, following the signing of an international agreement in 1963, testing was routinely done underground in vast tunnels
and chambers that had been excavated for that purpose. Thus another
category of skills, including those of Nevada's miners from the northern
camps, came into demand.

In fact, an entirely new kind of "camp" appeared on the desert at the
south edge of the test site. Camp Mercury was built by the government
to provide housing and basic services for those who worked at the site.
This camp, like the entire test site, was subjected to close security restrictions to protect the public and to seal the area from potential spies
and intruders.

By the late 1980s, about 8,000 people had jobs with the Department of
Energy or with contractors and agencies that worked with it at the test
site. Many lived in Las Vegas and rode buses to and from their work each

day, even though in some cases this meant travel of a hundred miles each way and several hours on the road.

## The Quest for Other Industries

Even though the economic history of Las Vegas seemed to be clearly successful in retrospect, the city's business leaders often felt a sense of frustration because their area did less well than other Sunbelt cities, such as Phoenix and Albuquerque, in attracting conventional industries. The fact that it did not have a well-developed institution of higher education until the 1970s, that it could not use its full allotment of Colorado River water until 1982, that it had no ready supply of natural gas and (in spite of the proximity of Hoover Dam) a shortage of electrical power available for industrial use—all these factors made the valley less attractive to potential private investors. And the reputation for crime associated with the gambling business had an unfavorable influence in the conventional financial circles of the nation.

In addition, according to Eugene Moehring, the city's search for a broader industrial base was stymied until the 1960s by an

old elite—consisting mainly of longtime businessmen who, though meaning well, were novices at big-time city building. . . . These leaders, while eager to promote the area, nevertheless tended to view urban problems through a small-town lens. To some extent, the steady growth of Las Vegas's resort economy was enough progress for them. (Moehring, *Resort City in the Sunbelt*, pp. 229–230).

## The Worldwide Reputation

So the post-1940 Las Vegas became not one city but many, a metropolis in the original Greek sense of that term. It was the mother city, or at least the elder sister, of a cluster of communities and industries. It was far more diverse and diversified than most people who knew only about its glittering show business could appreciate, but not as diversified as its thoughtful citizens wanted it to be.

It was show business and the entertainers who made Las Vegas famous, in spite of some of the negative publicity associated with gambling. The movie stars, comedians, and rock artists marched through in clusters. Massive stage shows formed a central part of the ordinary scene, with casts and crews rivaling those of Paris and New York. To "play Vegas" became the highest aspiration of a generation of young performing artists. McCarran Airport opened new runways in 1963, capable of handling more than one hundred flights a day.

Sporting events were a speciality of those who promoted Las Vegas most effectively, and here there were some encouraging precedents from upstate. Boxing matches had long been used by Nevada towns to attract attention to themselves. Carson City witnessed the championship match between Bob Fitzsimmons and James J. Corbett in 1897. The much-publicized Joe Gans–Battling Nelson match in Goldfield in 1906 did much to promote that town in the national press. Jack Johnson and Jim Jeffries fought for the world heavyweight championship in Reno in 1910. Las Vegas followed these examples in the contemporary era with a vengeance.

The first important event of this kind for Las Vegas came in 1965, when Mohammed Ali successfully defended his heavyweight title against Floyd Patterson at the Convention Center. Thirteen years later, Ali lost his title to Leon Spinks, also in Las Vegas. After 1980, Las Vegas became the favorite site in the nation for the staging of heavyweight matches, and bouts were held nearly every year, with massive electronic audiences catching glimpses of Las Vegas as well as of the fights.

The individual who brought Las Vegas its strangest publicity in the late 1960s was the billionaire industrialist Howard Hughes. One of the outstanding aircraft designers and contractor-builders of World War II airplanes for the U.S. government, Hughes also produced movies and owned a major airline. As early as the 1940s, Hughes had made large purchases of land in Las Vegas Valley. In later years these areas became urban suburbs known as Green Valley and Sun City–Summerlin. In later years he made Las Vegas the base for his vast financial operations. He became a recluse and chose one of the Strip hotels as a place for his intense seclusion from 1966 until 1970. During that time, he transferred hundreds of millions of dollars into Nevada and built an empire consisting of seven hotels and casinos, an airport and an airline, a television station, and hundreds of mining claims.

At first Nevada's politicians and businessmen welcomed Hughes and his millions, as they had traditionally done with all investors who seemed likely to stimulate the economy. The Hughes organization did appear eager to improve Nevada's reputation in the gambling business by crowding out some of the suspected underworld elements, and it made generous contributions to the University of Nevada's medical school and community colleges. But Hughes soon proved to be the strangest oligarch that Nevada had ever attracted. His self-imposed isolation and the very size of his financial empire in Nevada, estimated by some at $500 million, made it difficult for the state agencies responsible for gambling control to deal with him and to understand what was happening within his sprawling organization. When his business empire was rocked by nasty internal fighting and he seemed not to be in control, the nationwide publicity became an embarrassment.

Late one night in 1970, Hughes secretly left Nevada in disguise, just as he had arrived, and spent some of his last years hiding in Nassau or London. The struggle over his Nevada wealth and other holdings did not end even with his death in 1976, and the Hughes organization continued to play an important role in the economy, especially that of southern Nevada.

No city in America had gained a more glamorous or a more contra-dictory reputation in the sixty years between 1940 and 2000. Las Vegas rivaled New York, Hollywood, and Paris as a center for dazzling enter-tainment and elegant living. Its casinos and theaters attracted tens of millions of visitors every year, and it became common for Americans traveling abroad to hear foreigners say that the place they most wanted to see — or return to — was Las Vegas.

But for Nevadans, the razzle-dazzle of Las Vegas had become com-monplace. The "locals" typically regarded the casinos and stage shows as the domain of the tourists — something outsiders noticed and wrote about in a distorted way, and which local residents rarely indulged in. Behind and beyond the neon in the Las Vegas Valley, a population of more than one million people was performing essentially the same do-mestic roles as other Americans, and those who looked closely at Las Vegas seemed surprised to discover this fact.

Fifty years after the beginnings of the Strip and Henderson and Nellis, and forty years after the opening of the Nevada Test Site, Las Vegans could legitimately emphasize, instead of their status as an isolated oasis, their situation as a hub city of the booming Southwest. Their city was setting standards that many cities in various parts of the world sought to follow. During the 1990s the population of Clark County grew beyond the one-million mark; about 420,000 residents lived within the city limits. Ex-pansive and expensive business and residential districts stretched west-ward toward the Spring Mountain Range where the early Mormons had first looked for their timber and where they tried to develop their ill-fated lead mine in 1856.

But back in the center of the city, there were serious problems of urban blight on the very edge of the downtown resort area. East Fremont Street beyond the Casino Center was gradually becoming a slum. South Fifth Street, renamed Las Vegas Boulevard, had several unsightly blocks of decay and clutter. Like many wealthy cities of past eras—Rome, Paris, London, and New York—this new metropolis had to learn how to cope with urban deterioration, poverty, and crime, even as it enjoyed a higher level of wealth and a faster rate of growth than any other city in its class.

Las Vegas approached its aesthetic problems with a determined strategy based upon the concepts of modern municipal planning. In 1985, the Las Vegas City Council committed the community to the re-building of the central part of the downtown business district that had begun to crumble. The planners designated a 2.5-square-mile section— essentially the old original township of Senator William A. Clark—for comprehensive redevelopment, with earliest attention directed at the areas of greatest decay. The original railroad yards west of Main Street— including a 300-acre site that had remained largely undeveloped—was designated a zone for high-quality commercial and tourist facilities, with emphasis on visual appeal. In the deteriorating region north and south of Fremont Street (in the vicinity of Fourth and Fifth streets), city planners conceived of a "festival marketplace" called Winchester Station. The objective was to transform the entire downtown region into an attractive showplace.

As could be expected in such a diversified community, the basic idea generated controversy. One problem with this approach was that some private property owners who were reluctant to sell their stores or homes might be required to do so, at prices they considered inadequate, in order to allow new commercial enterprises to rise. The government's right of eminent domain—the right to condemn private property for public use—has long been recognized as an essential power of cities and states. But the condemnation of private property to erect casinos was a concept of which Las Vegas was a pioneer.

The growth and expansion of Las Vegas has obliterated most of the structural reminders of its railroad-era past. By the late 1980s the visual heritage of old Las Vegas was confined to a handful of historic sites that had survived from the pre-1940 period. A fragment of the old Mormon Fort of 1855 remained, and the 1989 legislature took steps to begin some reclamation and archeological work on that site. Lorenzi Park had been transformed into the home of the Nevada Historical Society and Museum

*Las Vegas Strip, 1997. (Las Vegas News Bureau)*

headquarters for southern Nevada. The Las Vegas High School on south Seventh Street and the neighborhood surrounding it continued to reflect the architectural charm and variety of the 1930s and 1940s. The 1933 neo-classical federal building/post office had been designated as the center of a historical district. Otherwise, Las Vegas managed to save few public monuments from the earlier eras.

At the other end of the spectrum, Las Vegas was recognized as a national leader in innovative architectural design, with its garish high-rise casinos and display signs, its neon extravagance, its defiant spreads of tropical landscaping on the bleak desert. The nation has been "learning from Las Vegas," as one group of architectural analysts wrote in 1977.

Those problems and challenges that Las Vegas could face as a city — relating to municipal services and planning — it handled reasonably well in the 1990s. For those that required state or federal assistance, as in gambling control, air pollution, and regional land-use planning, the record was not so clear.

The census figures for 2000 revealed that Washoe County's population had risen to 339,486, an increase of more than 33 percent since 1990. The growth in Clark County was even more imposing, to 1,375,765 — an increase of more than 85 percent. Most expansion occurred in the cities or their suburbs. Nevada once again faced the consequences of being the fastest growing state in the Union, with all the challenges that came with that fact.

## Suggested Supplementary Reading

Castleman, Deke. *Las Vegas*. Photography by Michael Yamashita. 2nd ed. Oakland: Compass American Guides, 1992.

Davies, Richard O., ed. *The Maverick Spirit: Building the New Nevada*. Reno: University of Nevada Press, 1999.

Hopkins, A. D., and K. J. Evans, eds. *The First 100: Portraits of the Men and Women Who Shaped Las Vegas*. Las Vegas: Huntington Press, 1999.

Hulse, James W. *Forty Years in the Wilderness: Impressions of Nevada, 1940–1980*. Reno: University of Nevada Press, 1986.

Moehring, Eugene P. *Resort City in the Sunbelt: Las Vegas 1930–2000*. Reno: University of Nevada Press, 2000.

———. "Suburban Resorts and the Triumph of Las Vegas," in Wilbur S. Shepperson, ed., *East of Eden, West of Zion: Essays on Nevada*. Reno: University of Nevada Press, 1989.

Myrick, David F. *Railroads of Nevada and Eastern California*. Vol. I, *The North-*

*ern Roads*; Vol. II, *The Southern Roads*. 1962-63. Reprint, Reno: University of Nevada Press, 1992.

Paher, Stanley W. *Las Vegas: As It Began — As It Grew*. Las Vegas: Nevada Publications, 1971.

Parker, Robert E. "Urban Growth Management in Southern Nevada," in Dennis L. Soden and Eric Herzik, eds., *Towards 2000: Public Policy in Nevada*. Dubuque: Kendall Hunt, 1997.

Rowley, William D. *Reno: Hub of the Washoe Country*. Woodland Hills, Calif: Windsor Publications, 1984.

Sheehan, Jack, ed. *The Players: The Men Who Made Las Vegas*. Reno: University of Nevada Press, 1997.

Stevens, Joseph E. *Hoover Dam: An American Adventure*. Norman: University of Oklahoma Press, 1988.

Titus, A. Costandina. *Bombs in the Backyard: Atomic Testing and American Politics*. Reno: University of Nevada Press, 1986.

Townley, John M. *Tough Little Town on the Truckee: Reno 1868-1900*. Vol. I. Reno: Great Basin Studies Center, 1983.

Venturi, Robert, Denise Scott Brown, and Steven Izenour. *Learning from Las Vegas: The Forgotten Symbolism of Architectural Form*. Cambridge: MIT Press, 1977.

# 15

# Land and Water

## *Changing Policies and Uses*

L ET US return to the basic thesis of this narrative: the region named Nevada is a desert land, and the society in Nevada came into existence, survived, and evolved by a series of adaptations to that condition. The Native Americans, prospectors, ranchers, and town builders all made strategic decisions about how to deal with this rugged terrain. All fashioned their communities around the fact that the land was vast and arid and the water scarce.

There were many more people bearing the label "Nevadan" in 1990 than there were in 1864, or 1900, or even 1960, so the uses of the land and water have been a matter of continuous concern. Nevadans have repeatedly been challenged to make new discoveries about the possibilities that their state offers.

To be effective, land and water policies should be interlocking, but in the Far West they have evolved in separate political jurisdictions. The basic land policies have been made in Washington, because the federal government controls the public domain, the forests, and the military-defense installations that cover about 86 percent of Nevada. But water policies have traditionally been a matter of state and local administration, at least until the 1980s. Thus there is an inherent conflict between planners, users, and different levels of government.

# The Search for a Land Policy: Part Two

It is a fundamental fact of Nevada history that the state and federal governments have never developed a satisfactory land policy that had broad public support. As we saw in chapter 10, Nevada's land policy evolved by a process of trial and error during the first thirty years of statehood, based upon existing federal grants. From the earliest days, both federal and state governments encouraged settlement and "improvement" of the land. When Nevada became a state, a settler could try to get some acreage in one of several ways. A family could simply occupy a site, start a home, and indicate an intention to use it; by doing so an individual acquired a "squatter's right." This was encouraged by the Pre-emptive Act passed by Congress in 1841, which said a squatter could claim up to 160 acres at a minimum price of $1.25 per acre. Some people persisted and eventually got title to their land; many others never "proved-up on," or improved, their acres, and eventually they moved onward in the continuous migration. The title to the land usually reverted to the government.

The same principle applied for miners, who could stake a claim as soon as they found a lead, file a statement with the district or county recorder, and thereby obtain title to the mineral rights. The claim continued to be valid as long as the locator worked on it regularly in accordance with local regulations. Senator Stewart of Nevada wrote the bill, which became law in 1866, assuring that local mining regulations would be valid in the western states.

A similar pattern eventually emerged with regard to water rights: a person established property rights to a flow of water simply by diverting it from the streambed and putting it to "beneficial use" over a period of time. So it was also on the livestock ranges; the herders made their claim to a spread by putting their cattle or sheep on it, and thinking about the legal questions later.

There was another way to obtain land title in the earliest years of settlement—directly from the federal government. A pioneer settler in some parts of the West could buy land at a public auction, if and when the U.S. General Land Office held one, but this was practically unknown in Nevada. There was also the possibility of taking up a homestead under the famous act of 1862. This offered a person ownership of 160 acres after five years of residence and payment of a fee, if the settler had proved up on the parcel. But 160 acres was not nearly enough to raise livestock or to produce a marketable crop in most parts of Nevada.

A third option available to a settler was to get a land title from the state, based upon one of its land grants. We have seen (in chapter 10) that this option did not help many people because the land was hard to sell and Nevada "traded" more than half of its 3.9-million-acre school grant back to the federal government in exchange for a more flexible plan of selection. Few settlers were able to take advantage of this opportunity before the turn of the century.

The improvement in the general economic picture after 1900, with the opening of Tonopah, Goldfield, the White Pine copper industry, and renewed interest in the possibilities of irrigating limited parts of the desert, eventually reversed the land-use trend of pioneer days. Much of the reverted land that had been claimed and abandoned by the original pioneers found a market after 1904, but that did not help those who had lost their property in the depression of the 1890s.

By 1900, the basic land-use map of Nevada was fixed for nearly a hundred years. Nevada has about 70.7 million acres of land. Of that, the Central Pacific (later the Southern Pacific) Railroad owned more than 5 million; only about 2.7 million acres had been transferred to the state for selection and sale to private owners. About 86 percent of the land within Nevada's borders remained under the control of the federal government or the Indian tribes—and little had changed in the 1980s. The Bureau of Land Management of the U.S. Department of the Interior, successor to the Public Land Office, assumed responsibility for administering more than 46.3 million acres in 1946. Large portions of the mountain terrain—more than 5.1 million acres—had been placed under the Forest Service of the U.S. Department of Agriculture.

## Water Policy: The Carson River, 1864–1902

For the first few years after 1864, Nevada legislators and judges tried to handle water disputes according to the laws of England and eastern states. The principle of *riparian rights* governed property rights in water matters. This meant that a settler was entitled to use a stream that flowed through or adjacent to his or her land, but must leave it undiminished for other users downstream. In Nevada's canyons and valleys, this was obviously impossible because for land to be productive, a stream usually had to be dammed, diverted, and spread out across many acres.

From the beginning of the state's history, bitter quarrels arose over water rights. The earliest notable disputes occurred along the Carson River, because that area attracted the first settlers and this was also the watershed where several large Comstock mills operated. When the ranchers built ditches upstream in the Carson Valley, they took water that would otherwise have flowed downward to the mills.

Even before Nevada became a state in October 1864, the struggle between the Comstock mill owners, led by William Sharon, and the Carson Valley ranchers came before the territorial courts. In dry years, there was simply not enough water for all users. At first the courts tried to apply the riparian principle, but when it was interpreted in a manner to deny water to farmers who had been using it effectively for many years (*Van Sickle v. Haines,* 7 Nevada 249, 1872), a popular and legislative reaction followed, and Nevada gradually moved toward a different principle.

This alternate policy, which evolved in the American West, became known as the *doctrine of prior appropriation.* The standard for settling disputes in this case asserted that the first person to apply water to a beneficial use gained a property right to the amount of water used, and one retained that right as long as that use continued. Later users of a stream had lower priority rights, based upon the time when the beneficial use began. In times of water shortage, if there was not enough for all claimants, those with the later appropriation dates were obligated by law to stop using the water, even if this meant their crops and livestock died. The oldest rights had to be honored first, in order of date of appropriation. The federal and state courts held, however, that the principle of beneficial use did not confer the right to waste water. A famous case which consolidated much of this principle after more than twenty-five years of intermittent litigation was *Union Mill and Mining Co. v. Dangberg* (81 Federal Reporter, 73, 1897).

The doctrine of prior appropriation did not apply generally in communities founded by members of the Latter-day Saints church. They employed a communal, cooperative system for sharing the scarce resource. Mormons generally did not divide the rights in strict chronological order; rather they divided the settlers into "primary" and "secondary" users, who had older and newer rights, respectively. And within each of these categories, all water was divided equally, or proportionately according to land holding, on a rotating basis. When the flow of the stream decreased, the amount of water available to each of the members of the community was reduced to assure that all shared equally in the benefits or the shortage—or at least this was the intention. At times, the Mormons had their water rustlers and water wars, just as their nonchurch counterparts did, but not as often.

The doctrine of prior appropriation proved to be an effective rule for settling disputes over water in most parts of the state until the early twentieth century—or so long as the population of the state was small and the claims for water relatively uncomplicated. But as Nevada became more fully developed and as the federal government became more actively involved in managing western resources, complex new problems arose.

## The Newlands Project: Fallon and Fernley

At the beginning of the twentieth century, when the mining booms of Tonopah and Goldfield were in full swing, western Nevada enjoyed an economic bonus in the form of one of the first federal experiments in arid-land reclamation.

The lower portion of the Carson River Valley had been one of the first successful agricultural districts in the western Great Basin, not far behind Genoa about 30 miles upstream. Farmers had established successful hay-raising enterprises in the 1860s, selling their services and produce to the Pony Express riders, the builders of the first telegraph lines, the emigrants, and the Comstock mining towns. But the numbers of those who could make a living by these means on the lower Carson were very small. Only about a dozen families had been able to establish themselves there by 1870. For a number of years, Churchill, one of the original nine counties but with no large-scale mining industry, had the smallest population of any county in the state. In 1880, it had only 479 residents and in 1900 only 830.

The Carson River region—along with the rest of the state—suffered from a prolonged drought in the late 1880s and 1890s; both the hay-raising and the cattle-grazing operations felt the pinch. As the nineteenth century ended with the mining business still languishing, Nevadans became more committed to the idea of a large-scale irrigation project that would store the excess water during the wet years for use during the dry seasons. But the impoverished state and local governments had no means of achieving this, and it was too costly for private landowners.

Senator Stewart had been an advocate of this idea for many years and tried to convince Congress in 1888 to donate irrigable public land to the arid western states to assist their development. The senator became involved in a nasty political battle with John Wesley Powell, the flamboyant director of the U.S. Geological Survey, who wanted to reserve western water for national purposes. The Stewart-Powell conflict was a fight which everyone lost, because Powell was forced to resign his position and Stewart could not get his preferred water policy passed in a badly divided Congress.

The most effective champion of federally financed reclamation was Congressman Francis G. Newlands, who made his home in Reno by 1888 and who studied the entire water and land system of western Nevada. Newlands was the most successful congressman in the state's history, but it required several years for him to win support for his ideas. Soon after his arrival in Nevada, he had conceived of projects that would divert waters of the Carson River onto arid land, but he had met much opposition from ranchers in Carson Valley. In the meantime, he acquired some strategic lands along the Carson and Truckee rivers for himself.

When Newlands entered politics, he identified his politics with the Silver Crusade in 1892 and was elected to Congress, winning more than 70 percent of the votes cast. For several years he was a political ally of Senator Stewart in the leadership of the Silver movement, but when that cause failed, he returned with new vigor to his earlier interest in water resource development. Within a few years he was able to change the economic map of western Nevada.

In 1901, during Newlands's fifth term in the House, an unprecedented new opportunity appeared for his irrigation concepts. When Theodore Roosevelt became president of the United States, there was, for the first time, a man in the White House who believed in aggressive national policies to develop the arid regions of the West. With his help, and by adopting some ideas from his congressional colleagues, Newlands was able to draft the legislation which went into the Reclamation Act of 1902. He also won the honor of having his home territory—the Carson and Truckee basins—selected for one of the first projects of the newly established United States Reclamation Service.

The plan identified about 450,000 bleak desert acres in the vast valley into which the Carson River emptied, and designated it for small farms (160 acres maximum for each individual). It was to be irrigated not only by water from the Carson River, part of which would be held in a proposed reservoir upstream, but also by approximately half the flow of the Truckee River, which was to be diverted from its channel into the Carson River basin. Some of this land was to be used on the benchlands east of Wadsworth (where the new town of Fernley appeared), but most was to be carried further east to the new community of Fallon—63 miles east of Reno and more than 30 miles east of Wadsworth.

For western Nevada this seemed to be the long-awaited deliverance from economic troubles. Within a year, hundreds of men were building Derby Dam on the Truckee River and the 30-mile canal to take the water into the Carson River. The construction camps at the dam and along the canal were as violent and rowdy as the older mining towns had been. Scores of people squatted on the desert acreage of Fallon even before the U.S. Reclamation Service offered plots for sale. By 1905, the Newlands Project was delivering water to the new farms—but not enough to serve all those who had bought or broken ground. The public response to this new program was greater than the government was able to accommodate.

During the first few years, the Newlands Project planners encountered innumerable problems. Efforts to acquire storage rights in Lake Tahoe for future use brought bitter opposition and prolonged lawsuits from lakeshore property owners and upstream users. The soil of the Carson Valley around Fallon was high in alkali and poorly drained, so it required much more investment and ground preparation than expected. Early farmers raised primarily alfalfa hay which brought a good price in the mining towns, until the mining towns went into borrasca. The Reclamation Service soon urged farmers to diversify—to raise more dairy herds and more types of fruits and vegetables, which eventually many of them did successfully.

In 1911–1913, construction crews built the crucial Lahontan retaining dam, thus making it possible to hold as much as 300,000 acre-feet of water and to generate electrical power. By 1914, Fallon and Fernley had become reasonably prosperous, orderly towns, comprising several hundred farming families and the usual service establishments.

The Newlands Project never served nearly the number of acres or people that its designers intended. The initial plan for 450,000 acres of reclaimed land was adjusted to 87,500 acres in 1925–1926 because experience had shown that no more than that could be irrigated from the two rivers. Whether the Newlands Project was a success in view of these figures is a debatable question because there has been interminable litigation and argument about whether this was the best use of the water that otherwise would have been available to the Paiute Reservation on Pyramid Lake or upstream users on the Carson and Truckee rivers. But thousands of new homes, newly cultivated acres, and more farm produce than Nevada had ever known before resulted from this pioneering experiment in desert irrigation. And over the years the users of the Newlands Project waters gradually repaid the federal government for its investment.

## The Truckee River, Lake Tahoe, and Pyramid Lake

The history of the Truckee River in the past hundred years demonstrates how protracted the struggle over the water from a small river can become. During the nineteenth century, when Reno had fewer than 15,000 people, the normal flow of this small waterway from Lake Tahoe to Pyramid Lake served the region and the people well, but problems were already appearing. Scores of fine ranches existed in the Truckee Meadows south and east of Reno, with a network of ditches to divert water outward to the pastures and hay fields. Lake Tahoe was already becoming a resort area, electrical power stations were appearing at various points along the river, lumbering operations were dumping excessive amounts of polluting sawdust along the river, and Pyramid Lake Paiutes complained that in some years not enough water reached their reservation to enable their farmers to irrigate the acres that had been set aside for their crops and cattle.

The problems escalated with the establishment of the Newlands Project, which as we have seen diverted about half of the Truckee's flow southeastward to serve the new communities of Fernley and Fallon and adjacent farms. In 1913, the U.S. government filed a "friendly lawsuit" to establish what appropriated water rights existed along the Truckee River in Nevada and to learn how much unappropriated water was available for the Newlands Project. United States attorneys represented both the Bureau of Reclamation and the Pyramid Lake Indians.

This was the beginning of the famous *Orr Ditch Case,* which lasted from 1913 until 1944 and then seemed to be resolved by agreement among nearly all the parties according to the doctrine of prior appropriation. In 1973, however, the entire controversy over the distribution of Truckee waters arose again because of complaints by the Pyramid Lake Paiutes that their ancient fishery rights had not been sufficiently protected, and the U.S. government filed suit against all others with water rights. This case finally went to the U.S. Supreme Court in 1983—seventy years after the original Truckee River suit had been filed. By the time the litigation had run its course, tens of thousands of water users were involved. Most Nevada interests won their case, and the allotments of water assigned in the *Orr Ditch* ruling were confirmed. But the basic fact remained that in dry periods when the Sierra snowpack was inadequate, there was not enough water to meet the legal rights of everyone, even though several additional reservoirs had been constructed upstream in the 1930s, 1940s, and 1950s. Population growth ran ahead of the water resources of western Nevada and in most of the rest of the Far West.

The history and the problems of Lake Tahoe are intimately linked with those of the Truckee River. In the 1860s, a San Francisco business-man named Alexis von Schmidt acquired property rights to the Truckee outlet near the north shore of the lake. In 1870, he built a dam to raise the lake level about five feet and proposed to divert and sell the addi-tional stored water to central California and the Bay Area. It would have been a vast and costly reclamation project for that time and would have taken surplus water in the opposite direction from the natural chan-nel. Nevada water users effectively fought back to prevent this, but von Schmidt's dam, with some improvements, became a permanent feature of the Tahoe-Truckee system. Although it was puny by comparison with Hoover Dam and small even by comparison with the Lahontan Dam, it had major significance for the future of western Nevada.

During the water disputes over the Truckee, the size and use of the dam engaged the attention of all parties. As part of the *Orr Ditch* decree, the federal court set maximum and minimum levels of the lake to allow water to be stored during the wet winters for use in dry periods and to try to assure that property and the natural beauty of the Tahoe region would not be damaged by either too much or too little water.

Yet Tahoe continued to be threatened by uncontrolled commercial and residential growth along its ecologically delicate shoreline. Increas-ing pollution of the lake became evident in the 1960s as resort casinos, ski facilities, boating marinas, and other businesses and homes prolifer-ated. California and Nevada agreed to the creation of the Interstate Com-pact Commission in 1971 to try to manage growth more effectively and protect the land and water, but this compromise encountered trouble in Congress, and basic problems were still unresolved in 1989, despite repeated attempts to settle them. Voters of both Nevada and California first rejected and then approved large bond issues in the early 1980s to enable their governments to buy some of the sensitive private land for environmental protection.

At the other end of the Truckee River, the people who relied upon the resources of Pyramid Lake had a different kind of problem. The Pyramid Lake Paiutes, whose aboriginal home had been on the lower Truckee and near the lake, had watched their beloved waters recede as the upstream diversions occurred. The Paiutes who lived at Wadsworth, Nixon, and along the river between these two towns tried for decades to irrigate their small plots and catch and sell trout to local markets. Gradually the

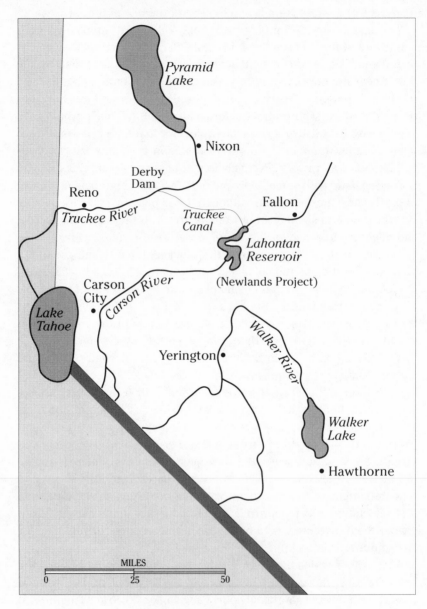

*Waterways of Western Nevada*

fisheries failed because of pollution, upstream diversions, and excessive fishing, and the agricultural opportunities were too few to support the entire band. In the 1970s more substantial federal support sought to reverse this trend by installing facilities to encourage the spawning runs of endangered fish populations.

Another downstream problem for the Truckee-Carson river complex involved the Stillwater Wildlife Management Area, a federal reserve northeast of Fallon. This marshland region is one of the important places used by migratory waterfowl on their north-south flights between Canada and Mexico. In recent years, the diminished flow of water into the refuge and upstream pollution have damaged the populations of pelicans, geese, and other wildlife—another instance of the costs of expanding human civilization on the natural environment.

In the meantime, as Reno-Sparks grew, thousands of residents resisted one reform that would ease the situation—the general installation of meters to measure the volume of water used by individual homes and businesses and to charge fees according to the quantity used. An archaic law from the 1920s prohibited such devices and made conservation more difficult to achieve, and wasteful practices were common throughout the valley.

## The Humboldt River Country

The Humboldt Basin communities had water and land problems, of course, but they did not reach the dimensions of those in the Truckee basin because there was not as much population pressure and not so diverse an economy as that of the Carson-Truckee watershed. Land-use patterns changed little between 1900 and 1980. Livestock raising and the affiliated activity of hay raising continued to be primary activities in the regions around Lovelock, Winnemucca, Battle Mountain, and Elko.

The basic water-rights questions on the Humboldt went before the Nevada State Engineer's office beginning in 1903, and they gradually worked their way through the courts during the next thirty years. In 1935, the Nevada Supreme Court issued the so-called Bartlett Decree, which established rights of all users according to the doctrine of prior appropriation. The Humboldt basin provided an example of how this water-distribution system could operate effectively.

Hundreds of farmers in the lower Humboldt valley—in the Big Meadows where the original pioneers had paused to rest and take on water before crossing the Forty Mile Desert—prospered at the turn of the century with their hay and cattle crops, and with the opening of new mining towns. Lovelock attracted enough new settlers to demand and get its own county—Pershing—in 1919. These same settlers watched their water supply dwindle in the 1920s as a result of drought and more upstream diversions.

In 1933, Lovelock valley ranchers took cooperative steps to meet their water problem. They borrowed money from the U.S. government, purchased upstream water rights, and prepared to store the additional water in a reservoir at the northern edge of their meadows. With government aid, they built the Rye Patch Dam in 1937, and the reservoir behind it provided insurance water for many dry seasons. During the next fifty years, the cost of this project was repaid several times in increased agricultural productivity in the Big Meadows.

Further up the river, Winnemucca and Humboldt County residents used their land and water resources effectively to generate a productive potato-raising business in the northern valleys, taking a cue from their neighbors in Oregon and Idaho. Winnemucca continued to be a livestock-shipping town and a contact point between Nevada and its northern neighbors, as it had been for a hundred years.

Battle Mountain likewise enjoyed a modest prosperity, based primarily upon its traditional railroad-and-livestock economy. Since it had continued to grow while Austin, its elder sister in Lander County, declined, the citizens of Battle Mountain repeatedly tried to win the county seat. Finally, in 1979, when the population of Battle Mountain exceeded that of Austin by more than four to one, the legislature approved the relocation of the county offices to the northern community.

Elko emerged, in the latter part of the twentieth century, as the most successful of the railroad-ranching towns of the northern tier. It had the largest and richest grazing acreage in its hinterland, and in the 1960s it claimed to be the second largest cattle-exporting county in the nation. As in the pioneer era, its very isolation was an advantage, because it became a strategic stopping place for motorists and truckers between Reno and Salt Lake City as highway traffic increased over the decades. It cultivated the Basque sheepherder heritage and the cowboy tradition more effectively than any other community in the state. And nowhere did a more conservative political agrarian spirit evolve than in this northeast corner.

In this region the much-publicized Sagebrush Rebellion began at the end of the 1970s. Elko County livestock owners, angered by the passage of the Federal Lands Policy and Management Act of 1976 and by the Bureau of Land Management's efforts to regulate the public domain more carefully to prevent overgrazing and pollution, led the movement for the state government to claim title to the unappropriated government lands—the more than 46.3 million acres managed by the BLM. The Elko leadership persuaded the legislature to appropriate more than a quarter million dollars to bring a lawsuit against the United States to assert Nevada's title to this land, on the grounds that Nevada had been improperly forced to "disclaim" its rightful title in the Enabling Act of 1864. The fact was that Nevada had accepted the reality of federal land ownership in the state constitution of 1864, and it had traded away much of its original land entitlement in 1880. The suit went nowhere; there was much national publicity and other western states gave lip service to the Sagebrush Rebellion, but it never got to court.

## From Bootstrap to Billions: The New Gold Rush

One of the ironies of Nevada's economic life in the 1980s arose from the fact that, just as some historians and economists had begun to write obituaries for the mining business, the northern and central part of the state began slowly to move toward new prosperity in that very industry. And the "hottest" mineral product was also the oldest in the western mining quest—gold. By the end of the decade, the wealth that had resulted from the new mining methods far exceeded all the money that had been produced in all the Nevada mining towns in the previous hundred years, and the Humboldt River towns were alive with miners and mining speculation.

The first glimmer of the new bonanza occurred near Carlin in 1955, when Marion Fisher, a miner from Battle Mountain, took over a long-neglected prospect called the "Bootstrap" mine. He got some promising assays from six virtually abandoned claims and tried to interest the largest companies in the West in the property, but he had no success for several years because the ore was of low-grade quality and the milling presented many problems. Eventually, in the 1960s, Fisher and his associates sold the property to the Newmont Mining Corporation, which led the way in mining and processing microscopic ore—sometimes called "no-see'um gold" because it can be identified only by high-powered microscopes.

For most of the state's history, gold was a secondary product. Only at Goldfield and two or three other places was the yellow metal more important than silver, copper, lead-zinc, or the more mundane industrial minerals. But suddenly, in the early 1980s, with the price of gold hovering around $450 per ounce after having soared much higher, prospectors with new technology spread out across the northwestern corner of the Great Basin, looking for the most glamorous of metals in a new way. They were searching for "microscopic" gold, which is scattered across vast areas in quantities so small that the original prospectors could not have dreamed of mining it, even if they had identified it. Most of the activity was in the northern half of the state, on the northwestern side of a line drawn diagonally from about Goldfield to Midas—as if those names had been chosen with foresight.

After 1980, Nevada was consistently the leading gold-producing state in the Union; the number of operating mines and the level of production expanded regularly through the early 1990s. With modern earth-moving and refining equipment, a greater volume of gold-bearing ore was being mined in a single year than during the entire history of the Comstock Lode and Goldfield. In 1995 alone, Nevada's mines yielded nearly $2.6 billion, producing nearly two-thirds of the nation's new gold, and the United States was the second-largest producer in the world. Geologists with advanced exploratory techniques reported new discoveries every year. After the initial period in which open-pit surface mining was the primary technique for extracting the precious metal, large corporations returned to the time-honored procedure of probing the deeper levels with drilling and shafts, often with considerable success. This industry accounted for tens of thousands of jobs across rural Nevada, not only in mining-related fields but also in secondary supply and service businesses.

While more than 70 percent of Nevada's $3.3 billion mining business was dedicated to gold in 1997, both silver and copper had once again become important mineral products. Mercury and barite, for which Nevada mines were noted in the 1980s, were much less important in the 1990s.

Oil was the mineral resource that caught most of the international headlines from the 1970s through the early 1990s, because America was running out of its own "liquid gold." The main supplies for the Western industrial world came from the Middle East. Nevada had produced oil in small quantities since the 1950s, and some petroleum engineers believed the geological conditions existed in the central Great Basin for the development of major oil sources. Six new fields were discovered between 1975 and 1985, but exploration slowed after the Gulf War of 1990–91 because the price of oil on the world market was relatively low. The quantity of petroleum yielded by Nevada wells has always been small, but a few firms continued to hope that oil, like gold, was a "sleeper" in the Great Basin.

## The Southern Nevada Land Rush, 1940s–1980s

One of the most remarkable land booms in the history of the Far West (not in the field of mining) occurred in the valleys around Las Vegas in the middle of the twentieth century, and it was still under way at the end of the 1980s. As the population of Clark County exceeded the half-million mark, the state and local government faced unprecedented challenges as they tried to maintain the "Nevada life-style" of expansive and comfortable living, which the prosperity of the region had encouraged.

The land policies within Nevada underwent an important change in 1938 when Congress initiated the Small Tract Program to encourage the sale or lease and development of lands in the Far West. The law had its greatest influence in Alaska and the Southwest, and in the deserts of California, Arizona, and Nevada. The program went into effect slowly, partly because the events of World War II diverted local and regional energies to military matters. With the return of the veterans and the increased westward migration of the nation's population after 1945, the Small Tract Program focused attention once again on the Southwest. Within the next two decades, more than ten thousand individuals selected tracts of two and a half, five, or ten acres for homesites in Nevada—most of them in the south. By 1976, when the Small Tract Policy was repealed, more than 46,500 acres of Nevada land had been classified as eligible for purchase. This amounted to another small land grant from the federal government, in the tradition of the earliest gifts of real estate from Congress to Nevada.

Many of the tracts that the Bureau of Land Management opened for sale or lease were situated around the edges of Las Vegas, but were not commonly contiguous to the city. As government agents opened the land for purchase, they attracted speculators—as in the land sales of the nineteenth century—who had little interest in municipal planning. The subdivision parcels were usually too small for effective planning, and Nevada's archaic land laws, which had been enacted for ranching and rural conditions of the previous century, provided little help. The irregular growth that resulted became a headache for city and county

planners in Clark County because of the difficulty of providing standard community services—utilities, sewers, police and fire protection,
streets, and parks—to the scattered outlying areas. In addition, some
large parcels of land within the developed area remained under federal
control.

In 1979, Congressman Jim Santini made an effort to address this Las
Vegas land problem and to relieve some pressure on Lake Tahoe in one
stroke. The outcome was one of the more creative legislative initiatives
in recent Nevada history. Together with Congressman Philip Burton of
California, he drafted legislation which gradually put some of the federal
land in Clark County on sale for private ownership, with the provision
that the money be transferred to the Department of Agriculture for the
purchase of sensitive lands in the Lake Tahoe Basin. The Santini-Burton
bill became law in 1980, and within two years this tandem measure
started to serve the interests of both Las Vegas expansion and Lake
Tahoe conservation.

Between 1982 and 1988, the Bureau of Land Management sold parcels
in Las Vegas worth about $26.6 million, and it transferred nearly $4 million to Las Vegas, Clark County, and the state of Nevada for parks and
education. At the same time, it allowed the federal government to acquire 8,500 acres of sensitive land at Lake Tahoe, which might otherwise
have been developed.

The Santini-Burton Act was a good example of statewide planning
and interstate cooperation, but it did not solve the basic problem of
regional planning in the Las Vegas Valley. This had become a valley
of fragmented jurisdictions. There were four incorporated cities—Las
Vegas, North Las Vegas, Henderson, and Boulder City. In addition, there
existed five unincorporated towns—Winchester and Paradise (which include the Las Vegas Strip casinos), East Las Vegas, Sunrise Manor, and
Spring Valley—whose property owners did not want annexation to the
city of Las Vegas. These five have been governed by the county commissioners with the assistance of advisory town boards, without sharing all
of the city's concerns and interests.

Long-range, systematic planning was complicated by another development in 1979. In that year, acting on the advice of Governor Robert
List, the legislature revised the Nevada tax base by reducing property
taxes 27 percent, removing the sales tax on food, and placing a ceiling
on certain state and local government expenditures. The idea was to
reduce the tax burden on Nevadans (which was already quite low compared with other states) and to restrict local governments' planning and

spending authority. This legislation hit Clark County governments at the worst possible time, when population growth was high and the need for planning and services was increasing. Yet this shift reduced the main traditional source of income for the local governments without providing a reliable replacement, and it greatly restricted local governments' flexibility in solving their own problems.

In the previous chapter, we considered the phenomenal population growth of Las Vegas and the surrounding communities due to tourism, the industrial complex at Henderson, the Nellis air base, and the Small Tract Program of the U.S. government. Most of this would not have been possible if government officers had not found a solution to the water problems that had become apparent in the 1940s and 1950s.

## The Southern Nevada Water Project

Because thoughtful state and local leaders recognized early the growing need for water, Las Vegas voters approved the creation of a local water district in 1948, and the first water from Lake Mead—which had originally been available to the Henderson industrial complex—was pumped to Las Vegas in 1955.

A crucial boost to the expansion of the Clark County economy came in the mid-1960s, when Senator Alan Bible of Reno managed the congressional legislation that made the Southern Nevada Water Project a reality. The 300,000 acre-feet that Nevada had been promised in the 1922 Colorado River compact was still a hypothetical asset in 1965, except for the relatively small amount that had been pumped and piped to Henderson. Senator Bible, by a series of skillful legislative moves, disentangled the Nevada water problem from a long-standing controversy between California and Arizona, and won presidential approval and congressional appropriations for the construction of the first phase in 1969–1971. He had the assistance of Senator Howard Cannon of Las Vegas, but nearly lost his struggle because of the administration's resentment of Congressman Walter Baring in the House of Representatives.

This initial stage of construction involved the boring of a four-mile tunnel through the mountains that separate Las Vegas Valley from the Colorado River. It took Adolph Sutro's crews nine years to dig a similar tunnel into the depths of the Comstock Lode a hundred years earlier. In this case, with the help of a giant mechanical "mole," the job was done in four months.

Stage One of the Las Vegas Valley Project provided for the installation of pumps and purifying agents that could deliver 135,000 acre-feet per year of clean river water into the growing urban area. Stage Two, completed ten years later, finished the highly sophisticated system which could distribute most of the remainder of Nevada's 300,000-acre-feet entitlement to those parts of the valley where the need was greatest. By 1982, more than one quarter of a billion dollars had been invested in the Southern Nevada Water System and an additional $70 million for the water treatment plant, and Clark County had one of the most modern and effective water-distribution systems in the country.

All northern Nevada communities had been yearning for a hundred years for a bountiful, dependable supply of water, but none had resources like the Colorado River and Hoover Dam in their neighborhoods. A combination of natural resources and effective politics had given one of the driest parts of Nevada the most reliable, long-term supply of the precious liquid in Nevada—and perhaps in the Far West.

In the early 1980s, another complication arose over the use of land and water resources, because the federal government announced a plan to file more than 6,000 applications for water rights on behalf of the federal government under Nevada law. This was a move by the Bureau of Land Management to exercise still more control over publicly owned resources. Then, in 1989, the Las Vegas Valley Water District (LVVWD) proposed a $1.5 billion project to drill 140 wells in Lincoln, White Pine, and Nye counties and to transport massive amounts of underground water to Las Vegas Valley through 1,000 miles of pipeline. It was a scheme much more ambitious than the Southern Nevada Water Project. LVVWD spokesmen referred to this as the Cooperative Water Project, but property owners and government officials in the three rural counties vigorously opposed the project because of fears that it would deplete surface and underground water supplies for their towns and farms. Strong resistance also came from California and from the federal government.

## Suggested Supplementary Reading

DeVine, Kelly, and Dennis L. Soden. "The Public Lands Controversy," in Dennis L. Soden and Eric Herzik, eds., *Towards 2000: Public Policy in Nevada.* Dubuque: Kendall Hunt, 1997. Pp. 121–42.

Elliott, Gary E. *Senator Alan Bible and the Politics of the New West.* Reno: University of Nevada Press, 1994.

Knack, Martha C., and Omer C. Stewart. *As Long as the River Shall Run: An Ethno-*

*history of Pyramid Lake Indian Reservation.* Berkeley: University of California Press, 1984.

Rowley, William D. *Reclaiming the Arid West: The Career of Francis G. Newlands.* Bloomington: Indiana University Press, 1996.

Strong, Douglas H. *Tahoe: An Environmental History.* Lincoln: University of Nebraska Press, 1984.

Tingley, Joseph V., Robert C. Horton, and Francis C. Lincoln. *Outline of Nevada Mining History.* Special Publication 15. Reno: Nevada Bureau of Mines and Geology, 1993.

Townley, John M. *Turn This Water into Gold: The Story of the Newlands Project.* Reno: Nevada Historical Society, 1977.

# 16

## Nevada Governments

### *Federal, State, and Local*

THE CONSTITUTIONAL system in the United States makes a basic assumption about the American people; they prefer to scatter their governmental assignments widely among those who exercise the public trust. Political responsibility is divided, by the people's choice, between the federal and state governments, and the state's authority is further subdivided into local governmental units. The citizen owes allegiance to both the federal Union and the state, and gets services from and pays taxes to both. This distribution of authority has evolved over two centuries, since the time when the original thirteen states created the federal Union to assure greater cooperation and a "common defense" in a threatening world. The Union is a remarkably flexible arrangement that has worked well for two hundred years, except for the tragic period of the Civil War.

In Nevada, this federal-state partition of powers is the source of continuous quarrels that have shaped much of the state's political and legal history. In addition, the state and local responsibilities have been distributed broadly among cities, counties, school districts, hospital trustees, administrative officers, airport trustees, assessment districts, and so on—all creatures of the state government.

Nevada was admitted to the Union during the Civil War, not because it was politically ready to pass from territorial status to equal footing with other states, but because President Lincoln and his party needed its votes in the electoral college and in Congress. No American state was ever born so prematurely or had so much trouble coming of age economically and socially. No other far western state except Oregon has continued to operate for so long under essentially the same constitutional structure. Few states have ever been so dependent on the national government for their political and financial well-being because Nevada is poor in most of the common natural resources—water, agricultural soil, forests, fisheries, and fossil fuels.

Because of the secessionist challenge to the Union, the drafters of Nevada's Constitution provided that citizens of the new state owed the "paramount allegiance" to the federal government "in the exercise of all its constitutional powers, as the same have been, or may be, defined by the supreme court of the United States." Also, Nevada's founders renounced all rights of rebellion and secession, and as we have seen, they also "forever disclaim(ed) all right and title to the unappropriated public lands . . . " within its borders.

Yet the history of the state might be regarded as a continuing tennis match between (1) those government officers who implement *federal* policies, and (2) local people and state officers, who have wanted to chart their own course according to local preferences. Or it could be defined as the account of a people who have repeatedly sought and often received federal aid, but who resent most forms of supervision or control from Washington. We have already noted examples of this in disputes over the Newlands Project and the later quarrels over water, the Sagebrush Rebellion, and the disagreements over use of the public lands. This also applies in fields such as environmental law, gambling and crime-related matters, and legislative apportionment.

In many ways, Nevadans are closer to their governments and public officeholders—federal as well as state and local—than most Americans are. Anyone who has made a reasonable effort has normally been able to have personal contact with the senators, congressman, governor, county commissioner, city officer, or school-board members who happen to be serving at the time. Direct access to the political process has usually been easy and often quick, if not always rewarding, because the population is small.

## The Washington Scene

Because Nevada, like New York or California, elects two United States senators, its citizens have traditionally had easy access to the federal bureaucracies. A letter or phone call to Capitol Hill for many years brought a prompt personal response and occasionally a favor, until the days of computerized responses to mail. In the era since the direct popular election of senators began in 1912, incumbents have made it a practice to cultivate this close relationship with the "folks back home." Senators like Francis G. Newlands (1903–1917), Key Pittman (1913–1940), Tasker L. Oddie (1921–1933), Pat McCarran (1933–1954), Alan Bible (1954–1975), Howard Cannon (1959–1982), Paul Laxalt (1975–1986), Richard Bryan (1989–2000), and Harry Reid (1987– ) — all of whom were elected to two or more terms — knew personally a large percentage of their constituents and courted their support by giving close attention to their local political needs. Most achieved enough personal influence in Washington to be able to gain some substantial political and economic benefits for Nevada from the federal treasury. Laxalt had a close relationship with President Reagan dating from the 1960s when they were governors of neighboring states. He became Mr. Reagan's national campaign manager in three different elections. Senator Reid, elected to a third term in 1998, became assistant majority leader in the Senate in 2001, the most influential position ever held in Congress by a Nevadan.

A senator's job, of course, should have a broader purpose than merely doing favors and acquiring federal benefits for the home state and its citizens. One who rises above the role of "errand boy" for constituents and helps to shape national and international policy in Washington has a claim to historical attention. Senator Pittman did so as chairman of the Foreign Relations Committee and as author of monetary legislation, Senator Oddie with his work on federal highway legislation, and Senator McCarran with his work on the judiciary committee and his authorship of controversial legislation on national security and immigration.

Because Nevada had only one congressman in the 435-member House of Representatives until 1983, its influence there has been small. No Nevadan rose to a position of leadership in the House in the first 125 years of the state's history, and except for Newlands and the Reclamation Act of 1902, none ever won recognition for designing a piece of legislation of national importance. Even those who served several terms — such as E. E. Roberts (1911–1919), Samuel S. Arentz (1921–1923, 1925–1933), James G. Scrugham (1933–1942), Walter Baring (1949–1952, 1957–1972), James Santini (1975–1982), James Bilbray (1987–1994), and Barbara Vucanovich (1983–1996) — received relatively little attention outside the state or within Congress for their legislative accomplishments. Due to its rapid growth, Nevada gained a third seat in the House in 2002.

## The State Government

Those who wrote the Nevada Constitution of 1864 did their work well. More than 140 years later, the state and county governments still functioned generally according to the original charter. There had been more than a hundred amendments to the constitution that was first framed during the Civil War, but most were minor. A few changes have occurred within the administrative system without the need for constitutional amendment and without altering the basic structure of the 1864 document. Nevada's Constitution has proved more adaptable than the basic written codes of most other states.

## The Legislature

When the Nevada legislature met in Carson City in February of 2003, the 139th year of statehood, most of the essential restrictions that the original state convention placed upon the legislature and the governor were still intact, and the public suspicions that had been written into the constitution originally had not diminished. Mark Twain, who observed the 1861 session and became a clerk and recorder for the 1863 session of the territorial legislature, was a keen skeptic about its activities; a later generation of legislature watchers in the early 2000s was little different.

The first territorial legislature remained in session for only sixty days. The original constitution limited the length of a regular session to sixty days and specified that regular sessions be held only every other year, on the assumption that this was sufficient time to do the state's business and that the lawmakers should not stay in Carson City any longer than was necessary. They could meet in late January after each general election and go home to their domestic duties in late March, presumably having put the state's government in order in the interim. Legislative matters could move at a leisurely pace during the winter months, when little work could be done on the ranches and the pace was slower in the mining towns.

There was not a large amount of money to be spent and not many political jobs to be dispensed. Probably no one who attended the sessions of the territorial legislature or the first state legislature in 1864–1865 had ever heard of a "lobbyist," because the term did not become common until later (its first recorded use was in 1863). But the species existed, nonetheless, as Nevadans were to learn to their dismay within

*State capitol building, Carson City, completed in 1871.*
*(Nevada Historical Society)*

*State legislative building, Carson City, 1997. (Photo by John Biale,*
*Legislative Counsel Bureau)*

a short time. Scores of petitioners sought charters for toll rolls, because that was an attractive way of making private money from a government privilege. We have already referred to the machinations of the mining companies and the railroad barons who twisted arms in Carson City to assure favorable legislation, and those who manipulated the elections of the United States senators for the benefit of special mining or railroad interests in the nineteenth century.

The sixty-day limit on the length of legislative sessions remained in the constitution until 1958, and even then the voters of Nevada, while removing that outmoded restriction, maintained a sixty-day limit during which the legislators could receive a salary. (They do receive per diem living expenses for as long as the session continues, and they do have the option of raising the salaries of future members of the legislature.) The voters obviously did not want to give the lawmakers a financial incentive to stay in session any longer than necessary.

Even in the 1980s, when the legislative business was much heavier and the duties of the senate and assembly more burdensome than it had been in the 1860s, there was pressure on the legislators to finish their work as soon as possible. The 1989 session lasted for 159 days, from January until July 1, and there was a flood of legislation during the last days as senators and assemblymen competed to get their favorite bills through the process before adjournment. In that session, the legislators introduced nearly 1,500 bills, enacted more than half of them into law, and considered more than 200 resolutions of various kinds. In 1998, voters approved a constitutional amendment limiting the session to 120 days, and the legislature took steps to limit the number of bills and to process them more systematically. Late session logjams, however, continued to occur.

## Taxation and Budget Making

The constitution makers of 1864 wrote into their document rigid limitations on the financial powers of the legislature. The legislators are required to raise the revenues for the general-fund expenditures that they authorize; there is no latitude for deficit financing of general government or education operations in Nevada. The original constitution writers anticipated that the property tax would be the main source of governmental revenue, but the constitution writers established a maximum tax levy of five cents on each dollar of assessed valuation for all governmental purposes. The authors of the constitution also set a limit on the state government's bonded indebtedness of 1 percent of the assessed valuation of the taxable property. (This limit remained in effect for 124 years, until the voters raised it to 2 percent in 1988.) These and other provisions mandated frugal policies on the state's budget makers from the outset, and they remained in effect in 2000.

There was no legal prohibition in the original constitution against sales taxes, income taxes, inheritance taxes, gambling, or other special-use assessments, but successive legislatures have usually been reluctant to use such implicit authority as they had in the taxing field. They have exercised their discretion to impose taxes almost under duress as public needs have grown. Nevada initiated a statewide tax on gambling only in 1945, imposing a 1 percent assessment on the gross winnings of gambling–license holders. This amount has increased gradually in the intervening years, reaching a top level of 6.25 percent for some larger casinos in 1987.

The legislature initiated a 2 percent retail sales-and-use tax for the first time in 1955, and the voters of Nevada overwhelmingly affirmed it in 1956 after a campaign in which the importance of this revenue for the schools became the main issue. Over the years, other sales-based taxes were added for schools and local governments, increasing the original 2 percent levy to 6 percent. The justification for expanding such taxes rested upon the growing population and the demand for more and better services. One rationale was that tourists helped pay a large part of the sales-and-use taxes. The legislature made a significant addition to these taxes in 1981, increasing them from about 3.5 to 6 percent, but at the same time it softened the impact of this increase because it removed the sales tax on food and substantially reduced property taxes.

For many years, taxes and fees levied on legal gambling institutions have constituted the largest single source of revenue for the state government. During the 1990s, gambling, entertainment, and sales taxes provided more than three-fourths of the state general fund income. Such revenue was unreliable in times of economic recession, causing much concern to budget makers. Most of the property tax revenue, formerly a large part of the state budget, was assigned to local governments and school districts.

At several points in their history, Nevadans have debated the question of how mines should be taxed. This issue divided the constitution writers of 1863 and delayed ratification of the fundamental law of the state. The controversy arose again in the 1980s, during the latter-day gold rush of that period. Governor Bob Miller told the 1989 legislature that the mining companies were paying far less than their fair share of the state's taxes, in view of the huge quantities of ore they were taking from Nevada earth. He presented evidence to show that gambling casinos were paying more than 7 percent of their gross revenues under Nevada law, but that the prosperous gold mines were paying less than 1 percent. The question of the appropriate level of taxation for mines was an emotional one, and could not be resolved without a long process of amending the constitution. A modest increase in the mining tax went before the voters and won approval in 1989.

The largest single category of expenditures of the state legislature in the general fund recently has been for education. Financial support for the public schools and the University of Nevada System accounts for nearly 58 percent of the regular budget in a typical biennium. The Department of Human Resources — embracing branches for health, aging, youth services, rehabilitation, welfare, mental health, and others — absorbs another 20 percent of the expenditures. The total expenditures by the state government for 1987–1988 fiscal year exceeded 1.5 billion dollars. In the 1988–1989 fiscal year, more than 10,000 people worked for the state government in scores of scattered agencies, not including more than 3,000 who were employed in the university system.

Under the constitutional requirements and the traditions that prevailed in 2003, all the major fiscal decisions had to be made during the crowded biennial session, and most of the work was left to the Senate Finance Committee and the Assembly Ways and Means Committee. The pressures and responsibilities on these people were great during the legislative term.

Nevadans have frequently debated the question of whether there should be annual sessions of the legislature in order to relieve the workload on the senators and assemblymen in the odd-numbered years. Voters voiced their agreement with such an experiment when they approved a constitutional amendment in 1958 and then repealed that same provision in 1960. There was little support for it again for the next thirty years. However, it has frequently been suggested that a regular session may be desirable in the even-numbered years for fiscal and budgetary matters only. One of the awkward results of the biennial system is that large budgetary costs — i.e., for education — must be projected more than two years in advance, and often the growth of the educational obligations has greatly exceeded the funding available by the end of the biennium. The funds appropriated for education in the 1985 session, for example, proved to be sadly inadequate for the 1986–1987 school year when thousands of unexpected students appeared in the schoolrooms of Las Vegas and Reno. The drafters of the constitution did not anticipate such rapid change. More than two-thirds of the other states have regular annual sessions of their legislatures.

The 2003 session produced the most remarkable confrontation between the branches of government and the citizens in more than a century. Governor Kenny Guinn, facing the facts of population growth and unmet needs, called for substantial tax increases. Most legislators agreed, but because of a recent constitutional amendment, it was necessary to have a two-thirds vote in each house to raise taxes. The session ended after 120 days in a deadlock without a completed budget. Governor Guinn called two special sessions and took the matter to the Nevada Supreme Court, which ruled that the legislature was required to pass a budget to fund educational needs, despite the two-thirds provision. Opponents asked the federal court to intervene, which it declined to do. Finally, the legislative minority broke ranks and the tax increase became law, apparently putting Nevada's government on a more stable basis.

The Nevada founding fathers of 1864 wrote some commendable features into the constitution which have stood the test of time. One example is the manner in which a legislative proposal is transformed from a bill into a law. The procedure is well designed to give the voting public a chance to follow the progress of a bill and to monitor the actions of their legislators with regard to it. Each bill must have three readings in each house, it must be printed and made available to the public, and the votes must be recorded — "yes," "no," or "not voting" — for each legislator on final passage. It is much more difficult for a legislator to "dodge an issue" in Carson City than it is in many other state capitals or in Washington, because her or his vote or absence will be recorded on final reading and possibly during the course of amendment and debate if the issue is a controversial one. One important constitutional safeguard in Nevada is that every bill must have a majority of all the elected members of each house recorded as voting "yes" on final passage; the absence of a member or an abstention is equivalent to a vote of "no." Thus, it is not possible for a bill to become a law in Carson City with only a handful of senators or assemblymen on the floor. In addition, recent sessions of the legislature have usually tried to assure that their committee hearings were well publicized.

Yet the constitutional framework of the legislature made its members vulnerable to outside pressures. Because the legislature is small in comparison to the law-making bodies in most other states, because the sessions are relatively short, and because the pay of legislators has usually been low and limited to a sixty-day time period, there has been a danger that undue outside financial pressure can be exercised, as was the case in the nineteenth century when railroad and mining interests "bought" legislative influence with large contributions to lawmakers.

In the 1970s and 1980s, it was the gambling casinos that made the most frequent large contributions to legislative and other electoral races. Many candidates for state and national office came routinely to depend upon contributions from the gamblers to finance their political campaigns, and it was obviously difficult to disregard those contributions when votes were cast in the assembly and senate.

Some popular reformers tried to legislate remedies by requiring candidates to reveal all large contributions and disclose their expenditures in seeking political office. Organizations dedicated to honesty and full citizen participation in government energetically publicized the problem on the local and national level, and some modest campaign finance reform was achieved. But the results were slow and insignificant both in Nevada and in Washington.

## Apportionment of Legislative Seats

The original Constitution of 1864 provided that the counties be represented in both houses on the basis of population, as determined every ten years during the regular federal census. For the first half century of the state's history, this practice was followed. However, in 1915, the legislature passed a law which provided that every county was entitled to one — and only one — senator, regardless of population. For another fifty years, this provision remained in effect, and citizens in the more heavily populated counties were denied representation in the upper house based upon population. Also, because each county was entitled by law to at least one assemblyman, this compounded the malapportionment and gave the rural counties virtual control of both chambers of the legislature. In theory, it would have been possible for 8 percent of the population to elect a majority of the members of the state senate.

This situation did not cause controversy when all the counties were relatively small and the state's population was widely scattered. With the rapid growth of Las Vegas and Reno after 1950, complaints grew about the underrepresentation of the urban areas. A similar problem existed in other states, and this inequity provoked a nationwide reform.

In 1962, the U.S. Supreme Court ruled in *Baker v. Carr* that federal courts could intervene in states where unfair apportionment existed in order to assure more equitable representation in the legislatures. Two years later, the same court decreed in *Reynolds v. Sims* that the one-person, one-vote principle must guide states in the apportionment of both houses of their state legislatures.

Nevada's legislators were forced to confront this problem when Flora Dungan, a Las Vegas reformer, filed a suit in federal court which resulted in a hearing and a court order in 1964 to reassign the seats of both houses on the basis of population—which had obviously been intended by the original framers of the Nevada Constitution. In 1965, the Nevada legislature faced the challenge of reapportioning itself in accordance with the rulings of the U.S. Supreme Court. In that year, there were seventeen counties and seventeen senators. Clark County, with about 44 percent of the people in the state (more than 137,000), had the same representation in the upper chamber as Esmeralda County with fewer than 500 people. Following the reapportionment, Clark County received eight senators out of a total of twenty, and the smaller counties were consolidated into legislative districts, in which a single senator represented two or more counties. A similar pattern emerged for the assembly.

In the next quarter century, there were two more reapportionments, which necessarily reflected the continued growth of the urban centers and the relative decline in the political influence of the rural counties. In the 1981 realignment of seats, Clark County was entitled to twelve of the twenty-one senate seats and twenty-four of the forty-two assembly seats — a majority in each house — because the 1980 census showed that it had more than 58 percent of the state's population.

Before and during the reapportionment of 1965, many citizens who lived in counties with small populations feared that once the more populous cities gained control of the legislature, or once the balance of power shifted southward, there would be neglect and disregard of rural interests and institutions. In general, this did not happen, at least through the 1990s. While there were some outbursts of sectional rivalry, most legislators felt responsible for all parts of Nevada. In the 2001 reapportionment, approximately 70 percent of the seats were assigned to Clark County because of its rapid population increase.

The legislature and other government agencies function best when citizen interest and participation in their affairs is high. One of the most effective public service and public information organizations in Nevada during the 1990s was the Progressive Leadership Alliance of Nevada (PLAN), a coalition representing a cross-section of ethnic, social, and economic groups whose needs are not often well addressed by lobbyists for the gaming and other profit-oriented commercial groups. PLAN worked for legislation to serve people in need of better public services. In the twenty-first century, Nevada legislators were still accessible to the citizens who wanted to contact them.

## The Governor and the Executive Branch

The constitution of Nevada, following the federal pattern, created a clearly separate branch of government for the executive. Since colonial times, there had been a suspicion of putting too much authority in the hands of the executive. Nevadans were no more willing to tolerate an autocrat in the state house than their ancestors were.

In the first 140 years of its history, Nevada had twenty-six governors or acting governors. (When a lieutenant governor finishes the term of an elected governor in Nevada, he is officially known as "acting governor.") In the earliest days of statehood, voters tended to select cattlemen for the chief executive office; as we have seen, Governors Bradley, Adams, and Sparks made their nonpolitical reputations in the livestock business, and Reinhold Sadler (1897–1902) was known for his activities in both mining and livestock raising. In the early twentieth century, people associated with mining or engineering were preferred for the executive mansion—men such as Tasker L. Oddie (a mining promoter and attorney, 1911–1914), Emmet D. Boyle (a mining engineer, 1915–1922), and James G. Scrugham (a mechanical engineer, professor, and conservationist, 1923–1926). In more recent years, the governors have usually been former newspapermen—i.e., Vail Pittman (1946–1950) and Charles Russell (1951–1958)—or attorneys, as in the cases of E. P. "Ted" Carville, (1939–1945), Grant Sawyer (1959–1966), Paul Laxalt (1967–1970), Robert List (1979–1982), Richard Bryan (1983–1988), and Robert J. (Bob) Miller (1989–1998). Mike O'Callaghan (1971–78) had been a former schoolteacher and welfare administrator. Kenny Guinn (1999– ) was a respected utility company executive and school board member before becoming governor.

Eleven of the first twenty-six governors were elected to a second term; none was ever elected to a third term, although four of them tried when that was still possible under the constitution. During the 1970s, the Nevada voters—following the national example set by the Twenty-second Amendment to the United States Constitution—changed the state constitution to prevent a third term.

Although the governor's office has considerable prestige, it is a relatively weak administrative instrument. The incumbent can make a few political appointments, but aside from those on the gambling boards, there is little discretionary authority that has much importance. The Nevada governor does not have line-item veto power in budgetary matters, as most other state chief executives do. The executive staff presents a budget to the legislature but, unless he is effective at personal "arm twisting" or public relations, the governor has little control over what the legislators do with it. The statutory law has imposed the state personnel office in the appointment field, and public opinion limits the executive options elsewhere. He has the usual veto power, of course, but it has been used sparingly in Nevada, and the legislature can override a veto by two-thirds votes of all the members in each house. The Nevada governor does not have a "pocket veto," i.e., the power to kill a bill by inaction after the adjournment of the legislature. In those instances when Nevada governors have been regarded as "strong," it has been because of their powers of persuasion with the public, rather than the inherent powers of the office.

One area in which the governor exercises significant discretion is in the field of gambling control—a responsibility which the framers of the Nevada Constitution did not contemplate. Licensing and policing of the gambling business is the responsibility of two agencies—the Nevada Gaming Commission and the Gaming Control Board—appointed by the governor. But increasingly, the growing influence of the gambling business in the state through payrolls and large political contributions to candidates has thrown the exercise of this control under a cloud.

## The Judicial Branch

Nevadans have usually been much more conscious of their state and local courts than they have of the federal court which functions within their borders. While the local municipal and justice courts and the state district courts operate nearer to the common concerns of the average citizen, the federal judges in Nevada play a crucial role in defending individual rights and in resolving disputes involving constitutional questions and matters relating to federal law. The state judges have received more attention in the local communities, but the federal judges have made far more history and have defended citizens' rights in the more conspicuous cases.

At the state level, Nevada has traditionally had an uncomplicated judicial organization. Although there have been several efforts to expand it, the voters proved reluctant to make large adjustments in the original provisions until 1976, when a "court system" received the approval of the electorate. The system has had to be expanded over the years to accommodate a growing caseload, but it bears the essential features of the 1864 model.

The original constitution provided for a supreme court comprised of three members (with the option of increasing the number to five), nine district courts, and an unspecified number of justice courts to be assigned to the various towns. It also allowed for the establishment of municipal courts in the cities. All judges were to be chosen by popular vote at regular elections.

The legislature enlarged the supreme court to five members in 1967. Justices originally were elected by the people to terms of six years; this continues to be the case at the beginning of the 1990s. A sitting justice who seeks reelection has often been challenged, and there have been some bitter electoral contests, especially at times when there was public quarreling among the members of the court. Some legal authorities have expressed serious misgivings about the process that subjects justices to the political arena because of the possibility that it might lead to improper popular or financial influence on the court. It seems obvious that a sitting judge should not be placed in the position of soliciting or accepting campaign contributions from business or private interests. Yet in 1988 the voters rejected a proposed constitutional amendment which would have allowed the Missouri Plan to be implemented. This would provide for the initial appointment of a judge to a vacant bench from a list prepared by the state bar association and for regular opportunities for voters to express their approval or disapproval of a sitting judge without requiring a political campaign.

In 1976, voters of the state approved a constitutional amendment which modified the judicial branch by creating a court system, with the chief justice of the supreme court having the authority to assign cases within the system. This change also provided a more professional manner for filling vacancies and established the Commission on Judicial Discipline, which consists of seven persons: two judges, two attorneys from the state bar association, and three lay citizens appointed by the governor. This commission has the authority to censure, retire, or even remove a judge in the event of misconduct in office. Although the Nevada court system had a stormy beginning in territorial days when there were bitter disputes and charges of corruption over mining litigation, the state and federal judiciary has had a commendable record for most of the last 125 years. The responsibilities of the court have expanded greatly in the recent era. In 1960, the supreme court disposed of about 100 matters per year; in 1996 it issued rulings in 1,307 cases.

The network of district courts, which handles most of the trial work in the state judiciary, has expanded with the population and the growing caseload. The original constitution provided for the establishment of nine judicial districts, and at the beginning of statehood the legislature authorized twelve judges to preside in these districts. In 1989, there were still nine districts, although much changed in their boundaries and greatly expanded in the number of sitting judges. After a hundred years of judicial evolution, in 1964 there were only twenty district judges, but the number had grown to thirty-nine by 1997, and another nine judges served in a division devoted to family court matters.

## The Federal Judiciary in Nevada

Federal judges are appointed by the president of the United States, normally on the recommendation of one or both senators from the state in which the vacancy occurs. They hold one of the most sensitive and responsible positions in the entire governmental establishment, as they receive cases which involve questions on the U.S. Constitution, the federal statues and the federal criminal code, and litigation between citizens or corporations of different states. The men who have served on the federal bench in Nevada in the past 100 years have invariably been individuals who have had distinguished careers in the bar, which usually means that they performed effectively as attorneys and won much respect from their colleagues in the process.

Only fifteen persons had served as federal judges within Nevada between 1864 and 1989, and in the latter year five of them were still serving. With one notable exception (to be considered later), the men who have served on the Nevada federal district bench in this century have grown in stature within the judicial fraternity. Some have had distinguished careers extending over twenty-five years—including Roger T. Foley (1945–1974), Roger D. Foley (1962–1996), and Bruce A. Thompson (1963–1992).

Once they have assumed the judicial robes, the judges have usually lapsed into historical obscurity—except when they have presided over a sensational case or have made a controversial ruling—because they have lifetime appointments and are removed from most political conflict. Yet upon these men has rested primary responsibility for the defense of the system of justice designed by the framers of the U.S. Constitution. The workload of the federal district court and federal magistrates who handle specialized matters for Nevada has grown phenomenally in recent years, embracing such widely diverse matters as federal criminal charges, bankruptcy, credit-card fraud, tax matters involving the Internal Revenue Service, civil rights, water rights, mining law, environmental law, and others. Death penalty cases from the state courts almost always reach the federal district bench, and Nevada state courts have imposed a remarkably high number of death sentences in recent years.

## The County and City Governments

Nevada's seventeen counties have been a familiar part of the governmental structure for more than seventy years. Since 1968, when the legislature combined Carson City and Ormsby County to form a single administrative unit, the state has technically had sixteen counties plus one city-county, but it is still common to use the former terminology. The 1987 legislature tried to create an eighteenth county—a tiny, unpopulated entity known as "Bullfrog" within Nye County around the proposed Yucca Mountain nuclear waste site—to assure that federal revenues which might be generated by such a project would be available to the state treasury rather than to the county. This legislation, which was hastily written and legally awkward, was eventually found to be unconstitutional.

In much of rural Nevada, the most tangible and familiar monument to government is the county courthouse. Some of the most widely admired symbols of the state's heritage are the buildings that house the local county officers, and the variety of architecture in the existing court buildings is one the testimonials to Nevada's eclectic heritage. In connection with the bicentennial of the Constitutional Convention of 1776, Ronald M. James, supervisor of the Nevada Division of Historic Preservation and Archaeology, assembled a handsome collection of photographs and texts on the theme of Nevada's courthouse traditions. James wrote:

> During the past 125 years, Nevada's seventeen counties have erected more than thirty courthouses, most of which survive today as monuments to years of local law and order. Some counties built

simple brick buildings while others designed structures with grand Greek columns and marble staircases. As a whole, they are imposing buildings constructed to provide a dignified setting for local courts and government. (James, *Justice in Balance: The Courthouses of Nevada*. Reno: Nevada Historical Society, 1986, p. 2.)

In the early local history of Nevada, the most frequent intracounty controversies were waged over which town(s) should have the honors and privileges that the county seat bestowed as the mining and railroad frontier moved inland. The courthouse was the home base of the county clerk, treasurer, recorder/auditor, assessor, sheriff, and district attorney—all of whom did much of the state and federal business for local people in a time when both Carson City and the federal authorities were far distant. The courthouse generated much business because it drew scattered prospectors and settlers like a social magnet. Miners went there to register their mineral claims, ranchers to record their land and water rights, voters to register and occasionally to cast their ballots, victims of violence to find the sheriff or district attorney, and property owners to pay their taxes. Young couples normally went to the courthouse for their marriage licenses and often for the matrimonial ceremony, and the district judges invariably held court there. Distinguished visitors usually made a call at this political hub of the county as they passed through. In pioneer Nevada and until the rise of the larger cities, the courthouse was a social center as well as the governmental seat on the frontier.

Nevada originally had eight counties; it reached the present number of seventeen in 1919. Only one community that was designated as a county seat by the territorial legislature of 1861, Virginia City, retained that role unchanged in 1989. (As we have seen, Carson City, originally the county seat of Ormsby County, was consolidated into a single municipal government in 1969.) Nearly all the other county-seat towns witnessed nasty local disputes to win or hold this status. Only once between 1920 and 1990 was there a change in county seats; that occurred in 1979 when the legislature approved the transfer of Lander County offices from Austin to Battle Mountain.

The city governments have been more diverse in their structures because their charters have been issued separately by the legislature and the communities in which they have developed are so dissimilar. Among the eighteen cities, there is a range in size from Las Vegas—with about 420,000 people—to Caliente, Wells, Carlin, and Mesquite, each of which had about 1,000 in 1990. In general, municipal governments have been

*Grant Sawyer State Office Building, Las Vegas.*
*(Rich Johnson, State Photographer)*

much more modest in designing their public offices than have the county governments, and city halls have generated less public pride than court-houses. A notable exception, however, is the Las Vegas City Hall, an eleven-story, bronze and marble tower constructed on Las Vegas Boulevard between 1971 and 1973. This $8 million triangular high rise is one of the most striking public buildings in the state, symbolizing the contemporary dynamics of Las Vegas as well as any other building in the city.

Eight county-seat communities serve "double duty" in government, having municipal offices as well. Las Vegas, Reno, Elko, Ely, Fallon, Lovelock, Winnemucca, and Yerington all divide the responsibilities of local government between county and municipal officers. Carson City has a unique arrangement of county and city governments blended into one; the former Ormsby County no longer exists. Some of the older towns like Virginia City, Pioche, Eureka, Battle Mountain, Minden, Tonopah, Goldfield, and Hawthorne have not felt the need for separate municipal governments, but these and other locales have often formed town boards — advisers to the county commissioners — who have exercised some influence over local affairs.

Large and small communities other than county seats have often wanted the benefits of municipal government to assure themselves of greater control over their local affairs. Places such as North Las Vegas, Boulder City, Henderson, Mesquite, Sparks, Carlin, Wells, Gabbs, and Caliente have all tried to affirm a community identity separate from both their mother county and the county seat by seeking incorporation under state law.

## The Expanding Role of Women

As the 20th century approached its end, women were playing increasingly prominent roles in Nevada's governments. In 1982, Barbara Vucanovich of Reno was the first woman to be elected to Congress from Nevada; she served seven terms before retiring. Sue Wagner, also of Reno, was the first woman elected lieutenant governor in 1990, and Miriam Shearing of Las Vegas set two precedents as the first woman to sit on the state supreme court (1993) and the first to serve as chief justice (1997–98). Frankie Sue Del Papa won election as secretary of state in 1986 and as attorney general in 1990, 1994, and 1998. In the 1995 and 1997 sessions of the legislature approximately one-third of the seats were held by women.

## Suggested Supplementary Reading

Atkinson, Glen. "State Finance and Revenues," in Dennis L. Soden and Eric Herzik, eds., *Towards 2000: Public Policy in Nevada.* Dubuque: Kendall Hunt, 1997. Pp. 185–200.

Bowers, Michael W. *The Sagebrush State: Nevada's History, Government, and Politics.* Reno: Universitiy of Nevada Press, 1996.

Driggs, Don W., and Leonard E. Goodall. *Nevada Politics and Government: Conservatism in an Open Society.* Lincoln: University of Nebraska Press, 1996.

James, Ronald M. *Temples of Justice: County Courthouses of Nevada.* Reno: University of Nevada Press, 1994.

Soden, Dennis L., and Eric Herzik, eds. *Towards 2000: Public Policy in Nevada.* Dubuque: Kendall Hunt, 1997.

# 17
## Gambling and Tourism

I N THE last half of the twentieth century, Nevadans have found a distinctive way to combine the peculiar geography of their region with the benefits of the federal system and their own individualistic esprit to form a prosperous economy. We have briefly touched on these developments earlier in our study of the growth of Las Vegas and Reno. Underlying this new economy is the evolution of the tourist business, stimulated by the expansion of legalized gambling. After much ambivalence to social policy for the first seventy years, Nevada then led the way for the next fifty years in making acceptable a business that was widely regarded elsewhere as socially improper.

## The Early History of Nevada Gambling

The first session of the territorial legislature in 1861 proclaimed gambling illegal, and the first session of the state legislature reaffirmed this prohibition in 1865. Yet games of chance persisted as a way of life in the early mining camps and railroad towns, even as it was being outlawed in other parts of the nation. It was a common form of entertainment and relaxation for men on the frontier, and it survived in bad times as well as in bonanza years in Nevada, even though some influential voices were raised against it.

Governor Henry G. Blasdel, the first elected chief executive, was not a man to mince his words on the subject. In his 1867 message to the legislature, he recognized that although gambling had been pronounced illegal by the original state legislature two years earlier, it continued to flourish. He proposed stronger legislation to the law. He said:

> Gaming is an intolerable and inexcusable vice. It saps the very foundation of morality, breeds contempt for honest industry, and totally disqualifies its victims for the discharge of the ordinary duties of life. Every energy of the State should be invoked to suppress it. (*First Biennial Message of Governor H. G. Blasdel . . . , January 10, 1867, p. 14.*)

Governor Blasdel, a devout Methodist, vetoed a bill that would have made gambling legal, and the 1867 legislature sustained his action.

In 1869 the issue arose once more, and again he deplored the survival of the games of chance and pointed out some basic defects in the law. Enforcement was a dead letter because the justices of the peace of the various townships had original jurisdiction, the law imposed no penalty upon anyone except dealers in a game, and the offense was treated only as a misdemeanor, the governor argued. Yet in that very session, the legislature passed the first Nevada law legalizing and presumably regulating gambling by requiring those who offered betting games to be licensed by the county sheriffs. Blasdel vetoed the bill, but both houses of the legislature voted overwhelmingly to override, and legalized gambling became the law of the state.

In his veto message, Governor Blasdel expanded on his ethical objections to gambling in trenchant, biting sentences that built to a crescendo:

> I know of no greater vice than gambling. It is against public morals. It saps the very foundations of society. It induces intemperance. It begets idleness. It fosters immorality. It multiplies crime. It leads to reckless extravagance, and unfits its unhappy victim for any position of business usefulness. In short it is the root of all evils—the highway that leads to immorality and crime. For centuries it has been the aim and effort of Christian men and women to uproot and destroy it; and to-day I believe there is not a State in this Union whose criminal statutes do not pronounce it a crime and punish it with heavy penalties. (*Journal of the Assembly . . . , Fourth Session, 1869, p. 282.*)

The governor's emotional rhetoric had no effect in the era of Comstock prosperity, and his point of view did not have any active disciples until the early 1900s. The efforts of the Nevada legislature to police and regulate gambling are a lesson in frontier laissez-faire. The state government provided no control mechanism beyond the level of the county sheriff, who was the licenser and fee collector when he took the trouble to perform that duty. He had the responsibility of collecting $100 per month for the first month and $75 per month thereafter for each game, the money to be divided between the county and state treasuries. There were also provisions in the law that attempted to keep the games off the first floors of buildings which fronted on a street, and to discourage persons under twenty-one years of age from being influenced by the games.

Nevada's government was not then dependent upon gambling revenue for its basic operations; gambling was a man's sport, widely regarded as the avocation of a "ne'er do well." Few people cared much about the back-room poker and fan-tan games because they were not conspicuous. They were considered to be unfit activities for ladies, and respectable women were almost never seen in the rooms where a game such as poker or panguingue was played.

After 1900, with the rise of the Progressive and other reform movements, a handful of outspoken moralists organized themselves to address the ethical questions about institutionalized gambling. The womens' clubs of Reno and President Joseph Stubbs of the University of Nevada revived the long-dormant sentiments of Governor Blasdel. In 1909 they got a law passed in the Nevada legislature prohibiting gambling, and the back-room poker and panguingue games were told to close their tables in 1910. A person found guilty of running any kind of game of chance was pronounced guilty of a felony and could be sent to the state prison for a term of one to five years.

Did this reflect the will of Nevada's 81,000 people at that time? The evidence is not clear, but gambling continued in the back rooms of many saloons in defiance of the law, and Nevada officialdom was ambiguous about enforcement. The legislature relaxed the rules slightly in 1911, tightened them again in 1913, relaxed them again in 1915. When Governor Tasker Oddie lost his bid for reelection to Emmet D. Boyle in 1914, he attributed his defeat to the fact that he had opposed the return of open gambling.

In 1919, Governor Boyle, one of Nevada's most honest and progressive governors, made a brief reference to gambling in his remarks to the legislature:

> The present gambling law, though aimed to prevent exploitation
> by commercial gamblers, has failed to accomplish this purpose. A

rigid enforceable law designed to prohibit gambling in all forms, including slot machines and race-track betting, should be enacted at this session.

There was new vocabulary here, reflecting new devices and new forums which the free-lance style of Nevada society had been unwilling or unable to control. But until this time, gambling was defined, by the leading politicians, as a departure from the norm, as a social evil to be carefully restricted and, if it got out of hand, eradicated.

During the 1920s, the back-room betting flourished in most of the mining and railroad towns, and there was no effective mechanism for controlling it. It was the economic downturn that followed the stock market crash of 1929 which prompted the Nevada legislature to take another chance with the tantalizing business. For the first time, Nevada approached the problem of its disreputable back rooms as a possible economic opportunity.

## The First Year of Decision: 1931

In 1931, several legislators discussed a legal-gambling bill outside the chambers without introducing it because it was thought to be unpopular, but finally Phil Tobin, a first-term assemblyman from Humboldt County, put it in the hopper. It passed both houses with little vocal opposition during the last days of the session, and Governor Fred Balzar signed it into law. Once again licensing and control were left to city or county officers. The business grew little and changed only slightly during the depression years of the 1930s.

Nevada already had a dubious reputation for its toleration of prostitution, easy six-week divorces (also authorized by the 1931 legislature), and permissive marriage license laws which required no waiting period. Several popular books appeared in the 1930s and early 1940s which made the state—and especially Reno—seem daring and glamorous for the casual attitude that existed toward the prevailing social mores of the day. The gambling halls that stood between the railroad depot and the courthouse seemed to be an outpost of sinfulness in an America that still believed, outwardly, in the mores of the Puritans.

But observers from the outside helped brighten the image. Richard G. Lillard's thoughtful book entitled *Desert Challenge: An Interpretation of Nevada*, published in 1942 by a leading New York book company, encouraged those who read his easygoing prose to feel better about the toleration of gambling:

The general atmosphere is that of any legitimate business patronized by the general public. The mood is that of an ultraserious carnival. There is none of the exclusive, aristocratic air of the Monte Carlo tradition. The atmosphere is businesslike, lacking in style and glamour. . . .

There are no steerers or criers. Visitors are never urged to play, and are at liberty to look on or linger. Women receive normal courtesies. No drinking is allowed except at the bar. The crowds are quieter than shoppers in a department store. They are as quiet as church congregations. (Lillard, *Desert Challenge*, pp. 321–322.)

Reassurances such as this, appearing in scores of books and magazines across the country, gradually convinced Nevadans and citizens of the other forty-seven states that the unusual experiment with legal games of chance on the sagebrush frontier had some virtues.

## The Second Year of Decision: 1945

It was not Las Vegas or Reno that led Nevada into the business of taxing gambling casinos for the benefit of their own community interests. Rather, it was the small-county legislators who produced the crucial legislation that linked the state's economy to the games and the gamblers.

One of the most ingenuous bills in the history of the Nevada legislature was that sponsored by Senators Fred Dressler of Minden, Ken Johnson of Carson City, Walter Cox of Yerington, Al Haight of Fallon, and John Robbins of Elko in 1945. This became the law that gave the state government the responsibility for licensing gambling and for collecting a 1 percent gross revenue tax. The state got only one-fourth, and the counties, towns, and cities enjoyed the remainder. It was a local government-funding measure that got the state of Nevada—and specifically the Nevada Tax Commission, which had been established for a totally different purpose—into the field of regulating and taxing gambling.

That 1945 bill, like several other fateful proposals in the history of Nevada gambling, was enacted into law during the rush toward adjournment in the last days of the legislative session; it reached the governor's desk with a flood of other legislation. It was probably the most momentous decision in the history of Nevada gambling—more pregnant with results for the future than the gambling legislation of 1869, 1909, or 1931. Its ramifications were not seriously discussed; some of its provisions were written into the law in a "free" conference between senators and assemblymen who were eager to adjourn and go home.

In this case, the governor was E. P. (Ted) Carville (1939–1945), a conscientious and thoughtful attorney from Elko. He did not sign the bill, but he did not veto it. He simply allowed it to become law without his signature, and then explained his inaction in a message to the secretary of state, hoping that his reservations would get transmitted to the next legislature. He wrote:

> I feel . . . that with the State making this departure from its fixed past policy, the effort will be made to extend the imposition of this type of taxation, and that the wiser course would have been to avoid this type of taxation, and obtain a just contribution from the gambling business by imposing a higher license fee. (Appendix to the *Journal of the Senate*. Carson City: State Printer, 1945.)

Governor Carville had raised a pertinent issue, but again there was no public discussion of it. The gambling business grew because it was attractive for tourists, profitable for the investors, and modestly helpful to the local and state budgets. Governor Carville's question soon became moot. Under normal circumstances, he might have been around to urge his point of view upon the legislature two years later, but his political aspirations carried him to the U.S. Senate. He was not in the governor's office in 1947, and the genial, relaxed Vail Pittman—a brother of the late Senator Key Pittman—followed an easier path.

Governor Pittman recommended, in 1947, not a review of the policy which had been initiated in 1945, but rather the possibility of an increase in the gambling and liquor taxes as a means of meeting the state's growing needs for revenue in the postwar economy. Most Nevada gambling-house owners obeyed the law and paid their fees and taxes without question. They and Governor Pittman thereby set an expectation that became standard for state budget makers during the next forty years.

The Pittman era was crucial in the history of Nevada gambling. It was during this administration that the first troubles began to appear in Nevada's uncontrolled, unsupervised style of gambling. Pittman was a man who believed in the "traditional, time honored ways of operating the state government," according to his biographer Eric Moody. He trusted in unregulated business, and he was not one to raise basic questions about the social consequences of the state's policy of benign indifference. As a result, several underworld figures, with criminal records in other states, staked their claims on Nevada's gambling frontier much as the old prospectors had done on the public domain in pioneering days.

During the Pittman years, the state government began to feel its way toward control of this unusual business, but it was too late to be effective because certain notorious criminal elements had begun to acquire a small number of popular casinos.

The first strong prompting toward self-analysis by Nevadans occurred as a result of a congressional report of 1950–1951, based upon an investigation of the rise of organized crime. Headed by Senator Estes Kefauver of Tennessee, this report charged that systematic criminal groups were flourishing in America and that some of the revenue on which they depended had originated in a few of the Nevada casinos. This startled the Nevada public and at least some of their officers, and led to more systematic efforts at policing the business after 1953.

When Governor Charles Russell asked the legislature in 1953 to grant the tax commission "complete power to deny and revoke any and all licenses," it was already too late to eradicate the criminal element easily. Russell's effort to close the door to the mobsters was an admirable one; he recommended a six-month residence period for any person seeking a gambling license, for more openness in licensing procedures, for the mandatory maintenance and state inspection of casino financial records, and for fingerprinting and background checking of casino personnel. Many of his recommendations were adopted, including the creation of the Gaming Control Board in 1955, yet Russell's remedies were procedural, not substantive. The moral questions were not raised, or even implied. Russell was one of the most responsible governors in the state's history, but it seemed not to be within his domain to raise the ethical or social questions about the long-range implications of the business.

The popular journalistic historian Oscar Lewis came through Nevada and wrote an entertaining book in the early 1950s. It had the engaging title *Sagebrush Casinos*. He made the erroneous assumption that the people of Nevada had voted for gambling in a referendum and could vote it out of business again if it became corrupt. But the electorate had never had the opportunity to vote directly on gambling, and as the casinos grew as a source of employment, the public support and dependency— in the press, the legislature, and the public at large—grew as well.

## The Third Year of Decision: 1957

The legislative session of 1957 produced a crisis in the gaming business and in the state's control mechanism. The owners of the Thunderbird Hotel in Las Vegas, accused of having formed illegal connections with criminal elements in other states, were faced with the suspension of their gambling license by the Nevada Tax Commission. One of the license holders was Lieutenant Governor Cliff Jones, and another was a former member of the Nevada Tax Commission. The Thunderbird owners persuaded their friends to introduce a bill—which became famous as Senate Bill 92—in which they tried to strip the Nevada Tax Commission and newly created Gaming Control Board of all authority to revoke or suspend licenses and to transfer basic responsibility to the courts. The bill passed both houses of the legislature, met a veto from Governor Russell, and returned to both houses for reconsideration. The legislature failed to override the veto because of the switch of a single vote in the senate.

The Thunderbird case was of special interest during the legislative session because a crucial lawsuit relating to it was pending at the same time in the Nevada Supreme Court. When the tax commission had ordered revocation of the Thunderbird license, its owners had gone to a district court and persuaded a rural judge to issue a restraining order against the commission to prevent it from closing the casino. The question of whether the commission had the authority to suspend a license without a full court hearing became the central issue. The supreme court ultimately ruled that the tax commission did have the authority to put gamblers who acted improperly out of business, but that it had not acted according to its own rules in the Thunderbird case. The result of this notorious 1957 controversy, therefore, was to sustain the power of the tax commission and Gaming Control Board, but also to prevent the immediate closure of the casino on technical grounds. Supreme Court Justice Charles Merrill wrote an opinion which contained a warning to the people of Nevada that they had undertaken a dangerous experiment and that gambling was not a right, but a tolerated nuisance that needed careful supervision.

In that same 1957 session, the legislators from the small counties devised a way of distributing part of the gambling-fee revenues among the rural areas, even though most of the income was generated in Las Vegas and Reno. A simple table-tax revision bill, introduced by Assemblyman John Giomi of Yerington, became an instrument for both decreasing the table-tax fees levied on large casinos and simultaneously distributing the fees equally among the seventeen counties. Thus the less populous rural counties, which were often poor in property tax opportunities, were offered a windfall, which their officers and legislative representatives were happy to accept. This change obviously came before the legislative reapportionment of the 1960s occurred.

This three-part policy refinement in 1957 set the direction for legalized gambling in Nevada for more than a quarter century. The showdown in the legislature over S.B. 92 demonstrated that a small bloc of casino owners might exercise extraordinary influence in the legislative halls, that the governor had special responsibility in the field of gambling control, and that the courts were willing to insist upon both the inherent police powers of the state and the procedural privileges of the gamblers.

## The Dominance of the Casino Business, 1959–1989

From the 1950s onward with the growth of tourism, Nevada had not only a thriving business in gambling, but an economic system to publicize it, school and university programs that relied upon it, and a state control mechanism that tried to protect as well as to police the casino owners. In the meantime, the mining business—which had long been the bellwether of the economy of the Silver State—became relatively less important to the business climate in most rural counties.

The next three governors—Grant Sawyer (1959–1966), Paul Laxalt (1967–1970), and Mike O'Callaghan (1971–1978)—all won reputations for diligence in gambling control. The agencies that evolved to police the business—the Gaming Policy Committee (an advisory group chaired by the governor), the Nevada Gaming Commission, and the Gaming Control Board—functioned efficiently and avoided major scandal, but questions continued to be raised about their effectiveness in keeping organized crime out of the business. Scores of agents worked in the field, investigating the suitability of applicants for licenses and checking on the compliance of casinos with state taxing and operational laws, but doubts persisted that Nevada had enough gaming control personnel, authority, and determination to do the job effectively.

An important new departure in the business came in 1969, when the state government agreed to issue corporate gambling licenses. Previously, the gaming control agencies had been willing to issue licenses only to individuals, on the theory that it was easier to check the backgrounds of those individuals who sought the privilege of operating a casino. This change had the effect of attracting several large corporations into the business, but it also complicated the state's responsibility for fighting organized crime. As historian Russell R. Elliott wrote:

> The Corporate Gaming Act of 1969 was a mixed blessing: although it encouraged conservative banking institutions to invest in gambling, it also created some problems of its own. According to

one official it opened a "can of worms" by forcing control officials
to distinguish between active and passive stockholders, in effect
causing the state to lose control of the passive stockholders and
making it more difficult to find hidden interests. (Elliott, *History of
Nevada*, 2d ed., p. 335.)

Yet this act clearly stimulated investment in Nevada's peculiar industry.
There was a rapid expansion of casino building in Las Vegas, Reno, Lake
Tahoe, and other parts of the state. During the 1980s, the passion for
casino building had reached some of the most remote outposts along the
state's borders—i.e., at Laughlin on the Colorado River at the extreme
southern tip, at Wendover on Interstate 80 on the Utah-Nevada border,
and at Jackpot on the Idaho border. By 1986, Las Vegas casinos were
attracting 15 million visitors a year who were leaving several billions
of dollars annually in the casinos and auxiliary service organizations,
and many of the large casinos had come under the ownership of giant
out-of-state corporations.

Although Nevada authorities continuously reported that their gambling control agencies were reasonably effective, the reputation of
Nevada as a source of revenue for unsavory activities persisted. Several
Las Vegas casino owners were convicted of felonies in the 1970s and
1980s, and others were targets for investigations by the FBI and the Internal Revenue Service. This affected the careers of some of the state's
leading political figures because the national news media took a keen
interest in Nevada. Three leading Nevada officials received unfortunate
nationwide attention in the 1980s.

## Howard Cannon

Senator Howard Cannon was the first resident of Las Vegas to build a
highly successful political career from a base in Clark County. A native
of Utah, he came to Nevada in the 1940s, established a law practice in
Las Vegas, and became city attorney. In 1956, he ran unsuccessfully for
the House of Representatives and, in 1958, he defeated two-term Senator George Malone by a large margin. Senator Cannon won his next
three races for reelection to the Senate. In his twenty-four-year career
in the upper house of Congress, he became one of the most influential
Democrats from the Far West by giving much of his attention to military and aviation affairs. He held the rank of brigadier general in the air
force reserve and served as a member of the Armed Services Commit-

tee. Nevadans generally gave him credit for bringing large military and atomic research projects to the state by virtue of his influence on Capitol Hill. He also became chairman of the Senate Commerce Committee.

In general, Nevadans welcomed the military-related appropriations that brought thousands of jobs to Nellis Air Force Base and the Nevada Test Site. Cannon also gained approval for obtaining federal assistance for the expanding Nevada airports. But in the early 1980s, he also identified himself with another military enterprise that became very unpopular—the proposal to deploy hundreds of M-X intercontinental ballistic missiles across the state—and this cost him much of his regular support.

In addition, as the years passed Senator Cannon had to bear the burden of another reputation that Nevada had acquired, one associated with the continuing presence of organized crime in Las Vegas. Although his associations with the unsavory figures were tenuous and indirect, he received political support from them and found his name linked with theirs in national investigations.

In 1982, when Senator Cannon was seeking reelection to his fifth term in the Senate, there were embarrassing news reports to the effect that the Teamsters' Union in 1979 had offered him a bribe to try to persuade him to block some legislation which the Teamsters opposed. The Justice Department had brought criminal indictment against the president of the Teamsters and four associates, charging them with having offered Cannon several acres of prime Las Vegas real estate in exchange for his help in killing the measure that they opposed. The trial began in Chicago in late October, only a few days before the general election in which Cannon was seeking his fifth term. Although the senator was not charged and he had not blocked the legislation as the Teamsters desired, his name was associated with the union, and he lost the election. Cannon ultimately appeared on the witness stand in defense of the accused Teamsters after his defeat and testified that he could not remember crucial aspects of the bribe offer, but the Teamster leaders were convicted and sentenced to prison. There is no doubt that the news reports hurt Cannon's political chances at a crucial time in the campaign.

The lesson from this series of events seemed to be that a political figure—even one who had a long and successful career of public service—was vulnerable if his name became too closely associated with questionable segments of society.

## *Paul Laxalt*

Of those Nevadans who have reached the national spotlight, none did so more rapidly or more completely than Senator Paul Laxalt, who received much publicity because of his close friendship with President Ronald Reagan. In his twelve-year career on Capitol Hill (1975–1986), Laxalt became more prominent in national politics than any Nevadan since Pat McCarran. He never held any important committee chairmanships in Congress and did not draft any important legislation, but he served as Mr. Reagan's frequent spokesman in the Senate and as his campaign manager in three elections. In the final analysis, Laxalt's star rose and declined with that of Mr. Reagan, and his abortive effort to become a presidential candidate in 1988 never got successfully started because he found himself fighting to avoid the taint of undesirable associations in the gambling business.

Laxalt's rise to prominence in national politics was almost unprecedented for a westerner from a small state. He won his first statewide office as lieutenant governor in 1962, his second as governor in 1966, and then retired temporarily from state politics in 1970. During his term as governor, he developed his friendship with Mr. Reagan, who was then governor of California. In 1974, he won a narrow victory for the United States Senate seat which had been abandoned by Alan Bible, and he devoted much time to Reagan's bids for the presidency in 1976 and 1980. When Mr. Reagan won in the latter year, Laxalt—although a junior member of the Senate—was in a position to wield unusual influence there. At the president's behest, he became national chairman of the Republican party.

During the hiatus in his political career between 1970 and 1974, Laxalt had entered the gambling business. He was the main promoter and developer of a hotel-casino in Carson City, and he raised much of the capital which allowed the business to begin. The question of his relationship with this gambling enterprise became national news when, in 1983, *The Sacramento Bee* and two other California newspapers published an article implying that profits may have been illegally "skimmed" from the operation before being reported for tax purposes. The news story did not assert that Laxalt knew of the skimming or had any role in it.

Nevertheless, Laxalt took personal offense at the story, and in 1984 he filed a $250 million libel suit against the *Bee* and its owners, demanding a retraction as well as damages. For three years, the suit attracted national publicity as lawyers for both sides maneuvered and sparred over legal matters. During the course of the depositions and discovery, there was much discussion of Laxalt's alleged dealings with individuals associated with disreputable elements of society, including Jimmy Hoffa, the notorious leader of the Teamsters' Union.

Just as the case was about to go to trial in Reno in 1987, there was a abrupt out-of-court settlement, in which the *Bee* said it did not have conclusive evidence that the skimming had occurred (and it had from the beginning been willing to assert that Laxalt was not involved), but it did not retract the story and did not apologize. Laxalt dropped his suit and proclaimed that he had won, even though his basic demands for a retraction and damages had not been met. It was widely presumed that Laxalt had dropped the suit because the continuing references to the case would be harmful to his campaign for the presidency. In the course of his planning for the presidential campaign, Laxalt acknowledged that the "Nevada image" would be a problem for him in his race for the highest office in the land. He occasionally affirmed that there was a singular "Nevada standard" for ethics, which much of the rest of the nation did not understand. Only a short time later, however, Laxalt abandoned his candidacy for the presidency because he did not have the financial support to continue it.

## Harry Claiborne

In the long history of Nevadans' embarrassments, no series of episodes has been more troublesome for the state's reputation than the highly publicized criminal conviction and impeachment of Federal District Judge Harry E. Claiborne of Las Vegas. In 1984, Judge Claiborne, who had been appointed to the federal bench in 1978, was found guilty of a felony for concealing personal income from the Internal Revenue Service and failing to pay income taxes on more than $106,000 in legal fees that he had earned as a prominent lawyer in Las Vegas. Originally Claiborne was also charged with soliciting and accepting a bribe from a brothel owner, but after an initial trial and a hung jury, those charges were dropped and he faced charges only on the indictments relating to false income tax returns. After his conviction, he was sentenced to a two-year term in a federal prison.

When Judge Claiborne refused to resign his federal judgeship following the conviction, the House of Representatives voted 406 to 0 to impeach him, and the U.S. Senate, in its first impeachment trial in decades, convicted him and removed him from his judicial office, which carried a salary of $78,700 per year. Claiborne was serving his term in a federal prison in Alabama when his nationally publicized impeachment trial proceeded. The nation could thus witness the spectacle of a Las Vegas judge sitting in the marble-columned Senate caucus room, trying to rationalize his conduct and explain the reasons for his conviction.

In his appearance before the Senate, Claiborne invoked a uniquely Nevadan defense. He charged that the justice department had singled him out for prosecution because he was a Nevadan and had been zealous as a judge in restricting federal investigations in the state. He said that federal agents had gone to Las Vegas to "plant the American flag in the Nevada desert" in an arrogant manner. His defense reminded reporters of the stance of a western gunfighter, romantically standing alone against outside troublemakers.

Claiborne's attitude, adopting provincial state's rights rhetoric in order to explain his conduct and the government's prosecution of him, troubled many Nevadans by the late 1980s. There was no substantial question that Claiborne's tax returns were incorrect, and whatever the attitude of the federal investigators, he could not escape responsibility by trying to shift the blame to incompetent tax accountants, as he had done. A federal vendetta, if it existed, was not an adequate excuse for the conduct to which Claiborne admitted. That he tried to use the state's sovereignty as part of his defense aroused the resentment of many of his fellow Nevadans.

Yet Claiborne was not alone in his assertion that federal authorities, especially the FBI, had employed unfair tactics in pursuing him. The case did not end with his conviction and removal from office by the U.S. Senate. After he had been released from prison, he applied for readmission to the Nevada bar. The Nevada Supreme Court and the Board of Governors of the Nevada Bar Association therefore had to face the question of whether Claiborne should be allowed to resume the practice of law in Nevada. Much of the legal profession and the press obviously favored his permanent removal from the bar after he lost his judgeship, but Claiborne also had some vocal supporters within the legal profession.

The Nevada Supreme Court took the position that Claiborne had been punished enough with his criminal conviction in federal court, his imprisonment, his impeachment by the House of Representatives and trial in the Senate, and the resulting humiliation. After a brief hearing, that Court quickly readmitted Claiborne to the state bar and faced a storm of criticism. The Supreme Court produced a written opinion explaining its action several months later.

With three of the five justices participating, the Court issued a 126-page brief in 1988, defending its decision to allow Claiborne to resume the practice of law in the state courts and accepting his assertions about the federal vendetta. Claiborne had been investigated by four separate grand juries before he was indicted, and the federal government had relied upon the testimony of a notorious prostitution merchant—himself a convicted felon and fugitive from justice—to get an indictment.

The Nevada Supreme Court's opinion—written by Justice Thomas Steffen—read in places like a brief for the defense of Claiborne. It found him irresponsible in his duties as a citizen, but it was keenly troubled by the conduct of the government officers who investigated and prosecuted him:

> We conclude, therefore, that respondent (i.e., Claiborne) slighted his responsibilities . . . by virtue of his negligent and careless attention to his legal obligations as a taxpayer during the years 1979 and 1980.
>
> In so concluding, for perhaps the first time throughout the tortured history of respondent's travails, respondent has been extended the benefit of the doubt. Based upon our extended consideration of the record, we have emerged with an abiding doubt as to respondent's guilt under a criminal standard of proof.[*]

The Court concluded that the facts of the case did not prove that Claiborne had willfully intended to defraud or that "he was intentionally dishonest for the purpose of personal gain."

If the justices of the Supreme Court meant to put the issue to rest, they failed, because their opinion enflamed the controversy once again within the legal community. When Claiborne sought readmission to the federal bar so he could practice law before U.S. courts, the process was more deliberate, and in this instance he failed. U.S. District Judge Robert C. Broomfield ruled in 1988 that Claiborne could not resume practice in federal courts for at least another year because public confidence in the court system might be weakened if there were no professional discipline for the convicted judge. He criticized the Nevada Supreme Court on the grounds that it "did not sufficiently consider the public confidence in the integrity of the bar and the courts as a whole."

Thus Nevada's peculiar social structure, economy, and the values

---

[*]State Bar of Nevada, Petitioner, v. Harry Eugene Claiborne, Respondent, 104 Nevada, Advance Opinion 22, p. 99.

identified with them frequently received unfavorable national attention, and the most engaging social questions of the late twentieth century had forced themselves into the center of the state's civic affairs.

During the late 1980s, Nevada's tourism business learned to develop a broader view of the state's attractions, reaching out beyond casinos to the natural wonders and cultural resources of the state. Governor Bryan's administration emphasized the need to diversify not only Nevada's economic base but also to emphasize the historical heritage of the state. The Nevada Humanities Committee and the Nevada State Council on the Arts provided hundreds of programs that served Nevadans and visitors from throughout the world with a brilliant menu of Silver State culture. Governors Miller and Guinn both continued this policy of trying to promote Nevada's natural resources and attractions.

## Suggested Supplementary Reading

Burbank, Jeff. *License to Steal: Nevada's Gaming Control System in the Mega-resort Age*. Reno: University of Nevada Press, 2000.

Denton, Sally, and Roger Morris. *The Money and the Power: The Making of Las Vegas and Its Hold on America, 1947–2000*. New York: Alfred A. Knopf, 2001.

Findlay, John M. *People of Chance: Gambling in American Society from Jamestown to Las Vegas*. New York: Oxford University Press, 1986.

Lewis, Oscar. *Sagebrush Casinos: The Story of Legal Gambling in Nevada*. Garden City, N.Y.: Doubleday, 1953.

Moehring, Eugene P. *Resort City in the Sunbelt: Las Vegas 1930–2000*. Reno: University of Nevada Press, 2000.

Moody, Eric N. "The Early Years of Casino Gambling in Nevada, 1931–1945." Ph.D. dissertation, University of Nevada, Reno, 1997.

———. *Southern Gentleman of Nevada Politics: Vail M. Pittman*. Reno: University of Nevada Press, 1974.

Sawyer, Grant. *Hang Tough: Grant Sawyer, An Activist in the Governor's Mansion*. Interviews by Gary E. Elliott; narrative compiled by R. T. King. Reno: University of Nevada Oral History Program, 1993.

Sheehan, Jack, ed. *The Players: The Men Who Made Las Vegas*. Reno: University of Nevada Press, 1997.

Skolnick, Jerome H. *House of Cards: The Legalization and Control of Casino Gambling*. Boston: Little, Brown, 1978.

# 18

# Community Building in the Silver State

E VERY GROUP of people who live together in a republican or democratic system must face basic questions about the conduct of their civic life. How will they educate their children and meet the need for trained specialists for the future? What will they do about those unfortunates among them who are in need, those who have acted violently, or those who are socially incompetent? Will the society take any steps to cultivate the arts and sciences and to preserve their heritage in an orderly way?

A civilized community will do more than exploit the land and move on like a wave of grasshoppers through a grainfield. Nevada, which has always been a place that attracts more transients than settlers, has had to fashion its public institutions on a foundation of sand. Its agencies of public service have always been poor because they have been dependent upon an island of more-or-less permanent residents in a moving stream of humanity bound for somewhere else.

## Education: The Frontier Experience

One fundamental test of a civilized society is the provisions it makes for its children. Since the beginning of frontier society in Nevada, a continuing concern has been the education of its young citizens-to-be. Before the state government existed, when the territorial government had no authority to tax efficiently or otherwise to impose its will, local communities either voted taxes on themselves or worked privately to raise money for schools. The necessity for teachers and classrooms became obvious before there was a tax structure to support it. The needs of the schools always ran ahead of the public financing for teachers, books, and buildings.

Virginia City had only 17 children in school in the fall of 1862; a year later there were 360. No resources of government existed to meet the unexpected shortage of teachers. This pattern, with constantly growing statistics, has been a recurring feature of Nevada's history; the same problem was evident 125 years later on a much larger scale.

The authors of the Nevada Constitution recognized the need for a system of public schools, but could not agree upon whether children in the scattered hinterlands should be required to attend them. Because schools were so few and the locations of many ranches and mines so remote, the members of the 1864 convention decided that the issue of compulsory or voluntary attendance should not be addressed in the constitution, but should be left to the legislature.

No state ever had more meager resources for starting a public school system. The constitutional framers mandated a State Permanent School Fund, thanks to grants that the Congress had given to Nevada upon its admission to the Union. Nevada, like other western states, was entitled to two sections of land in every township from the federal government to be sold for an endowment for school purposes. However, as we have seen, little of the land to which Nevada was entitled had any market value, so little was sold. Early legislatures also provided that 5 percent of all taxes collected by the state should be distributed among the counties for school purposes. In spite of this, the entire amount of support for schools from the state government was barely enough to operate the classrooms more than one or two months out of the year. Counties had the right to impose school taxes, but they acted inconsistently and irregularly, depending on the will of those in office. The admission of Nevada to the Union coincided with a modest burst in school building at the local level. In 1864, there were 34 school districts but only 17 school buildings in the 10 counties—with only 940 students in average daily attendance. Two counties had no schools at all, and at least half the schools did not have enough money to offer classes for more than a few months during the normal school year. Half of the school buildings in the state had been constructed during the previous year, and several more were under construction.

No dependable source of money existed to pay teachers' salaries. Outside Storey County, the average salary of a teacher was about $48 per month—half of a miner's wage. Often those who accepted teaching jobs did so only as a makeshift arrangement; a teacher seldom remained for as long as a year at any school.

A handful of private educational establishments did provide some opportunities beyond those available from the public schools. Hannah K. Clapp, the educator and woman suffrage leader whom we discussed in chapter 11, was the founder of the first private school in 1861. She dedicated herself to the Carson City children through her Sierra Seminary as long as the prosperity of the 1860s and 1870s lasted. Later there were private Catholic schools in Virginia City, inspired by Father Patrick Manogue, and a preparatory school for girls in Reno, founded by the Episcopal Bishop Ozi W. Whitaker. At times local citizens necessarily banded together to raise money for the education of their children.

This basic condition existed through the bonanza era. Some wealthy school districts provided fine buildings, like the Fourth Ward School in Virginia City, and the teachers and books to give them pedagogical integrity. Others, more remote from the rich ore bodies, functioned by hook or crook in log cabins.

## The Fundamental Law of 1907

Even in the earliest years on the frontier, a few towns or clusters of scattered ranches tried to hire teachers for their children. During many years before 1900, only about half the state's children were in school, and many had no books. In 1887, the legislature designated the district attorney of each county as ex officio superintendent of schools. Most of these men had no professional training in pedagogy and few were interested in school matters. As one state superintendent wrote, "As there was no required course of study, each school was a law unto itself as to what it should do and how much."

Not until 1907 did the architects of Nevada educational policy face the fact that the anarchistic system in education that had existed for more than forty years needed some refinements. Here, as in so many areas, the influence of the Progressive movement was a factor in focusing the attention of the people and the politicians on the basic problem.

In that year the legislature enacted laws that provided for a plan of unified state supervision of schools, established a state board of education responsible for a standard course of study, required the certification of teachers, and set the stage for better communication among teachers and with supporting agencies at the state level, including the university.

In 1909, the legislature acted to stimulate practical industrial training. The second- or high-school movement, which barely existed before 1900, also received a boost from the Progressives. There was a surge of investment by local districts in improved buildings and facilities. The most effective leaders in this reform movement were Superintendent of Public Instruction Orvis Ring and Professor Romanzo Adams of the university.

The 1907 law, with frequent modifications and improvements, provided the foundation for the educational system until 1955. During most of this period, the state granted only about 30 percent of the revenue to operate the schools, and local districts or counties provided most of the remainder from property taxes. During much of this period, Nevada's revenue ranked quite well when compared to other states in the area of educational support. During the depression year of 1932, for example, Nevada ranked third among the states in per capita expenditures per child in average daily attendance. This excellent record did not survive into the more prosperous post–World War II era.

## Maude Frazier, A Heritage Builder

One person who distinguished herself for lasting contributions to the Nevada heritage in this middle period of Las Vegas history was Maude Frazier, a Wisconsin-born schoolteacher who arrived in Nevada to teach in Genoa in 1906 when she was about twenty-five years of age and who had a career of more than fifty years of community and state service.

In that era, schoolteachers were often as itinerant as miners, going where the jobs were and never knowing when their employers would be unable to pay their meager wages. She taught or served as school principal in several Nevada towns besides Genoa—Seven Troughs, Beatty, Goldfield, and Sparks—before she applied for the position as deputy superintendent of public instruction in Las Vegas in 1920. For a woman to seek such an administrative office in that era was a bold act indeed, but she was hired and soon won a statewide reputation for dedication to a better educational system.

*Fifth Street Grammar School, Las Vegas. (Ferron-Bracken Collection, University of Nevada, Las Vegas, Library)*

More than any politician or businessman of that time and place, Frazier shaped the lives of young people in southern Nevada. Her area of educational supervision covered 40,000 square miles. She visited school districts regularly, at first going to some of the remote towns and ranches by way of California or Utah because Nevada roads were so bad. When she observed promising high school students, she encouraged them to attend college, occasionally helping them to find loans and promising to guide them into teaching jobs after a few months of training. Thus she gradually built a cadre of teachers in the most isolated corner of the most arid state.

After a few years, Frazier became superintendent of schools in Las Vegas. In 1929, she planned the Las Vegas High School building for 500 students—an extravagant number, her critics said—and she supervised its construction. When she retired from that position in 1946, she was recognized as one of the few public officers of her time who had planned well for a burgeoning city. After her retirement from the school district, she served six terms in the Nevada legislature. In 1962, when she was eighty-one years old, a vacancy occurred in the office of lieutenant governor, and Governor Grant Sawyer appointed her to fill the position. The first building erected on the University of Nevada campus in Las Vegas was distinguished by her name.

## The Reforms of the 1950s

The perennial school crisis rose again in more acute form during the mid-1950s. Because of the growth of tourism and the defense industries in the south, Nevada's population had trebled since the days of the Tonopah-Goldfield bonanza, and doubled since the 1930s. The state faced not only the problem of more than 200 scattered school districts, but also of the expanding technical knowledge, higher job expectations among its young people, and a rapid influx of new residents. In January 1954, Governor Charles Russell called a rare special session of the legislature to confront these problems.

That session authorized the most thorough analysis of the Nevada public education system ever conducted. The state engaged the George Peabody College of Nashville, Tennessee, to make an analysis of not only the schools, but also of the state's mechanism for supporting them. After several months of study, the Peabody committee gave the people of Nevada some striking facts:

1. Nevada had far too many school districts, many of which were desperately poor: "150 of Nevada's 196 elementary schools are too small to provide a rich and varied instructional program."
2. Nevada had 36 high schools, but 22 of them were too small to be effective, with few vocational courses, little music and art, poor health service, meager library resources, and poor physical facilities.
3. The tax base for supporting education was inadequate and grossly unfair, because poor districts did not have sufficient help from the state or from any other source.

The Peabody team told Nevadans some things they did not want to hear. The state had the highest per capita income among the far western states, but it provided one of the lowest levels of support per pupil for its schools. This was embarrassing information, revealing that the state had a poorer record of support for its schools than had been the case in the 1930s.

Legislators such as Cyril Bastian of Caliente and Maude Frazier were leaders in the movement to enlighten the senate, the assembly, and the voters of the state about the plight of the schools. Bastian made a "facts of life" speech that was memorable in the annals of the legislature, pointing out how poorly many districts were financing their schools. Following the publication of the Peabody report, a citizens' movement arose to change the system of taxation and the school districts. Each of the seventeen counties became a single school district, replacing the more than two hundred fragmented districts and consolidating their resources. One of the by-products of this study was the approval in 1955 of a retail sales tax of 2 percent on most goods and services—the first tax of its kind in the state's history. This new revenue did much to put school financing on a sounder basis.

## School Desegregation in Clark County

Many American cities went through a social crisis in the 1950s and 1960s as the struggle to achieve equality of opportunity for minority groups unfolded. Nevada was spared the agony of the crisis, because its minority population was small, but it did share the learning process and the adjustments that the nation made during those years.

When the United States Supreme Court declared racial segregation in public schools to be unconstitutional in the famous case of *Brown v. Board of Education of Topeka* in 1954, Las Vegas was still at an early stage of its phenomenal growth. Yet a pattern of racial discrimination was emerging in the elementary schools there in the 1960s. The Clark County School District effectively achieved integration in the high schools of the Las Vegas area, but its elementary schools were severely segregated. In the Westside area in 1968, where the population was predominantly black, there were six schools in which the student enrollment was more than 97 percent black, and more than 80 percent of the county's black schoolteachers were assigned to those schools.

This condition resulted in the most notable civil rights case in Nevada history, *Kelly v. Guinn,* in which Federal Judge Bruce Thompson ruled in 1969 that a basic pattern of segregation did exist as a result of school-board policy, and he charged it "with the affirmative duty to take whatever steps might be necessary to convert to a unitary system in which racial discrimination would be eliminated root and branch." When the school district sought to soften the impact of the segregation and the court order with an optional program, the courts rejected the plan as inadequate. Judge Thompson's decisive rulings were affirmed by the Ninth Circuit Court of Appeals in 1972, and the school district then proceeded without delay to implement a more effective plan.

## The Challenge of the 1980s

Nevada's experience was not typical of the national school trend between 1975 and 1985. While public school enrollment declined by more than 9 percent nationwide in that decade, Nevada's enrollment increased slightly, and at the kindergarten and elementary levels the student population grew substantially. At the end of the 1970s, Nevada once again had one of the highest rates of per capita income in the nation, and yet it was 48th among the 50 states in the percentage of its per capita income that it expended on education.

Some other troubling facts appeared in the *Status Report* issued by the Nevada State Department of Education in 1987. Nevada ranked 19th among the states in teachers' salaries—a marked improvement over previous years—but it compared poorly with most other states in average class size. It had one of the highest student-teacher ratios in the nation in 1986. "We must work toward reducing the number of students each teacher is expected to teach, especially in the early elementary grades," Superintendent of Public Instruction Eugene T. Paslov wrote in the report.

In 1988, the Nevada State Education Association organized an initiative petition proposing a corporate income tax for Nevada to raise more funds for education, but voters rejected it in 1990.

## The Evolution of the University

The writers of the Constitution of 1864 were men of large vision; they wanted not only a public-school system, but also a university. The building of a rudimentary public-school system, though not an easy task, was a much more reasonable goal than the creating of a genuine university in which the various academic and professional fields of learning could be cultivated. As Albert T. Hawley, one of those who worked on the section that would establish a university, told the convention, "To create a state university, to build up its various departments, and fill it with professors, is a work of time." It was a painfully slow and often frustrating path from the constitutional ideals to the sprawling university and community college system of 1997, which enrolled more than 78,000 students.

Although the constitution provided for the establishment of a board of regents and authorized it to create an institution of higher learning, pioneer Nevada did not have the resources to do so immediately. In 1862, Congress passed the famous Morrill Land Grant Act, allowing each state to select and sell thousands of acres of public land to establish endowments for institutions of higher learning. This act specified that colleges receiving such support must provide instruction in "agriculture and the mechanic arts," occupations that were important to an expanding frontier society. But the money from this endowment in Nevada was very meager because there was little good land to be sold, and the state did not have a large enough tax base to begin the process until 1873.

Even then, when the legislature provided for a "University Preparatory School" in Elko, it was a modest effort. Its doors opened to 1 instructor and 7 students in the fall of 1874, and for ten years it functioned with only 1 or 2 teachers and never more than about 35 students. Since it was little more than a weak high school, the institution could not attract students from the more populous towns of western Nevada, and in any case few young people were prepared for the challenges of advanced study.

After the legislature and the regents moved the institution to Reno in 1886, a long, difficult period of academic experimentation followed.

For more than twenty-five years, the university struggled with a small faculty and a student body numbering between 150 and 350, trying to master the traditional liberal arts studies of older colleges, the needs of a teacher-training school, and the technical fields mandated by the Morrill Act. A learned president, Dr. Joseph E. Stubbs, provided the guidance that the young university needed to begin the research and service expected of such an institution. When he died in 1914, forty years after the official establishment of the university, higher education in Nevada had an intellectual, if not a fiscal, foundation.

For another forty years, from 1914 until 1954, the university marked time, enduring the restraints of two world wars and the Great Depression. It did not have more than about 2,000 students on the Reno campus (the only teaching unit of the university) even at the end of this period, and it remained primarily a training school for Nevadans interested in the provincial occupations. It did operate an agricultural experiment station with federal support, and gifts from the Mackay family enabled it to do pioneering work in mining and geology, but otherwise its faculty had little support for research ideas. Slowly, in the 1950s the university and the citizenry of the state began to discover the broader possibilities of higher education in research and service, and the institution broke out from the small Reno campus and the provincial orientation where it had germinated for seventy years.

Three important developments occurred in the 1950s. First, the university established an extension program and then a branch campus in Las Vegas—a move that was resisted by the academicians in the north but dictated by the realities of population and politics in the south. Second, the legislature and the regents in 1959 created the Desert Research Institute with a mission of investigating a broad spectrum of scientific problems for society. This was a formal recognition of the university's research role. And third, the university underwent a struggle for academic freedom, in which an aroused faculty and responsible citizens successfully fought against an ill-conceived administrative plan to muzzle debate and discussion of important ideas. In all three experiences, the university showed that it had achieved greater maturity in one decade than in the previous eighty years.

The establishment of a campus in Las Vegas was a decisive step. An informal beginning had been made in 1951 when a single class met at the Las Vegas High School. Local citizens and personnel at Nellis Air Force Base were searching for college-level classes, and institutions from California and Utah seemed ready to fill the gap in Nevada's higher educa-

*Honor Court and Morrill Hall, University of Nevada, Reno, campus.*
*(Photo by Ted Cook)*

tion. Three years later, the university established the Nevada Southern branch as a permanent unit, and in 1957 the state opened the first university building—Maude Frazier Hall—on a 60-acre campus on Maryland Parkway. Within the next decade, the Las Vegas branch was offering four-year degrees and preparing for autonomous status, which it achieved in 1968.

In the next few years, the University of Nevada, Las Vegas, emerged from its status as a colony of Reno with as much flair as the host city that grew up around it. It extended across a 335-acre campus with an enrollment of approximately 23,000 students each fall semester by the 2000s. It offered the community a young and academically talented faculty, a handsome performing arts complex, a key research center for the Environmental Protection Agency, the Desert Biology Center, and scores of other units that testified to the community's determination to build a "multi-versity." In 1987 the regents and legislature authorized an engineering school and in 1997 a law school. For nearly a decade the university

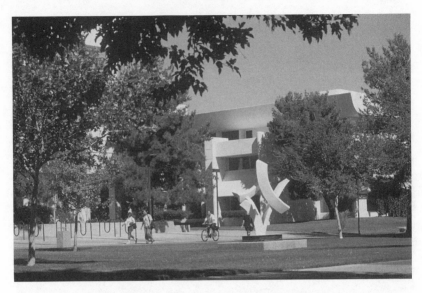

*University of Nevada, Las Vegas, campus.*
*(UNLV News and Public Information)*

was led by the dynamic Robert Maxson, who assumed the presidency in 1984.

In the early 1990s, UNLV was troubled by a series of controversies and scandals over its highly publicized basketball program. Jerry Tarkanian, the coach who built the "Runnin' Rebels" into one of the most impressive varsity teams in the nation, had a continuous battle with the National Collegiate Athletic Association (NCAA) over his recruiting methods and his special arrangements for athletes. His practices led to censure by the NCAA and a series of lawsuits against the university. In addition, longstanding conflict with President Maxson brought unwanted national publicity to the university. Despite this distraction, the improvement of the university's academic reputation continued, enhanced by the UNLV Foundation, which mobilized generous community support.

The older university in Reno grew at a more measured pace. In the mid-1950s it endured the troubled leadership of President Minard W. Stout, whose dictatorial practices brought reproach from the academic world until the Board of Regents fired him in 1958. Later leadership was more stable under presidents Charles J. Armstrong, N. Edd Miller, Max Milam, and Joseph N. Crowley. While Nevada-Reno served a smaller student population than UNLV, the momentum established in its professional schools and liberal arts during the earlier years allowed it to establish a national reputation for high-quality advanced education.

The Desert Research Institute, founded in 1959, is a specialized scientific unit of the University System that has raised most of its operating money for advanced research from government and private sources. It became famous worldwide for its studies of weather, environmental problems, and biology.

Before 1968, Nevada almost completely ignored the national trend that offered college-level occupational training for those who did not seek the full range of a university education — it was the only state without either a community college or a junior college. Beginning in the late 1960s, the legislature and Board of Regents embraced a community college experiment started by citizens of Elko and created a new division within the university system. By 1971, Elko Community College, Clark County Community College (CCCC), and Western Nevada Community College (with branches in Reno and Carson City) were in operation, offering both technical and occupational training and university-parallel courses. In 1979 Western was divided, and the Reno unit became Truckee Meadows Community College.

By the time the community college division approached its thirtieth anniversary in 1998, it was serving more than 45,000 students with modern facilities in a dozen communities. The Elko college had changed its name to Great Basin College and CCCC had become the Community College of Southern Nevada, reflecting the expanding range of their services. Even the name of the university system had been modified to reflect the new dimensions in higher education. All the units were now part of the University and Community College System of Nevada.

## Human Resources and Welfare

The state government has several agencies that are charged with helping communities, families, and individuals to attain and keep a reasonable standard of living. The most prominent of these offices are within the Department of Human Resources, which was handling more than $275 million in fiscal year 1988. While there were six divisions in this department, the clients who have the greatest need and receive most public attention usually become the responsibility of the Division of Welfare.

Nevada has a mixed history in welfare matters as in education. For the first half century of the state's history, there was no formal statewide program for assisting the needy, and it was usually families or local churches and fraternal orders that organized help for the widows, orphans, and indigents. Societies such as the Odd Fellows, Masons, Knights of Columbus, and others assumed much of the responsibility for such aid.

During the early twentieth century, Nevada became one of leaders among the states in giving help to the needy. In 1915, the legislature enacted a law authorizing aid to mothers of young children who had no support from a husband, and in 1923 it began to provide old-age assistance. During the early 1930s, Nevada was ahead of most other states in its assistance to the poor.

A significant change occurred after the New Deal programs began in the 1930s, when the federal government assumed more responsibility for welfare. The new programs initiated in Washington, the wartime economy, and the rapid increase in population which followed in the 1940s and 1950s were accompanied by less generous official policies. Not only did the Nevada legislature move away from the comparatively generous policies of the 1930s, but it was even slow to embrace some of the federal policies initiated by the New Deal. The Old Age and Survivors Disability Insurance program, enacted by Congress in 1935, did not become available to Nevada's elderly until 1953 because the legislature declined to accept responsibility for the state's share of the costs. Other programs for the totally disabled, for dependent children, and for food stamps were accepted only partially or belatedly, if at all, in Nevada.

Thus Nevada by the 1950s had gained a reputation for being stingy toward its welfare clients. In 1955, one widely read essayist, Albert Deutsch, wrote a scathing article in the popular magazine *Collier's* entitled "The Sorry State of Nevada," which included these lines:

> And so goes the dismal story of Nevada's niggardliness. Too rich to accept normal taxes, too poor to maintain its institutions and agencies on a decent twentieth century level, coddling known racketeers and making them respectable by legalizing their operations, while turning a cold poormaster's eye to its poor, its sick, its socially misshapen . . .
>
> There are, of course, many good people in Nevada, concerned about the deplorable neglect of child and adult unfortunates, and wanting to do something about it. But they don't set the effective health and welfare policies of the gambling state, nor have they been able to modify it much—as yet. (March 18, 1955, p. 85).

For much of the next quarter century, as the state became more prosperous economically as the tourist-gambling economy expanded, its welfare and human-assistance programs remained among the most poorly financed in the nation. In 1972, a group of welfare mothers in Las Vegas organized an "Eat-In" at local casinos to dramatize the fact that their children were hungry and that Nevada had not yet accepted a federal food stamp program that had been available for several years. The Nevada legislature adopted the federal Medicaid program to assist persons who needed long-term health care in hospitals or nursing homes, but it set assistance standards so rigid that only the very poorest were eligible for its benefits. Even so, Medicaid costs within the state rose rapidly—from approximately $5 million in 1967–1968 to more than $90 million in 1987–1988. The growth of population, particularly among the elderly, and rising health-care costs accounted for these dramatic increases. The costs for hospital care in Nevada were the highest in the nation.

A well-trained and highly motivated staff within the Department of Human Resources was often frustrated by the fact that funds were not available to meet the legitimate needs of those in society who require basic help, care, rehabilitation, or retraining.

In mental health as in many other fields, a few dedicated public servants tried to serve their clients well despite meager budgets and inadequate facilities. Facilities in Sparks and Las Vegas were overcrowded, and Nevada nearly lost federal assistance in this area in 1987 before it authorized new positions to give additional care. A nationwide study of mental health services in 1988 showed that Nevada was doing a less than adequate job of caring for those who had serious mental illness and who required institutional care. The report came from the National Alliance for the Mentally Ill and the Public Citizens' Health Research Group, and found that while Nevada ranked 13th in the nation in per capita income, it ranked 44th in the nation in terms of its financial commitment to the mentally ill.

## The Prison-Correctional System

One responsibility of the state government which the public is most likely to ignore or misunderstand is the punishment and rehabilitation of criminals. The Nevada prison is the oldest public institution in the state, but the one whose history has been most neglected. During much of

Nevada's early history, the penal system was understandably crude; during recent history, the policies of the prison administrators have usually been more enlightened, but with some grotesque exceptions. With the rapid growth of the prison population and the lack of adequate facilities, administrators of the penal system have faced a difficult challenge.

At the beginning of Nevada's history, the need for a prison was obvious. Abraham Curry, the founder of Carson City and the man who provided the territorial legislature with its first meeting place, was also the person who made his sandstone hotel available to imprison those people who had been convicted of crimes in 1862. This hotel, at Warm Springs about 2 miles east of Carson, became the first prison and Curry became its warden. Later, the state government bought his land and hotel, and gradually adapted it to prison use.

Nevada developed its penal system, like other institutions, by the cheapest possible methods and by trial and error. As there was a sandstone quarry on the property, early prisoners were assigned to cut the stone to build the permanent prison and many of the larger buildings in Carson City, including the capitol.

The prison's early history was as violent as that of the state itself. The original state law designated the lieutenant governor as ex officio warden. His job as warden was the most dangerous political assignment in state government because of the class of men he dealt with and the lack of secure facilities. Fire, prisoner escapes, and inmate uprisings marred the history of the institution. Lieutenant Governor Frank Denver and four guards suffered wounds during a breakout in 1871.

During the busiest bonanza years, when the prison was becoming overcrowded, the state purchased land on the Truckee River east of Reno for a larger detention facility. Construction proceeded slowly for several years, but the site was never used for a prison. Later it was adapted to become a home for the state mental hospital. The prison site near Carson continued to serve its original purpose—and as the place for imposing the death penalty—which it still serves today.

Only slowly did Nevada prison administrators adopt the attitude that prison should serve to rehabilitate the inmates by providing useful employment and training. For many years the prisoners produced license plates for automobiles, and the state eventually acquired a farm south of Carson City where men requiring minimum supervision could raise crops and livestock. During the administration of Governor Grant Sawyer and Warden Jack Fogliani (1959–1967), a constructive program of counseling, arts and crafts, recreation, rural honor camps, and education expanded to serve virtually all the inmates, and the legislature authorized a larger, separate facility for women.

Yet the overcrowding problem increased as the state's population grew and lawmakers mandated longer sentences for criminals than most other states did, and conditions for some inmates were barbaric. Crude forms of punishment caught the attention of the public in the late 1970s when two prisoners brought suit against the warden and prison administrators on the grounds that the institution was inflicting cruel and unusual punishment in violation of the Eighth Amendment of the Bill of Rights. Testimony in federal district court revealed that prisoners were sometimes confined to the "hole" for as long as a month with only crude sanitary facilities, with the privilege of shaving and taking a shower only once a week, with little or no clothing, and no chance for recreation or exercise. It was also revealed that some patients from the state mental hospital were occasionally confined to the state prison without adequate legal proceedings. "Shocking as this may be, the principal problem with the psychiatric ward [of the prison] is that there are many people incarcerated there who have never been convicted of any criminal offense," the court said. After hearing evidence, Judge Bruce Thompson ordered a modification of such procedures to assure that constitutional guarantees against cruel and unusual punishment would be honored. (*Craig v. Hocker,* 405 Fed. Supp. 656, 1975; consent decree filed Dec. 18, 1980.)

In another case, an inmate named Robert Stickney in 1979 brought a class-action suit against the governor, the attorney general, the secretary of state—who serve as prison commissioners—and the staff of the main Carson City prison, charging that the overcrowded conditions in the prison constituted "cruel and unusual punishment." At a trial held in 1980, Judge Edward C. Reed found that the combination of overcrowded conditions and inadequate numbers of supervisory personnel did create a situation that led to violence and molestation of some prisoners, and the court mandated that certain minimum numbers of personnel be housed in some prison blocks. The court-ordered standards worked well for several years, but they were neglected following a change of prison administration, and Judge Reed found the prison authorities in contempt of court in 1988. He appointed a special monitor to assure compliance. (*Stickney v. List,* 1982; *Stickney v. Bryan,* 1988.)

In the 1970s and 1980s, Nevada had a larger percentage of people in prison than any other state in the nation, and it faced extraordinary costs in supervising its inmates and building new facilities to hold them. The prison population in 1970 was less than 700. By the end of 1980, it had grown to more than 1,800, and by 1986, to more than 4,300. By 1987, there were fourteen detention facilities under the jurisdiction of the Nevada Department of Prisons—including the original prison established in 1862 and thirteen other centers scattered throughout the state—devoted to correction, restitution, and conservation. Half of these were established in the ten years between 1976 and 1986. In addition, the legislature authorized a new $30 million prison near Ely and planned to construct another large facility near Lovelock.

Enlightened social policy and new court rulings had begun to change the public attitudes about prisons by the late 1980s, but this had little impact on public policy in Nevada before 1989.

## The 1988 Fiscal Study

Nevada marked the beginning of the 125th year of its statehood with the release of a massive fiscal study dealing with the manner in which the state and local governments financed their activities. This 700-page document, which had been mandated by the 1987 legislature, was the most thorough analysis of state and local fiscal matters in the history of the state, and it was widely regarded as a possible guideline for future decision making on taxation and expenditures.

The legislature had arranged for two nationally known research groups, the Urban Institute of Washington, D.C., and Price Waterhouse, to make the study. The senior editor was Robert D. Ebel, and it became known as the "Ebel report." Although it had not been intended as a document to suggest policy for the legislature, it nevertheless drew some important conclusions and made thoughtful projections and suggestions about fiscal policies.

A central assumption of the Ebel report held that Nevada's population would continue to increase in the 1990s and into the twenty-first century. The number of residents had exceeded one million in 1986—the third highest growth rate in the nation in the recent period. The report said that Nevada's schools and agencies would need more revenue by the mid-1990s simply in order to provide the same kind of education and government that existed in 1988, even if economic conditions remained favorable for the next few years. (If there were to be a recession, the study warned, either services would have to be reduced or taxes would have to be raised earlier.) The growth of population—especially the increasing number of children, elderly, those in need of welfare, and those sentenced to prison—would require more tax dollars for comparable service.

The study showed that Nevada's taxes in the 1980s were low by comparison with those of fifteen other western states or states whose economies relied heavily on tourism. "When compared with other states in terms of the relationship between its potential fiscal capacity and its actual tax effort, Nevada has fiscal room to maneuver. When ranked with other states, Nevada is next to last in tax effort." The report offered several criticisms of the state's existing taxing policy, including the assertion that the retail sales tax was "regressive"—i.e., that it put an unfair burden on the poorest section of society. It argued that Nevada voters would be unwise to close the door on the possibility of a state personal income tax, as they voted to do in a proposed constitutional amendment in the 1988 election.

It had long been evident from other studies that Nevada's government was spending substantially less on education and welfare on a per capita basis than the national average. The Ebel report data confirmed that this was still the case. Across the nation, Americans spent an average of more than $600 per person for primary and secondary education; in Nevada the figure was $550. In higher education the average expenditure was $235 per person nationally, $198 in Nevada. In public welfare, Nevada's per capita deviation from the national norm was even more marked: the national average was $318, but Nevada's was only $155. Obviously Nevada's government gave a lower priority to education and welfare than most other states did.

The Ebel report did not win much praise when it was first released; there was sharp criticism of it from both official and unofficial sources, and the 1989 legislature virtually ignored it. But it did prompt the citizens of the state to begin a serious dialogue on social priorities and public finances for the first time in thirty years.

In several respects, Nevada of the late 1980s had characteristics similar to those of the era of the pioneers, when most of its residents were transient single people. The 1986 edition of the *Nevada Statistical Abstract*, prepared by the governor's office, showed that Nevada had the smallest percentage of native-born residents of any state in the Union. Among all the fifty states, Nevada also had the highest percentage of households with only one or two persons, and a very high percentage of people who had arrived only a short time earlier. The combination of these and other statistics suggested that Nevada had the highest percentage of people without families or roots in the nation. It was a way station for people on their way somewhere else, as it had been in the days of the early mining and railroad camps. The high rate of dropouts in schools, the high prison statistics, and the burgeoning welfare needs all reflected this central fact. Nevada is still a state undergoing rapid transition at the end of the 1990s.

## Suggested Supplementary Reading

Bowers, Michael W. *The Sagebrush State: Nevada's History, Government, and Politics*. Reno: University of Nevada Press, 1996.

Bushnell, Eleanore, and Don W. Driggs. *The Nevada Constitution: Origin and Growth*. 6th ed. Reno: University of Nevada Press, 1984.

Crowley, Joseph N. *The Constant Conversation: A Chronicle of Campus Life*. Reno: Black Rock Press, University of Nevada, Reno, 2000.

Hulse, James W. *The University of Nevada: A Centennial History*. Reno: University of Nevada Press, 1974.

Hulse, James W., with Leonard E. Goodall and Jackie Allen. *Reinventing the System: Higher Education in Nevada, 1968–2000*. Reno: University of Nevada Press, 2002.

Nicoletta, Julie. *Buildings of Nevada*. Photography by Bret Morgan. New York: Oxford University Press, 2000.

Shepperson, Wilbur S., ed. *East of Eden, West of Zion: Essays on Nevada*. Reno: University of Nevada Press, 1989.

Soden, Dennis L., and Eric Herzik, eds. *Towards 2000: Public Policy in Nevada*. Dubuque: Kendall Hunt, 1997.

Watson, Anita Ernst. *Into Their Own: Nevada Women Emerging into Public Life*. Reno: Nevada Humanities Committee, 2000.

# 19
## The Struggle for Equal Rights

ONE OF the most difficult challenges that Nevada's civic institutions have faced in their 125 years of history has been to offer the fundamental rights and privileges of society to all its citizens. The frontier experience did not guarantee equal rights to all; from the beginning, many elements of society were systematically excluded from political and economic opportunities that white men took for granted. For decades, women and nonwhite males fell beyond the protection of the law.

As we study the background of Nevada's social policies, we must frequently remind ourselves of the fact that the state achieved its political identity during the Civil War—the most traumatic time in the history of the American Republic. Its leaders and most of its citizens were committed to the most conservative of purposes—the preservation of the federal Union that had been fashioned by George Washington, John Adams, Ben Franklin, Thomas Jefferson, James Madison, and John Marshall, among others.

That Union and Nevada's state institutions were presumably committed to a very liberal constitutional principle—that all men were created equal, and that they were endowed by the Creator with inalienable rights, and that among these rights were life, liberty, and the pursuit of happiness. In the 1860s, informed citizens did not see a sharp distinction between such liberal and conservative purposes, because they were complementary. They were meant to establish and defend the basic rights of the individual.

On the other hand, the men of that day did not regard the principle as applicable to women and minority races. These were ambiguities that the early citizens of Nevada brushed over lightly. The Nevada Constitution affirmed that:

> All men are, by nature, free and equal, and have certain inalienable rights, among which are those of enjoying and defending life and liberty; acquiring, possessing, and protecting property, and pursuing and obtaining safety and happiness. (Article I, Section 1, *Constitution of the State of Nevada.*)

Yet in later sections of that same constitution, the framers provided that only *white males* had the right to vote; therefore only they could hold office or serve on juries. Women, Asian-Americans, blacks, and Native Americans all remained outside the political process, except that most of them (excluding Indians) paid taxes and were subject to the laws. For most of these groups, decades—or, in some cases, more than a century—passed, and the goal of equal standing within society still had not been completely achieved. The roles of both women and the ethnic minorities have changed rapidly, especially in the second half of the twentieth century.

## The Struggle for Women's Rights

Nevada was, in the beginning, a man's state. The early explorers, prospectors, and railroad builders were virtually all men. A significant number of women traveled on the emigrant wagons, but a proportionally small number followed the early miners and railroad men as wives and homemakers. These were often culture builders, but not often participants in the political decision-making process because they did not have the right to vote until 1914—exactly fifty years after the admission of Nevada to the Union.

There were few professions in which women could exercise their talents without seeming unnatural, and the gender barriers fell slowly. They were almost universally accepted as schoolteachers and as caretakers/ nurses, but only gradually as clerks, secretaries, and journalists. We have seen in chapter 11 that little progress was made by women seeking greater political rights in the nineteenth century.

The outstanding pioneer for women's rights in Nevada in the early twentieth century was Anne Martin, born in 1875 in the little Carson River town called Empire, near the capital city. She received a good education at Stanford University, taught briefly at the University of Nevada in the 1890s, and later went on to an active career in politics.

Martin's father, a Carson City wood merchant and one-term state senator, had been successful enough to leave her a modest inheritance. She traveled several times to Europe between 1900 and 1910, and also to Egypt and the Orient—an unusual opportunity for a young woman in that era. Then in her middle thirties, she took up the cause of woman suffrage. The key group dedicated to this cause was the Nevada Equal Franchise Society, which was founded in 1911, with supporters in all parts of the state.

Martin emerged as the leader of this society and its successful effort to amend the state constitution to extend voting rights to women—a process that was completed in 1914. She had traveled throughout the state over rough roads in a primitive automobile to carry the suffrage campaign into remote towns and ranches. Her dedication paid dividends because it was the male voters of the remote mining and railroad towns and the ranches who provided many of the votes toward the victory in the crucial election. Nevada granted women the right to vote six years before the Nineteenth Amendment to the federal Constitution extended the franchise to all women in 1920.

Martin had many associates and allies across the state, one of the most active of whom was Bird Wilson, one of the state's first woman attorneys and stockbrokers. She practiced her professions for a time in Goldfield and was responsible for organizing the suffragist groups in Las Vegas and other parts of southern Nevada. Another influential organizer was Delphina Squires of Las Vegas, whose husband published the newspaper *The Las Vegas Age.*

In spite of the success of the suffragist movement, Martin regarded her life as a failure because she personally never won political office. She was the first woman ever to run for the U.S. Senate, and she did so twice, getting nearly 20 percent of the Nevada vote in 1920. She became a leading advocate of social reform and had a reputation as a radical in her own time. History writers have only belatedly given her the recognition that most of her contemporaries withheld. She died in California in 1950, sensing that she had been forgotten by history. More than thirty years later, however, an energetic organization called the Anne Martin Chapter of the Nevada Political Caucus was pressing forward on behalf of the movement that she had led in the first two decades of the century.

Those men who most actively opposed woman suffrage anticipated

**VOTE FOR**

# ANNE MARTIN

———

**Other Candidates for U. S.
Senate Support Big Business**

**She's For YOU**

*Campaign card from Anne Martin's senate race.
(Nevada Historical Society)*

that if women gained the right to vote, they would press for other reforms, such as closing the saloons and forbidding the sale of alcoholic beverages. They were correct, and women did actively participate in Prohibition, using an initiative petition in 1918 to outlaw the sale of liquor. Some political leaders were afraid that when women could vote, it would give additional political strength to manual laborers and thereby challenge the control exercised by the old oligarchies.

Even after women won the right to vote in 1914, progress toward political parity with men came slowly. The first woman elected to the Nevada legislature was Sadie D. Hurst, an assemblywoman who represented Washoe County in 1919. Frances Friedhoff of Hawthorne was the first woman to serve in the senate; she was appointed in 1935. One of the first successful newspaperwomen was Florence Lee Jones Cahlan, who became a prominent reporter in Las Vegas in the 1930s. Mildred Bray of Carson City broke another barrier when she won statewide elective office as superintendent of public instruction three times between 1938 and 1950. It was still unusual for women to hold statewide public office in the 1940s and 1950s, but later it became more common for them to win office in city and county governments as judges, administrators, and legislators. Barbara Vucanovich became Nevada's first congresswoman in 1983.

During the 1970s, the proposed Equal Rights Amendment (ERA) to the U.S. Constitution became a recurring issue in Nevada politics. This simple recommendation, passed by Congress in 1971, would merely have placed language in the Constitution that no person could be denied equal rights on the basis of sex, but it created a blizzard of misunderstanding and controversy because of a perception that it might diminish the status of women rather than assure their rights on the same basis as men's. Much of the controversy centered in Nevada because most other states of the North and West ratified quickly in the early 1970s, and favorable action by only three additional state legislatures would have added the ERA to the basic laws of the land. The Nevada legislature debated and declined to ratify in 1973, 1975, and again in 1977, then submitted the question to the electorate, who voted against the amendment by a majority of more than two to one. Political analysts speculated that the combined opposition of major religious denominations (including the Catholics and the Latter-day Saints) and the gambling-resort industry accounted for the defeat. Advocates of equal rights for women felt the same frustrations that Anne Martin and her contemporaries had known for several years before 1914.

Even though the Equal Rights Amendment failed in Nevada, the debate and publicity surrounding it led to important changes in the law which benefited women. The provisions of the minimum-wage law, previously applicable only to men, were extended to all workers. Women won equal rights with men in the control of community property. Legislative leaders such as Mary Gojack, Jean Ford, and Sue Wagner demonstrated admirable political skills in advancing a wide range of social reforms in a social climate that was not always friendly to their efforts.

## The Native Americans

In Nevada, as in several other western states, the status and the neglect of the rights of the American Indians have been the oldest ethnic problems. Although their numbers have been small by comparison with the Caucasian population, the Indians have presented the most persistent challenge to the sense of social justice in Nevada. Indians have at various times been treated as members of separate nations, as citizens, as uncivilized barbarians, and as wards dependent on the government. Federal and state policies have often been inconsistent. Their cultural achievements and ecological sensitivity have often been ignored.

From the beginnings of white settlement, there were a few individuals who tried to assure that Indians were fairly treated, but even those who intended to be their benefactors—such as the Mormons at the Las Vegas Mission in 1855–1858 and Warren Wasson, who became an agent for Territorial Governor James W. Nye in the 1860s—participated in their displacement from their native grounds. In most cases, white immigrants, workers, or settlers drove them from the land and water and killed the game without regard for the consequences those acts would bring to the Native Americans.

We mentioned in chapter 5 that President U.S. Grant, by executive order, established two reservations for the Northern Paiutes in 1874 at the lower ends of the Truckee and Walker rivers. Each embraced more than 300,000 acres that were presumably set aside for the bands that had traditionally lived in those regions. The Pyramid Lake Reservation remains much the same in scope as it was at that time, in spite of some intrusions by squatters. The boundaries of the Walker River Reservation, on the other hand, have been greatly altered due to policy changes over the years. Through much of their history, each of these reservations has served as home to anywhere from 400 to 700 Native Americans and, as custodians of the Native American heritage, for thousands more.

Elsewhere, the assurances of the government agents were less well honored. In southern Nevada, government officers initially offered the Southern Paiutes a reservation encompassing more than 30,000 square miles, but they eventually received only about 1,000 acres in the Moapa Valley in 1875. The Shoshones of northern and northeastern Nevada likewise endured broken promises and broken treaties as the Anglo-American frontier expanded; (see the mention of the Te-moak treaty in chapter 2). The federal government established a reservation at Duck Valley in the Owyhee River area of Elko County for these bands in 1877. In the 1980s, this was the most populous reservation in the state, with more than 800 people living within its boundaries in Nevada. However, all these reservations that were formed in the nineteenth century were able to serve fewer than a third of the Native Americans in the state.

One factor that kept the Indian people outside the mainstream of American life was the lack of standard education. Indian children were generally not accepted in the public schools of Nevada until the 1920s, and occasional effort to open Indian schools failed. Senator William M. Stewart played an important role in establishing the Stewart Indian School south of Carson City in the 1890s, but often the price of a rudimentary education was the separation of children from their widely scattered families.

In 1887, Congress passed the controversial Dawes Act, which intended to break up the reservations, divide the lands among individual tribal members, and accelerate the process of integrating them into the larger society. This principle was initially accepted for the Walker River Reservation in 1906, and later reversed; Pyramid Lake Indians never agreed to the process. The entire policy was rejected with the so-called Indian New Deal Act of 1934, which was based on the theory that the Native American heritage should be preserved and protected, and that Indian lands not yet distributed should be retained and expanded. During this era, an energetic female Indian agent named Alida Bowler worked diligently to try to protect the rights of local tribes.

In the meantime, Nevada's congressional delegation had taken direct interest in the problems of Native Americans whose ancestors had been displaced and who were often living in poverty on the fringes of the towns. In the early twentieth century, the U.S. government created several "colonies," or Indian communities within or near the towns where numbers of them lived. Helen Stewart, the noted Las Vegas Rancho owner, provided land from her property on her own initiative for such a colony in 1911. The government created colonies near Reno, Gardnerville, Winnemucca, Ely, Fallon, Yerington, and in other scattered places. There were more than twenty such communities in the late 1980s.

Congress recognized in 1946 that the aboriginal peoples throughout the country had been wrongfully displaced from much of their land by the pioneers in the mid-1800s. A federal statute enacted in that year created the Indian Claims Commission. After extensive hearings, the commission made determinations on the value of the land that was taken from the Indians in the last century and offered payments amounting to millions of dollars in compensation to Nevada tribes. In some cases, most notably in the instance of the Western Shoshones, the Native Americans denounced the money offer and affirmed that the land in question was still theirs, and not for sale.

The political influence of Nevada's Indians was small, because their numbers were few (only about 2 percent of the state's population), they were widely scattered, and their average incomes were lower than those of their fellow citizens. In some communities a few families were benefiting from small industry or business ventures, or from agriculture, but many others lived—like their forerunners for two or three generations— in chronic poverty. Neither Nevada nor the federal agencies had found a formula for both preserving the rich Indian heritage and providing the contemporary Indians with the benefits and amenities of the larger society.

## The Chinese Immigrants

When the Central Pacific company was building its railroad across Nevada in 1867–1869, most of the heavy manual work was performed by Chinese laborers who had been brought in for the construction crews. These men were tolerated while their services were needed to build the line as long as their presence seemed temporary; at least 10,000 to 12,000 of them prepared the roadbed and laid the rails. When, after the completion of the railroad, hundreds of them sought work in towns and on ranches, bitter hostility arose among the majority of the white population throughout the West. Hundreds of Chinese congregated in Carson City and the old mining town of Tuscarora in Elko County, and many scattered to other towns to establish restaurants and laundries.

One of Nevada's best-known Chinese immigrants was Gue Gim Wah. She arrived in Nevada with her husband Tom Wah in 1917 and became legendary for the Chinese cuisine she prepared for workers in a mining

*Tom and Gue Gim Wah. (Elizabeth Gemmell Frizzell Collection, University of Nevada, Las Vegas, Library)*

camp near Pioche. Gue Gim Wah remained a Nevada resident for over seventy years until her death in the late 1980s.

The Chinese population declined sharply in Nevada between 1880 and 1900, partly because of the general depression and partly because of the hostility against them. Hundreds of individual acts of violence were committed against peoples from the Far East in a score of Nevada towns. During the Tonopah bonanza years, a mob murdered a Chinese man who had lived in the state peacefully for more than thirty years, and the killers escaped punishment. In Reno a few years later, other vandals burned most of Chinatown. The population of this ethnic group declined to fewer than 300 in the 1940s. The tiny Japanese contingent also endured humiliating discrimination early in this century.

As the number of people of Asian descent increased after 1950, the old patterns of bigotry evaporated. Contemporary peoples from the Far East, including several thousand Vietnamese, Filipinos, and Japanese, as well as Chinese, have made their homes and found good employment opportunities in Nevada. The Nevada Equal Rights Commission, established in 1961, found no notable pattern of discrimination against these peoples in the first twenty years of its operation. Asiatics did claim, however, that they were barred from middle-management jobs in the Las Vegas resort industry. In 1964, the state officially recognized and honored its pioneers of Chinese descent for their contributions to society.

## The Blacks, or African-Americans

The problems for Nevada's black population have been different from those of other minority groups because through most of the state's early history this segment was so small that it was politically insignificant. Only since 1960 has Nevada been forced to face the fact that it had allowed unfair practices to develop that were harming its growing number of black citizens.

Nevada was the first state in 1869 to ratify the Fifteenth Amendment—which provided that no citizen could be denied the right to vote on the basis of race—and some African-Americans had the franchise as early as 1870. The clause in the original state constitution that granted voting rights only to white males was removed in 1880 by a popular vote of 14,215 in favor, 672 against. A companion measure granted the right to vote and hold office to all male citizens regardless of race. Yet this did not assure social or economic equality to black citizens because many carried the social scars of slavery, and because unofficial barriers existed in the major employment fields throughout the nation. For example, it was virtually impossible for blacks to find work in most mines or on the railroad construction and maintenance crews.

As Professor Elmer Rusco has shown in his book *"Good Time Coming?" Black Nevadans in the Nineteenth Century*, there was a pattern of discrimination against blacks in the 1860s, not only because the Nevada Constitution extended political rights to white males only, but also because minority children were forbidden by law to attend school with white children, and other racist barriers existed in the workplaces. The law which mandated separate schools was declared unconstitutional in 1872.

Yet the experiences of black people during the period of the depression in the 1880s and 1890s were apparently not as humiliating as those of the Indians and Chinese. Nevada's official and unofficial policies toward blacks gradually became more enlightened in the 1870s, 1880s, and 1890s. Perhaps because the African-American population was so small (there were about 396 blacks in Nevada in 1880 and only 134 in 1900), less apparent discrimination existed in those years, but few of them ever held well-paying jobs.

After 1900, however, with the new mining booms and railroad building, bitter and degrading racist statements against blacks appeared in the newspapers, and they were forcefully expelled or prohibited from settling in some towns. This was a period when discriminatory "Jim Crow" legislation became popular across the nation, and Nevada's congressman and senator Francis Newlands joined the chorus of bigotry. Still, Nevada's black population remained very small.

Because of its growth patterns, Las Vegas became the focus of interest in race relations in twentieth-century Nevada. Walter Bracken, the influential officer of the Las Vegas Land & Water Company, tried to segregate blacks in a single section of the town (Block 17 adjacent to the red-light district). However, many Las Vegas businesses, including most places of entertainment and recreation, accepted their trade through the 1920s, and this remained true of the gambling clubs in the early 1930s. While blacks seldom held the better jobs, there was no blatant policy of discrimination in hiring and employment.

The first overt pattern of general discrimination came in 1931, when the Six Companies, builders of Hoover Dam, refused to hire blacks on their construction crews. This unofficial policy provoked the creation of an association to work against discrimination in employment.

The building of Hoover (Boulder) Dam in the 1930s brought the first few hundred black workers to southern Nevada, and subtle patterns of discrimination emerged there in employment and housing. When World War II introduced new military and industrial activities to Clark County, several hundred more African-American citizens arrived, mostly from Louisiana and Arkansas, and a serious pattern of residential segregation emerged in Las Vegas that forced most blacks into the Westside (formerly the old McWilliams' Township). This rapidly became an overcrowded ghetto, with inferior public services. As we have seen in chapter 18, the schools that served the black children there were markedly inferior to those available elsewhere in the city until the federal court intervened.

At Henderson, as the U.S. government built the Basic Magnesium plant in the early 1940s, the contractors established housing on a segregated basis, setting aside an area named after George Washington Carver, a noted black scientist, for blacks. The contractors segregated the workplaces and the dining halls, and the housing accommodations in Carver Park were inferior to those provided for white workers.

Later, as the Strip expanded southward and the Las Vegas hotel-casino business flourished, African-Americans were systematically relegated to the lower-paying service jobs, such as maids and maintenance people. In most casinos, blacks were denied the privilege of dining, gambling, or attending the shows, even in places where black entertainers were performing. Thus in the 1940s, de facto racial discrimination grew to an extent that had never existed previously. It extended, informally and by gradual stages, to swimming pools and hospitals, and the Las Vegas police force remained almost entirely white in spite of the growth of minority populations. By the 1950s, some journalists and critics were calling Nevada "the Mississippi of the West." This was not a totally accurate description, because Nevada had no official statewide policy of segregated schools, separate sections of buses, and separate restrooms and water fountains. The discrimination that existed in Nevada was real, but it was erratic and not institutionalized by law.

There were a few pioneering efforts to have laws passed in Carson City to deal with these inequities. The legislature of 1939 received the first bill, introduced by the Clark County delegation, intended to bar discrimination in places of public accommodation. This measure failed quickly, as did several similar measures introduced between 1947 and 1963. As early as 1949, a group of University of Nevada students and professors in Reno pressed for a civil rights law because of the obvious discrimination in Reno, but no response came from Carson City.

The legislature delayed the passage of a state civil rights act for several reasons. In the first place, Nevada did not immediately have the social pressures that were becoming obvious in the South and East, where demonstrations and occasional violence erupted in the wake of the U.S. Supreme Court's ruling in *Brown v. Board of Education of Topeka,* the decision which held racial segregation in schools was unconstitutional.

In the middle 1950s, a determined contingent of civil rights advocates formed in Las Vegas, including a dentist, Dr. James McMillan, and a physician, Dr. Charles West, both articulate and respected blacks. Using the growing voting power of the minorities and the national publicity on racial disturbances in other parts of the country, they pointed the way toward a reversal of the city's growing "Jim Crow" attitude. In 1960, in the midst of racial tension in the South and East, Dr. McMillan threatened passive resistance and demonstrations on the Las Vegas Strip if local businesses did not end their discriminatory policies by March 26. The city political and business leaders at first resisted, but hours before the deadline, they announced a policy of nondiscrimination in places of public accommodation. The owners of the Strip resorts followed their example, and a racial crisis was averted, for the time being, in Las Vegas.

More serious demonstrations for minority rights in Nevada occurred in 1961, when a few blacks staged a "sit-in" in Reno and marched before the capitol building in Carson City to protest discrimination. In that year, the legislature created a weak and poorly financed Equal Rights Commission to make inquiry about whether a pattern of racial discrimination existed. This was merely a delaying tactic, because the fact of increasing segregation was obvious.

Nevada did not act officially to prohibit racial discrimination in housing, employment, and places of public accommodation until after Congress had passed the landmark federal Civil Rights Act of 1964 and a widely publicized demonstration against Las Vegas casinos threatened to bring federal intervention. Nevada was one of the last states in the North and West to fashion a meaningful policy to discourage racial bigotry.

The most severe crisis in race relations in Nevada history occurred in Las Vegas in 1969 and 1970, when a series of riots and disorders occurred at local schools and eventually spilled over to the streets of the Westside. At the peak of the crisis, Governor Paul Laxalt placed the Nevada National Guard on alert. But a series of compromises that provided for the hiring of more black teachers, plus the effective court decisions of Judge Thompson (discussed in chapter 18), allowed the passions to subside without the level of violence that several other cities had experienced.

Although substantial progress was made thereafter, even at the end of the 1980s many remnants of the backward policy of the 1950s remained. As a result, the majority of Nevada's 50,000 black citizens had employment opportunities and incomes below the average level for Caucasian workers, and the unemployment rate of blacks was chronically higher.

An important court case involving the rights of minorities in Nevada came before Federal Judge Edward C. Reed, Jr., in 1980. The plaintiff, Willie Washington, was a black man who had sought employment with the Reno City Fire Department and who filed a class-action suit on the grounds that the written test given to job seekers discriminated against minority-race applicants. After hearing evidence and reviewing the facts, Judge Reed agreed with the plaintiff; the city had never hired a black fire fighter in the century-long history of the department, and the test results indicated a pattern of discrimination. Under the court's direction, a compromise procedure provided for two hiring lists to be used alternately until a reasonable ratio of minority employees had been hired.

## The Hispanics

The fastest-growing ethnic minority in Nevada in the 1980s was the Hispanic people—those from Mexico, Central America, and other parts of the Spanish-speaking world. In less than a decade, this section of society had grown from a few thousand to more than fifty thousand, mostly concentrated in the Las Vegas area, but with increasing numbers on the livestock and potato-raising ranches of the north.

At the beginning of the 1990s, the census officers counted 124,418 Hispanic residents in the state, with more than 82,000 living in Clark County and nearly 23,000 in the Reno-Sparks area. There were indications that many people in this ethnic category were not counted. Thousands of Hispanics may have avoided the census takers in 1980 because they were in the country illegally. Later federal legislation enabled many of these people to seek permanent immigration status and to regularize their presence in the United States.

Because Nevada is on the fringe of the southwestern border states through which much of the immigration from Mexico has come, it faces similar but smaller challenges than its neighbors. Southern California and Arizona have received hundreds of thousands who have fled the poverty of Mexico or the political turmoil of Central America to seek homes and jobs in the United States. Las Vegas, with its abundance of employment opportunities in the service businesses, has been especially attractive to these individuals. A study by Professor Tony Miranda of the University of Nevada, Las Vegas, predicted that Hispanics would be the fastest-growing ethnic minority for many years in the future, because the tourist industry offered many chances to those who did not speak English, as well as the possibility of "upward mobility" for those who are bilingual.

The newly arrived Hispanics did not face overt discrimination in Nevada comparable to that which faced the Chinese in the nineteenth century or the blacks in the early twentieth century, but the official statistics revealed several problems. Per capita income of Hispanics was lower than that of whites, housing was more crowded, and the school dropout rate was higher. The fact that many Hispanics came from backgrounds of poverty and had low expectations of future success preconditioned some young people to accept less attractive positions in society.

Yet Professor Miranda observed that many Hispanic immigrants arrived with dreams of a better life—the dream that brought thousands of the original settlers to the Far West. Some segments of this group— notably the Cuban-Americans—have fared quite well within the state. And the political awareness and activity of the Hispanics increased notably as their numbers grew.

Nevada, like the rest of the nation, made much progress in most areas of civil rights since the Supreme Court's ruling in *Brown v. Board of Education of Topeka*. At the very least, the passive indifference that had allowed for segregated schools and places of opportunity was widely recognized as a social mistake, and important strides were made in offering employment and housing opportunities to people of all ethnic backgrounds on a more equal basis. While supporters of the Equal Rights Amendment were bitterly disappointed by the defeats they suffered in the 1970s, no one could confidently assert that their movement was dead. The proponents for ethnic and sexual equality across the spectrum of society seemed poised for new efforts at the beginning of the 1990s.

# Suggested Supplementary Reading

Crum, Stephen J. *The Road on Which We Came: A History of the Western Shoshone*. Salt Lake City: University of Utah Press, 1994.

Hopkins, Sarah Winnemucca. *Life Among the Piutes: Their Wrongs and Claims*, ed. Mrs. Horace Mann. 1883. Reprint, Reno: University of Nevada Press, 1994.

Howard, Anne Bail. *The Long Campaign: A Biography of Anne Martin*. Reno: University of Nevada Press, 1985.

Knack, Martha C., and Omer C. Stewart. *As Long as the River Shall Run: An Ethnohistory of Pyramid Lake Indian Reservation*. Berkeley: University of California Press, 1984.

McMillan, James B. *Fighting Back: A Life in the Struggle for Civil Rights*. Interviews by Gary E. Elliott; narrative compiled by R. T. King. Reno: University of Nevada Oral History Program, 1997.

Miranda, M. L. *A History of Hispanics in Southern Nevada*. Reno: University of Nevada Press, 1997.

Moehring, Eugene P. *Resort City in the Sunbelt: Las Vegas 1930–2000*. Reno: University of Nevada Press, 2000.

Rusco, Elmer R., and Sue Fawn Chung, eds. *Ethnicity and Race in Nevada*. Special issue of *Nevada Public Affairs Review* 2 (1987).

Zanjani, Sally. *Sarah Winnemucca*. Lincoln: University of Nebraska Press, 2001.

# 20

## The Twelve
## Northern Counties

I
N THE previous chapters, we have explored many dimensions of the
Nevada experience. The terrain of this state was once infamous as a
dangerous barrier for emigrants on their way to California. Later it
became the site of several silver and gold bonanzas. It has been regarded
both as a lonely outback suitable only for sheepherders and prospectors,
and also as a mecca for experimenters and bettors. It has a reputation
as the world's foremost nuclear-testing laboratory, and its citizens are
recognized as highly creative promoters of tourism and gambling. It is
frontier country for organized crime and also for those who would eliminate the mobsters. In population, Nevada is one of the smallest of the
fifty states in the Union, but it invites and receives more intense national
publicity than many others. It is a testing ground for unorthodox social
theories and an outpost of solid American conservatism. Because the
state is so large and its centers of population so widely scattered, no
single generalization about it will suffice for a historical summary. It is
not, in the broadest sense, a single commonwealth, but rather a kalei-
doscope of variety and change.

Nevadans have become accustomed to thinking of the seventeen
counties as fixed units in the social and political spectrum; it will be
convenient here to speak rather of geographical regions as we summa-
rize the Nevada heritage at the beginning of the 1990s. Every section of
the state, whether or not it has been directly affected by the changes

that touched Las Vegas and the Reno-Carson-Tahoe area, has shared the transformation of the late twentieth century. Every town and region represents a different response to the challenge of maintaining a society in the rugged terrain of the Basin and Range topographical province. Previously, we discussed the evolution of both Reno and Las Vegas. In this chapter and the next, we shall begin a descriptive tour of some of the twelve northern counties, beginning in the corner of the state with the communities that were the earliest to be identified as "Nevada."

## Carson City

The town that was built around the optimism of Abraham Curry and the political preferences of Territorial Governor James Nye and Senator William M. Stewart contains the finest collection of architectural and historical monuments to Nevada's early heritage, in spite of a recent history of ungainly growth that has diluted its traditional charm.

Yet Carson City continues to be, 150 years after its founding, one of Nevada's most appealing communities. It has its share of eclectic "casino modern" architecture, but as of 2000 this had not become the dominant presence within the community. The towering backdrop of the Sierra Nevada has not been obscured or spoiled by the intrusion of neon. The old heart of the capital city still has dozens of well-maintained public and private edifices dating from the nineteenth century, and the state museum holds the best single collection of Nevadiana in existence. But the visitor must now pass through miles of urban sprawl to reach them from the north, east, or south, because Carson City's population has grown to over 50,000.

Although Carson City has long since been outdistanced by Las Vegas and Reno as a commercial and entertainment center, it has been more fortunate and successful in retaining the monuments of its earlier prominence. No other community has a finer structural heritage in a small space. The old capitol building—the center of which dates from the 1870s—was substantially modernized in the 1970s without disturbing the exterior and while successfully leaving much of its interior elegance intact. The handsome legislative building (1971)—designed by Reno architect Graham Erskine in collaboration with David Vhay and Raymond Hellman—is a stately complement to the capitol complex. In the heart of the city there is still the noble, three-story, red brick federal building that once served as the post office and U.S. courthouse, built in the 1890s and recently the home of the state library. The state museum—which once housed the U.S. Mint where famous silver dollars were produced from 1870 until 1894—has likewise been restored and expanded. The governor's mansion, built in 1906, has been refurbished in a Georgian style that reflects the tastes of Carson designers at the turn of the century. The Capitol Complex was enlarged by the construction of the new supreme court and library buildings on the quadrangle that includes the legislative building and the old capitol. The legislative building itself was remodeled and expanded in 1996.

No city in the state, large or small, has been more fortunate in the preservation of historic homes from the pioneer era. An official "historic district" has identified more than a hundred buildings that are architecturally significant in the center of the city, including scores of residences representing ten major domestic architectural styles that were popular between 1850 and 1940. It boasts the oldest Nevada newspaper still published in the same town, the oldest fire engine company, and the most authentic items associated with the era of Mark Twain.

Carson remained the nerve center of the state government despite the expansion of many administrative responsibilities to Las Vegas, Reno, and elsewhere. At legislative time—during the winter and spring of the odd-numbered years—its temporary population expands considerably.

## Virginia City

Although it is now one of the smallest county seats in Nevada, Virginia City has survived as a viable community better than most of the mining towns of the 1870s because it is just near enough to and far enough from the crowds and commerce of Reno and Carson City. The tourists can reach it easily, and although they sometimes overwhelm it at noon, they usually leave before sundown. It had—at least until the early twenty-first century—survived the constant threat of fire and the ravages of the new gold miners. (Gold Hill, on the other side of the "divide," was not so fortunate, having been scarred by a great open-pit mining operation during the 1970s. Only a handful of the original buildings and authentic restorations outlasted this calamity.)

It was on the slopes of Mt. Davidson that the second Nevadans (the Native American bands were first) generated the social standards, political expectations, and speculative fever that became characteristic of the Silver State. Virginia City attracted, produced, or gave notoriety to most of the men who laid the foundations of the state in the late nineteenth century. Few of its monuments and artifacts from the 1860s survive, but as of the early 2000s, it still proudly displayed two score buildings that were erected in the bonanza days of the 1870s and shortly thereafter. Such structures as the Storey County Courthouse, Piper's Opera House, St. Mary's in the Mountains Catholic Church, St. Paul's Episcopal Church, the Presbyterian Church, the Miners' Union Hall, and a score of the surviving bonanza-era buildings along B and C streets must now compete with dozens of more recent commercial intruders for the attention of the visitors, but the heritage of the most romantic period of Nevada's mining camp history is well represented nonetheless. Virginia City was at the heart of one of the largest federally recognized historic districts in America.

More than any other town of Nevada, this one has been regarded as having charm, character, and faded glamour. It was not uncommon in decades past to refer to Virginia City as a grand lady or a dowager queen; she is the great-grandmother of modern Nevada. For Nevadans with a sense of history, to visit her at a quiet time is like a visit home, for it reminds us of how and why we began our experiment as a commonwealth.

The Comstock is perched on the slopes of Mt. Davidson, to the northeast of Carson City. West of the capital, on much higher terrain, is Nevada's most beautiful, most popular, and most vulnerable lake.

## The Tahoe Basin:
## Development versus Conservation

The most tangled and frustrating history of change in northern Nevada has been written on the shores of Lake Tahoe, the once-pristine mountain lake in the high Sierra that is shared by Nevada and California. For more than a century there has been a series of skirmishes among those who live and own property in the basin, those who use its waters in the Truckee River downstream, conservationists and naturalists who want to preserve its natural beauty, and the various government agencies who control most of the land around it.

From the 1870s until the 1940s, there were recurring legal battles over the uses of Tahoe water. In the 1860s, an enterprising California engineer named Alexis von Schmidt proposed to divert much of the lake's water to the California Central Valley and San Francisco, and built a dam at the lake's outlet for this purpose. This dam, located at the point where the Truckee River leaves the lake, never served its original purpose, but it did raise the level of the lake six feet above its natural rim—thus creating a reservoir "on top" of the lake that could store large quantities of water for later downstream use. Eventually, homeowners, ranchers, utility companies, Indians at Pyramid Lake, and government agencies came to rely upon this source.

After long and costly litigation, the Tahoe-Truckee water disputes seemed to be resolved in 1944 with the so-called Orr Ditch decree issued by the U.S. District Court for Nevada, in which all the major claimants to Truckee River water rights agreed to a formula for storing and distributing the water (see chapter 15). At that time, Tahoe and its surrounding mountains were largely unspoiled. Some families had summer cabins there, and small ski clubs made occasional excursions to the nearby slopes, but there was little commercial development and little expectation that there would be much because roads were poor in the best of weather and hazardous in winter. The year-round population of the Tahoe Basin was about 2,000 or 3,000 people; the summer population did not exceed 20,000.

During the first fifteen years after World War II, the skiers, gamblers, and developers "discovered" Tahoe and transformed it into a world-famous resort center. One of Reno's largest casino operators, William Harrah, extended his gambling empire onto the lake's south shore in 1955, and other resort promoters followed. Soon there were clusters of casinos, motels, and other ancillary businesses crowding the north and south ends of the lake. The crowning achievement of those who wanted to promote Tahoe's beauty and the recreational opportunities of the region was the successful bid to host the 1960 Winter Olympics at nearby Squaw Valley. Thousands of visitors, countless newspaper columns, and hours of television publicity followed. Visitors arrived at Tahoe by the thousands in both winter and summer after 1960. As a sensitive historian of the Tahoe region, Douglas H. Strong, wrote in 1984, the basin had become afflicted by "runaway growth," with urban sprawl damaging much of its natural beauty and polluting its waters.

Fortunately, a defensive action had been mounted by several individuals and groups to resist the destruction, but it was only partly successful in retarding the excessive development. Much of the adjacent land had been designated as national forest by the mid-1950s, and Nevada acquired much of the eastern shoreline and mountains for a state park. Through additional acquisitions, public agencies acquired about 70 percent of the land in the basin by the 1970s.

Yet the effort to develop a basinwide plan for orderly growth foundered. Because the state boundary runs through Lake Tahoe and because the two states share many streams outside the basin, Congress had authorized a California-Nevada Interstate Compact Commission in 1955 to settle questions relating to all the waters of the Truckee, Carson, and Walker rivers. The legislatures of the two states had endorsed the commission in a spirit of hope, but it took the members thirteen years to prepare a report, which finally won ratification by the two legislatures in 1971. However, Secretary of Commerce Walter Hickle opposed the compact, asserting that the rights of Pyramid Lake Indians had not been sufficiently addressed, and Congress delayed action. Nearly twenty years later, the matter was still unresolved, several lawsuits had been initiated, and the development of Tahoe's shoreline had proceeded.

In the meantime, the summer population of the basin had grown to approximately 200,000 — including 60,000 permanent residents — by the 1980s, a ten-fold increase within four decades. Incline Village at the north end of the lake and Stateline on the southern fringe had become medium-sized communities which straddle the border. Traffic around the lake had increased to a point that exhaust fumes were damaging the flora, the quality of the lake's water had measurably declined, and air pollution had become oppressive and unhealthful. The voters of both Nevada and California at first rejected and then approved large bond issues in the 1980s to allow their governments to purchase some environmentally sensitive lands. The Nevada bond issue, authorizing $31 million, won approval in 1986, but ten years later the clarity of the water was still declining. In 1997 a major environmental conference, attended by President Bill Clinton, tried to find new ways to reduce the pollution that was threatening to destroy a natural treasure.

## Carson Valley and Douglas County

Situated in that idyllic corner where the western boundary of Nevada ceases to follow the meridian and becomes a diagonal pointed toward the Colorado River is Douglas County, which includes most of Carson Valley—the birthplace of Nevada. The high, rugged Sierra peaks that encircle Tahoe drop sharply on their eastern escarpment, providing a distinct punctuation mark between the desert of the Great Basin and the towering mountain wall. There are few more pleasant settings in Nevada than this well-watered enclave, framed by the snowcapped highlands to the west and the gray-brown Pine Nut Mountains to the east.

There is little reason to wonder why settlers from Utah chose this valley for a station in 1850, though it was 500 miles from Salt Lake City. It was on the main emigrant trail to California, it seemed promising for agriculture, and its location close against the Sierra foothills seemed to be as far westward as they could reasonably hope to establish their projected state of Deseret (see chapter 5). Nearly a century and a half later, this valley remains one of the favored localities of the inland West for its beauty and bucolic charm.

As the decades passed and the mining booms came and went, Carson Valley endured more commercial disappointments but fewer drastic changes than its neighbors to the north and east. The earliest residents of Genoa regarded their town successively as a mission station for the church, as a county seat, and as a potential commercial center. But the Mormons retreated, and when Nevada Territory came into existence in 1861, the political headquarters soon shifted a dozen miles northward to Eagle Valley (Carson City). Shortly thereafter, the commercial and industrial heart of the territory shifted to the Comstock Lode and the Truckee Meadows.

Genoa and Carson Valley became commercial backwaters in the human flood that swept across Nevada during the bonanza years, but that fact allowed those who settled the region to transplant and cultivate a style of life that had more in common with Europe or the Midwest than with the bonanza camps. Henry F. Dangberg, a German immigrant who had come west in the 1850s, was one of few tenacious early settlers who held onto his land when the early prosperity faded, and he encouraged more of his fellow countrymen to join him. These and other farmers produced and sold crops and dairy products to the Comstock towns and Carson City, and a thriving lumber industry harvested timber from the Sierra for the mines. The prosperity of Carson Valley rose and fell with the mining communities, but it was not totally dependent upon them.

In the 1880s, the new town of Gardnerville emerged on the east fork of the Carson River because there was need for a commercial core in the center of the valley. Within a decade, it had virtually replaced Genoa as the local marketplace. Farmers and traders came from as far as Bishop and Bridgeport in California to buy and sell.

The Dangberg family emerged from the depression of the 1880s and 1890s with an extensive ranching empire intact, and set a patriarchal style reminiscent of Central Europe. In 1905 they founded the town of Minden—named for the German birthplace of H. F. Dangberg—to serve as the southern terminus of the Virginia & Truckee Railroad, which was then under construction in the valley. Within a few years it had won the county seat from Genoa, where the genteel decay had become a way of life. All these changes occurred gradually, under local, private initiative or neglect, and the valley assumed a conservative social attitude that did not always match that of the more dynamic, younger regions. The valley had the service of the Virginia & Truckee for as long as it survived — until 1950.

Douglas County contains only 751 square miles — less than 1 percent of the total area of the state. Yet by 2000, the population within the Nevada portion of Carson Valley approached 35,000, and several thousand more had crowded onto the Nevada side of the line at the south end of Lake Tahoe. In addition, subdivisions were appearing in and near the Pine Nut range to the east. Carson Valley acquired some light industry in the 1980s and felt the early pangs of commercialization, but it had established two of the finest museums in the state at Genoa as testimonials to its ties with the pioneer past.

Carson Valley is near the verdant upper end of the Carson River system where the two forks debouch from the Sierra. Here the nineteenth-century pioneers found inviting surroundings for their labors. It was much more challenging for others to build an agricultural community in the bleak and alkaline lower reaches of the same valley in the early part of the twentieth century.

## Fallon and the Newlands Project

In chapter 15 we dealt with the beginnings of the Newlands Project and the establishment of the towns of Fallon and Fernley as a result of the new irrigation possibilities. Here there grew a society eager for experimentation — both social and agricultural. The building of Derby Dam, the Truckee Canal, and the Lahontan Reservoir between 1905 and 1915 promised a regular supply of water in the lower Carson Valley where agriculture had been virtually impossible earlier. Patches of green pasture and cropland appeared here, in one of the poorest counties in the state and one of the most barren valleys. At first most farmers produced the old Nevada staple — alfalfa — as their basic cash crop. The agricultural districts developed slowly before 1920 because of the excessive alkaline in the soil, uncertain pricing conditions, and the difficulty of marketing their crops in distant regions.

For a brief period during World War I, a socialist colony existed within the Newlands Project area. Its members hoped to develop a cooperative society that would work for world peace and mutual assistance rather than war and economic competition. Those who came to Fallon and Fernley were initially responsive to such social reform ideals, but these notions did not survive the local violence and patriotic zeal provoked by the war.

Fallon producers and businessmen engaged in more agricultural experiments than any other comparable group in the state during the next half century. They assumed local control from the federal government for the management of the Truckee-Carson Irrigation District. In the 1920s, they won attention throughout the West for the production of a special variety of cantaloupe, which were widely publicized as "Heart-O-Gold" melons from the Lahontan Valley. Production and marketing were successful for a few years, but the drought and depression of the early 1930s dampened hopes. Another venture, stimulated by George Wingfield of Goldfield and Reno, promoted the dairy business on a grand scale, and this continued more or less successfully for more than a half century. Beef production also became an important segment of the local economy, with some of the largest feeding and breeding operations in the state located here. Fallon also became the state's main region for the production of turkeys, chickens, and eggs during the 1920s, but once again the depression did permanent damage to the original optimism.

After more than fifty years of trying, with mixed success, to build its economy on agriculture, Fallon—like so many other communities—found prosperity as a defense-industry community. During World War II, the U.S. Navy chose Fallon as the site for an aerial gunnery training station because of the good flying conditions and the nearby open spaces available for target practice. The base became inactive in 1946 after the war ended, but the navy restored it to wartime status in 1951 during the Korean conflict. During the Vietnam War of the 1970s, more than 2,300 military personnel were regularly stationed there, causing the Fallon economy to expand as never before.

# Lyon County

For 125 years, Lyon County has been on the edge of Nevada's history, but it has also been a microcosm of what turn-of-the-century Nevada wanted to be. For its size, the county has more sagebrush-state history confined within its ragged borders than any other. The county contains only 2,024 square miles—less than 2 percent of Nevada's total area—

yet it shares some part of all three of the western Nevada rivers — the Truckee, the Carson, and the Walker. It also claims the old emigrant trail market town of Dayton and a corner of the Comstock Lode at Silver City. It shared the copper-mining boom of the 1950s and 1960s with the Anaconda operation at Weed Heights. At its northern tip, there is a piece of the Newlands Project adjacent to Fernley; at its southern end a part of the Toiyabe National Forest. Old Fort Churchill of Civil War fame serves as its heart, and the well-watered Mason Valley as its midsection. It has its own sprawling example of desert suburbia at Silver Springs and a corner of the Walker River Indian Reservation in the northeast.

Yerington is only about 35 air miles from Carson City, but it seems more remote because of the intervening mountains. It is more than 65 miles by regular highway from the capital. In 1989, it was still more rural and bucolic than either Carson City, Minden-Gardnerville, or Fallon because it was more remote from the tourist arterials, and the agricultural environs still dominated the landscape. Throughout its mid-century history, Lyon County ranchers have typically irrigated more than 80,000 acres and tended more than 45,000 head of livestock in their relatively small valleys. At times there have been as many as 400 working farms and ranches in the county. Time has not stood still in Lyon County, but it has been merciful.

Fernley, only 30 miles east of Reno-Sparks and 50 miles from Carson City, lost its identity as an agricultural center and increasingly became a "bedroom" community for those larger urban areas in the 1980s. Most of the farmland had been subdivided into lots for single-family homes, and Fernley claimed a population of more than 8,500 as the century ended. Most of the local residents in the work force preferred to live there and commute to their employment because buying and renting homes was much less costly in Fernley; at least 70 percent of the population had jobs in the cities to the west. Studies conducted for the local school board, based on the experience of the early 1980s, projected a doubling of the population within the near future.

## Sparks as a Commercial Center

No city or county in Nevada has been as successful as its boosters would like it to be in attracting new business and diversifying its economy, but in the late 1990s the community of Sparks had one of the most enviable records in the state in attracting new businesses outside the dominant tourist-gambling sector. Its political and business interests have been able to preserve its identity separate from Reno even as the two cities grew to be contiguous along a common border.

At the end of the 1990s, Sparks was a warehousing and light industry city of considerable regional importance. It shared this role with Reno because, fundamentally, the Truckee Meadows region is a single geographical and economic unit, but with more than 130 companies, Sparks enjoyed a higher percentage of diversified nontourist businesses than Reno, and its spokespeople were eager to cultivate their distinctiveness.

The crucial stimulant for this business was the enactment of a "freeport" law by the Nevada legislature in 1949, which provided a property tax exemption for goods in transit. This allowed large companies that planned to distribute and sell their products in other parts of the West to store and assemble them in Nevada warehouses without the payment of heavy property taxes that were standard in other states. The legislature gradually refined and improved this law, and in 1960 the voters added it to the state constitution, which provided an assurance that the policy would not rapidly be changed. A dozen Nevada towns tried to take advantage of the freeport provision and attract businesses on the basis of it, but none was more successful on a proportional basis than Sparks.

Among the industries located in or near Sparks is a diving-board manufacturer (14 miles east), a company engaged in the harnessing of thermal energy, a pillow maker, and a venetian blind factory. Within the city's boundary is a 450-acre industrial park with a substantial amount of available space for development.

The local governments of Reno, Washoe County, and Sparks had chronic problems trying to cooperate and coordinate their planning to manage growth in a responsible way. Their records of performance were not as chaotic as those of the Las Vegas and Clark County governments in the 1970s and 1980s, but only because the population growth was not as great in the Truckee Meadows as it was in the Las Vegas Valley.

## The Changing Scene along Highway 50

In the stretch of land due east of Sparks, Fernley, and Fallon, lies the region that the promoters of tourism call Pony Express Territory, because the famous riders and horses of 1860 and 1861 crossed it before the days of the railroad and the telegraph. Three of the earlier mining rushes — at Austin, Eureka, and Hamilton — put their marks on these environs in the 1860s, and the great copper district near Ely led the state's mineral industry for more than a half century. But it was a land of little change for more than a hundred years, until the gold rush of the 1980s.

When an eastern journalist described Highway 50 across the center of the state as "the loneliest highway in America" in the early 1980s, local businessmen rallied to turn the indictment into an asset, and apparently it had beneficial commercial effects in the advertising which followed. Once called the Lincoln Highway, it crosses ten rugged mountain ranges and as many serene valleys, an appealing alternative to thousands of motorists who want to avoid the pressures of the freeways.

Neighbors are far apart along Highway 50. Three or four hundred residents of Austin preserved their town almost in the exact center of the state more than a century after its original mines fell dormant and even after it could no longer sustain its claim to a county seat. Yet its livestock ranges, the occasional mining operations, and the thin thread of the "loneliest road" enabled this matron of the eastern Nevada mining frontier to repel the "ghosts" who had taken over hundreds of other pioneer camps.

Eureka, a ninety-minute drive eastward from Austin, was the best preserved 1870s mining town in central Nevada, with its handsome, red brick courthouse, an opera house, newspaper building, and other ornaments from the bonanza days—a three-dimensional museum town of 750 people set in the piñon-juniper forest of the high desert. No town in the state made the transition from the 1880s to the 1980s with a finer core of its bonanza-era business district intact.

In the last half of the 1980s, this idyllic picture was altered by the gold rush, which was centered in northern Eureka County but which stretched southward through the Roberts range virtually to the outskirts. The throngs of miners and construction workers, the site of bulldozers clearing ground for mobile homes, the water shortages, and the crowded schools all marked the end of one historical era and the beginning of another.

Even those central Nevadans who prospered from the gold rush of the 1980s were sensitive to the ephemeral nature of such phenomena because of the history of the Ely region. With the collapse of the copper industry in White Pine County in the 1970s, the people of this rugged enclave faced the challenge of finding alternate economic opportunities. In the 1860s, this area won notoriety because of Hamilton, one of the richest silver-mining towns in the West (chapter 8). Then for sixty years it was an important source of copper for the American industrial markets (chapter 12). But the Kennecott Copper Corporation, which had been the district's primary employer for decades, closed its mining operations in 1978 and its reduction plant in 1983. The huge metallurgical facility at McGill gradually rusted, and the younger generation began the exodus that has become familiar in many parts of industrial America.

By 1980, the local people who remained recognized that the earth could no longer yield the metal in the quantities and of a value that the world market would buy. The population had dropped by more than 20 percent—from 10,100 to 8,100—during the decade of the 1970s. School enrollments declined from 2,600 in the mid-1970s to about 1,600 in 1983. McGill and Ruth endured more severe demographic declines than Ely because they were more completely dependent on the mining and smelting business. Economically, White Pine was on the ropes.

Yet there were a few consolations during the most difficult period of the late 1970s and early 1980s. Kennecott, which had built a reputation in Nevada as an industrial giant with a humanitarian face, was characteristically generous in its departure, giving the local government much of the equipment of its defunct railroad plus some artifacts to encourage the appreciation of its historical assets. White Pine offered good hunting, fishing, and other outdoor sports, but these were hardly sufficient to assure economic prosperity in a remote area of the mountain West. The state government tried to lend assistance by choosing a site north of Ely for a large prison complex, the first phase of which was constructed in the middle 1980s. This maximum-security facility was capable of holding 500 men, with the possibility of adding accommodations for another 500 at a later date. While the long-range economic impact continued to be problematical, the construction of the first phase gave some short-term relief to the county's business community.

Through the 1980s, White Pine residents nourished the hope that one of their valleys would become the locale for the construction of a massive coal-burning, steam-generated electrical power plant, which was proposed and sponsored by a group of Nevada and California utility companies, but which had not received final approval by the end of the 1980s. Local residents also hoped that there might one day be an oil boom in the valleys to the west of Ely, where a few wells had been producing petroleum for more than a quarter century. At the end of the 1980s, Ely was getting economic benefits from the gold rush that was centered in Eureka and Elko counties.

Among the assets that this county of 8,900 square miles could still rely upon—even after the mineral resources were subtracted—were the excellent grazing ranges, which produced more than 12 million pounds of beef and 1.8 million pounds of sheep and wool in 1987. This was the realm where Jewett Adams and Billy McGill had built their livestock empires three generations earlier, and ranchers still had large herds of cattle and sheep in the high sagebrush-covered valleys and canyons. The outside world finally began to appreciate the scenery of its mountains—especially the magnificent Snake Range and the Great Basin National Park—and Ely profited commercially. (See chapter 1.)

Ely was also the place where U.S. Highways 93, 6, and 50 intersected, carrying a small fraction of the nation's regional traffic. These did not have the high volume of tourism of U.S. 40 (I-80) to the north or of U.S. 91 (I-15) to the south, but they offered a commercial lifeline to Ely as the mines of Ruth and the smelters of McGill fell silent. Motor lodges flourished as the old mining-town hotels faded. By the late 1980s, the White Pine population had inched upward beyond 10,000 once again and had become less dependent on gambling and less tied to a single industry than most other regions of the state.

## Diversification in the Upper Humboldt Basin: Elko County

The transportation revolution of the nineteenth century created Elko County; its sequel in the twentieth century transformed it. We considered in chapter 9 how the builders of the transcontinental railroad established the town in 1868, and how the cattle barons of the next generation gave it a prominence that greatly exceeded its size. In the twentieth century, it had advantages over White Pine because it has even more expansive rangelands and it is bisected by both the transcontinental railroad, which gave it its origins in the 1860s, and the Interstate 80 freeway, which gave it new life a hundred years later. From the beginning, the northeast corner had been the section most fully endowed with small streams; thus it continued to be the most important livestock-raising section of the state. The promotional brochures sometimes called Elko "the last real cow town in the West."

Elko County, with its 17,127 square miles, was the only part of Nevada's northeastern quadrant to enjoy consistent growth through the middle years of the twentieth century; by the late 1990s its population exceeded 45,000, with about half of them living in the city of Elko. Less dependent on metal mines through most of its history than Lincoln, White Pine, Lander, and Eureka counties, more fortunate in its water supply and more imaginative in the development of historical resources, Elko County was more successful at keeping pace with the expanding economic movement in the Far West.

The Elko region had several other economic advantages that its neighbors to the south lacked. The livestock business, which for all its hazards was a more dependable resource than the mining industry, gave Elko the distinction of being the capital of Nevada's cowboy culture, with a popular annual poetry festival. The construction of the Interstate 80 for more than 130 miles across its midsection in the 1950s, 1960s, and 1970s poured millions of dollars into the economy, and the ever-increasing flow of traffic sweetened the mixture further.

Local businessmen successfully promoted the majestic Ruby Mountains, the Ruby Lake Wildlife Refuge, and other natural features for the visitors' market. Citizens developed the finest locally sponsored museum in the state under the leadership of Howard Hickson, and in 1967 Elko became the home of the first community college within the University of Nevada System.

Elko has regularly played a larger role in the state's political history than its relatively small size would suggest. As we have seen, it was the home base of the first reformist governor, L. R. "Broadhorns" Bradley (1871–1878), who tried to force the large mining companies to pay their fair share of taxes in the 1870s. The state's tenth governor, John Sparks (1903–1908), had extensive rangeland operations around Elko, as we have also seen. Three Elko attorneys served in the executive mansion in Carson City in later years—Morley Griswold, who became acting governor in 1934, E. P. "Ted" Carville (1939–1945), and Grant Sawyer (1959–1966). Governor Charles Russell (1951–1958) also spent some of his early years here. Its citizens have often been leaders in the legislature.

In the history of Nevada gambling, Elko introduced some innovations that were later followed by Reno and Las Vegas. Hotel owner Newton Crumley has often received credit for bringing the floor show into the gambling business in 1941 with a week-long orchestra and stage show under the direction of jazz director Ted Lewis. A parade of famous show-business personalities followed, proving that even a small, remote hotel-casino could attract visitors from afar. Singer Bing Crosby became a regular visitor and a publicity attraction for the Crumley enterprises and for Elko.

Capping the economic expansion of the recent period has been the remarkable gold rush of the 1980s, which affected all of the Humboldt Basin and extended southward into Eureka, Lander, and Nye counties. The most active field of development was adjacent to Elko and Carlin (see chapter 15).

Through the mid-1980s Elko and adjacent regions of Eureka, Lander, and Humboldt counties were the center of the gold rush—the largest of its kind in American history. Nevada was producing more than half of the nation's "yellow metal"—with an estimated value of nearly $1.5 billion in 1987. There were common predictions that the known reserves of "microscopic gold"—which had previously been little known in the mining world—were sufficient to last for twenty or twenty-five years, if 1988 world prices were maintained. People with long mining experience knew, however, that the prices of raw materials—and especially of the precious metals—are impossible to predict.

Thousands of people were employed in mining and related fields in northern Nevada in the 1990s — many more than were engaged in the traditional agriculture businesses. Local schools enrolled increasing numbers of students, and the demand for housing forced prices upward at an unprecedented pace. Late in the decade, however, with the price of gold falling, the gold producers and the local communities were retrenching.

## Initiatives on the Lower Humboldt: Battle Mountain, Winnemucca, Lovelock

The three other principal communities along the old Humboldt Trail shared a modest measure of the economic vitality of Elko and northern Eureka as the twentieth century entered its final decade. Lander, Humboldt, and Pershing counties had a much smaller portion than Elko of the economic benefit from the freeway and—at least until 1989—from the gold rush, but their benefits were large by the standards of rural Nevada. They too constructed reasonably prosperous communities from a combination of agriculture, tourism, and—in the 1980s—accelerated production of and exploration for gold. With the assistance of the state government, they cooperated in the establishment of a Tri-County Development Authority to seek economic expansion and diversification. This region embraced nearly 20 percent of the state's land area but only about 2 percent of its population.

Battle Mountain, which had been established as a shipping point on the Central Pacific Railroad in 1868, warranted little historical attention for decades. It had less success than either Elko or Winnemucca as a trading and transfer center because it had no arterial to the north and its hinterland produced a modest amount of mineral wealth from a small copper mine, a few turquoise properties, and some barite mines.

Battle Mountain's southern connection to Austin via the Reese River Valley was crucial in the years of the early mining boom, but this became less vital as Austin declined and as northern Lander County residents focused their attention on the east-west traffic. Businessmen like Dan Shovelin and William Swackhamer struggled through the depression, with the help of highway patronage, to reap the benefits of the postwar tourist boom. Austin, the old "mother of counties" in eastern Nevada, had no such advantage. In the late 1970s, when the population of Austin had shrunk to about 400 while that of Battle Mountain had increased to about 2,500, voters of Lander County finally decided to move the county seat to Battle Mountain.

In the 1970s and 1980s, the Sierra Pacific Power Company constructed two coal-burning electrical generating plants at Valmy, only about 12 miles west of Battle Mountain. This construction work and the operation of the plant enhanced the industrial possibilities of the entire north-central sector. Such a reliable source of energy, together with the employment it provided, gave the middle Humboldt a kind of insurance policy that few other parts of rural Nevada had.

Winnemucca continued to be the most prosperous town in north-western Nevada for the same reasons that put it on the map in the days of the pioneers and early traders. It was still the southern gateway to the resources of eastern Oregon, still the most probable stopping point for tourists along the middle Humboldt, and still the market center for a vast livestock-raising dominion. Its business leaders tried with modest success to promote a tourist highway from "Winnemucca to the Sea," a route that would encourage traffic across northern Humboldt County along Highway 40 and through southern Oregon. But Winnemucca, like its sister cities, found its prosperity in the late 1980s in the new mining activity; its population increased by nearly 50 percent during the decade.

Lovelock, the smallest of the county seats in the Tri-County Development Region, had the greatest struggle finding its economic legs in the 1980s. It was probably more diversified in the early part of the decade with the agricultural enterprises served by the Rye Patch Reservoir and its mining and earth-processing plants, but it felt the economic recession of the 1980s more severely than most towns, and its labor force declined sharply before 1985. The gold rush of the late 1980s enabled it to recover the lost momentum.

Like its sister cities along the Humboldt corridor and elsewhere, Lovelock was eager to diversify its economy by attracting industry. Its businessmen tried to promote their railroad and freeway connections, their relative proximity to the Reno-Sparks area (90 miles), their pleasant desert climate, and their open spaces as economic assets. Similar enterprising activity had a history in this valley that reached back as far as George Lovelock himself, who settled there in 1862.

If motorists proceed in a historical tour along the route used by the Donner party—now Interstate 80—they cross the Forty Mile Desert, which looks as barren and forbidding as it did 150 years ago, except for the freeway. They approach the Truckee River near Wadsworth, which never recovered from the loss of the railroad shops removed by the Southern Pacific in 1904 (see chapter 13).

# The Basque Phenomenon

One fascinating part of the Nevada mosaic is the persistence and the flowering of Basque culture and pride on the livestock ranges and in the towns of the north. More than any other ethnic group that came from the old world to the new to share in the building of this western state, the Basques have retained the colorful traditions of their Pyrenees homeland and have transported them to the Great Basin.

The figure of the solitary Basque sheepherder along the eastern slopes of the Sierra Nevada and across the mountains and valleys of the Great Basin was familiar a hundred years ago, and it was still a living memory as these lines were written. The early Basques usually did not become owners of ranches, but they persisted as a cultural group with a distinct identity partly because some of their men and women established distinctive hotels and eating places, partly because they frequently renewed their ties to their European homeland, and partly because they produced an unusual number of political and social leaders who persistently identified themselves with their Pyrenees ancestry. Nevada Basques pioneered regional festivals, first in Sparks in 1959 and later in Elko in 1964. In 1989, a powerful sculpture entitled *Solitude*, created by Nestor Basterretxea, was erected in Reno's Rancho San Rafael Park to honor their special subculture.

## Contemporary Native Americans

In addition to the Basques, there is another category of Nevadans who have maintained parts of their distinct culture even as they have shared the transitions of the contemporary era. The peoples who were introduced in chapter 2—the Southern Paiutes, the Mohaves, the Shoshones, the Washos, and the Northern Paiutes—have struggled rather successfully to retain their rights and identities in the context of rapid social changes that have swept over Nevada in the past half century. Native Americans constitute less than 2 percent of the state's population, but their role in the region's history has been profound.

There were approximately thirty locations where Native Americans operated reservations or colonies with legally recognized rights and privileges at the end of the 1980s; all except two of them are scattered across the northern counties and adjacent states where their ancestors once roamed. (The exceptions are the Moapa River Reservation and the Las Vegas Colony in Clark County.)

Only three or four had as many as 500 residents or enrolled members, but all had some rights of self-government that had been established by federal law and affirmed by the federal courts. The Indian peoples therefore exercised a dual sovereignty and had an importance larger than their numbers. A combination of grass-roots initiative and governmental changes between the 1930s and 1990s enabled many of these groups to reaffirm their tribal heritage even as they took a larger place in the mosaic of modern Nevada.

The largest and oldest of these enclaves were the Pyramid Lake and Walker River Indian reservations, at or near the sites where Indian Agent Frederick Dodge had proposed the establishment of "Indian farms" in 1859 (see chapter 5). Each of these had been home to several hundred Northern Paiutes throughout the historical period, and the reservation status had allowed them to affirm special privileges. The Pyramid Lake Paiutes waged a successful fight to prevent their lands from being divided and allotted in the early twentieth century. Although the Walker River Paiutes accepted allotments and surrendered most of their lands in 1906, they maintained their tribal identity, regained other lands along the river suitable for agriculture in the 1930s, and maintained a functioning community at Schurz.

Other medium-sized jurisdictions—such as the Duck Valley Reservation in northern Elko County, the Goshute Reservation on the Nevada-

Utah border northeast of Ely, the McDermitt Reservation along the Nevada-Oregon border, and the Moapa Valley Reservation northeast of Las Vegas — combine modest agricultural developments with commercial enterprises. In addition, there are small colonies, established by acts of Congress and operating under their own constitutions, in Las Vegas, Carson, Reno-Sparks, Dresslerville, Ely, Lovelock, Fallon, Elko, Wells, Winnemucca, Yerington, and other scattered rural areas. Thousands of Native Americans have taken their places in the larger society and have reduced their ties with tribes.

Self-government and the assertion of tribal rights have been encouraged by congressional legislation such as the Indian New Deal of the 1930s (which made local constitutions possible), by the granting of additional trust lands to various groups, and by creation of the Indian Claim Commission in 1946. This latter agency had responsibility for establishing facts regarding lands that had been illegally taken from Indians in the nineteenth century and providing compensation to contemporary Indian groups for those seizures. By the 1980s, most claims had been settled and several groups had received some form of payment.

The most important exception involved claims of some Western Shoshone Indians, who received national attention for their long-standing assertion that they had never formally yielded their aboriginal lands in south-central and eastern Nevada. They refused a payment of more than $26 million and continued to fight for their rights to graze cattle, hunt, and fish according to their own tribal regulations, and resisted military and other exploitation of the lands. A passionate love of their prehistoric domain lay behind their tenacious struggle against modern abuses of the countryside.

## Suggested Supplementary Reading

Crum, Stephen J. *The Road on Which We Came: A History of the Western Shoshone.* Salt Lake City: University of Utah Press, 1994.

d'Azevedo, Warren, ed. *Great Basin,* Vol. 11 of *Handbook of North American Indians,* William Sturtevant, gen. ed. Washington: Smithsonian Institution Press, 1986.

Douglass, William A., and Jon Bilbao. *Amerikanuak: Basques in the New World.* Reno: University of Nevada Press, 1975.

Strong, Douglas H. *Tahoe: An Environmental History.* Lincoln: University of Nebraska Press, 1984.

Tingley, Joseph V., and Kris Ann Pizarro. *Traveling America's Loneliest Road.* Reno: Nevada Bureau of Mines and Geology, 2000.

# 21

# The Five
# Southern Counties

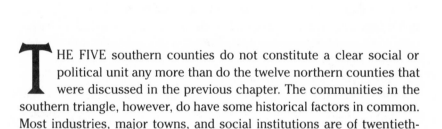

T HE FIVE southern counties do not constitute a clear social or
political unit any more than do the twelve northern counties that
were discussed in the previous chapter. The communities in the
southern triangle, however, do have some historical factors in common.
Most industries, major towns, and social institutions are of twentieth-
century origin, and this region has been more dramatically transformed
by the defense-related activities of the U.S. government than have the
northern counties.

In 1940, fewer than a third of the people of the state lived in Mineral,
Nye, Esmeralda, Lincoln, and Clark counties, and they had almost no
industries except the traditional mining and railroading. By the 1990s
the impact of the federal defense industry had reconstructed the economies of nearly every subregion, and the population explosion in the Las
Vegas Valley could be felt throughout the southern triangle.

## Hawthorne and Mineral County

The first of such developments came in the arid land south of Walker
Lake, and it occurred because one of the small railroads dating from
the days of the first mining boom still penetrated an isolated part of the
desert.

Just before 1900, when little was happening in the depressed, half-forgotten western half of the Great Basin, one of the old patriarchs of the Central Pacific railroad empire—Collis P. Huntington—became interested in the region. The Carson & Colorado Railroad had been constructed southward from Candelaria, across Montgomery Pass, into the Owens Valley and the high Sierra in the 1880s and then had operated at a loss because it had no rich mining or agricultural districts to serve. The enterprising Huntington had a dream of extending it further southward toward the Mojave, where he could connect it with his Southern Pacific lines. He bought the stock and assets from H. M. Yerington of Carson City and his associates, and eventually absorbed the old Carson & Colorado into the Southern Pacific's vast transportation network.

This gave little immediate benefit to Hawthorne; indeed the first consequences were negative. As the Southern Pacific undertook modernization of the old narrow-gauged line, it bypassed the town in order to get a straighter and shorter route to Tonopah and Goldfield. But it established a new community, named Mina, 34 miles east of Hawthorne, and that town, too, still clung tenaciously to life in the last decade of the twentieth century because minerals continued to be extracted and shipped from the region.

Hawthorne's population dwindled to about 250 people in 1920. It seemed destined to follow hundreds of other Great Basin camps into oblivion. But almost miraculously, the U.S. government discovered a need for the vast stretches of desert that surrounded it. A destructive explosion in a navy ammunition compound in New Jersey persuaded the government to look for a more remote area with plenty of open space and the advantages of a railroad. Senator Tasker L. Oddie and Congressman Samuel S. Arentz urged the navy to locate its storage and processing center near the south end of Walker Lake, and construction began in 1929. With the rapid expansion that occurred during World War II, the Hawthorne Naval Ammunition Depot became one of the largest in America.

Because Hawthorne was not large enough to serve all the people who arrived to work at the depot, the navy established a nearby community of its own, named Babbitt, with several hundred family units. At the peak of its activity during World War II, some 13,000 people lived in the Hawthorne/Babbitt area. Inside the sprawling compound, the government built large concrete storage bunkers, more than 200 miles of railroad tracks, and 550 miles of paved roads.

The ammunition depot provided Mineral County with its main economic asset for fifty years. In 1977, the navy turned its operation over to the U.S. Army, and three years later, the government reassigned major responsibility for its management to a private organization under the army's supervision. During the 1980s, the operation was greatly reduced and much of Babbitt was dismantled like an abandoned mining town of the previous era. Some of the former military facilities remained, however, including parks and recreation facilities that provided a welcome oasis.

Hawthorne, in the meantime, gradually developed a tourist business based in part on gambling and in part on the excellent fishing and water-sport activities at Walker Lake. And at least at the end of the 1980s, its railroad connection offered the region a benefit that few of the older towns of the Great Basin still had. Yet ironically, Hawthorne was virtually landlocked by the surrounding ammunition depot, and it had less flexibility in planning its future than its leaders wanted. The population in the late 1980s had stabilized at about 4,000.

## Tonopah and Goldfield

The prominence of Tonopah and Goldfield in politics in the early 1900s and the hundreds of millions in ore production did not save them from the gradual decay which has usually been the fate of post-bonanza mining towns.

Tonopah made a successful transition from a mining economy to one based upon tourism and the growing atomic energy and defense industries. The U.S. Army established and operated a large air base nearby during World War II, and because the town is situated near the northwestern corner of the Nevada Test Site, it shared the benefits of some of the high-technology industries relating to rocket testing in the 1970s and 1980s. The U.S. Air Force conducted experiments with the highly secret Stealth bomber (based at Nellis Air Force Base) at the range near Tonopah in the 1980s, and the exploratory search for a possible nuclear depository at Yucca Mountain drew hundreds of new workers onto the streets where Senator Oddie and Senator Pittman began their political careers.

Mineral industry investors returned to the Tonopah district in the 1980s, including the giant Anaconda Company, which was in search of molybdenum and copper. When that enterprise closed in 1985, the town learned anew the lessons of the cyclical nature of mining. An Australian company resumed operations late in the decade.

Tonopah has been from the beginning a way-station community, roughly equidistant between Reno and Las Vegas; its importance grew in the era of heavy trucking between Los Angeles, Sacramento, and Salt Lake City. Truckers who use U.S. Highways 95 and 6 often make this a stopping point. The long-abandoned army air base continued to serve small commercial, government, and private planes, and the county offered industrial sites nearby.

More than most Nevada mining camps, Tonopah found a place for itself as a service center for federal enterprises without losing its identity as an early twentieth-century boomtown. Its sister cities and neighboring counties had struggled for decades to find a similar compromise.

Goldfield suffered two disastrous fires in the 1920s and deteriorated more rapidly than Tonopah after its bonanza period, and by the World War II era it had few remaining artifacts of the boom years. Still the county seat of Esmeralda County, it maintained its antique courthouse and hoped for restoration of the monumental, vacant Goldfield Hotel, while the remainder of the town slowly crumbled. Much of the tourist bonanza of the late twentieth century passed it by, and efforts of local citizens to have a direct road built from the Tonopah test site were unavailing. Goldfield boasted seven antique/gift stores at the end of the 1980s, which was perhaps a record for an old mining town of 500 people.

## Lincoln County

Lincoln County, with its cluster of four small towns located 100 to 175 miles north of Las Vegas, is the parent of Clark County, but it shared almost none of the prosperity or glamour of the younger offspring at the end of the 1980s. The communities of Alamo, Caliente, Panaca, and Pioche embraced a combined population of about 4,000, composed mostly of older citizens, clinging to the mining and farming traditions of the past and to hopes that some new industrial or commercial development would come their way and revive a dormant economy. Because of their proximity to southern Utah, they had closer business and cultural ties with Cedar City and St. George than with other Nevada communities.

Pioche was unique among the older Nevada mining towns because it had been a silver boomtown in the 1870s, had barely survived as a county seat for sixty-five years, and then enjoyed a second boom, this time in nonprecious metals that were required by the defense industries during

*Downtown Pioche, circa 1906. (Nevada Historical Society)*

World War II. It had been widely known in the 1870s that potentially valuable veins remained in the lower depths and that there were other ores—especially lead and zinc—below the water level. The building of Hoover Dam and a federally funded power line made cheap electrical power available in the 1930s. By this time a Utah mining entrepreneur named Ed Snyder proved the value of the large deposits of low-grade, lead-zinc-silver ore at the deeper levels, and from 1939 to 1957, his Combined Metals Reduction Company extracted more than $50 million in industrial metals. In their first eighty years, the Pioche mines yielded more than $100 million in ore.

Like all the other older mining camps, Pioche fell on hard times again in the last half of the twentieth century. It survived primarily because it was the seat of Nevada's third largest county and because it was a supply and shipping point for the extensive livestock ranges of east central Nevada. Like its neighbors Panaca and Caliente, it offered a historically interesting way station for thousands of tourists from southern California and southern Nevada on the way to the new Great Basin National Park in White Pine County.

Lincoln County's other towns had less dramatic histories, but they also reflected pages from the region's past that proved interesting to some of the newer residents of Clark County who sought impressions of pioneer Nevada. Panaca, founded by Mormons in 1864, was the oldest community in eastern Nevada whose history of settlement was continuous; it celebrated its centenary and that of Nevada with an enthusiasm that was not matched anywhere else in the eastern counties. Its tall, old poplar trees, a few original pioneer buildings, the wide streets, and pastoral setting constituted the best reminder in eastern Nevada of the foundations that the early Latter-day Saints had laid.

Caliente, with its handsome 1905 depot building, its railroad houses, and its sprawling commercial district, is a living museum of the turn-of-the-century railroad era in which it was born. It was a division point on Clark's Salt Lake line and later on the Union Pacific for more than fifty years, but when the railroad companies shifted from steam to diesel locomotives after World War II, Caliente was one of the victims of the modernization. Its civic leaders looked desperately for industries that would replace the lost railroad payrolls. They even entertained ideas about seeking a toxic waste depository.

Alamo, located in the Pahranagat Valley 90 miles north of Las Vegas and 80 miles south of Pioche, was one of those towns founded by the Mormons in 1905–1906, when the church reached once again into the dominions beyond Utah that Brigham Young had once staked out for it. The settlers bought the few fertile acres of this slender, remote valley, brought their sheep and pioneer implements, and waited with patience for the bounty.

It came slowly. The Pahranagat district—tested by Governor Blasdel in 1866 and found wanting—provided a livelihood for a few ranching families but not much other economic opportunity until the era of the Nevada Test Site, of which it was a northeastern neighbor. A few families, mostly Mormon, drew their livings from this oasis with a solemn tenacity similar to that of desert tribes across the world, and registered little surprise when the nuclear experimentation came to their vast neighborhood. Alamo is the nearest downwind neighbor to the Nevada Test Site.

Lincoln and Nye counties were at the heart of the region that the U.S. Air Force selected for the M-X intercontinental missile system in 1979. Under a plan that aroused great controversy before it was abandoned in 1981, the Pentagon announced its intention to build 4,600 missile-launching sites to be scattered across southern Utah and southeastern Nevada. For several months this region was the focus of intense study and publicity. When the federal government eventually scrapped the plan in the wake of a strong public protest, these communities returned to the obscurity that had been standard with them for decades.

## Nuclear Testing: Clark and Southern Nye Counties

The most complex chapter in recent Nevada history relates to the experiments with atomic weapons and other nuclear devices in southern Nevada. This part of the state's experience is one of the most important because it has consequences not only for national defense, but also for the future of humankind. In nuclear science as in entertainment, Nevada is at center stage in the theater of the world. Most of the area of the Nevada Test Site is located within Nye County; most of the economic impact has been in the Las Vegas Valley.

We discussed the Nevada Test Site in a preliminary way in chapter 14 in connection with the growth of Las Vegas. A more detailed consideration of its impact and significance is appropriate as we approach the conclusion of our study of Nevada and its relationship to the Southwest in general and the nation as a whole.

In 1945, the United States raised the curtain on the nuclear age with its first tests near Alamogordo, New Mexico. Soon thereafter, American planes dropped atomic bombs on the Japanese cities of Hiroshima and Nagasaki, where more than 100,000 people died instantly. When the atomic age was still in its infancy in 1950 and the population of Nevada was only 160,000, the United States government selected the isolated southern desert region northwest of Las Vegas for a testing ground, and within a short time this barren expanse became a laboratory of unprecedented scientific importance. Earlier tests had been conducted on isolated atolls of Micronesia in the South Pacific.

The Nevada Proving Grounds—later expanded and renamed the Nevada Test Site—became a focal point of world scientific attention in the search for understanding of nuclear devices. This was the same land where Governor Blasdel had trekked in 1866—then called "Death Barren"—in an unsuccessful effort to establish a county government in Pahranagat Valley.

The Atomic Energy Commission selected and developed the Nevada Test Site in such a remote area because the Soviet Union had exploded its first atomic device in 1949, the Korean War had erupted in 1950, and the American political leaders felt new urgency to prepare the country for possible military threats from abroad. The Pacific site seemed too distant and too vulnerable to the spying of potential foes. The first tests in Nevada were conducted with great secrecy.

As we saw in chapter 14, scientists detonated forty-five atomic experimental devices between 1950 and the spring of 1955, virtually all of them above the earth or on towers, where their spectacular predawn explosions could be witnessed hundreds of miles away in the cities and towns of Nevada, Arizona, Utah, and California. Nevadans learned to take the tests for granted; many enjoyed the publicity and the excitement of the fireballs and mushroom clouds produced by the experiments. Some military units that came to Nevada to be trained in simulated "combat zones" were proud to have been so close to the atomic action. Las Vegas casinos sold "atomic cocktails" as promotion stunts. Only after several years of testing did a significant part of the public become worried about the possibility that radioactive contaminated dust particles might present a hazard to the health of people hundreds of miles away. In 1979, twenty-four "down-wind" residents of southern Utah sued the federal government, alleging that they and their families had been unnecessarily exposed to radiation hazards without due caution and warning, and many members of their communities had died from cancer as a

*Early atomic bomb test in Clark County. (Nevada Historical Society)*

result. Similar lawsuits and debates over the long-range effects of the atomic testing continued into the 1990s without a clear consensus.

In the meantime, the plan of operation changed during a "thaw" in the international Cold War and as a result of new scientific data. The government suspended testing from 1955 to 1957 and then resumed its experiments mostly in underground caverns, where the danger of radiation exposure to individuals was much smaller. At the time testing began in 1950, little was known about the geology of that region of southern Nevada and even less about the effects of nuclear contamination on plant and animal life. Utah ranchers reported unusual burns and deaths among their sheep in the mid-1950s, and a few sought compensation. As the testing proceeded and controversy grew, Camp Mercury on the test site became a center of unique scientific studies of several new fields, but the research into human vulnerability lagged.

The United States detonated 135 explosions underground between the summer of 1961 and 1963, when President John Kennedy signed a Limited Nuclear Test Ban Treaty with the Soviet Union and the United Kingdom. The treaty contained a pledge that there would be no more testing in the atmosphere—which caused the Atomic Energy Commission to expand its program of underground experimentation. Occasionally the blasts beneath the earth were of such magnitude that they broke through to the surface, thus "venting" small amounts of radioactive pollution into the air, but usually the contamination was contained within deep caverns.

Economically, the test site gave southern Nevada another kind of bonanza. Thousands of workers benefited monetarily from the paychecks that the well-financed government bureaus provided. Because housing was minimal and most workers preferred the amenities of Las Vegas and other communities, thousands of people made long commuting trips from the city or from other towns of the region. Miners and engineers who could not find work in the declining metals districts to the north were delighted to find employment at NTS.

For more than twenty years—from the mid-1960s until the late 1980s, there was a virtual deadlock in U.S.-Soviet negotiations over the control and limitation of atomic testing and the deployment of nuclear weapons. Yet during that period, the public debate expanded over continued testing both in parts of Nevada and elsewhere. Hundreds of American citizens who had been exposed to radiation dangers either from fallout or from having participated in military and civilian experiments at the test site sought information and compensation from the government. In the late 1980s, a series of pacifist groups and other protestors picketed the entrance to the test site and established a "peace camp" on Highway 95 near Mercury to bear witness against the nuclear experimentation. In 1997 the National Cancer Institute confirmed that tens of thousands of cases of thyroid cancer in the United States had been traced to fallout from the tests of the 1950s.

Another act in the continuing drama began early in 1988 when the National Resources Defense Council, a private American environmental organization, and the Soviet Academy of Sciences agreed to cooperate in monitoring underground explosions by use of seismic devices. Two geophysical engineers from the University of Nevada, Reno, Professors James Brune and Keith Priestley, were part of the first international teams who carried sensitive instruments for measuring earth tremors to the Soviet nuclear testing areas and who helped Soviet scientists install their instruments in Nevada and California. The cooperation between two groups of scientists and private citizens from both countries was believed to have advanced the spirit of mutual trust which had long been lacking in the atomic test negotiations.

The improvement of relations with Russia brought a change in emphasis in U.S. nuclear-defense policy. President William J. Clinton declared a moratorium on nuclear testing in 1993 and signed a comprehensive test-ban treaty in 1996. Instead of exploding nuclear devices, scientists planned experiments sending shock-waves through plutonium to test the quality of old stored bombs at NTS without detonating them. The proposal was strongly supported by the Department of Energy but was controversial within the peace movement and among environmentalists.

## Laughlin, the Northern Valleys, and Pahrump

In chapter 14 we also discussed the evolution of Las Vegas and its neighboring cities—North Las Vegas, Henderson, and Boulder City, and the townships which are suburbs within the metropolitan area. Although these accounted for most of the people in the region, the outlying areas of Clark County included several communities that tried to follow the Las Vegas pattern.

The most surprising development in the 1980s in southern Nevada—a community that is not easily surprised by growth and change—was the development of Laughlin at the extreme southern tip of the state, 90 miles south of Las Vegas and reflecting the Las Vegas motifs. Below Davis Dam on the Colorado River, sandwiched between the Mojave National Scenic Area of California and the Kingman region of Arizona, Laughlin rapidly developed into one of the most successful resort areas in the state after Las Vegas and Reno, with seven major resort casinos built in the span of five years. Nearer than Las Vegas to some major tourist markets of southern California and Arizona, it attracted investments from several of the largest resort companies in America, and by 1990 it was offering more than 3,000 hotel rooms and glittering entertainment to a swelling clientele of visitors.

Even those valleys in northeastern Clark County that had been settled by Mormon colonizers in the last century felt the impact of the expanding casino business to a more limited extent. Overton and Logandale in the Moapa Valley and Mesquite and Bunkerville in the Virgin Valley continued through most of their history to be predominantly agricultural communities, with many of the families that settled there a century ago still well represented.

After the turn of the century, with the early, modest growth of Las Vegas, the Moapa and Virgin River communities had a new and much closer market for their foodstuffs, and with the building of Highway 91 in the early twentieth century, access to towns both north and south was greatly improved. The building of Hoover Dam and the rise of Lake Mead inundated the site of old St. Thomas, but the other communities enjoyed a modest prosperity in the new Nevada; about 5,000 people lived in the towns of this region in the early 1980s. During that decade, a border-town casino rose from the sands of Mesquite to beckon the automobile trade to the slot machines as soon as it entered the state from Utah. Yet these towns continued to be, more than a century after their founding, living reminders of the legacy of the Mormon subculture of the "Dixie" of Brigham Young's Zion.

Likewise to the west, beyond the Spring Mountain Range on the way to Death Valley, the long-neglected Pahrump Valley experienced a long-awaited cycle of development relating to the growth in Las Vegas. A paved road was completed in 1954, and a community electrical system and telephones came into operation only in the 1960s, but the tourist investment was already under way in Pahrump.

Although located in the southern tip of Nye County, Pahrump has been much more closely tied to Las Vegas commercially than to Tonopah, and has become a virtual suburb of that urban complex. Once a Nevada

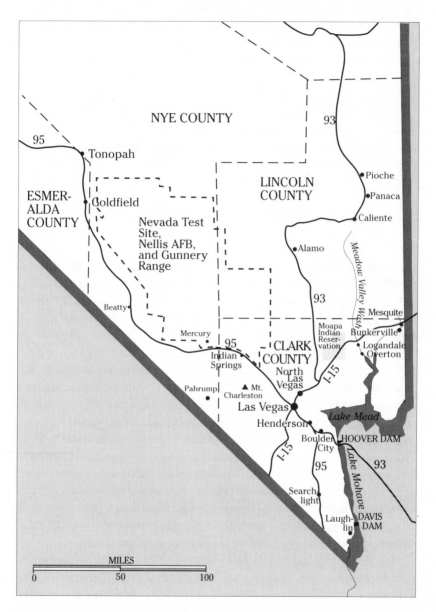

*Southern Nevada (1980s)*

curiosity as a place where cotton could be grown because of the long, hot season, it expected in the 1990s to be the first Nevada community to have a bonded winery. The cultivation of grapes had been tried in the 1890s, but the transportation and technical problems of that era did not allow the viniculturists to prosper. In view of the recent history of southern Nevada, it would not be wise to predict failure in this enterprise a hundred years later.

Pahrump in the 1980s had become a community for spacious lots, sprawling homes, and casinos, with a population that was challenging that of Tonopah (164 miles away) and was seeking a county or city government of its own.

## The Las Vegas Phenomenon: A Last Word

Any effort to identify the essential changes in Las Vegas at the end of the 1990s is doomed to failure. The speed with which the metropolitan area has expanded for fifty years and the fact that the pace was accelerating even as this text went to press suggest that in this valley much of the future of the state of Nevada and the entire Southwest will be fashioned. Only the broad outlines of the possible future additions to Nevada's heritage can be suggested.

On the threshold of the 1990s, the much-celebrated gambling and show business continued to flourish in Las Vegas despite the competition from legalized lotteries and other forms of gambling in several other states. Fears that the introduction of casino gambling in Atlantic City, New Jersey, in the 1970s would reduce the appeal of Las Vegas to eastern gambling clients proved unfounded; except for a short recession in the early 1980s, the gambling-tourist economy continued to grow. There were even indications that some easterners who tasted the attractions of casino gambling in Atlantic City were more inclined after that experience to risk their luck in Las Vegas. Reno did not experience a comparable expansion of its gambling-resort business in the same period.

The growth of Las Vegas was also fueled in the late 1980s by unprecedented success in attracting other businesses and industries. One example was the decision of Citicorp, one of the nation's largest financial institutions, to operate a major credit card processing plant in the area. Companies such as GTE-Sylvania, Ford Aerospace, Tungsten Carbide, Ethel M Chocolates, and others either opened or expanded industrial facilities because of favorable land, water, and tax incentives offered by state and local governments. The fact that the 1987 legislature authorized the development of a college of engineering and computer science at the University of Nevada, Las Vegas, provided a promise that future industrial installations would have the advantages of specialized higher education and research facilities. The land acquired by Howard Hughes west of Las Vegas in the 1940s promised to be the site of extensive residential, industrial, and commercial development in the 1990s.

A leading historian from Las Vegas, Eugene Moehring, reflected the optimistic spirit of the community when, in his 1989 book, he catalogued the recent expansion and competition for land in the Las Vegas Valley. This included the massive Downtown Transportation Center and monorail system linking the Convention Center, the downtown casino center, Cashman Field, and possibly the Strip and McCarran Airport. And characteristically he included a slight note of concern that all this emphasis on growth was "perhaps overly ambitious" (*Resort City in the Sunbelt,* p. 267).

For two generations, Las Vegas grappled with its reputation as the most sinful and unorthodox place in the U.S. At times its permanent residents deplored the slanders hurled at the town because of the mobsters who operated there, but occasionally they recognized the bonuses that flowed from the notoriety. During the 1990s, however, this most maligned of American cities assumed a new and paradoxically different community image. It evolved as a family vacation center, with theme parks and other attractions for all ages and for foreign visitors. The weekly news magazine *Time,* featuring Las Vegas in a cover story in one of its first issues of 1994, proclaimed it in racy prose "The New All-American City." The key message was that "Las Vegas has become Americanized, and, even more, America has become Las Vegasized."

Although Las Vegas gained respectability in the arts, it did not downplay the gambling nucleus of its operation; it simply provided more imaginative enticements to draw potential bettors to the Strip. Americans of the late twentieth century had become more acclimated to immediate consumption and risk-taking to accommodate their whims. America's gamblers wagered a record $330 billion in 1992 — an 1,800-percent gain since 1976. Slot machines — of which Nevada was a leading manufacturer as well as promoter — accounted for $252.9 billion. Nevada casinos accounted for more than half the entire amount, or $165.6 billion, of the total net winnings.

By the early 1990s other jurisdictions had learned to imitate Nevada rather than to scorn it. Much of this new betting was in the form of state and local lotteries, in which bettors could wager small amounts in the hope of winning super jackpots and in the belief that their losses would go into state coffers for education or other public services. New Hampshire led the way with a lottery of this kind in 1964. In the next thirty years, two-thirds of the states in the Union introduced some form of gambling in order to help their budgets. This was a less painful way to collect revenues than raising taxes, and it gradually made other forms of gambling, which had previously been widely condemned, more palatable. Scholars even produced studies arguing that there were social virtues to gambling as entertainment, as a social safety-valve, and as a rational, "victimless" method of seeking gain and profit.

Since casino gambling continued to be regarded as a "growth industry" even during the listless economic period of the early 1990s, Las Vegas found another demand for its specialized talents. The casinos along the Strip were exporting experienced gaming supervisors and workers with their arcane skills to other parts of the country as the casino business proliferated. The "pool of talent" trained in Las Vegas was a major resource for investors who opened new betting parlors in several regions where gambling had recently been introduced.

The spread of legalized gambling coincided with the growing respectability of the business. For decades, the perception of Las Vegas as a center for organized crime and as a source of revenue for mobsters apparently restrained other states and regions when they considered gaming as a source of revenue. But this perception gradually weakened when larger, better-known, and respectable corporations such as Hyatt, Hilton, Metro-Goldwyn-Mayer, and Ramada Inn entered the business in Nevada. As the collective profits of the Nevada-based casinos climbed dramatically through the 1970s and 1980s, gambling as a source of revenue for public purposes became more attractive.

Gambling fever had spread to hundreds of places at home and abroad by the mid-1990s. More than sixty Indian reservations established casinos, sometimes subcontracting with professional gamblers who had Nevada experience. At least that many more Indian tribes or units were considering casinos in the mid-1990s. The international market was expanding as well, but this only seemed to enhance the attractiveness of Las Vegas, because the city offered a variety of new mega-resorts.

Las Vegas has never been deterred from taking big gambles, and it would be difficult to find a city with a more successful economic record in the last half of the twentieth century. Whether it and the state it is now leading can fashion social and ethical policies equal to the economic success stories will be one of the major questions for the next century.

Las Vegas is not merely the fastest growing metropolitan area in the nation. An entertainment magnet for the world, it is also near ground zero of the most formidable nuclear laboratory on the planet. Nevada is host to the most dazzling entertainment and the most deadly environmental experiments in the experience of modern civilizations. Las Vegas and the new Nevada in the south are having an impact on the world.

## Suggested Supplementary Reading

Castleman, Deke. *Las Vegas*. Photography by Michael Yamashita. 2nd ed. Oakland: Compass American Guides, 1992.

Gallagher, Carole. *American Ground Zero: The Secret Nuclear War*. Cambridge: MIT Press, 1993.

Gottdiener, M., Claudia C. Collins, and David R. Dickens. *Las Vegas: The Social Production of an All-American City*. Malden, Mass.: Blackwell, 1999.

Land, Barbara, and Myrick Land. *A Short History of Las Vegas*. Foreword by Guy Louis Rocha. Reno: University of Nevada Press, 1999.

McCracken, Robert D. *Las Vegas: The Great American Playground*. Expanded ed. Reno: University of Nevada Press, 1997.

Moehring, Eugene P. *Resort City in the Sunbelt: Las Vegas 1930–2000*. Reno: University of Nevada Press, 2000.

Solnit, Rebecca. *Savage Dreams: A Journey into the Hidden Wars of the American West*. San Francisco: Sierra Club Books, 1994.

Tronnes, Mike, ed. *Literary Las Vegas: The Best Writing about America's Most Fabulous City*. Introduction by Nick Tosches. New York: Henry Holt, 1995.

Venturi, Robert, Denise Scott Brown, and Steven Izenour. *Learning from Las Vegas: The Forgotten Symbolism of Architectural Form*. Cambridge: MIT Press, 1977.

# Selected Bibliography

Abbe, Donald R. *Austin and the Reese River Mining District: Nevada's Forgotten Frontier*. Reno: University of Nevada Press, 1985.

Angel, Myron, ed. *History of Nevada, 1881, with Illustrations*. Introduction by David Myrick. 1881. Reprint, Berkeley: Howell-North, 1958.

Arrington, Leonard J. *Brigham Young: American Moses*. New York: Alfred A. Knopf, 1985.

———. *The Mormons in Nevada*. Las Vegas: Las Vegas Sun, 1979.

Ball, Howard. *Justice Downwind: America's Atomic Testing Program in the 1950s*. New York: Oxford University Press, 1986.

Bancroft, Hubert Howe. *History of Nevada: 1540–1888*. Originally published as part of Volume XXV, *The Works of Hubert Howe Bancroft*. 1890. Reprint, Reno: University of Nevada Press, 1981.

Barlett, Donald L., and James B. Steele. *Empire: The Life, Legend, and Madness of Howard Hughes*. New York: W. W. Norton, 1979.

Bowers, Michael W. *The Sagebrush State: Nevada's History, Government, and Politics*. Reno: University of Nevada Press, 1996.

Boyer, Florence M. "Las Vegas: My Home for Sixty Years." Unpublished oral history, University of Nevada, Reno, 1967.

Brown, Mrs. Hugh. *Lady in Boomtown: Miners and Manners on the Nevada Frontier*. 1968. Reprint, Reno: University of Nevada Press, 1991.

Burbank, Jeff. *License to Steal: Nevada's Gaming Control System in the Megaresort Age*. Reno: University of Nevada Press, 2000.

Bushnell, Eleanore. *Crimes, Follies, and Misfortunes: The Federal Impeachment Trials*. Urbana: University of Illinois Press, 1992.

Bushnell, Eleanore, and Don W. Driggs. *The Nevada Constitution: Origin and Growth*. 6th ed. Reno: University of Nevada Press, 1984.

Canfield, Gae Whitney. *Sarah Winnemucca of the Northern Paiutes*. Norman: University of Oklahoma Press, 1983.
Carlson, Helen S. *Nevada Place Names: A Geographical Dictionary*. Reno: University of Nevada Press, 1974.
Castleman, Deke. *Las Vegas*. Photography by Michael Yamashita. 2nd ed. Oakland: Compass American Guides, 1992.
Chan, Loren B. *Sagebrush Statesman: Tasker L. Oddie of Nevada*. Reno: University of Nevada Press, 1973.
Cline, Gloria Griffen. *Exploring the Great Basin*. Norman: University of Oklahoma Press, 1963.
————. *Peter Skene Ogden and the Hudson's Bay Company*. Norman: University of Oklahoma Press, 1974.
Coray, Michael. "African-Americans in Nevada." *Nevada Historical Society Quarterly* 35 (winter 1992): 239–57.
Crowley, Joseph N. *The Constant Conversation: A Chronicle of Campus Life*. Reno: Black Rock Press, University of Nevada, Reno, 2000.
Crum, Stephen J. *The Road on Which We Came: A History of the Western Shoshone*. Salt Lake City: University of Utah Press, 1994.

Dangberg, Grace. *Conflict on the Carson: A Study of Water Litigation in Western Nevada*. Minden, Nev.: Carson Valley Historical Society, 1975.
Davenport, Robert W. "Early Years, Early Workers: The Genesis of the University of Nevada, Las Vegas." *Nevada Historical Society Quarterly* 35 (spring 1992): 1–20.
Davies, Richard O., ed. *The Maverick Spirit: Building the New Nevada*. Reno: University of Nevada Press, 1999.
Davis, Sam P., ed. *The History of Nevada*. 2 vols. Reno: Elms Publishing Co., 1913.
d'Azevedo, Warren, ed. *Great Basin*. Vol. 11, *Handbook of North American Indians*, William Sturtevant, gen. ed. Washington: Smithsonian Institution Press, 1986.
Denton, Sally, and Roger Morris. *The Money and the Power: The Making of Las Vegas and Its Hold on America, 1947–2000*. New York: Alfred A. Knopf, 2001.
De Quille, Dan (William Wright). *The Big Bonanza*. 1876. Reprint, New York: Alfred A. Knopf, 1947.
DeVoto, Bernard. *Mark Twain's America*. Boston: Houghton Mifflin Co., 1932.
Dobra, John L. *The Economic Impacts of Nevada's Mineral Industry*. Nevada Bureau of Mines and Geology, Special Publication 9. Reno: University of Nevada Mackay School of Mines, 1988.
Dombrink, John, and William N. Thompson. *The Last Resort: Successes and Failures in Campaigns for Casinos*. Reno: University of Nevada Press, 1990.
Douglass, William A., and Jon Bilbao. *Amerikanuak: Basques in the New World*. Reno: University of Nevada Press, 1975.
Driggs, Don W., and Leonard E. Goodall. *Nevada Politics and Government: Conservatism in an Open Society*. Lincoln: University of Nebraska Press, 1996.

Ebel, Robert D., ed. *A Fiscal Agenda for Nevada: Revenue Options for State and Local Governments in the 1990s*. Reno: University of Nevada Press, 1989.

Edwards, Elbert B. *200 Years in Nevada: A Story of People Who Opened, Explored, and Developed the Land. A Bicentennial History*. Salt Lake City: Publishers Press, 1978.

Edwards, Jerome. "Nevada Gambling: Just Another Business Enterprise." *Nevada Historical Society Quarterly* 37 (summer 1994): 101-14.

————. *Pat McCarran: Political Boss of Nevada*. Reno: University of Nevada Press, 1982.

Egan, Ferol. *Sand in a Whirlwind: The Paiute Indian War of 1860*. Foreword by A. B. Guthrie, Jr. Garden City: Doubleday, 1972.

Elliott, Gary E. *Senator Alan Bible and the Politics of the New West*. Reno: University of Nevada Press, 1994.

Elliott, Russell R. *Growing Up in a Company Town: A Family in the Copper Camp of McGill, Nevada*. Reno: Nevada Historical Society, 1990.

————. *Nevada's Twentieth-Century Mining Boom: Tonopah, Goldfield, Ely*. Reno: University of Nevada Press, 1966.

————. *Servant of Power: A Political Biography of Senator William M. Stewart*. Reno: University of Nevada Press, 1983.

Elliott, Russell R., and Helen J. Poulton. *Writings on Nevada: A Selected Bibliography*. Reno: University of Nevada Press, 1963.

Elliott, Russell R., with the assistance of William D. Rowley. *History of Nevada*. 2nd ed. Lincoln: University of Nebraska, 1987.

Erikson, Kai. "Out of Sight, Out of Our Minds." *New York Times Magazine*, 9 March 1994.

Fatout, Paul. *Mark Twain in Virginia City*. Bloomington: Indiana University Press, 1964.

Fiero, Bill. *Geology of the Great Basin*. Reno: University of Nevada Press, 1986.

Findlay, John M. *People of Chance: Gambling in American Society from Jamestown to Las Vegas*. New York: Oxford University Press, 1986.

Fitzgerald, Roosevelt. "The Evolution of a Black Community in Las Vegas: 1905–1940," and "The Demographic Impact of Basic Magnesium Corporation on Southern Nevada." In Rusco and Chung, eds., *Ethnicity and Race in Nevada*. *Nevada Public Affairs Review* 2 (1987): 23-35.

Forbes, Jack D., ed. *Nevada Indians Speak*. Reno: University of Nevada Press, 1967.

Ford, Jean. *A Nevada Woman Leads the Way*. Interviews and editing by Victoria Ford. Reno: University of Nevada Oral History Program, 1998.

Ford, Jean, and James W. Hulse. "The First Battle for Woman Suffrage in Nevada: 1869-1871 — Correcting and Expanding the Record." *Nevada Historical Society Quarterly* 38 (fall 1995): 174-88.

Fradkin, Philip L. *Fallout: An American Nuclear Tragedy*. Tucson: University of Arizona Press, 1989.

————. *A River No More: The Colorado River and the West*. Tucson: University of Arizona Press, 1984.

Frémont, John Charles. *The Expeditions of John Charles Frémont*. Edited by Donald Jackson and Mary Lee Spence. Vol. 1, *Travels from 1838 to 1844*. Urbana: University of Illinois, 1970.

Gallagher, Carole. *American Ground Zero: The Secret Nuclear War*. Cambridge: MIT Press, 1993.

Gerlach, Andrea K. "Political Culture and Water Politics in Nevada: Las Vegas Attempts to Quench Its Thirst." M.A. thesis, University of Nevada, Las Vegas, 1992.

Glad, Betty. *Key Pittman: The Tragedy of a Senate Insider*. New York: Columbia University Press, 1986.

Glass, Mary Ellen. *Nevada's Turbulent '50s: Decade of Political and Economic Change*. Reno: University of Nevada Press, 1981.

———. *Silver and Politics in Nevada: 1892–1902*. Reno: University of Nevada Press, 1969.

———. *Water for Nevada: The Reclamation Controversy, 1885–1902*. Reno: University of Nevada Press, 1964.

Glasscock, Carl B. *Gold in Them Hills: The Story of the West's Last Wild Mining Days*. Indianapolis: Bobbs Merrill, 1932.

Goldman, Marion. *Gold Diggers and Silver Miners: Prostitution and Social Life on the Comstock Lode*. Ann Arbor: University of Michigan Press, 1981.

Gottdiener, M., Claudia C. Collins, and David R. Dickens. *Las Vegas: The Social Production of an All-American City*. Malden, Mass.: Blackwell, 1999.

Hafen, LeRoy R., and Ann W. Hafen. *Old Spanish Trail: Santa Fe to Los Angeles*. Glendale: Arthur W. Clark Co., 1954.

Hansot, Elisabeth, Jill M. Winter, and Charlotte Word, eds. "Beyond ERA: A Women's Agenda for Nevada." *Nevada Public Affairs Review* 2 (1983).

Hardesty, Donald L. *The Archaeology of the Donner Party*. Reno: University of Nevada Press, 1997.

———. *The Archaeology of Mining and Miners: A View from the Silver State*. Pleasant Hill, Calif.: Society for Historical Archaeology, 1988.

Harnar, Nellie Shaw. *Indians of the Coo-yu-ee Pah (Pyramid Lake): The History of the Pyramid Lake Indians, 1843–1959 and Early Tribal History, 1825–1834*. Sparks: Dave's Printing and Publishing, 1974.

Hart, John. *Hiking the Great Basin: The High Country of California, Oregon, Nevada, and Utah*. San Francisco: Sierra Club Books, 1981.

Heizer, Robert F., and Martin A. Baumhoff. *Prehistoric Rock Art of Nevada and Eastern California*. Berkeley: University of California Press, 1962, 1984.

Heller, Dean. *Political History of Nevada: 1996*. 10th ed. Carson City: State Printing Office, 1997.

Highton, Jake. *Nevada Newspaper Days: A History of Journalism in the Silver State*. Stockton: Heritage West Books, 1990.

Hohmann, John W., comp. *The Old Las Vegas Mormon Fort: The Founding of a Desert Community in Clark County, Nevada*. Carson City: Department of Conservation and Natural Resources, 1996.

Hopkins, A. D., and K. J. Evans, eds. *The First 100: Portraits of the Men and Women Who Shaped Las Vegas*. Las Vegas: Huntington Press, 1999.

Hopkins, Sarah Winnemucca. *Life Among the Piutes: Their Wrongs and Claims*. Edited by Mrs. Horace Mann. 1883. Reprint, Reno: University of Nevada Press, 1994.

Houghton, Ruth M., and Leontine B. Nappe, eds. *Nevada Life-styles and Lands*. Reno: University of Nevada Bureau of Governmental Research, 1977.

Houghton, Samuel G. *A Trace of Desert Waters: The Great Basin Story*. Foreword by Samuel I. Zeveloff. 1976. Reprint, Reno: University of Nevada Press, 1994.

Howard, Anne Bail. *The Long Campaign: A Biography of Anne Martin*. Reno: University of Nevada Press, 1985.

Hulse, James W. *Forty Years in the Wilderness: Impressions of Nevada, 1940–1980*. Reno: University of Nevada Press, 1986.

———. *Lincoln County Nevada: The History of a Mining Region*. Reno: University of Nevada Press, 1971.

———. *The Nevada Adventure: A History*. 6th ed. Reno: University of Nevada Press, 1990.

———. *The University of Nevada: A Centennial History*. Reno: University of Nevada Press, 1974.

———. "W. A. Clark and the Las Vegas Connection." *Montana: The Magazine of Western History* 37 (winter 1987): 48–55.

Hulse, James W., with Leonard E. Goodall and Jackie Allen. *Reinventing the System: Higher Education in Nevada, 1968–2000*. Reno: University of Nevada Press, 2002.

Hundley, Norris, Jr. *Water and the West: The Colorado River Compact and the Politics of Water in the American West*. Berkeley: University of California Press, 1975.

Israel, Fred L. *Nevada's Key Pittman*. Lincoln: University of Nebraska Press, 1963.

Jackson, W. Turrentine. *Treasure Hill: Portrait of a Silver Mining Camp*. Tucson: University of Arizona Press, 1963.

James, Ronald M. "Drunks, Fools, and Lunatics: History and Folklore of the Early Comstock." *Nevada Historical Society Quarterly* 35 (winter 1992): 215–38.

———. *Justice in Balance: The Courthouses of Nevada*. Reno: Nevada Historical Society, 1986.

———. *The Roar and the Silence: A History of Virginia City and the Comstock Lode*. Reno: University of Nevada Press, 1998.

———. *Temples of Justice: County Courthouses of Nevada*. Foreword by Cliff Young. Reno: University of Nevada Press, 1994.

James, Ronald M., and C. Elizabeth Raymond, eds. *Comstock Women: The Making of a Mining Community*. Reno: University of Nevada Press, 1998.

Jensen, Andrew, comp. "History of Las Vegas Mission." *Nevada State Historical Society Papers*. Reno: Nevada State Historical Society, 1926. Pp. 117–284.

Johnson, David A. *Founding the Far West: California, Oregon, and Nevada, 1840–1890*. Berkeley: University of California Press, 1992.

Johnson, Edward C. *Walker River Paiutes: A Tribal History*. Schurz, Nev.: Walker River Paiute Tribe, 1975.

Johnson, Leroy, and Jean Johnson. *Escape from Death Valley: As Told by William Lewis Manly and Other '49ers*. Reno: University of Nevada Press, 1987.

Kaufman, Perry Bruce. "The Best City of Them All: A History of Las Vegas, 1930–1960." Ph.D. dissertation, University of California, Santa Barbara, 1974.

Kelly, J. Wells. *First Directory of Nevada Territory*. Introduction by Richard Lingenfelter. 1862. Reprint, Los Gatos, Calif.: Talisman Press, 1962.

Knack, Martha C., and Omer C. Stewart. *As Long as the River Shall Run: An Ethnohistory of Pyramid Lake Indian Reservation*. Berkeley: University of California Press, 1984.

Kneiss, Gilbert. *Bonanza Railroads*. Stanford: Stanford University Press, 1941.

Knepp, Donn. *Las Vegas: The Entertainment Capital*. Menlo Park, Calif.: Lane Publishing, 1987.

Kroeber, A. L. *Mohave Indians: Report on Aboriginal Territory and Occupancy of the Mohave Tribe*. New York: Garland Publishing Inc., 1974.

Laird, Charlton G., ed. *Walter Van Tilburg Clark: Critiques*. Reno: University of Nevada Press, 1983.

Lambert, Darwin. *Great Basin Drama*. Niwot, Colo.: Robert Rinehart Publishers, 1991.

Land, Barbara, and Myrick Land. *A Short History of Las Vegas*. Foreword by Guy Louis Rocha. Reno: University of Nevada Press, 1999.

———. *A Short History of Reno*. Reno: University of Nevada Press, 1995.

Lanner, Ronald M. *Trees of the Great Basin: A Natural History*. Reno: University of Nevada Press, 1984.

Larson, Andrew Karl. "I Was Called to Dixie." In *The Virgin River Basin: Unique Experience in Mormon Pioneering*. Salt Lake City: Deseret News Press, 1961.

Laxalt, Robert. *Nevada: A Bicentennial History*. New York: W. W. Norton, 1977.

Legislative Commission of the Legislative Counsel Bureau. "Blue Ribbon Commission on Legislative Process." *Bulletin 89-7*. Carson City: State Printing Office, 1988.

Lewis, Marvin. *Martha and the Doctor: A Frontier Family in Central Nevada*. Reno: University of Nevada Press, 1977.

Lewis, Oscar. *Sagebrush Casinos: The Story of Legal Gambling in Nevada*. Garden City, N.Y.: Doubleday, 1953.

———. *The Town That Died Laughing*. Boston: Little, Brown, 1955.

Lillard, Richard G. *Desert Challenge: An Interpretation of Nevada*. New York: Alfred A. Knopf, 1942.

Lingenfelter, Richard E. *Steamboats on the Colorado River*. Tucson: University of Arizona Press, 1978.

Long, Walter S. *Brushwork Diary: Watercolors of Early Nevada*. Text by Michael J. Brodhead and James C. McCormick. Reno: University of Nevada Press, 1991.

Loomis, David. *Combat Zoning: Military Land-Use Planning in Nevada*. Reno: University of Nevada Press, 1993.

Lord, Eliot. *Comstock Mining and Miners*. Introduction by David F. Myrick. 1883. Reprint, Berkeley: Howell-North, 1959.

Mack, Effie Mona. *Nevada: A History of the State from the Earliest Times through the Civil War*. Glendale: Arthur H. Clark, 1936.

Madsen, David B., and James F. O'Connell, eds. *Man and Environment in the Great Basin*. SAA Papers No. 2. Washington: Society for American Archeology, 1982.

Magnaghi, Russell M. "Virginia City's Chinese Community, 1860–1880." *Nevada Historical Society Quarterly* 24 (summer 1981): 130–57.

Martin, Anne. "NEVADA: Beautiful Desert of Buried Hopes." *The Nation* 115 (26 July 1922): 89–92.

Mathews, Mary McNair. *Ten Years in Nevada: or, Life on the Pacific Coast*. Foreword by Mary Lee Spence and Clark C. Spence. 1880. Reprint, Lincoln: University of Nebraska Press, 1985.

McBride, Dennis. *In the Beginning: A History of Boulder City, Nevada*. 2nd ed. Boulder City: Boulder City/Hoover Dam Museum, 1992.

McCracken, Robert D. *A History of Tonopah, Nevada*. Tonopah: Nye County Press, 1992.

———. *Las Vegas: The Great American Playground*. Expanded ed. Reno: University of Nevada Press, 1997.

McLane, Alvin R. *Silent Cordilleras: The Mountain Ranges of Nevada*. Reno: Camp Nevada Monograph No. 4, 1978.

McMillan, James B. *Fighting Back: A Life in the Struggle for Civil Rights*. Interviews by Gary Elliott; narrative compiled by R. T. King. Reno: University of Nevada Oral History Progam, 1997.

McPhee, John. *Basin and Range*. New York: Farrar, Straus, Giroux, 1981.

Miller, Max. *Reno*. New York: Dodd, Mead & Co., 1941.

Miranda, M. L. *A History of Hispanics in Southern Nevada*. Reno: University of Nevada Press, 1997.

Moehring, Eugene P. *Resort City in the Sunbelt: Las Vegas 1930–2000*. Reno: University of Nevada Press, 2000.

Molinelli, Lambert. *Eureka and Its Resources*. 1879. Reprint, Reno: University of Nevada Press, 1982.

Moody, Eric N. "The Early Years of Casino Gambling in Nevada, 1931–1945." Ph.D. dissertation, University of Nevada, Reno, 1997.

———. *Southern Gentleman of Nevada Politics: Vail M. Pittman*. Reno: University of Nevada Press, 1974.

Mooney, James. *The Ghost Dance Religion and Wounded Knee*. 1896. Reprint, New York: Dover Publications, 1973.

Morgan, Dale. *The Humboldt: Highroad of the West*. 1943. Reprint, Lincoln: University of Nebraska Press, 1985.

———. *Jedediah Smith and the Opening of the West*. Indianapolis: Bobbs Merrill, 1953.

Mozingo, Hugh N. *Shrubs of the Great Basin: A Natural History*. Reno: University of Nevada Press, 1987.

Myrick, David F. *Railroads of Nevada and Eastern California*. Vol. I, *The Northern Roads*; Vol. II, *The Southern Roads*. 1962–63. Reprint, Reno: University of Nevada Press, 1992.

Nash, Gerald D. *World War II and the West: Reshaping the Economy.* Lincoln: University of Nebraska Press, 1990.

Nevada Bureau of Mines and Geology. *The Nevada Mineral Industry: 1986.* Special Publication MI-1986. Reno: Nevada Bureau of Mines, 1987.

Nevada State Museum. *Pleistocene Studies in Southern Nevada.* Anthropological Papers No. 13. Carson City: Nevada State Museum, 1967.

Nicoletta, Julie. *Buildings of Nevada.* Photography by Bret Morgan. New York: Oxford University Press, 2000.

Nielson, Norm. *Reno: The Past Revisited.* Norfolk, Va.: The Donning Co., 1988.

Ostrander, Gilman. *Nevada: The Great Rotten Borough 1859–1964.* New York: Alfred A. Knopf, 1966.

Paher, Stanley W. *Las Vegas: As It Began — As It Grew.* Las Vegas: Nevada Publications, 1971.

Patterson, Edna B., Louise A. Ulph, and Victor Goodwin. *Nevada's Northeastern Frontier.* Sparks, Nev.: Western Printing and Publishing Co., 1969.

Paul, Rodman W. *Mining Frontiers of the Far West: 1848–1880.* New York: Holt, Rinehart and Winston, 1963.

Pisani, Donald J. *Water, Land and Law in the West: The Limits of Public Policy.* Lawrence: University Press of Kansas, 1996.

Raymond, C. Elizabeth. *George Wingfield: Owner and Operator of Nevada.* Reno: University of Nevada Press, 1992.

Read, Effie O. *White Pine Lang Syne: A True History of White Pine County, Nevada.* Denver: Big Mountain Press, 1965.

Reid, Harry. *Searchlight: The Camp That Didn't Fail.* Reno: University of Nevada Press, 1998.

Reisner, Marc. *Cadillac Desert: The American West and Its Disappearing Water.* New York: Viking, 1986.

*Reports of the 1863 Constitutional Convention of the Territory of Nevada,* as written for *The Territorial Enterprise,* by Andrew J. Marsh and Samuel L. Clemens, and for *The Virginia Daily Union* by Amos Bowman. Edited by William C. Miller and Eleanore Bushnell; general eds., Russell W. McDonald and Ann Rollins. Carson City: Legislative Counsel Bureau, 1972.

Reps, John W. *Cities of the American West: A History of Frontier Urban Planning.* Princeton: Princeton University Press, 1979.

Reynolds, Deon, and Jon Christensen. *Nevada.* Portland, Ore.: Graphic Arts Center Publishing, 2001.

Richnak, Barbara. *Silver Hillside: The Life and Times of Virginia City.* Incline Village, Nev.: Comstock Nevada Publishing Co., 1984.

Rodriguez, Thomas, and M. L. Tony Miranda. *Hispanic Profiles in Nevada History: 1829–1991.* Las Vegas: Latin Chamber of Commerce, 1991.

Rolle, Andrew F. *John Charles Frémont: Character as Destiny.* Norman: University of Oklahoma Press, 1992.

Ronald, Ann, and Stephen Trimble. *Earthtones: A Nevada Album.* Reno: University of Nevada Press, 1995.

Roske, Ralph J. *Las Vegas: A Desert Paradise*. Tulsa: Continental Heritage Press, 1986.

Rowley, William D. *Reclaiming the Arid West: The Career of Francis G. Newlands*. Bloomington: Indiana University Press, 1996.

———. *Reno: Hub of the Washoe Country*. Woodland Hills, Calif.: Windsor Publications, 1984.

———. *U.S. Forest Service Grazing and Rangelands: A History*. College Station: Texas A&M University Press, 1985.

Rusco, Elmer R. *"Good Time Coming?": Black Nevadans in the Nineteenth Century*. Westport, Conn.: Greenwood Press, 1975.

———, project director, Nevada Black History Project. "Nevada Black History: Yesterday and Today." Reno: Nevada Humanities Committee, 1992.

———. "Welfare in Nevada: The Great Anomaly." *Nevada Public Affairs Review* 1 (1980): 8–80.

Rusco, Elmer R., and Sue Fawn Chung, eds. *Ethnicity and Race in Nevada*. Special issue of *Nevada Public Affairs Review* 2 (1987).

Ryser, Fred A., Jr. *Birds of the Great Basin: A Natural History*. Reno: University of Nevada Press, 1985.


Sawyer, Grant. *Hang Tough: Grant Sawyer, An Activist in the Governor's Mansion*. Interviews by Gary E. Elliott; narrative compiled by R. T. King. Reno: University of Nevada Oral History Program, 1993.

Scott, Lalla. *Karnee: A Paiute Narrative*. Reno: University of Nevada Press, 1966.

Scrugham, James G., ed. *Nevada: A Narrative of the Conquest of a Frontier Land*. 3 vols. Chicago: American Historical Society, 1935.

Shamberger, Hugh A. *Goldfield: Early History, Development, Water Supply*. Sparks, Nev.: Western Printing & Publishing Co., 1982.

Sheehan, Jack, ed. *The Players: The Men Who Made Las Vegas*. Reno: University of Nevada Press, 1997.

Shepperson, Wilbur S. *Restless Strangers: Nevada's Immigrants and Their Interpreters*. Reno: University of Nevada Press, 1971.

———. *Sagebrush Urbanity: Nevada's Humanities*. Reno: Nevada Humanities Committee, 1990.

———, ed. *East of Eden, West of Zion: Essays on Nevada*. Reno: University of Nevada Press, 1989.

Shepperson, Wilbur S., with Ann Harvey. *Mirage-Land: Images of Nevada*. Foreword by Ann Ronald. Reno: University of Nevada Press, 1992.

Shepperson, Wilbur S., with the assistance of John G. Folkes. *Retreat to Nevada: A Socialist Colony of World War I*. Reno: University of Nevada Press, 1966.

Sigler, William F., and John W. Sigler. *Fishes of the Great Basin: A Natural History*. Reno: University of Nevada Press, 1987.

Skolnick, Jerome H. *House of Cards: The Legalization and Control of Casino Gambling*. Boston: Little, Brown, 1978.

Smith, Grant H. *The History of the Comstock Lode: 1850–1920*. Reno: Nevada State Bureau of Mines, 1943.

Smith, Harold Truman. "New Deal Relief Programs in Nevada, 1933 to 1935." Ph.D. dissertation, University of Nevada, Reno, 1972.

Smith, Jedediah S. *The Southwest Expedition of Jedediah Strong Smith: His Personal Account of the Journey to California — 1826–1827*. Edited with an introduction by George R. Brooks. Glendale: Arthur H. Clark Co., 1977.

Smith, John L. *Running Scared: The Life and Treacherous Times of Las Vegas Casino King Steve Wynn*. New York: Barricade Books, 1995.

Smith, Scott T. *Nevada: Magnificent Wilderness*. Foreword by Hal Rothman. Englewood, Colo.: Westcliffe Publishers, 1996.

Soden, Dennis L., and Eric Herzik, eds. *Towards 2000: Public Policy in Nevada*. Dubuque: Kendall Hunt, 1997.

Solnit, Rebecca. *Savage Dreams: A Journey into the Hidden Wars of the American West*. San Francisco: Sierra Club Books, 1994.

Stevens, Joseph E. *Hoover Dam: An American Adventure*. Norman: University of Oklahoma Press, 1988.

Stewart, George R. *The California Trail: An Epic with Many Heroes*. New York: McGraw Hill, 1962.

———. *Ordeal by Hunger: The Story of the Donner Party*. New ed. Boston: Houghton Mifflin, 1960.

Stewart, Robert E., Jr., and Mary Frances Stewart. *Adolph Sutro*. San Francisco: Howell-North, 1962.

Stewart, William Morris. *Reminiscences of Senator William M. Stewart of Nevada*. Edited by George Rothwell Brown. New York: Neal Publishing Co., 1908.

Stone, Irving. *Men to Match My Mountains: The Opening of the Far West, 1840–1900*. Garden City, N.Y.: Doubleday, 1956.

Strong, Douglas H. *Tahoe: An Environmental History*. Lincoln: University of Nebraska Press, 1984.

Swainston, Harry W. "Nevada Water Law: A Shift to Riparianism?" *Nevada Public Affairs Review* 1 (1986): 15–19.

Thompson, David. *Nevada: A History of Change*. Reno: Grace Dangberg Foundation, 1986.

Tingley, Joseph V., and Kris Ann Pizarro. *Traveling America's Loneliest Road: A Geologic and Natural History Tour through Nevada along U.S. Highway 50*. Reno: Nevada Bureau of Mines and Geology, 2000.

Tingley, Joseph V., Robert C. Horton, and Francis C. Lincoln. *Outline of Nevada Mining History*. Special Publication 15. Reno: Nevada Bureau of Mines and Geology, 1993.

Titus, A. Costandina. *Bombs in the Backyard: Atomic Testing and American Politics*. Reno: University of Nevada Press, 1986.

———, ed. *Battle Born: The Federal-State Conflict in Nevada During the Twentieth Century*. Dubuque: Kendall Hunt, 1989.

Totton, Kathryn Dunn. "Hannah Keziah Clapp: The Life and Career of a Pioneer Nevada Educator, 1824–1908." *Nevada Historical Society Quarterly* 20 (fall 1977): 167–83.

Townley, Carrie Miller. "Helen J. Stewart: First Lady of Las Vegas." *Nevada Historical Society Quarterly* 16 (winter 1973): 214–44; 17 (spring 1974): 2–31.

Townley, John M. *Alfalfa Country: Nevada Land, Water and Politics in the Nine-*

*teenth Century*. Reno: University of Nevada Agriculture Experiment Station, 1981.

———. *Conquered Provinces: Nevada Moves Southeast, 1864–1871*. Charles Redd Monographs in Western History. Provo: Brigham Young University Press, 1973.

———. *Tough Little Town on the Truckee: Reno 1868–1900*. Vol. I. Reno: Great Basin Studies Center, 1983.

———. *Turn This Water into Gold: The Story of the Newlands Project*. Reno: Nevada Historical Society, 1977.

Trimble, Stephen. *The Sagebrush Ocean: A Natural History of the Great Basin*. Reno: University of Nevada Press, 1989.

Tronnes, Mike, ed. *Literary Las Vegas: The Best Writing about America's Most Fabulous City*. Introduction by Nick Tosches. New York: Henry Holt, 1995.

Twain, Mark. *Roughing It*. Vol. II of *The Works of Mark Twain*. Berkeley: University of California Press, 1972.

Underhill, Ruth Murray. *The Northern Paiute Indians of California and Nevada*. 1941. Reprint, New York: AMS Press, 1980.

Unruh, John D., Jr. *The Plains Across: The Overland Emigrants and the Trans-Mississippi West, 1840–1860*. Urbana: University of Illinois Press, 1979.

Venturi, Robert, Denise Scott Brown, and Steven Izenour. *Learning from Las Vegas: The Forgotten Symbolism of Architectural Form*. Cambridge: MIT Press, 1977.

Warren, Elizabeth von Till. "Armijo's Trace Revisited: A New Interpretation of the Impact of the Antonio Armijo Route of 1829–1830 on the Development of the Old Spanish Trail." M.A. thesis, University of Nevada, Las Vegas, 1974.

Watson, Anita Ernst. *Into Their Own: Nevada Women Emerging into Public Life*. Reno: Nevada Humanities Committee, 2000.

Wheat, Margaret M. *Survival Arts of the Primitive Paiutes*. Reno: University of Nevada Press, 1967.

Wheeler, Sessions. *The Nevada Desert*. Caldwell, Id.: Caxton Printers, 1971.

Wheeler, Sessions, with William W. Bliss. *Tahoe Heritage: The Bliss Family of Glenbrook, Nevada*. Foreword by Robert Laxalt. Reno: University of Nevada Press, 1992.

White, Michael C. *Nevada Wilderness Areas and Great Basin National Park: A Hiking and Backpacking Guide*. Berkeley: Wilderness Press, 1997.

Winter, Jill M. "Nevada Welfare Policies, and the New Federalism: Untangling the Alphabet Soup." *Nevada Public Affairs Review* 2 (1983): 15–20.

Worster, Donald. *Rivers of Empire: Water, Aridity, and the Growth of the American West*. New York: Pantheon Books, 1985.

Young, James A., and B. Abbott Sparks. *Cattle in the Cold Desert*. Logan: Utah State University Press, 1985.

Zanjani, Sally Springmeyer. *Goldfield: The Last Gold Rush on the Western Frontier*. Athens: Ohio University Press, 1992.

———. *A Mine of Her Own: Women Prospectors in the American West, 1850–1950.* Lincoln: University of Nebraska Press, 1997.

———. *Sarah Winnemucca.* Lincoln: University of Nebraska Press, 2001.

Zanjani, Sally Springmeyer, and Guy Louis Rocha. *The Ignoble Conspiracy: Radicalism on Trial in Nevada.* Reno: University of Nevada Press, 1986.

Zauner, Phyllis. *Carson City.* Tahoe Paradise, Calif.: Zanel Publications, 1984.

# Index

Abraham, Spencer, 15
Adams, Jewett, 139, 253, 326
Adams, Romanzo, 280
admission to the Union: California, 54–55; Nevada, 83–84, 242–43
African-Americans, 298, 306–10. *See also* Clark County, desegregation
agriculture: Anasazi, 21–23; Humboldt River, 122–23, 233–35; Las Vegas, 63–65, 99–100, 145–48, 185; Muddy Mission, 93, 95–98; Reno, 119, 140, 142; Southern Paiutes, 23, 27; Virgin Valley, 142–44, 344; western valleys, 134–36, 225–29, 318–23. *See also* livestock business
air bases, military: Fallon, 207, 321; Las Vegas, 211, 214–15, 271, 286, 335, 343; Reno, 206–7, 214; Tonopah, 335
Alamo, Lincoln County, 336, 339
Alamo ranch (near Reno), 140, 142
Ali, Mohammed, 217
Amargosa River, 10, 13, 172
American Museum of Natural History, 18
American River, 52
Anaconda Copper Company, 179, 335
Anasazi, 20–23, 26
Angel, Myron, 119
Anthony, Susan B., 159
anthropology and archeology: historic, 25–32, 219; prehistoric, 18–25

architecture: Carson City, 314–15; courthouse, 257–60, 336; Eureka, 324; Las Vegas, 196, 219–21, 260; Virginia City, 316
Arentz, Samuel S., 193, 244, 334
Armijo, Antonio, 39–40, 42
Armstrong, Charles J., 288
Arrington, Leonard, 51, 97
Ashley, Delos R., 89
Asian-Americans, 298, 304–6. *See also* Chinese
*Atlantic to the Pacific: What to See, and How to See It,* 120
Atomic Energy Commission, 215, 340–42
atomic test site. *See* Nevada Test Site
Aubrey, Francis Xavier, 91–92
Aurora, 78–81, 86–88, 135
Austin: county seat, 81, 112, 124, 258; discovery and early development, 78–79, 81, 162; heritage, 108, 323–24; pioneers, 88–89; railroad, 114, 127

Babbitt, 334–35
Babcock, Eliza, 159–60
*Baker v. Carr,* 252
Balzar, Fred, 264
bank crowd, 103–5
banking, 160, 198, 200
Bank of California, 103–4, 127
Bannock Indians, 69

Bannock War, 154
Baring, Walter, 239, 244
Bartleson, John, 44–46, 55
Bartleson-Bidwell party, 44–46
Bartlett Decree, 233
Bartley, David, 174
Basic Magnesium, 213–14, 308
*Basin and Range,* 5
Basques, 206, 234, 330
Basterretxea, Nestor, 330
Bastian, Cyril, 283
Battle Mountain: agriculture, 233–34; county seat, 234, 258, 329; economy in the 1980s, 328–29; founded, 124; mining, 235, 329; railroad to Austin, 127, 328
Baumhoff, Martin A., 24
Beatie, Hampton S., 58
Beatty, 55
Beaver Dam Canyon, 53
Belmont, 109, 112
Bible, Alan, 239, 244, 272
Bidwell, John, 44–46, 55–56
Big Bonanza, 75, 101–3, 106–8, 127, 162, 167
Big Meadows, 122, 233–34
Bilbray, James, 16
*Birds of the Great Basin,* 7
Blackburn, Abner, 58–59
Black Rock Desert, 16, 182
blacks. *See* African-Americans
Blasdel, Henry G., 84, 89, 261–63, 339–40
BLM. *See* Bureau of Land Management
Board of Regents. *See* University of Nevada
Bodie, California, 135
Bonelli, Daniel, 144–45
Bonneville, Benjamin, 40
Bonneville Salt Flats, 10, 48, 182
Bootstrap mine, 235
Boulder City, 90, 194, 238, 260
Boulder Dam. *See* Hoover Dam
boundary: with Arizona, 89–90, 98; with California, 55, 86–88; with Utah, 89–90, 94, 96–97
Bowers, Lemuel (Sandy), 66–67
boxing, 170, 217
Boyle, Emmett D., 193, 253, 263–64
Bracken, Walter, 192, 307
Bradley, L. R. "Broadhorns," 125, 138–39, 141, 150–51, 253, 327
Bray, Mildred, 301
Brier, Julia, 53
Bringhurst, William, 62–65
Broomfield, Robert C., 275

Brown, Mrs. Hugh, 165–66
*Brown v. Board of Education of Topeka,* 284, 309, 311
Brune, James, 343
Bruneau River, 39
Bryan, Richard, 16, 244, 253, 276
Bryan, William Jennings, 153
Buchanan, James, 60, 72, 75, 80
Buck, Franklin, 139
Buckland's, 80
Buena Vista Valley, 79
Bullfrog district, 172, 181
Bunker, Edward, 142
Bunkerville, 37, 142, 344
Bureau of Land Management (BLM), 225, 235–40
Bureau of Reclamation, 194
Burton, Philip, 238
Bush, George (H. W.), 17
Bush, George W., 15
Butler, Belle, 163
Butler, Jim, 163–67, 171

Cahlan, Florence Lee Jones, 301
Caliente, 19, 24, 114, 132, 184–85, 258, 336, 338
California: boundary, 55; constitution making, 54–55, 81; Donner party, 48–49; explorers, 33–35, 38–40; gold rush, 52–53; Mexican War, 51; statehood, 54–55; western movement, 44–50, 55–56
California-Nevada Interstate Compact, 318
Call, Anson, 95
Callville, 95, 98
Camp Mercury, 215, 342–43. *See also* Nevada Test Site
Candelaria, 128
Cannon, Howard, 239, 244, 270–71
Caples, Robert Cole, 202
Carlin, 124, 235, 260
Carson, Christopher "Kit," 39, 41–42
Carson & Colorado, 128–29, 131, 135, 164, 180–81, 315, 334
Carson City: in bonanza era, 136–37; boxing, 217; capital, 80–81; capitol, 68, 136–37; Chinese in, 131, 304; described by Mark Twain, 85; early education, 279; founded by Abe Curry, 68; local government, 257–58; railroad, 104, 120, 127–28, 130
CCC. *See* Civilian Conservation Corps
Central Pacific: across northern Nevada,

121-26; business practices, 129-30, 150-51, 180; financing and construction, 114-17, 304; land grant, 115, 137, 225; link with Virginia & Truckee Railroad, 103-4, 120-21

*Century in Meadow Valley,* 94

charcoal burners, 110

Charleston, Mt., 8, 10

Chiles, Joseph B., 46

Chinese, 117, 122, 130-31, 135, 304-6. *See also* Asian-Americans

Church, James Edward, 206

Churchill County, 19, 80, 227

*City of Trembling Leaves,* 206

Civilian Conservation Corps (CCC), 201

Civil Rights Act, 309

Civil War, 74, 84, 98, 115, 242-43

Civil Works Administration, 201

Claiborne, Harry E., 273-75

Clapp, Hannah K., 159-60, 279

Clark, Walter E., 198

Clark, Walter Van Tilburg, 35-36, 200, 206, 209

Clark, William (explorer), 36

Clark, William A. (railroad promoter), 148, 185-92

Clark County: community college, 289; desegregation, 283-84; economic factors, 339-47; established, 189; land rush, 237-39; population, 192, 221, 252; reapportionment, 251-52. *See also* Nevada Test Site

Clemens, Samuel L. *See* Twain, Mark

Clinton, President Bill, 318, 343

Clover Valley, 184

Clovis points, 19

Cobre, 175

Cohn, Abe, 29

Colcord, Roswell, 152

Colorado River, 4, 6, 8, 190; boundary change, 89-90; compact, 192-93, 239; described, 10-11; development, 25, 192-94, 343-44; exploration, 37-40, 46, 91-92; Hoover Dam, 193-96, 239-40; Mohave Indians, 26, 30; navigation, 92, 95

Columbia River, 4, 13, 36, 41

Columbus, Christopher, 1

Combined Metals Reduction Company, 338

community colleges, 217, 288-89, 327

Comstock, Henry Paige, 67

Comstock Lode: bonanza period, 101-8; decline, 108, 112; early development, 75-77; litigation, 71-73, 82; post-1880 developments, 162, 315-16; prospecting and discovery, 57, 61, 66-68

*Comstock Mining and Miners,* 72

Condor Canyon, 24

Congress, U.S.: authorizes Colorado River expedition, 92; California-Nevada Interstate Compact, 318; California statehood and Utah Territory, 55; Civil Rights Act of 1964, 309; creates Great Basin National Park, 15; creates Nevada Territory, 83; established Indian colonies, 331-32; Indian Claims Commission Act, 30-31; interstate commerce legislation, 130; land-grant legislation, 137-38; National Mining Law (1866), 103; Nevada enlarged, 89; Nevada statehood, 84; Pacific Railroad Act (1862), 115; stops minting silver dollars (1873), 108; Taylor Grazing Act, 141-42; wilderness legislation, 16-17; Yucca Mountain study, 14

Consolidated Virginia, 106

Constitution, Nevada, 234-35, 245-49, 251-54, 278, 297-98

Constitution, U.S., 30, 84, 301

constitutional conventions, Nevada, 81-84

constitutional structure (Nevada's), 242-43, 245-49, 251-53

Coolidge, Calvin, 193

copper mining: Lyon County, 178-79, 322; White Pine County, 173-78, 324-25

Corbett, James J., 217

Corporate Gaming Act, 269-70

cotton mission, 95

courthouses, 257-60, 316, 324, 336

court system. *See* judiciary

Cox, Walter, 265

Cradlebaugh, John, 71-72

*Craig v. Hocker,* 293

crime, organized, 267-71

Crocker, Charles, 117-19, 121-25

Crosby, Bing, 327

Crowley, Joseph N., 288

Crumley, Newton, 327

Curry, Abraham, 68, 136, 292

Cutler, Winifred, 143

Daggett, Rollin, 129-30, 151

Dangberg, Henry F., 135, 319-20

Dat-so-la-lee, 29

Davidson, Mt., 66–68, 75–77, 86, 105–8, 315–16
Davis, Jefferson, 115
Davis Dam, 11, 344
Dawes Act, 303
Dayton, 58, 77, 80, 105, 135, 322
Death Valley, 10, 21, 26, 53
Death Valley party (1849), 10, 53
Deidesheimer, Philip, 76
Delamar, 163
Demont, Joseph, 58
Dempsey, Jack, 170
Denver, Frank, 292
Department of Energy (DOE), U.S., 14, 215, 343
Department of Human Resources, Nevada, 249, 289–91
Depression, Great (1930s), 171, 194, 201–2. *See also* New Deal
Derby Dam, 229, 320
desegregation, 283–84
Deseret, 51, 319
*Desert Challenge: An Interpretation of Nevada,* 264–65
Desert Research Institute. *See* University of Nevada
Deutsch, Albert, 290
Devil's Hole, 7–8
DeVoto, Bernard, 86
divorce, 196, 199–200, 264
Dixie Mission, 95–96
doctrine of prior appropriation, 226–27, 230–31, 233, 240
Dodge, Fredrick, 61, 331
DOE. *See* Department of Energy
Dominguez, Francisco Atanasio, 34–35
Donner Lake, 48
Donner party, 48–50, 61
Donner Summit, 47, 117
Douglas, Stephen A., 72
Douglas County, 80, 135, 318–20
Dressler, Fred, 265
Duck Valley, 303
Dungan, Flora, 252

Eagle Ranch, 68
Eagle Valley, 29, 58, 136
East Ely, 176
East Las Vegas, 238
Ebel, Robert D., 294–95
education, 249–50, 277–89, 295. *See also* University of Nevada

Eisenhower, Dwight, 209
Eldorado Canyon, 92, 98, 148
Eldorado County, Calif., 98
Elko: community college, 197, 285, 289; county seat, 125, 260; described, 326–28; early years, 124–26, 138–40; economy, 233–35; railroad, 114, 125–26
Elko County, 124–26, 326–28; explorers and emigrants, 39, 45; livestock raising, 138–40
Elliott, Russell R., 178, 269–70
Ely: copper industry, 173–78; county seat, 111, 260; described, 324–26; prison, 294; railroad, 132, 175–76
emigrants: Death Valley party, 10, 53; Donner party, 48–50; early 1840s, 44–47; gold rush, 52–53; Latter-day Saints, 50–52; westward movement, 43–44, 55–56
Equal Rights Amendment, 301–2, 311
Equal Rights Commission, 306
Erskine, Graham, 314
Escalante, Francisco Silvestre Velez de, 34–35
Esmeralda County, 78, 80, 129, 170, 252
Etna Cave, 19
Eureka: decline, 112; discovery and early development, 108–10; gold rush (1980s), 324; railroad, 114, 127–28
Eureka & Palisade, 127–28, 174
Eureka County, 109, 324–25
*Eureka Sentinel,* 109
explorers, 33–43, 91–92

Fair, James G., 106, 112, 150
Fallon: county seat, 260; described, 320–22; Naval Air Station, 207, 321; Newlands Project, 227–29; population, 192
Fallon Naval Air Station, 207, 321
FBI, 270, 274
Federal Works Projects Administration, 173, 202, 211
Fennimore, "Old Virginny," 67
Fernley, 227–29, 320–22
Fiero, Bill, 4
Fifteenth Amendment, 306
Fillmore City, Utah, 59
*First Directory of Nevada Territory,* 77
Fish Creek war, 110
Fisher, Marion, 235
Fitzpatrick, Thomas "Broken Hand," 44
Fitzsimmons, Bob, 217

Flenniken, Robert P., 72
Flood, James C., 106
Fogliani, Jack, 292
Foley, Roger D., 256
Foley, Roger T., 256
Foote, Joseph Warren, 95–97
Ford, Jean, 302
forest service. *See* U.S. Forest Service
Fort Churchill, 24, 70, 322
Fort Mojave, 128
Forty Mile Desert, 45, 47–48, 53, 122, 330
Fourth Ward School, Virginia City, 279
Franciscans, 33–34, 65
Franktown, 60
Frazier, Maude, 280–83
Freeport law, 323
freeways. *See* highways
Frémont, John: California rebellion, 51; explorations, 41–42, 47, 55, 122; and Native Americans, 26, 61
Frenchman Mountain, 18–19
Frenchman's Ford, 123
Friedhoff, Frances, 301
fur trading, 36–37

Gabbs, 213, 260
Galley, James, 88
Galley, Martha, 88
gambling: history of, 261–70; in Las Vegas, 193, 211–13, 216–18, 346–49; legalized by legislature, 192, 200; made illegal by legislature, 198; political influence, 250–51; in Reno, 198, 207–9, 317; taxation, 248–49
Gaming Commission, 254, 269
Gaming Control Board, 254, 267–69
Gans, Joe, 170
Garcés, Francisco, 34–35
Gardnerville, 127, 322
Gass, Octavius and Mary, 98–100, 145–46, 185
General Land Office, U.S., 224
Genoa (Mormon Station): agriculture, 133–35, 227, 319; county seat, 60, 72, 80, 319–20; museums, 320; Orson Hyde at, 59–60; political role declines, 135, 319–20
*Geology of the Great Basin,* 4
Gerlach, 182
"Ghost Dance Religion," 156–57
Gila River, 91
Ginacca, Joseph, 123

Giomi, John, 268
Glyn, Elinor, 173
Godbe, William S., 163
Gojack, Mary, 302
Gold Canyon, 58–59, 66–68, 71
Goldfield: county seat, 170, 260, 336; discovery and early development, 167–70, 236; population, 181; railroads, 114, 181, 189; recent years, 335–36
Goldfield Consolidated Mining Company, 168, 170
Goldfield Women's Club, 170
Gold Hill, 68, 75–77, 106–7, 112, 119, 130, 315
gold mining, 92, 109; in Goldfield, 167–70; of the 1980s, 235–36, 324, 328. *See also* mining
gold rush: California, 52–54; of the 1980s, 235–36, 324, 328
Goodhue, Bertram G., 196
Gorbachev, Mikhail, 343
Goshute Indian Reservation, 331
Gould, George, 182
Gould, Jay, 182
government, federal, 242–44, 256–57
government, local, 242, 257–60
government, state, 242–43, 245–56
governor, office of, 253–54
Grand Canyon, 6
Grant, U. S., 61–62
Grant Canyon, 236–37
Gray, Edwin, 174
Gray, Robert, 127
Great Basin National Park, 15, 17, 326, 338
Great Salt Lake, 37–38, 44, 51
Green Valley, 217
Greenwood, Caleb, 47
Griswold, Morley, 200, 327
Grosh, Ethan Allen, 66
Grosh, Hosea Ballou, 66
Guadalupe Hidalgo, Treaty of, 51
Guggenheim family, 174–75
Guinn, Kenny, 250, 253, 276
Gypsum Cave, 18

Haight, Al, 265
Hamilton, 110–12, 164, 174, 324
Harolds Club, 207
Harrah, William, 317
Harrell, Jasper, 139–42
Harriman, Edward H., 182–84
Harrington, Mark, 25
Hastings, Lansford, 48

Hawley, Albert T., 285
Hawthorne: early development, 128–29; later developments, 260, 333–35; railroad, 114, 128
Hawthorne Naval Ammunition Depot, 207, 334–35
Heizer, Robert F., 24
Hellman, Raymond, 314
Henderson, 213–14, 238–39, 260, 308, 343
Herlong Ordnance Depot, 207
Hickle, Walter, 318
Hickson, Howard, 327
Hidden Cave, 19
highways, 204, 207, 209, 212, 323–24, 326, 329, 336
Hillyer, C. J., 157–59
Hispanics, 310–11
Historic Preservation and Archaeology, Nevada Division, 257
*History of Nevada* (Elliott), 270
*History of Nevada 1881* (Angel), 119
Hoffa, Jimmy, 273
Homestead Act, 224
Hoover, Herbert, 192–93
Hoover Dam, 11, 21, 93, 193–94, 201, 211, 240, 307–8, 338
Hopkins, Mark, 117
Houghton, Samuel G., 12
Hudson's Bay Company, 37, 39
Hughes, Howard, 184, 217–18
Hulse, Benjamin R., 65
Humboldt, Alexander von, 42
Humboldt County, 80, 85, 123, 234, 328
*Humboldt: Highroad of the West,* 13
Humboldt Range, 79, 123
Humboldt River: described, 13; economic development, 328–30; emigrant trail, 45, 47–48, 52–53; explorations of, 39–40, 42; Native Americans, 19, 154; railroad building, 122–25, 138; water rights, 233–34. *See also* livestock business
Hunt, Jefferson, 53
Huntington, Collis P., 117, 180, 334
Hurst, Sadie D., 301
Hyde, Orson, 59–60, 95

immigrants, 112–13; Basque, 206, 234, 330; Chinese, 117, 122, 130–31, 135, 304–6
impeachment, 273–74
Incline Village, 318
Indian Claims Commission Act, 32, 304, 332

Indian New Deal Act, 303, 332
Indian reservations and colonies, 61–62, 331–32
Indians. *See* Native Americans
Industrial Workers of the World (IWW), 168–69
initiative petition, 160
intercontinental ballistic missile. *See* M-X
Internal Revenue Service (IRS), 270, 273
Interstate Compact Commission, 231
Interstate Highway Act, 209
Irish Mountain, 92
IRS. *See* Internal Revenue Service
Irving, Washington, 40
Ives, Joseph C., 92
IWW. *See* Industrial Workers of the World

Jackpot, 270
James, Ronald M., 257
Jarbidge Cave, 19
Jarbidge River, 13
Jefferson, Thomas, 36
Jeffries, Jim, 217
Jensen, Andrew, 64
Johnson, George A., 92
Johnson, J. Neely, 84
Johnson, Jack, 217
Johnson, Ken, 265
Johnston's army, 94
Jones, John E. (governor), 112, 144
Jones, John P. (senator), 112, 130, 150, 152–53, 162
Jones, Nathaniel V., 64–65
Judah, Theodore, 115
judiciary: federal, 254–57, 273–75, 293; local, 255; state, 254–56; territorial, 71–73
Justice Department, 271, 274
*Justice in Balance: The Courthouses of Nevada,* 257–58

Kefauver, Estes, 267
Kelly, J. Wells, 77
*Kelly v. Guinn,* 284
Kelsey, Benjamin, 45
Kelsey, Nancy, 44–45
Kennecott Copper Company, 178, 325
Kennedy, John, 342
Kimberly, 175–76
Kinkead, John, 110
Kyle Canyon, 8

*Lady in Boomtown,* 165–67
Lahontan basin, 6, 10
Lahontan Reservoir, 229, 320
Lake, Myron, 117, 120
Lake Bonneville, 6
Lake County, 80, 88
Lake Lahontan, 6
Lake Mead, 6, 21, 93, 95, 214, 239
Lake Mojave, 10
Lake's Crossing, 117
Lake Tahoe, 12, 16, 26, 29, 51, 134, 230–31;
    conservation, 238, 316–18; described by
    Mark Twain, 85
Lander County, 79, 81, 124–25, 258, 329
land grants, federal, 115, 137–38
land policy, 137–38, 224–25, 237–38
Lanner, Ronald M., 6, 8
Larson, Andrew Karl, 144
Lassen-Applegate Trail, 53
Las Vegas: development (1920–1940),
    192–96; ethnic problems, 307–11; ex-
    plorations, 39–41, 51; gambling and
    tourism, 204, 211–13, 216–21, 269; land
    problems, 237–39; Mormon mission, 51,
    62–65, 185; railroad town, 114, 132, 185–
    92; Rancho, 97–98, 145, 148, 303; recent
    developments, 346–49; water needs,
    187–88, 192, 239–40
Las Vegas Indian Colony, 331
Las Vegas Land and Water Company, 189,
    192
Las Vegas Mission and Fort, 62–65, 95, 185,
    219
Las Vegas Valley, 8, 10, 11, 53, 98; atomic
    testing, 215–16; industry, 213–16, 346–47;
    land, 237–39; railroad, 132, 184
Las Vegas Wash, 92, 95
Latter-day Saints: arrival in Utah, 51; be-
    ginnings, 50–51; in Carson Valley, 58–60;
    and Equal Rights Amendment, 301; in
    Las Vegas, 62–65; in Pahranagat Valley,
    338–39; in Virgin, Moapa, and Meadow
    valleys, 93–98, 142–45, 344
Laughlin, 270, 343–44
law and order. *See* judiciary
Laxalt, Paul, 244, 253, 269, 272–73, 309
Laxalt, Robert, 206
Lear, William, 206
Lee, Francis, 94
Lee, Ruth, 94
Lee, S. L., 29
legislature: apportionment, 251–53; civil

rights, 308–9; creation of counties,
    80–81, 89, 109, 111, 189–90; divorce, 199–
    200; education policy, 278–80, 282–85,
    289; 1861 session, 79–81; Equal Rights
    Amendment, 301–2; gambling policy,
    263–70; Goldfield labor trouble, 169;
    land policy, 137–38; law-making pro-
    cess, 250; legalized gambling, 192, 200;
    in the 1980s, 245–53; Progressive-Era
    legislation, 160–61; railroad company
    influence, 130; session limit, 247; and tax
    increase of 2003, 250; woman suffrage,
    157–59
Lehman Caves, 15, 19
Leland, Joy, 27
Lester, John Erastus, 120
Lewis, Marvin, 88
Lewis, Meriwether, 36
Lewis, Oscar, 267
Lewis, Ted, 327
Liberty Pit, 176
*Life Among the Piutes: Their Wrongs and
    Claims,* 156
Lillard, Richard, 265
Lincoln, Abraham, 72, 74, 80, 84, 242
Lincoln County, 53, 89, 96–97, 139, 144, 183,
    189–90, 336–39
List, Robert, 238, 253
livestock business, 123–25, 134–35, 138–
    42, 234, 319, 321–22, 326. *See also*
    agriculture
Logandale, 97, 344
Lord, Eliot, 72
Lorenzi, David, 193
Lorenzi Park, 219
"Lost City," 21–22
Lovelock, 114, 122, 156, 233–34, 260, 294,
    328–30
Lovelock, George, 122, 330
Lovelock Cave, 19, 24–25
Lux, Charles, 140–41
Lyon County, 80, 178–79, 321–22

McCarran, Patrick, 172, 201, 214, 244, 272
McCarran International Airport, 212, 217,
    346
McDermitt Indian Reservation, 332
McGill, 175–78, 325–26
McGill, William, 139, 175, 326
Mackay, John, 68, 75, 106, 108
McLane, Alvin R., 4
McLaughlin, Patrick, 67

McMillan, James, 309
McPhee, John, 5
McWilliams, J. T., 187
magnesium, 213–14
Malheur Reservation, 154
Manly, Lewis, 42, 53
Manogue, Patrick, 279
marriage laws, 199
Marsh, William, 167
*Martha and the Doctor,* 88
Martin, Anne, 160, 298–99
Mary's River. *See* Humboldt River
Mason, H. N. A. "Hock," 134, 141
Mason Valley, 12–13, 134–35, 138–41, 156,
    178–79, 322
Maxson, Robert, 288
Maynard, Mila Tupper, 160
Meadow Valley Mining Company, 111
Meadow Valley Range, 163
Meadow Valley Wash, 11, 24, 53, 93, 184,
    190
Medicaid, 291
mental health, 291
Mercury. *See* Camp Mercury
Merrill, Charles, 268
Mesquite, 93, 142–43, 258, 344
Mesquite Club, 190
Mexican-Americans. *See* Hispanics
Mexican War, 51
Mexico, 36, 38, 41, 46
military bases: Fallon Naval Air Station,
    207, 321; Fort Churchill, 24, 70, 322;
    Fort Mojave, 128; Hawthorne Naval
    Ammunition Depot, 207, 334–35; Her-
    long Ordnance Depot, 207; Nellis Air
    Force Base, 211, 214–15, 271, 286, 335,
    343; Stead Air Force Base, 206–7, 214;
    Tonopah Air Base, 335
Mill City, 123
Miller, Bob, 248, 253, 276
Miller, Henry, 140–41
Miller, Max, 205
Miller, N. Edd, 288
Mills, Darius O., 127–28
Mina, 334
Minden, 114, 127, 182, 260, 319
Mineral County, 129, 333–35
mining: bonanza era (1864–1878), 101–13;
    California gold rush, 54–55, 57–58; Com-
    stock discovery, 67–68; copper, 173–79,
    324–25; early Comstock period, 75–77;
    Eldorado Canyon, 91–92; gold, 167–70,

235–37, 324, 328; Las Vegas Mission,
    62–63; lead-zinc, 338; oil, 236–37, 325;
    other districts (1860–1863), 78–79, 85–
    90; placer, 58–60, 66–67; taxation, 82,
    84, 248–49; Tonopah and Goldfield era,
    162–70, 172–73
Mint, U.S. (Carson City), 136, 315
Miranda, Tony, 311
mission, revival style, 196
missions, California, 34–35
Moapa, 93, 184, 303, 344
Moapa River Indian Reservation, 331–32
Moehring, Eugene P., 213, 216, 347
Mohave, 26, 30, 35
Mojave Desert, 8–10, 26, 35, 53, 92
Mojave National Scenic Area, 344
Mojave River, 10
Monterey, Calif., 40, 54–55, 81
Moody, Eric, 266
Morgan, Dale, 13
Mormon church. *See* Latter-day Saints
Mormon fort. *See* Las Vegas Mission and
    Fort
*Mormons in Nevada,* 97
Mormon Station (later Genoa), 58–60
Mormon Trail, 40, 91, 93
Morrill Land Grant Act, 285–86
Moss, Johnny, 92
Mound House, 128
Mozingo, Hugh N., 7–8
Muddy Mission, 95–98
Muddy River, 11, 55, 95–98, 144
municipal planning, 209, 219–21, 237–39
Murphy, Martin, 47
M-X (experimental missile) 14, 271, 339

National Cancer Institute, 343
National Mining Law, 103
National Register of Historic Places, 196,
    315–16
National Resources Defense Council, 343
Native Americans, 2; Anasazi, 20–23;
    contemporary period, 331–32; earli-
    est evidence, 10, 18–19; explorers and
    emigrants, 40–41, 48, 61–62; modern
    period, 25–32, 61–64; Pyramid Lake,
    battles of, 69–71; rock art, 23–24; Sarah
    Winnemucca Hopkins, 154–57; struggle
    for rights, 30–32, 154–57, 302–4; Wovoka,
    156–57. *See also* Mohave; Paiute,
    Northern; Paiute, Southern; Shoshone;
    Washo

navy: air station at Fallon, 207, 321; ammunition depot at Hawthorne, 207, 334–35
Needles, Calif., 38
Nellis, William H., 214
Nellis Air Force Base, 211, 214–15, 271, 286, 335, 343
Nelson, "Battling," 170
Neolithic culture, 20
*Nevada: A Guide to the Silver State,* 173, 211
Nevada Bar Association, 274
Nevada Central, 127, 162–63
Nevada Consolidated Copper Company, 175–76
Nevada copper belt, 178
Nevada Equal Suffrage Association, 160
Nevada Historical Society and Museum, 219–21, 314
Nevada Humanities Committee, 276
Nevada Northern Railroad, 132, 175–76, 182
"Nevada's Fateful Desert," 35–36
Nevada State Council on the Arts, 276
Nevada State Education Association, 285
Nevada State Museum, 18, 21, 24, 131, 314
Nevada State Railroad Museum, 127, 131
*Nevada Statistical Abstract,* 296
Nevada Tax Commission, 265–68
Nevada Territory, 75, 79–83, 245
Nevada Test Site, 215, 271, 335, 339–43, 349. *See also* Camp Mercury
New Deal, 201–2, 290, 303
New Jersey, 346
Newlands, Francis G., 121, 152–53, 197–98, 228–29, 244, 307
Newlands Reclamation Project, 196, 227–30, 243–44, 320–21
New Mexico Territory, 55
Newmont Mining Corporation, 235
Nixon, 231
Nixon, George, 168, 170–71
North, John, 82–84
Northern Nevada Railroad Museum, 132
North Las Vegas, 238, 260, 343
nuclear testing. *See* Camp Mercury; Nevada Test Site
nuclear waste, 14–15, 17, 257
Nye, James W., 28, 80–84, 89, 109, 135, 302
Nye County, 139, 163, 167, 339

O'Brien, William, 106
O'Callaghan, Mike, 253, 269

Oddie, Tasker L., 163–65, 171–72, 244, 253, 263, 334
Office of Indian Affairs, 61
Ogden, Peter Skene, 1, 39–40, 42, 50–51
Ogden's River (Humboldt River), 40, 42. *See also* Humboldt River
oil, 236–37, 325
Old Red Ledge, 67
Old Spanish Trail. *See* Spanish Trail
Ophir mine, 67–68, 75, 82
Oregon, 51
O'Riley, Peter, 67
Ormsby, William, 69–70, 154
Ormsby County, 80, 104, 136–37
Orr, John, 59
*Orr Ditch Case,* 230–31, 317
Orrum, Eilley, 66
Overton, 97–98, 193, 344
Owens Valley, Calif., 128
Owyhee River, 13, 15–16, 39
*Ox-Bow Incident,* 206

Pahranagat Valley, 89, 92, 97, 108, 338–39
Pahrump, 344–46
Pah-Ute County, 98
Paiute, Northern, 19, 21–23, 26, 28–29, 61–62, 69–70, 154–57, 231, 303
Paiute, Southern, 21–23, 26–28, 303
Paleolithic culture, 18, 20
Palisade, 121
Panaca, 24, 93–94, 336–38
Paradise, 238
Paslov, Eugene T., 285
Paul, Almarin B., 76
Peabody family, 156
Peabody report on education, 282–83
Pershing County, 122, 328
Pilot Peak, 45
Pioche: county seat, 111, 146, 189–90; early developments, 94, 111–12, 144, 165; railroads, 114, 127–28, 185; recent developments, 337–38
Pittman, Key, 171, 201, 244, 266
Pittman, Vail, 253, 266–67
Pittman Act, 171
police force, state, 169
Polk, James K., 51–52
polygamy, 89
Pony Express, 70–71, 227
Pony Express Territory, 323–24
population, 192, 203, 221
populist movement, 130, 150–53

Potosi Mine, 65
Powell, John Wesley, 96, 227–28
Pre-emptive Act, 224
Preston, Morrie R., 169
Priestley, Keith, 343
primary election, 161
prisons, 291–94, 325
Progressive Era, 160–61, 197, 263, 280
Progressive Leadership Alliance of Nevada
    (PLAN), 253
Prohibition, 159, 198, 301
Promontory, Utah, 115, 126
prostitution, 107, 198–99, 204, 207
Prouse, William, 59
Public Land Office, 224–25
Public Service Commission, 160
Pueblo dwellers (Anasazi), 20–23
Pueblo Grande of Nevada, 21, 193
Pyramid Lake: battles of, 69–70; discovery,
    41, 47; fish, 7, 230; Truckee River inflow,
    12, 121; water litigation, 230–33
Pyramid Lake Reservation, 61–62, 154, 229,
    230–32, 302–3, 318, 331

Railroad commission, 161
railroads: in Clark County, 185–92; oli-
    garchy, 129–30; smaller lines, 126–29;
    through northern Nevada, 115–26, 176,
    178, 180–82; through southern Nevada,
    182–85; transcontinental built, 115–26;
    transcontinental proposed, 56, 114–15.
    *See also* Carson & Colorado; Central
    Pacific; Eureka & Palisade; Nevada
    Central; Nevada Northern; Salt Lake,
    Los Angeles & San Pedro; Southern
    Pacific; Tonopah & Goldfield Railroad
    Company; Union Pacific; Virginia &
    Truckee; Western Pacific
Ralston, William, 103–4
ranching. *See* agriculture; livestock
    business
Rancho Grande, 140
Rawhide, 172–73
Raymond-Ely Mining Company, 111
Read, Effie O., 174
Reagan, Ronald, 244, 272
Reed, Edward C., 293, 310
Reese River, 79, 127, 138
*Reese River Reveille,* 89
referendum, 160
Reid, Harry, 16, 244
Reno: early period, 114, 117–21, 279; growth

(1900–1940), 196–201; growth (since
    1940), 203–9; influence of Newlands,
    121, 152–53, 197–98; population, 181, 192,
    196, 209; railroads, 114, 117–21, 129, 204
*Reno* (book), 205
Reno, Jesse L., 117
*Reno: Hub of the Washoe Country,* 197
Requa, Isaac, 163
Requa, Mark, 163, 174–75
*Resort City in the Sunbelt,* 216, 347
*Reynolds v. Sims,* 252
Rhyolite, 172, 181
Rice, George Graham, 173
Rickard, Tex, 170, 173
Riepetown, 175
Ring, Orvis, 280
Rioville, 144
riparian rights, 225–26, 240
Rivera, Rafael, 40
Robbins, John, 265
Roberts, E. E., 198–99, 244
Robinson mining district, 174
rock art, 23–24
Rocky Mountain Fur Company, 37
Roosevelt, Franklin, 172, 200–201, 213
Roosevelt, Theodore, 142, 168–69, 228
*Roughing It,* 84–86
Rowland, John, 46
Rowland-Workman party, 46
Rowley, William D., 197, 198
Ruby Mountains, 16, 45, 48, 327
Ruby Valley, 28
Rusco, Elmer, 307
Russell, Charles, 253, 267–68, 282, 327
Ruth, 175–78, 325
Rye Patch Dam, 234, 329
Ryser, Fred A., 7–8

*Sacramento Bee,* 272–73
Sadler, Reinhold, 112, 253
*Sagebrush Casinos,* 267
Sagebrush Rebellion, 235–36, 243
St. Joseph, 95, 97
St. Thomas, 95, 97, 142
sales tax. *See* taxation
Salt Lake, Los Angeles & San Pedro, 184
San Antonio Range, 163
San Buenaventura River, 35, 38, 41
San Gabriel Mission, 35, 38, 40, 46
Santa Rosa Range, 123
Santini, James, 238, 244
Santini-Burton Act, 238

Sawyer, Grant, 253, 269, 292, 327
Schmidt, Alexis von, 231, 316
schools. *See* education
Schurz, 331
Scrugham, James G., 193, 244, 253
Searchlight, 173
senators, U.S.: elected by legislature, 84, 130, 150, 160–61; elected by the people, 160–61. *See also individual senators*
Serra, Junipero, 34, 65
Sevier River, Utah, 34
Sharon, William M., 68, 103–4, 108, 120, 127–28, 150, 152, 184
Shaw, Dr. Anna Howard, 159
Shearing, Miriam, 260
Sheep Range, 18
Shoshone, 26, 28–29, 64, 154, 303, 331
Shovelin, Dan, 329
*Shrubs of the Great Basin*, 7–8
Sierra Nevada, 2, 4–5, 12, 38, 52, 76, 88, 119
Sierra Seminary, 159
*Silent Cordilleras: The Mountain Ranges of Nevada*, 4
Silver City, 77, 107, 322
silver mining: central Nevada, 78–79, 88–89, 109–11; on Comstock, 66–68, 75–77, 103–6; eastern Nevada, 111–12; Tonopah, 163–67. *See also* mining
Silver party, 130, 150–53, 228
Silver Purchase Act (1934), 171, 201
Silver Springs, 322
Simpson, Mary Virginia, 98–100
Singatse Range, 178–79
Six Mile Canyon, 66–67
Small Tract Program, 237
Smith, Jedediah, 1, 37–40, 42, 46, 50–51, 55
Smith, Joseph (LDS leader), 50–51
Smith, Joseph W., 169
Smith, R. B., 134
Smith, Raymond I., 207
Smith, T. B., 134
Smith, Thomas S., 95
Smith Valley, 134–35
Snake Range, 15, 326
Snake River, 39
Snow, Erastus, 94
Snyder, Ed, 338
Sodaville, 164–65, 181
Southern Nevada Water Project, 239–40
Southern Pacific Railroad, 180–82, 225, 334
Spanish explorers, 33–36, 91
Spanish Trail, 40–41, 46, 62, 134, 212

Sparks: described, 322–23; development, 206–9, 260; on emigrant trail, 47; population, 181, 192; railroad, 114, 181
Sparks, B. Abbott, 6
Sparks, John, 140–42, 168–69, 253, 327
Spinks, Leon, 217
Spring Mountains, 8, 11, 63, 193
Spring Valley, 238
"squatters' government," 59–60
Squaw Valley, Calif., 207, 317
Squires, Delphina, 299
Stanford, Leland, 117
statehood. *See* admission to the Union, Nevada
Stead Air Force Base, 206–7, 214
Stealth bomber, 335
steamboats, 92, 95
Steffen, Thomas, 275
Stevens, Elisha, 47
Stevens-Murphy-Townsend party, 47, 115
Steward, Julian, 27
Stewart, Archibald, 146, 185
Stewart, H. E. (Reno mayor), 198–99, 204
Stewart, Helen, 145–48, 185, 303
Stewart, William Morris: advocate of reclamation, 227; Indian school, 303; law practice, 72–73; legislature, 68, 80–84; mining law (1866), 103, 224; as U.S. senator, 84, 89, 103, 130, 150–53, 159–60
Stewart Indian School, 303
Stickney, Robert, 293
*Stickney v. List/Bryan*, 293
Stillwater Wildlife Management Area, 233
Stimler, Harry, 167–70
Stokes, Anson Phelps, 127, 162–63
Stokes, J. G. Phelps, 162–63
Storey County, 80
Stout, Minard W., 288
Strip (Las Vegas), 211–13, 238, 308–9, 347
Strong, Douglas H., 317
Stubbs, Joseph E., 197–98, 204, 263, 286
Sun Mountain, 58, 66–68, 86. *See also* Davidson, Mt.
Sunrise Manor, 238
Sunrise Mountain, 8, 189
Supreme Court, Nevada, 233, 250, 255, 274–75
Supreme Court, U.S., 230–31, 243, 251–52, 283–84
*Surveyor General and State Land Register, Report of the*, 145
Susanville, Calif., 81, 88, 120

Sutro, Adolph, 68, 104–5, 108, 150, 239
Sutter, John, 48, 52
Sutter's Fort, 52
Swackhamer, William, 329

Tarkanian, Jerry, 288
taxation: corporate income tax proposed, 285; for education, 248, 249, 250, 278, 280; "freeport" law, 323; of gambling, 248, 249; increase in 2003, 250; of LDS communities, 97; of mines, 82, 84, 138, 151, 248–49; Nevada patterns criticized, 294–95; of property, 247–48; of retail sales, 248, 283
Taylor Grazing Act, 141–42
Teamsters' Union, 271, 273
Te-moak, 28
*Territorial Enterprise,* 86, 104, 151
Terry, David, 72
Thompson, Bruce A., 256, 284, 293
Thompson, Samuel, 65
Thunderbird Hotel, 267–68
Tinnan, John, 140
Tobin, Phil, 264
Toiyabe Range, 79
Tonopah: county seat, 167, 260; early development, 163-67, 170–72, 335; population, 192; railroads, 114, 181, 189; recent years, 335–36
Tonopah & Goldfield Railroad Company, 181
Toquima Range, 109
tourism, 205–9, 211–13, 216–18, 263–70, 317, 327, 343–50
Townsend, John, 47
*Trace of Desert Waters,* 12
*Track of the Cat,* 206
Treasure City, 110, 174
*Trees of the Great Basin,* 6
Tri-County Development Authority, 330–31
Truckee, Captain, 154
Truckee Canal, 320
Truckee Meadows, 12; emigrants, 47–48; Native Americans, 29, 61–62; railroads, 103, 117–19, 181. *See also* Reno; Sparks
Truckee River: agriculture, 137, 140, 142; described, 11–12; explorers and emigrants, 42, 47–48, 52; Native Americans, 26, 154, 302; railroad building, 117–19; 121; reclamation, 197, 227–33; rock art, 24
Tule Springs, 10, 18

Tuohy, Donald R., 24
Tuscarora, 126, 304
Twain, Mark (Samuel L. Clemens), 84–86, 98, 136, 245, 315

*Union Mill and Mining Company v. Dangberg,* 226
Union Pacific, 115, 122, 132, 145, 182, 185, 190, 192, 196, 338
Union party of Storey County, 83
Unionville, 78–80, 124
United Order, 142
U.S. Air Force, 214, 343
U.S. Army, 70, 93, 98, 206
U.S. Forest Service, 225, 317
U.S. Geological Survey (USGS), 227
U.S. government. *See specific agencies*
University of California, 18, 24
University of Nevada: Board of Regents, 285–89; community colleges, 217, 289, 327; Desert Research Institute, 286, 289; at Elko (preparatory school), 125, 159, 197, 285; establishment, 285–86; at Las Vegas, 286–89, 347; medical school, 217; at Reno, 126, 160, 197–98, 206, 217, 285–89; research, 19, 206, 286, 343; system, 249
USGS. *See* U.S. Geological Survey
Utah, 50, 96–97, 133, 163, 319
Utah Territory, 55, 58–60, 69, 92, 94, 97, 319
Utah War, 60

Valley of Fire, 24
V & T. *See* Virginia & Truckee
*Van Sickle v. Haines,* 226
veteran, 176
Vhay, David, 314
Virginia & Truckee (V & T), 103–4, 120–21, 126–27, 130–32, 136–37, 182, 315, 320
Virginia City: bonanza era, 101–9, 112, 120–21, 127, 131–32, 278; compared with Tonopah, 165–67; county seat, 80, 258–60; described, 315–16; early development, 67–68, 76–78, 84
Virginia Mountains, 66, 135
Virgin River, 20, 37–39, 55, 93, 95–96, 142–44, 334
Vucanovich, Barbara, 244, 260, 301

Wabuska, 131, 178
Wadsworth, 121–22, 181, 228
Wadsworth, Sylvia, 94

Wagner, Sue, 260, 302
Walker, Joseph R., 40–42, 46–47, 61, 126
Walker Lake, 13, 24, 38–39, 172
Walker River: agriculture, 134–35; described, 11–13; explorers, 38–39, 42, 47
Walker River Indian Reservation, 62, 302–3, 331
Wallace, C. C., 130
Walton, Richard Guy, 202
Warren, Elizabeth, 40
Washington, Willie, 310
Washoe City, 68, 77, 80, 120, 136
Washoe County, 80, 104, 182, 206, 221
Washoe Valley, 60, 67, 103, 135–36
Washo, 26, 29, 62, 154
Wasson, Warren, 62, 302
water policy, 188–89, 192–93, 223, 225–35, 239–40
Weaver, James B., 152
Weed Heights, 179, 322
welfare, 289–91, 295–96
Wellington, 135
Wells, 126, 258
Wendover, 182, 270
West, Charles, 309
Western Federation of Miners, 168–69
Western Pacific, 182
Westside, the, 187, 284, 308–9
Wheeler Peak, 5, 15
Whitaker, Ozi W., 120, 279
Whitehead, Stephen R., 196
White Pine County, 15, 19, 110–11, 126, 132, 139, 173–78, 324–26
*White Pine Lang Syne,* 174
Whitney, George B., 144
Whittemore, C. O., 187–89

wilderness, 16–17
Williams, James, 69
Williamson, Frances, 159
Wilmot Proviso, 54
Wilson, Bird, 299
Wilson, Jack. *See* Wovoka
Winchester, 213, 238
Wingfield, George, 168–71, 198–200
Winnemucca: county seat, 124, 260; early development, 123–24; explorers and emigrants, 39, 45; in the 1980s, 329; railroads, 114, 122–23, 182; water problems, 233–34
Winnemucca, "Old" Chief, 69, 154
Winnemucca, Sarah, 69–70, 154–57
Winnemucca Lake, 19
Winter Olympics (1960), 207, 317
Wolfskill, George, 40
women: in early Nevada, 113, 179; in government, 260
women's rights, 149, 157–60, 298–302
Workman, William, 46
Works Projects Administration (WPA), 173, 202, 211; guide to Nevada, 173, 211
Wovoka, 156–57
WPA. *See* Works Projects Administration

Yakima Reservation, Washington, 154
Yerington, 12, 135, 157, 178, 260, 322
Yerington, H. M., 130, 135, 334
Young, Brigham, 50–51, 56, 59–60, 62–65, 95–97
Young, Clara Kimball, 170
Young, Ewing, 39
Young, James A., 6
Yount, George, 40
Yucca Mountain, 14–15, 17, 257, 335